C0-AWT-230

The Psychopathology of Childhood and Adolescence

The Psychopathology of Childhood and Adolescence

Amy Beth Taublieb

 LONGMAN

An imprint of Addison Wesley Longman, Inc.

New York • Reading, Massachusetts • Menlo Park, California • Harlow, England
Don Mills, Ontario • Sydney • Mexico City • Madrid • Amsterdam

Acquisitions Editor: Catherine Woods
Supplements Editor: Cyndy Taylor
Text and Cover Designer: Amy Trombat
Cover Photo: © Rieder & Walsh/Photonica
Electronic Production Manager: Alexandra Odulak
Desktop Coordinator: Joanne Del Ben
Manufacturing Manager: Hilda Koparanian
Printer and Binder: RR Donnelley & Sons Company
Cover Printer: Phoenix Color Corp.

For permission to use copyrighted material, grateful acknowledgment is made to the copyright holders on pp. 263–265, which are hereby made part of this copyright page.

Library of Congress Cataloging-in-Publication Data

Taublieb, Amy Beth.
   The psychopathology of childhood and adolescence / Amy Beth
Taublieb.
     p. cm.
   Includes bibliographical references and index.
   ISBN 0-673-99035-4
   1. Child psychopathology.   2. Adolescent psychopathology.
   3. Clinical child psychology.   I. Title.
   [DNLM: 1. Mental Disorders—in infancy & childhood.   2. Mental
Disorders—in adolescence.   3. Child Behavior Disorders.
   4. Psychopathology—in infancy & childhood.   5. Psychopathology—in
adolescence.   WS 350 T222p 1997]
   RJ499.T348   1997
   618.92'89—dc20
DNLM/DLC   96-41472
for Library of Congress   CIP

Copyright © 1997 by Addison-Wesley Educational Publishers Inc.

All rights reserved. No part of this publication may be reproduced, stored in a retrieval system, or transmitted, in any form or by any means, electronic, mechanical, photocopying, recording, or otherwise, without the prior written permission of the publisher. Printed in the United States.

ISBN 0-673-99035-4

12345678910—DOC—99989796

Contents

Contents

160 Chapter eight
Disorders of Identity in Childhood and Adolescence

176 Chapter nine
Mental Retardation and the Pervasive Developmental Disorders

207 Chapter ten
Disruptive and Attention Deficit Behavior Disorders

231 Chapter eleven
Disorders of Eating and Elimination in Childhood and Adolescence

Preface

During my thirteen years of teaching undergraduate psychology courses, I was often called on to teach a class in child and adolescent psychopathology. Because much of my clinical practice is devoted to working with young people, this class was always one of my favorite teaching assignments. I was often frustrated, however, when looking for a good textbook to order for my students. Most of the books that were available assumed a developmental perspective. This approach would have been acceptable if crucial clinical topics had been addressed more than superficially. The only books that did contain the relevant clinical information were psychiatry textbooks, which unfortunately were not suitable for an undergraduate course. As I was bemoaning this situation to a publishing company representative at a psychology convention exhibition booth, he responded (I think halfheartedly), "Why don't you write one?" And so the story began.

As a clinician, I recognized the importance of integrating the clinical and developmental perspectives in this book. Indeed, a major part of my motivation for writing this textbook was to provide students with a sound clinical perspective. Writing, however, is a continuous process of learning, modification, and compromise, and my original "hard-line" clinical perspective metamorphosed into the developmentally informed clinical perspective presented here. Much of the content is based on the recently released *DSM-IV*, so this book is up to date in terms of its presentation of clinical material. Clinical information, however, is not limited to lists of diagnostic criteria. Each disorder is discussed in terms of clinical presentation, etiology, diagnostic criteria, assessment, epidemiology, and treatment approaches. Further, the symptoms of each disorder are conceptualized along the continuum of pathology to show how they vary according to the developmental stage of the child or adolescent patient. Further, to make this theoretical material more real to the reader, the chapters contain illustrative case studies.

Although the writing is extremely user-friendly, the tone is not at all condescending or superficial. Complex concepts are presented in a manner a lay reader can easily comprehend, but the book is by no means too simplistic for graduate students, medical students, nursing students, or professionals. A glossary of these key terms which are boldfaced in text, is provided at the end of the book. "Think About It" boxes present the reader with thought-provoking questions based on issues in recent research and clinical practice.

All of this material is presented within a developmental context, with particular emphasis on how the various psychopathologies present themselves in children and adolescents. Because of this integrated approach, the reader does not have to choose between the clinical and developmental perspectives. Indeed, current trends in teaching in this field do not support the idea that the two different perspectives are mutually exclusive.

The text is written so that students do not have to take prerequisite courses in psychology. Thus, this book can be used across different disciplines, not just in psychology courses. In addition, to meet the needs of students for independent study, the pedagogical devices allow the reader (student, professional, or lay parent) to assimilate the material without formal class instruction.

To assist the instructor in using this text, a companion *Instructor's Manual* is available. The manual includes a bank of test questions, which have been tested on my own students; lecture suggestions with project/discussion ideas, supplemental resource materials; and when relevant, a discussion of potential pitfalls, concepts which, in my experience, have been difficult for students to grasp.

One Final Point

I hope that I have provided the reader as well as the instructor with a textbook that competently addresses the clinical and developmental issues relevant to the psychopathology of childhood and adolescence. The quality of this book has benefited from opportunities to "test-market" revisions on several undergraduate classes. Input from students as well as from many reviewers has contributed to making the final product a better one. I believe that this unique book will meet the needs of students at various levels, instructors, professionals who work with young people, and interested lay readers. To determine how well this text succeeds in these endeavors (and how it can better meet such needs in subsequent editions), I require feedback from you. If you are so inclined, please take a minute to drop me a line or give me a call with your reactions. Feedback from its readers can help the book continue to improve and achieve its maximum potential.

Acknowledgments

It seems appropriate to acknowledge those professionals whose input and expertise helped this text become a finished product. First and foremost, it was Catherine Woods (Acquisitions Editor at Longman) who read a prospectus and a sample chapter and was willing to take a chance with a first-time author and a controversial project. Her support and guidance were omnipresent throughout the project and will be remembered long after the first edition computer disks have been filed away! Catherine Woods' assistant Erica Smith also deserves acknowledgment for her efficient management of all the necessary details, which, at times, I am sure were more bothersome than rewarding! Finally, acknowledgment is due to the reviewers who offered their input at the various stages of manuscript development:

Alan C. Butler, *University of Maine*
Albert Cain, *University of Michigan*
David Hansen, *University of Nebraska*
Vicki S. Harris, *Vanderbilt University*

Alan Kent, *Nova Southeastern University*
Catherine Koverola, *University of Manitoba*
Robin Morgan, *Indiana University*
George Vesprani, *University of Cincinnati*

Clearly, it was the thoughtful feedback of these professionals that contributed to the creation of the final product you hold in your hands.

Amy Beth Taublieb

Chapter one
Conceptualization of the Psychopathology of Childhood and Adolescence

Introduction

When you hear the phrase "psychopathology of childhood and adolescence," what are some of your associations? Some people imagine a "crazy" child, screaming hysterically behind the thick doors of an insane asylum. Maybe you envision a sociopathic substance abuser in a maximum security prison, obsessively contemplating his next heinous crime. Or perhaps you focus on a recent newspaper report of a preteen suicide, and you wonder how anyone could be so depressed that she would desire to terminate her life. Indeed, the word *psychopathology,* especially when applied to children and adolescents, evokes powerful, emotionally laden imagery.

As we begin a formal study of the topic, however, we need to depend less upon free associations to define the topic and more upon factually based principles. First, look at this definition of the term *psychopathology:*

1. The science dealing with the causes and development of mental disorders.
2. Psychological malfunctioning, as in a mental disorder.

This definition from *Webster's New World Dictionary of the American Language* is adequate if it is assumed that there is an accepted definition of "mental disorders" or "psychological malfunctioning." If we agree on definitions of those two terms and apply these definitions to children and adolescents, the term *psychopathology of childhood and adolescence* is appropriately defined.

Like the term *psychopathology,* however, the phrases *mental disorder* and *psychological malfunctioning* both have several images associated with them. How can we arrive at a single definition we can use in rigorous scientific inquiry? Yet one consistency that does seem to prevail is the equating of *psychopathology* with what is considered to be "abnormal behavior."

Conceptualization of Abnormality

But are there agreed-upon definitions for *abnormal behavior?* Is there agreement as to whether any given behavior in which a child or adolescent engages is to be classified as abnormal? Is there a single set of criteria upon which all such decisions can be based?

There is, at least, general agreement that certain behaviors are "just plain weird." Some children and adolescents who demonstrate behaviors that others find to be aversive or strange are perceived as a bit odd or perhaps even abnormal. But what criteria can we use to classify a particular behavior as abnormal? The ideal set of criteria could be used to evaluate any behavior, and every evaluator would come to the same conclusion with respect to normalcy.

In fact, however, the current manner in which abnormal behavior is conceptualized depends on the particular theoretical framework(s) employed. Whether a professional is working with a troubled adolescent or an agitated 5-year-old, what is deemed to be abnormal depends on the theoretical perspective from which the case is approached.

Accuracy of Diagnosis

In order to properly evaluate any approach to defining abnormality we need to know whether the method can accurately detect the presence of psychopathology. For any given clinical situation, there is a range of four possible outcomes (see Table 1.1). Correct classifications can fit into one of two categories: diagnosing pathology when it is present (**true positive**) or correctly determining that no pathology is present (**true negative**). Similarly, erroneous classifications can fit into one of two categories: diagnosing pathology when none is present (**false positive**) or diagnosing an absence of pathology when it is actually present (**false negative**). As we explore various theoretical approaches to defining abnormality, we will evaluate their validity in different situations.

Table 1.1 Outcomes of Diagnosis

	Diagnosis	
Reality	Pathology	No pathology
Pathology	True positive (accurate)	False negative
No pathology	False positive	True negative (accurate)

The Statistical Approach

The statistical approach to defining abnormality involves assessing the probability that a given behavior will occur. Based upon the mathematical assumptions of the Central Limit Theorem, the statistical approach envisions all behaviors in terms of the frequency of their occurrence. This probability is represented by a frequency distribution referred to as the **normal** or **bell curve.** Figure 1.1 represents a frequency distribution, illustrating how often certain behaviors are likely to occur. The horizontal axis lists the behaviors in question, and the vertical axis represents the frequency with which the specific behaviors actually occur. Clearly, those behaviors represented along the middle of the curve are more frequent, while those represented at either end occur considerably less often. At either extreme of the curve, the behaviors can be conceptualized as also being more "extreme." Behaviors represented at the two extremes (at a greater distance than two standard deviations from the mean) are generally considered to be abnormal.

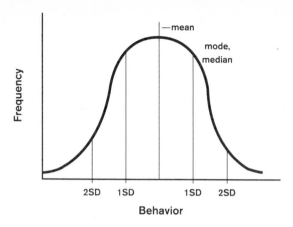

figure 1.1 Bell Curve: Frequency Distribution of Certain Behaviors
Behaviors represented at the two extremes are considered abnormal.

How can we use this information in the conceptualization of psychopathology in childhood and adolescence? To illustrate, consider 3-month-old Jenny, who cries whenever she is hungry. Is this behavior abnormal? More specifically, where is this behavior represented on the normal curve? We may not know the exact percentage of 3-month-old baby girls who cry when they are hungry, but we can safely assume that such behavior is very nearly universal. We can predict that this "hunger-crying" behavior would fall in the middle of the curve. Statistically speaking, then, the behavior in question would *not* be considered abnormal. By definition a frequently occurring behavior has a high probability of occurring in the population.

In contrast, consider 15-year-old John, who exhibits identical behavior. That is, whenever John feels hungry, he cries loudly, often screaming in a high-pitched voice. We know that such behavior is rare among healthy 15-year-olds in our population. Therefore, this example of "hunger-crying" behavior would fall in the tail of the frequency distribution—it occurs quite infrequently. Statistically speaking, then, a 15-year-old boy who cries whenever he is hungry would be considered to be "abnormal"; such behavior is relatively rare.

Other situations, however, are ambiguous. For example, the developmental literature reports that most children have a sense of gender identity at about 36 months of age. Thus, statistically speaking, we can say that it is normal for a child to be able to articulate his or her gender on or around the third birthday. Consider, however, the case of 2-year-old Pete, who is able to convince the clinician of a firm sense of gender identity. Operating from within a firm statistical framework, we would have to consider Pete's premature development of gender identity abnormal as its frequency is rather low.

Now consider the case of 2-year-old Ashley, who has no interest in stuffed animals or dolls. Rather, she carries a silver spoon from her grandmother's house, and she even sleeps with it. The developmental literature states that the majority of young children become attached to a special toy, usually a doll or animal, by 18 months of age. Ashley has never had such a relationship with a traditional toy. Statistically speaking, her behavior would be deemed abnormal.

Still another example is 8-year-old Brian, who has an IQ of 140. Using the statistical approach to defining pathology, Brian would be considered abnormal in this area, as his score does not fall within two standard deviations of the mean. Brian's IQ score is so high that it falls in the tail of the frequency distribution. The drawback to applying this approach is obvious: few parents would want their child of above-average intelligence to be considered abnormal.

Clearly, then, defining abnormal behavior from a statistical perspective has its limitations. Although most people tend to define normalcy within the statistical framework (either formally or informally), there are obvious problems in using the statistical approach as the sole or primary criterion. With this approach, we have to classify any uncommon behavior as abnormal and therefore pathological, whether the behavior is a delay in development, an acceleration in development, true pathology, or simply the manifestation of behaviors or characteristics not found in the majority of the given reference group.

A second difficulty with this method of defining pathology centers around the determination of the critical values along the normal curve. That is, what point along the normal curve (to the left and right of the median) is to be considered the cutoff point for determining pathology or abnormality? Is it appropriate to classify all behaviors two standard deviations to the left and right of the median as abnormal or pathological? Instead, should all behaviors with frequencies one standard deviation to the left and right of the median be considered abnormal? Clearly, the actual placement of the line of demarcation is arbitrary, yet the cutoff can have serious implications for classification and subsequent treatment of a child or adolescent.

The Cultural Approach

Another way to define abnormal behavior is to assess how the given behavior is perceived by the culture in which it is observed. Here, the issue is the degree to which the culture or society accepts the behavior or experiences difficulty with its manifestation. Is the behavior generally considered acceptable, or is it typically frowned upon or discouraged?

Again, it is useful to consider some examples. First, consider the case of Jonathan, an 11-year-old boy who, when not directly supervised, sets fires and burns magazines, books, and school papers. Of course, this is not a behavior that the majority of society would condone. Therefore, with minimal ambiguity, we can classify Jonathan's behavior as abnormal within the cultural framework. Similarly, the behavior of 8-year-old Emily, who is often involved in physical fights with her classmates, is not generally socially acceptable, so her fighting can be considered abnormal from the clinical perspective. These examples typify unambiguous situations that can be reliably classified by employing the cultural perspective to define psychopathology.

In some situations, however, the cultural perspective is not appropriate. There are behaviors that some members of a culture find unacceptable, yet that cannot be accurately classified as abnormal. Sixteen-year-old Richard, for example, calls himself an atheist, but American society is Judeo-Christian in orientation and adherence to an established religious system is generally reinforced as a positive value. Although many members of his society would not approve of Richard's atheism, he cannot be classified as abnormal.

When there is no consistent cultural position on an issue, an individual's value system must be incorporated into decisions about normalcy. Consider 15-year-old Beth, whose first sexual experience was a single act of unprotected sexual intercourse with her boyfriend. A few weeks later, Beth discovered she was pregnant, and she decided to abort the pregnancy. Although some people support Beth's decision, others question how she could have possibly proceeded as she did. Clearly, in this case the cultural approach cannot help us define what is normal.

Another issue in using the cultural perspective is that acts considered deviant in one culture can be viewed as perfectly appropriate in another. Consider 9-year-old Adam. As part of a clinical academic evaluation, Adam drew a picture of a person (see Figure 1.2). The school psychologist was pleased with Adam's attempt, perceiving it as an age-appropriate attempt to reproduce a human image. Being Amish, Adam has been taught that it is wrong to draw human figures with faces, that such images represent disrespect toward God.

However, if 9-year-old David from midtown Manhattan were to draw a similar picture, his school psychologist would rightly be alarmed. In most cases, a 9-year-old boy who does not incorporate faces in his human figure drawings is indeed exhibiting pathology.

Like the statistical approach to defining abnormality, then, the cultural approach has limitations. The reliability of the cultural approach is severely compromised when personal values and/or cross-cultural differences are involved.

figure **1.2**

Think About It

Ethnic Differences in Coping with School Stress

Research reported in the *American Journal of Orthopsychiatry* (Munsch & Wampler, 1993) looked at adolescents of different ethnicities in terms of their coping strategies for dealing with school stressors. The authors surveyed 51 African-American, 222 caucasian, and 159 Mexican-American students and analyzed their responses to stressful school events, their coping strategies, and their support networks. Minority students were more likely to have relatives as their support networks, while caucasians more often looked outside the family. If we take these data at face value, what are the implications in regard to psychopathology and normalcy?

The Biological Approach

The biological approach to defining abnormality and pathology attempts to be scientifically objective. From this perspective, psychopathology is caused by an anomaly in one or more systems—a chemical imbalance, a morphological variation, or any other deviation from normal biological status.

To apply this perspective to defining normalcy, we must accept the premise that psychopathology can be at least partially caused by physiological changes. This means that there is a direct connection between biological status and psychological functioning. Thus, when biological processes go awry, psychopathology results, and certain types of biological anomalies determine the presence or absence of pathology.

For a valid application of this model, consider 17-year-old Jasmine. Over the past six months, she has become extremely sensitive and moody; she sobs tearfully at the slightest provocation. Prior to this, Jasmine had been relatively stable emotionally and cried only three or four times a year. Seven months ago, at the recommendation of her gynecologist, Jasmine began taking oral contraceptives in order to regulate her painful, irregular menstrual periods. Hormonal assays indicated that the progesterone level in the birth control pills was too high for Jasmine, causing her moodiness. When her prescription was adjusted, the affective lability promptly disappeared. Approaching her problem from a biological perspective proved useful and appropriate. Clearly, the biological "abnormality" was the source of Jasmine's psychological symptoms.

In the case of 7-year-old Jimmy, however, the biological approach arrived at an erroneous conclusion. Several weeks ago, Jimmy was struck by an automobile, and he hit his head on the pavement. About a week after the accident, there was a dramatic change in Jimmy's behavior. Over the past several weeks, this child has become anxious and less independent; he is a more restless sleeper, often waking up at night screaming in terror; and he has become reluctant to leave his house alone. In an attempt to evaluate these symptoms, his physician sent Jimmy to the local children's hospital for a CAT scan, but the test showed no physiological abnormality. On this basis, Jimmy was diagnosed as having no demonstrable problem. Unfortunately, the physician did not look for other sources of Jimmy's symptoms. Jimmy has recovered physically, but he is still suffering psychologically. This child has Post-Traumatic Stress Disorder, a genuine psychopathological diagnosis.

As illustrated by these two examples, the biological approach to defining normalcy is appropriate when the cause of the behavior in question is at least partially biological. When the cause is not biological, however, or when there are multiple causes, it is imperative to investigate **psychogenic factors** as well. Failing to consider nonbiological factors will often lead to erroneous diagnoses.

The Functional Approach

If we can conceptualize the biological approach as the perspective that most clearly features scientific objectivity, we can characterize the functional approach as the perspective that most features practicality. The functional approach evaluates the degree to which the behavior in question interferes with the individual's optimal level of functioning.

The crucial question in the functional approach is whether or not, or to what degree, the symptoms in question affect the individual's day-to-day functioning. The severity of any given symptom is irrelevant in diagnosing pathology unless the behavior negatively affects the person's life. For example, a 13-year-old girl living in central Boston may possess all of the symptoms indicative of a clinical diagnosis of snake phobia. However, the chance that she will encounter a snake in her daily life is virtually nil, so her symptoms seldom if ever manifest themselves. Thus, using the functional approach, we would not consider this girl abnormal.

Eleven-year-old Reid, however, wets his bed nearly every night. Reid is often so upset in the morning he goes to school on the verge of tears and spends the first class period in the guidance counselor's office in order to calm himself down. In this situation, the behavior (bed-wetting) severely affects the quality of the individual's day-to-day functioning. This case of Nocturnal Enuresis would clearly be defined as pathological by the functional model.

In contrast, consider 8-year-old Josephine. She prefers to be called "Jo" because that sounds like a boy's name, and she insists that she is truly a boy. Jo wears androgynous clothing and has her hair cut short; she enjoys playing football, basketball, and baseball; and she insists that eventually her "pee-pee" (i.e., her vagina) will be replaced by a "wienie" (i.e., a penis). Academically, Josephine performs well; socially, she interacts well with her peers; and, aside from some arguments about her "true" gender, the little girl is no discipline problem to her parents. Josephine functions as well as most children her age. Although Josephine clearly exhibits symptoms of Gender Identity Disorder of Childhood, according to the functional perspective she does not exhibit pathology—her symptoms do not interfere with her day-to-day functioning.

Like the other perspectives, the functional approach has its limitations. Although this approach is pragmatic, there are situations in which diagnostic criteria for a given disorder are met, yet the individual's quality of life does not appear to suffer substantially. When there is no clear impairment in function, is it appropriate to apply a diagnostic label? And how much deviation from the "normal" level of functioning is required for a diagnosis of functional abnormality? The ambiguity inherent in such decisions limits the inter-rater reliability, and hence the validity, of the functional approach to defining abnormality.

The Clinical Approach

The clinical approach to defining normalcy and its converse, psychopathology, is the one employed most consistently by professionals. Although many professionals use other perspectives in their work in child and adolescent psychopathology, it is virtually impossible not to incorporate the clinical perspective as well.

The clinical approach to defining pathology is built around a diagnostic classification scheme. Criteria for the various diagnostic categories include a list of symptoms, and a certain number of symptoms must be present in order to diagnose an individual with that particular syndrome. The *Diagnostic and Statistical Manual of Mental Disorders (DSM-IV)* of the American Psychiatric Association (1994) is the most popular sourcebook in the United States. Chapter 2 discusses the *DSM-IV* and its predecessors in detail. Here, it is mentioned only to illustrate the clinical perspective. The *DSM-IV* lists every acknowledged psychopathological diagnostic category, with the essential criteria for each diagnosis. In addition, the *DSM-IV* addresses **differential diagnosis** so that pathologies with similar symptoms will not be misdiagnosed. The *DSM* is an atheoretical system, so there is little reference to **etiology** (causes).

Because the clinical perspective is so widespread in actual clinical practice, the issue of false negative and false positives becomes a moot point. In no way, however, is this to imply that by adopting the clinical perspective, a practitioner will make only accurate decisions. Indeed, clinicians, academics and researchers focusing on the inadequacies of the *DSM* system have questioned the validity and reliability of its diagnostic criteria. Yet because the clinical perspective is in many ways the cornerstone upon which all other approaches to defining pathology are based, to professionals working in the field, the clinical definition virtually defines the pathology. Professionals often turn to the clinical criteria in order to evaluate the accuracy of decisions reached via the other approaches.

To illustrate the use of the clinical perspective, consider the diagnostic category "Conduct Disorder." According to the *DSM-IV*, a child with this disorder must meet the following **exclusionary criterion:**

If eighteen or older, cannot meet the criteria for antisocial personality disorder.

The child must also have satisfied at least three of the following **inclusionary criteria** within the past 12 months, with at least one of the criteria present within the past 6 months.

1. Often bullies, threatens, or intimidates others.
2. Often initiates physical fights.
3. Has used a weapon that can cause serious physical harm to others (e.g., a bat, brick, broken bottle, knife, gun).
4. Has been physically cruel to people.
5. Has been physically cruel to animals.
6. Has stolen while confronting a victim (e.g., mugging, purse snatching, extortion, armed robbery).
7. Has forced someone into sexual activity.
8. Has deliberately engaged in fire setting with the intention of causing serious damage.
9. Has deliberately destroyed others' property (other than by fire setting).
10. Has broken into some else's house, building, or car.
11. Often lies to obtain goods or favors or to avoid obligations (i.e., "cons" others).
12. Has stolen items of nontrivial value without confronting a victim (e.g., shoplifting, but without breaking and entering; forgery).
13. Often stays out at night despite parental prohibitions, beginning before age 13 years.
14. Has run away from home overnight at least twice while living in parental or parental surrogate home (or once without returning for a lengthy period).
15. Is often truant from school, beginning before age 13 years.

In order to make a diagnosis of Conduct Disorder, a practitioner must determine that the individual's behavior "causes significant impairment in social, academic, or occupational functioning" (American Psychiatric Association, 1994).

The clinical approach, then, involves evaluating whether the individual possesses the relevant symptomatic criteria to the appropriate degree, so that the diagnosis can be applied. As in the case of Conduct Disorder, a set of criteria exists for each diagnostic category in the *DSM-IV.*

Are the *DSM-IV* criteria optimal? That is, for example, would there be a better way to define Conduct Disorder? The continuing revision of this diagnostic manual demonstrates the need to continually reevaluate these criteria. For the most part, however, the *DSM-IV* criteria are objective; inter-rater reliability is generally high; and this system is almost universally used by practitioners in the fields of psychology, psychiatry, and mental health in the United States.

The Dimensional Approach

As a means of bringing together all the approaches to psychopathology, Achenbach (1982) proposed a dimensional approach to conceptualizing psychopathology. Integrating the major theoretical models within a developmental context, the model was designed "to help us understand troublesome behavior in light of the developmental tasks and processes that characterize human growth." Using data obtained from child behavior checklists completed by parents (see Table 1.2), Achenbach and Edelbrock divided childhood and adolescence into four developmental periods characterized by the tackling of certain issues. Failure to resolve these issues can cause psychopathology.

Table 1.2 Syndromes Found Through Factor Analysis of the Child Behavior Checklist

Group	Internalizing Syndromes*	Mixed Syndromes	Externalizing Syndromes*
Boys aged 4–5	1. Social withdrawal 2. Depressed 3. Immature 4. Somatic complaints	1. Sex problems	1. Delinquent 2. Aggressive 3. Schizoid
Boys aged 6–11	1. Schizoid 2. Depressed 3. Uncommunicative 4. Obsessive compulsive 5. Somatic complaints	1. Social withdrawal	1. Delinquent 2. Aggressive 3. Hyperactive
Boys aged 12–16	1. Somatic complaints 2. Schizoid 3. Uncommunicative 4. Immature 5. Obsessive compulsive	1. Hostile withdrawal	1. Hyperactive 2. Aggressive 3. Delinquent
Girls aged 4–5	1. Somatic complaints 2. Depressed 3. Schizoid 4. Social withdrawal	1. Obese	1. Hyperactive 2. Sex problems 3. Aggressive
Girls aged 6–11	1. Depressed 2. Social withdrawal 3. Somatic complaints 4. Schizoid obsessive		1. Cruel 2. Aggressive 3. Delinquent 4. Sex Problems 5. Hyperactive
Girls aged 12–16	1. Anxious obsessive 2. Somatic complaints 3. Schizoid 4. Depressed withdrawal	1. Immature hyperactive	1. Cruel 2. Aggressive 3. Delinquent

*Syndromes are listed in descending order of their loadings on the second-order internalizing and externalizing factors.
Source: Achenbach, 1982.

Choosing a Theoretical Orientation

Despite the wide range of orientations toward childhood psychopathology, there is no single defining approach. Rather, each of the various approaches has its own merits and flaws. Of course, each of the approaches can yield reliable data in certain specific cases. However, in the more typical ambiguous situations, different perspectives are likely to yield different conclusions. To what degree, then, does a diagnosis depend on the definition of normalcy employed by the diagnostician?

The objectivity of the clinical perspective does yield results that are relatively consistent and reliable. Even when a practitioner does not agree with the particular criteria for any given diagnostic category, it is helpful to know that uniform criteria are being employed.

This is not to recommend using the clinical perspective to defining pathology to the exclusion of all the others. In fact, in the majority of clinical situations, most practitioners incorporate all the different perspectives. Competent professionals are aware that no single approach to defining pathology, be it statistical, functional, biological, cultural, or clinical, is able to stand on its own in every situation. Therefore, rather than attempt to determine which *one* of the given perspectives is optimal, we want to determine which *ones* are best suited for any given case.

It is often useful to think of psychopathology as a **continuous variable** as opposed to a **dichotomous variable.** In other words, rather than attempting to determine the presence or absence of pathology as an all-or-none concept, we can think of psychopathology as being present in virtually every individual, and then evaluate it as a matter of degree. We all have elements of "health" as well as elements of "pathology" in our psychological constitution, but in differential proportions. Some individuals might demonstrate a 50/50 split (i.e., 50 percent health, 50 percent pathology), whereas other individuals have a less even distribution. By approaching psychopathology as a continuum, rather than forcing an individual case into a positive-or-negative dichotomy, we can gain the most benefit from the myriad approaches defining pathology and normalcy. Practically speaking, a statement such as "The patient is manifesting psychopathology from a clinical and statistical perspective, but there does not seem to be any significant functional impairment" has more value than the statement. "The patient's behavior is normal" or "The patient's behavior is abnormal."

The next section on theoretical perspectives is presented against this backdrop of a continuous approach rather than a dichotomous, either-or approach. Again, there are several major theoretical approaches to explaining the etiology of psychopathological conditions in children and adolescents, and it is often most useful clinically to integrate several different perspectives in the conceptualization of a single case. Thus, we will focus less on the obvious differences between the various theoretical frameworks and more on how the approaches can be integrated.

Implications of Theoretical Perspectives

Virtually every textbook on psychopathology, whether its focus is on adulthood or on childhood and adolescence, discusses the various theoretical explanations of etiology. The theoretical approach chosen in any particular situation will affect the clinician's perspective on etiology, symptomatology, clinical treatment, and research. Just as the manner in which normalcy is defined influences how psychopathology is conceptualized, the theoretical approach provides the framework for treatment of pathological conditions.

Specific Theoretical Perspectives

Not surprisingly, the major theoretical approaches to the psychopathology of childhood and adolescence are the same ones applied to psychopathology in general. But it is not sufficient to merely "scale down" the theories that are applied to adults. Children are not "mini-adults," so it is imperative to consider any approach within a developmental context.

Theoretical perspectives can be classified as psychoanalytic theories; learning theories, including behavioral approaches and social learning theories; interpersonal theories, including systems approaches, attachment approaches, and temperament approaches; and biological theories, including physiological and genetic approaches. As we explore these perspectives, we will see that the boundaries separating these approaches are blurred. For example, the attachment approaches contain elements of learning theory, and virtually all the perspectives, with the possible exception of the biological approaches, could be classified as interpersonal. We will explore each of the major theoretical approaches separately and conclude with an integrative example combining elements of the different theories.

Psychoanalytic Theory

Psychoanalytic theories—especially the theory of Sigmund Freud—have exerted a strong influence on psychological thought. Our discussion of theoretical approaches begins with an exploration of the major components of psychoanalytic theory as it applies to the psychopathology of childhood and adolescence. Focusing on psychological functioning rather than behavior, psychoanalytic theory was developed primarily through clinical observation of young people with psychological problems (Marans & Cohen, 1991), though Freud himself never worked with children directly. Although current clinical work with children and adolescents generally involves behavioral or interpersonal approaches, the psychoanalytic school continues to exert a powerful influence.

Sigmund Freud's Psychosexual Theory An aspect of Freud's theory that is directly applicable to the psychopathology of childhood and adolescence is his **psychosexual model of development.** Freud conceptualizes human development as consisting of five consecutive stages through which every human being must pass in sequence in order to become psychologically healthy and mature. If, for some reason, an individual is unable to complete the tasks of any given stage, that individual is said to be *fixated* at that particular stage. According to Freud, it is the specific stage at which **fixation** occurs that determines the nature of an individual's personality or, in more severe cases, psychopathology. These stages are defined according to the body part that is the focus of the child's sensual gratification. According to Freud's theory, the **erogenous zones** change as the child matures, and the timely movement from one erogenous zone to another indicates psychological health and maturity.

During the first 18 months of life, the mouth is the primary source of gratification. The nature of the baby's experiences during this **oral stage** will determine some aspects of adult personality. For example, a baby whose oral needs are consistently frustrated will engage in aggressive oral behaviors (e.g., biting, loud crying, screaming) and may mature into an adult with an oral aggressive personality style. Such an adult often expresses anger verbally through sarcasm, yelling, and swearing; has a difficult time trusting others because of the betrayal associated with feeding needs as an infant; and tends to use the teeth in oral activities (e.g., chewing ice, biting a Popsicle rather than sucking it, or habitually chewing on pencils). Freudian theory tells us that an infant whose oral needs are consistently gratified will have pleasant associations with oral activities. As the child matures, he or she will use the mouth for oral erotic activities such as sucking, kissing, and eating. An infant who experiences the oral stage as excessively satisfying, however, may mature into an oral dependent personality. Characteristics of such a person include frequent eating, compulsive oral habits (e.g., thumb-sucking, inserting objects into the mouth, sucking on hard candies), and being extremely dependent and psychologically needy.

From 18 months to approximately 3 years of age, the child is confronted with two interrelated phenomena. First, the child is beginning to recognize his or her control over the process of having a bowel movement, a possible source of pleasure. And second, the parents are attempting to control that same process through toilet training. Power struggles that evolve during this **anal stage** lay the framework for the child's attitudes toward authority and control as an adult. Individuals whose anal period experiences were extremely strict and limiting will mature into what Freud labels anal retentive personalities. Such adults tend to focus on details, rigidly adhere to rules, are compulsively neat and orderly, and tend to be extremely frugal with their finances. In contrast, those whose experiences during this stage of development were rather unstructured and free from rules tend to mature into anal expulsive personalities. Anal expulsive types tend to be messy and disorganized; they rebel against authority, resent rules and regulations, and are careless with money. According to this theory adequate resolution of anal stage issues/conflicts result eventually in a mature adult with appropriately moderate approaches to money, organization, and authority.

Between the ages of 3 and 5 years, the child deals with the issues of the third stage of psychosexual development, the **phallic stage.** At this time, the child directs his or her erotic energies toward the genitalia (the penis in boys, the clitoris in girls), and masturbation becomes a more or less regular activity. During this stage, the child's conceptualization of the parents changes. Up until this time, the child perceived the parents as a single caretaking unit, but during the phallic stage, the child develops a sense of **gender identity** through identification with the parent of the same sex. This can prove to be a difficult task. Boys need to deal with their **Oedipus conflict;** they must move from feeling resentfully jealous of the father because of his relationship with the sexually desired mother to identifying with the father, a process referred to as identification with the aggressor. Girls need to deal with their **Electra conflict,** moving from jealousy of the mother because of her relationship with the sexually desired father to identification with the mother. Resolution of these conflicts marks the termination of this phallic stage and prepares the individual for heterosexual relationships later in life.

After the phallic stage, the child enters the **latency stage** of development. From about 6 to 12 years of age, there is no specific erotic focus. The child's sexual urges are attenuated somewhat, and he or she learns to channel sexual energies into more socially acceptable activities. For example, an anally fixated second-grader may become a sculptor who works with clay rather than playing with his feces. A third-grader who is orally aggressive may develop a strong preference for crunchy foods or gum chewing rather than biting everyone who angers her.

Upon reaching puberty, around 12 years of age, the preadolescent enters the **genital stage** of development. At this point the preteen embarks on a quest to fulfill the reproductive needs. The erotic focus returns to the genital area—back to the penis for the male, but requiring a shift from the clitoris to the vagina for the female. The maturing individual is preparing for the eventual formation of a mature marital relationship.

According to Freud's psychosexual theory of development, every child must successfully complete all five stages in order to become a psychologically healthy adult. Should an individual have particular difficulty with any one of these stages, this will evidence itself in maladaptive reactions during times of stress, or, in more severe cases, through full-blown psychopathology (S. Freud, 1920, 1940).

Case Study 1.1

The parents of 16-year-old Elias told a psychoanalyst friend that they were concerned because their son has not expressed any interest in girls. They suspected, however, that Elias masturbates for extended periods of time, and they have also found erotic poetry written by Elias with his mother as the object of his sexual desire.

The psychoanalyst conceptualized the described behavior as being characteristic of a fixation at the phallic stage of development. The masturbation represented a continued focus on the penis as a source of erotic pleasure. Similarly, the psychoanalyst interpreted Elias's sexual feelings toward his mother as being indicative of an unresolved Oedipus conflict.

Anna Freud Partly as a reaction to the theory of her father, Anna Freud (1895–1982) emphasized the necessity of focusing on the child's observable behavior, although she did not completely discount unconscious processes. Like her father, Anna Freud focused on the conflicts and tensions inherent in various stages of life, claiming that each stage of development has concomitant tasks that need to be accomplished. She also wrote of the role of the child within the sphere of the family, emphasizing the role of the family in the youngster's healthy or atypical development.

Anna Freud, too, believed that psychopathology emanates from the inability of a child to accomplish the tasks of development at the appropriate times. She distinguished between those psychopathologies that are a manifestation of developmental disturbances and those that are a manifestation of internal conflict. She classified the psychiatric disorders of children into the following categories: psychosomatics, neurotic symptoms, psychotic and delinquent symptoms, borderline symptoms, personality disorders, hypochondriasis, inhibited or destructive symptoms, infantile symptoms, symptoms resulting from organic causes, delays and failures in development, fears and anxieties, school failures, failures in social adaptation, and aches and pains (A. Freud, 1945, 1952, 1958, 1965).

Melanie Klein Melanie Klein (1882–1960) believed that Anna Freud placed too heavy an emphasis on overt behaviors. Focusing primarily on those instincts present from life's very beginning, Klein wrote of the instinctual urges that form the basis of the individual's development. These urges are associated with oral gratification obtained from the mother and the emotions associated with that process.

Klein spoke of the earliest part of life as a time when the infant is virtually totally dependent upon the mother or primary caretaker. The baby becomes aware of this dependence and vulnerability and develops a feeling of fear and hostility toward the mother. Kleinian theory postulates that the baby worries about abandonment during this phase and becomes overwhelmed with paranoid and persecutory feelings. By 6 months of age, these issues should resolve as the baby reaches the next phase of Kleinian development. This second stage is characterized by the baby recognizing the benevolence of the mother and feeling excessively guilty for the hostile feelings of the previous stage. This phase characterized by *depressive guilt* becomes a focal point for subsequent development throughout life. Klein considers the psychological processing of this guilt, a process referred to as *reparation*, to be a continuous task as the individual matures. With its accomplishment, the individual will be able to integrate the good and bad in a relationship. Failure, however, will result in pathological use of the defense mechanisms of projective identification, splitting, idealization, denial, and persecutory anxiety (Klein, 1948, 1952, 1958, 1984a, 1984b).

Klein is now viewed as a pioneer in the development of **object relations theory.** This theory focuses on how the internalization of an individual's experiences affects psychological development. For child and adolescent psychopathology, object relations theory provides a **schema** to explain how the young child copes with conflict with parental figures.

D. W. Winnicott's work (1953) is often conceptualized as combining that of Sigmund

Freud and Melanie Klein. His developmentally oriented object relations theory emphasized the psychological and environmental conditions necessary for a child to develop a sense of identity. Focusing on the close interrelationship between the mother and child, Winnicott wrote of the necessity of every child being exposed to a "perfect environment" and argued that the maternal figure serves as a virtual mirror for all of the infant's needs and desires. According to Winnicott, this temporary mirroring allows the infant to eventually become aware of his or her own needs. As the baby grows older, the mother should offer an unobtrusive presence when the child is not making requests. This combination of care and independence is "good-enough mothering," and, according to Winnicott, allows an individual to develop a psychologically healthy sense of self.

Case Study 1.2

Six-year-old Tasha is having problems in her kindergarten class. She did not attend preschool, and this is her first experience with spending any extended period separated from her mother. According to her teacher, for the first 45 minutes of class each day, Tasha cries hysterically, saying that she wants to return home. After she calms her down, Tasha remains shy, withdrawn, and aloof from the other children. She completes her assigned work but gives the impression that she is not actively involved. However, when Tasha's mother comes to take her home, the child resumes a lively demeanor.

After taking a lengthy history from Tasha's mother, an object relations therapist interprets Tasha's behavior as being a result of "too good" mothering; Tasha has not been sufficiently encouraged to engage in activities independently.

Erik Erikson The theory of Erik Erikson accepts the Freudian psychodynamic position, yet places more emphasis on the psychosocial components of development. His model proposes eight stages of development, extending from birth until late adulthood. Each stage presents the individual with specific age-appropriate conflicts to resolve. Like Anna Freud, Erikson emphasizes the family's ability to influence the progress of the child through the early stages. Healthy, nonpathological development is a direct result of the resolution of the conflicts inherent in each of the developmental stages. Erikson postulates that if a particular crisis is not resolved at its given time, the opportunity for its resolution is missed. Psychopathology is thereby explained as the inability to resolve one or more of the crises at the appropriate time of life.

Five of Erikson's eight stages involve childhood and adolescence. From birth until approximately 24 months of age, the infant is dealing with issues of *basic trust versus mistrust*. The resolution of this phase depends on the baby's relationship with the mother with respect to fulfilling the needs for oral gratification. Erikson's second stage (which corresponds chronologically with Freud's anal stage of development) involves the issue of *autonomy versus doubt*. As in Freud's second stage of psychosexual development, between 2 and 4 years of age the young toddler must cope with budding yearnings for independence, which are often stifled by parental limits. Between 4 and 6 years of age, the preschooler faces the conflict of *initiative versus guilt*. Erikson interprets this conflict in terms of oedipal issues, writing of the child's need to "sublimate" gender issues and the attraction to the opposite-sex parent, directing this energy into more socially appropriate channels. Erikson labels the major conflict of grade school as *industry versus inferiority*. During this time, the child's world of relationships expands beyond the family network, gender identity solidifies, and the child begins to become involved in more competitive activities. Next, adolescence requires formulation of a life plan, involvement in a peer group, and management of increasing sexual urges. Erikson refers to this phase as *identity versus identity diffusion*, emphasizing the necessity of repeated experimentation with different life roles in order to eventually achieve a comfortable identity (Erikson, 1963, 1968).

Learning Theory

In the late 1950s and early 1960s, largely in response to dissatisfaction with the available psychotherapeutic modalities (see particularly Eysenck, 1952), a new set of clinical approaches was introduced, based primarily upon learning theory. The basic premise of these **learning theories** is that all behaviors are learned and can therefore be "unlearned." Working from a self-proclaimed platform of scientific objectivity, behavioral theorists conceptualize and treat the presenting symptoms as *target behaviors*, not as indications or representations of some deeper, hidden psychopathology.

Traditionally, the pure behaviorist or learning theorist would focus almost exclusively on symptom amelioration rather than devoting time to exploring the dynamics behind the pathology. From this strict perspective, the symptoms are indeed the pathology, and the clinician will not probe beyond the acquisition of the information required to reduce the target symptomatology. Today's behavior therapist, however, does not limit his or her focus to symptoms but tries to change the environmental factors that affect the behaviors in question. In other words, the therapist does look at the *functional dynamics* of the pathology.

This approach to the understanding of psychopathology is based on the application of three major behavioral theories: classical conditioning theory, operant conditioning theory, and cognitive behavioral theory. Social learning theory is another type of learning theory that integrates the principles of the behavior theories with those of social interaction.

Classical Conditioning Theory Perhaps the oldest form of behavior theory, **classical** or **respondent conditioning theory,** dates back to the work of the nineteenth-century Russian researcher Ivan Pavlov. Pavlov demonstrated that after repeated pairing of a neutral stimulus (the *conditioned stimulus*, or CS) with another stimulus (the *unconditioned stimulus*, or UCS) that evokes a certain response (the *unconditioned response*, or UCR), the CS alone will elicit a similar if not identical response (the *conditioned response*, or CR). Pavlov's demonstration paired a buzzer (CS) with the presentation of meat (UCS) when feeding his laboratory dogs. The dogs would salivate (UCR) upon exposure to the meat. After repeated pairings, they would salivate (CR) at the sound of the buzzer alone (Pavlov, 1927).

In an experiment performed in the 1920s, classical conditioning was demonstrated in an 11-month-old baby referred to in the literature as Little Albert (Watson & Rayner, 1920). The researchers paired a white rat—a stimulus that previously evoked no startle response—with a loud noise, a stimulus that naturally induced a startle response in the young boy. "Little Albert" then demonstrated a startle response even when the white rat was presented without the loud noise.

Case Study 1.3

Four-year-old Benji was brought for a psychological consultation for an unusual problem. For the past few weeks Benji had cried whenever he saw a peanut-butter-and-jelly sandwich, previously a favorite of his.

Benji has been attending a preschool for the past eighteen months. After receiving consent from the parents, the psychologist consulted the preschool to see if any information could be obtained to explain Benji's behavior. Two months ago, a new child enrolled in Benji's class. Although this child is unremarkable in most aspects of his behavior, he consistently forces himself to vomit at lunchtime. When the psychologist presented this information to Benji's parents, they gave each other a knowing smile. Apparently, whenever Benji vomits or sees someone else do so, he begins to cry. Because his daily lunch is typically a peanut-butter-and-jelly sandwich, the sandwich has become a CS for Benji, evoking the CR of crying.

Operant Conditioning Theory The second form of behavioral theory views the organism as less of a passive participant simply reacting to environmental stimuli. **Operant conditioning theory** conceptualizes the organism and the environment as exerting reciprocal effects on each other. The behavior in question (the *operant*) both affects and is affected by the environment around it. Originated by Edward Thorndike (1932) and B. F. Skinner (1953), and then applied to child and adolescent psychopathology in the late 1960s and the 1970s (see Berger, 1977, and Eysenck, 1967), this theory posits that all behavior can be explained on the basis of four principles: positive reinforcement, negative reinforcement, punishment, and extinction. According to operant conditioning theory, these four principles account for the learning, maintenance, modification, and elimination of behavior patterns.

Reinforcement of any kind *increases* the frequency of the behavior it follows. *Positive reinforcement* works by the addition of a stimulus—the *positive reinforcer*—that will increase the frequency of the target behavior. For example, a reward of $10 for a high score on an arithmetic test is a positive reinforcer for a second-grader. Similarly, an experimenter might give candy to an autistic child after a certain period of non-self-destructive behavior.

Negative reinforcement also increases the frequency of a behavior, but it does so by removing some aversive stimulus from the environment. Thus, while positive reinforcement works by adding something positive to the environment following the target behavior, negative reinforcement works by removing something negative from the environment following the target behavior. As an example of the application of negative reinforcement, consider the following case study:

Case Study 1.4

Twelve-year-old Mike has been exhibiting difficult behavior at school. He repeatedly disrupts the class with obscene noises, silly gestures, and immature comments. The consulting psychologist recommends the following plan. The boy's mother or father will attend school with Mike daily and follow him around from class to class. The boy will find this situation extremely embarrassing and aversive. The parents will continue to do this until there is a five-day period when Mike behaves appropriately in all of his classes. At that point, the parents will stop attending school unless the misbehavior resumes.

In contrast to reinforcement, *punishment* is designed to *decrease* the frequency of the target behavior. Typical punishments are "grounding" a teenager for unacceptable behavior, withdrawing television privileges from a school-age child for failure to do homework, and giving a toddler "time out" for misbehaving.

The effectiveness of punishment versus reinforcement has been a much researched topic. Various aspects of the punishment (for example, its timing and nature) have been investigated (e.g., see Abramowitz & O'Leary, 1990; Little & Kelley, 1989). The ethical issues in the administration of punishment are even becoming controversial in day-to-day parenting situations. Indeed, several European countries have made physical punishment of children illegal, and some U.S. states are considering the same type of legislation.

Think About It

Right of the Parent or Right of the Child?

Research on behavioral theory shows that reinforcement is clearly superior to punishment in modifying behavior. Considering the reported increase in physical abuse of children, should parents or the government decide whether physical punishment of children is allowed? Do laws against corporal punishment protect children, or do they infringe on the rights of parents?

According to operant conditioning theory, behaviors are maintained and modified by reinforcement and punishment, so removal of reinforcing stimuli should result in elimination of a given behavior. This process of **extinction** is especially effective when a maladaptive behavior has inadvertently been reinforced, as in the following case study.

Case Study 1.5

Four-year-old Betsy begins to cry and scream whenever her mother is on the telephone. Often the screams are so loud that they can be heard in the adjoining apartments. Because the noise is so unpleasant, Betsy's mother gets off the phone after a few minutes to discipline Betsy, and within 90 seconds, the child stops crying. Inadvertently, Betsy's mother is reinforcing the child's tantrum behavior by providing Betsy with a positive response when she cries (i.e., getting off the phone and paying attention to the child).

It was recommended that the mother take the phone into another room when Betsy cries, and that she *not* get off the phone and interact with the child. After a week, Betsy's tantrums decreased, and after 19 days they ceased completely.

Kanfer and Phillips (1970) presented a five-part approach to conceptualizing behavior according to operant conditioning theory. Their S-O-R-K-C method was designed primarily for assessment. The letters represent the following concepts.

S (situation): Environmental factors (both internal and external) that influence the behavior

O (organism): The biological status of the child or adolescent

R (response): The primary response, whether overt or covert

K (contingency): The relationship between the behavior and its consequences, especially with respect to reinforcement schedules

C (consequences): The consequences of the behavior

Cognitive Behavioral Theory **Cognitive behavioral theory** differs from the other behavioral theories in that it incorporates the rather covert element of cognition into the theory. Kendall (1985) reviewed the basic assumptions behind the cognitive behavioral model. The underlying premise is that a person's cognitive interpretation of external events, and not the events themselves, determine the individual's response. Emphasizing the interrelationship between cognition and behavior, cognitive behavioral theorists maintain that the majority of human learning is indeed cognitively mediated.

Thus, according to this model, both adaptive and pathological behaviors arise from the manner in which we interpret external events. Maladaptive or irrational beliefs about the environment and external events are translated into maladaptive, pathological behaviors. Modification of maladaptive behaviors requires the identification, processing, and "reframing" of these cognitions (Ellis & Bernard, 1983).

Case Study 1.6

Thirteen-year-old Sarah is exhibiting the signs and symptoms of a public-speaking phobia. This is especially cumbersome because she is required to do several oral presentations in her eighth-grade English class. Her anxiety is so intense that she is unable to get out of her seat when she is supposed to speak in front of her class.

Sarah told the psychologist about her thoughts and feelings during these situations and revealed that one of her arms is slightly shorter than the other. Although this is barely noticeable, Sarah believes that if she speaks in front of the class, her classmates will notice her short arm and laugh at her. This unlikely, irrational cognition, not the actual act of speaking in public, proved to be the source of Sarah's fear.

Social Learning Theory Yet another variation of learning theory that incorporates some aspects of the various behavioral models is **social learning theory.** This approach focuses on environmental models of both desirable and undesirable behaviors. That aspect of social learning theory most applicable to the study of psychopathology in childhood and adolescence is **observational learning,** a process also referred to as *modeling,* proposed by Albert Bandura in the mid-1960s.

Bandura claimed that children learn various behaviors without ever having been reinforced in any way. This so-called no-trial learning occurs when the child observes another individual, referred to as a *social model,* performing a behavior. However, it is important to note that the issue of reinforcement is not moot with respect to social learning. Although in this model, reinforcement is not viewed as crucial to learning, reinforcement does influence which learned behaviors are actually performed. As we would expect, those behaviors perceived by the child to result in positive reinforcing consequences are the ones most likely to be actually carried out.

Subsequent investigations into the phenomenon of social learning revealed various interesting developmental trends. First, younger children tend to choose models whom they perceive as being kind and/or having a certain amount of legitimized power. Through a process of *deferred imitation,* toddlers imitate behaviors they observed some 6 or 8 months earlier. It is not at all uncommon for young children between the ages of 18 months and 3 years of age to view television characters as models. As children mature into the school years, however, it becomes important for the model to be their age or older and to be similar to them in as many ways as possible, especially with respect to gender.

Case Study 1.7

The teacher of 9-year-old Derrick telephoned the child's mother, sounding upset. He reported that over the past few weeks, Derrick has been getting into verbal arguments with some of the more assertive girls in the class. Although these confrontations never escalate to physical acting out, Derrick repeatedly engages in name-calling and uses some obscene phrases, many with sexual connotations. When Derrick's mother asked his teacher to repeat the phrases, she immediately recognized them as those used by her physically abusive husband when he became intoxicated.

Interpersonal Theories

Although all the theoretical perspectives we have discussed acknowledge the role of interpersonal interaction in the development of psychopathology, the theoretical models to be explore in this section feature this interaction in their constructs. These theories explain both adaptive and pathological behavior in terms of interpersonal interactions between individuals, most often family members. With respect to the psychopathology of childhood and adolescence, the most prominent of the interactional theories are systems theory, attachment theory, and temperament theory.

Systems Theory Systems theory, which focuses on the entire family within a *systems* framework, is often applied to the psychopathology of childhood and adolescence. In systems theory, no single individual in a family is labeled as the identified patient or as suffering from some psychopathology. Rather, the entire family is the patient, even though one individual may represent or manifest the pathology of the entire system.

Often incorporating other approaches, systems theory examines the family's system in terms of its psychodynamics, behavioral patterns, attachment issues, and certain biological factors in an attempt to explain the manifest pathology. In addition, systems theory often goes beyond the overt symptomatology and probes into deeper dynamics to explore the interactions between family members. Relationships between the parental figures, the siblings, each parent and each child, and often members of the extended family are all examined.

Systems theory postulates that all systems, including families, tend to maintain a *homeostasis*—that is, they tend to maintain the status quo. Healthy families, however, can change to accommodate the physical, social, and cultural development of family members. The ability of the family to withstand disruptions and to be flexible enough to integrate developmental changes into the system determines its relative health or pathology. Because all family members are participants within the system, the behaviors and responses of each family member affect the others (Ravenscroft, 1991).

The two major approaches to family systems therapy are the structural and strategic approaches. Salvatore Minuchin (1974) is recognized as the primary proponent of the *structural family systems approach,* which explains psychopathology as a result of a dysfunctional degree of involvement. In a healthy family, as each individual progresses through development, family members maintain a balance between becoming involved with each other and not intruding on each other's personal space. In contrast, psychopathology results from inappropriate enmeshment with or detachment from other family members.

With Jay Haley (1973) and Milton Erikson (1963) as its primary proponents, *strategic family therapy* focuses on the problem-solving abilities of the family. Effective problem solving is so crucial, according to the strategic model, that the inability to do so solve problems leads to psychopathology among family members. Thus, this approach views the therapist as an instructor who helps the family by teaching more effective problem-solving strategies.

Case Study 1.8

The upper-middle-class Jonesman family lives in the suburbs of an eastern city. The two older children are Justin, a 7-year-old boy, and Julia, a 12-year-old girl. After Jack, the new baby, had been home for a couple of weeks, Justin began acting different. He was previously a well-behaved little boy, but now whenever his mother is caring for the newborn, Justin begins to play in the baby's crib. He throws toys out of it, often breaking some. When Mrs. Jonesman puts the baby down and attends to Justin and disciplines him, Julia laughs hysterically.

Consultation with a systems therapist revealed that the new baby has disrupted the homeostasis of the family system. Justin, who was accustomed to being the "baby," is attempting to restore the homeostasis by engaging in immature behavior that forces his mother to decrease her involvement with the newborn. Julia, who has always assumed the role of the family clown, is attempting in her own way to restore the previous homeostasis by laughing loudly.

Attachment Theory Attachment theory focuses on the relationship between the child and his or her primary caretaker, from birth onward. First proposed by psychoanalyst John Bowlby, the basic premise behind attachment theory is that from birth, the infant innately engages in certain behaviors in an attempt to guarantee proximity to the mother (Bowlby, 1958). Subsequent work has identified some 15 types of attachment behavior, including greeting responses, differential crying, differential vocalization, differential smiling, and reactions to the mother's leaving (see Ainsworth, 1963). The caretaker's responses reinforce certain behavior patterns to varying degrees, so attachment behaviors vary, with intensities at either extreme indicating psychopathology (see Marin & Solomon, 1986).

Think About It

How Important Is Mom?

Bowlby revised his theory considerably throughout his career. Initially, in a monograph published by the World Health Organization (WHO), Bowlby stated that appropriate mothering by the biological mother is necessary for mental health. However, practitioners in many countries objected to his position. Bowlby later revised this conservatively narrow position.

Attachment theory delineates different stages: the first phase, from birth to 3 months, is characterized by undiscriminating social responsiveness; the second phase, from 3 to 7 months, is characterized by discriminating social responsiveness; the third phase, from 7 months to 3 years, is characterized by the child taking initiative in seeking proximity to and contact with the primary caregiver; and the fourth phase, beginning at approximately age 3, is characterized by goal-directed partnership behavior.

Bowlby writes that the behaviors of the caretaker and infant are reciprocal and that the quality of this relationship determines the child's subsequent psychological adjustment. Inner distress signals cause the child anxiety, and the extent and duration of the anxiety are directly determined by the quality and rapidity of the caregiver's response. According to attachment theory, the response pattern determines the child's subsequent expectations and therefore patterns of interaction with others in later life (Bowlby, 1958, 1969).

Think About It

Attachment and Depression

Empirical data support the theory that childhood attachment affects relationships in adult life. Pearson, Cowan, Cowan, and Cohn (1993) assessed the recollection of childhood and adolescent attachment experiences of 53 adults. The authors also collected data about current depressive symptomatology. Results indicated that poor attachment in childhood was positively correlated with depression in adulthood. How would you interpret this study?

Case Study 1.9

Eight-month-old Alice is considered by her parents and relatives to be an especially well-behaved baby. She seldom cries unless she is hungry or needs a diaper change, she sleeps an uninterrupted eight hours every night, and she eats quite well. However, Alice is noticeably uncomfortable when held, and she shows no special affection for either of her parents. Indeed, she manifests as much enthusiasm when a stranger approaches her as she does when her mother approaches. Overall, she shows very little affective response. Attachment theorists would consider Alice to have severe difficulties with attachment because she has not achieved the expected level of attachment for a child of her age. (Alice was later diagnosed with Pervasive Developmental Disorder.)

Temperament Theory **Temperament theory** focuses on the child's innate modes of interacting with his or her environment. Like attachment theory, this is a reciprocal model in that it also integrates the environment's responses to the child. Temperament theory states that each individual has a characteristic pattern of interacting with specific environmental stimuli. In a cyclic pattern, the child's inborn tendency to react in a certain way elicits predictable reactions from the external world, in turn eliciting specific behaviors from the child. Temperament theory hypothesizes that psychopathology results when there is a poor "fit" between a child's temperament (i.e., manner of interacting with the environment) and the expectations and reactions of the caretakers. Empirical data also exist that relate dimensions of temperament to quality of coping abilities and responses to stress (e.g., Carson & Bittner, 1994).

A 25-year longitudinal study (Thomas & Chess, 1977) distinguished nine dimensions of behavior in children: (1) activity level, (2) rhythmicity, (3) approach or withdrawal response, (4) adaptability, (5) intensity of reaction, (6) threshold of responsiveness, (7) quality of mood, (8) distractibility, and (9) attention span and persistence. The researchers proposed connections between the child's score on each of these dimensions, parenting patterns, and development of subsequent psychopathology.

Case Study 1.10

A couple consulted a behavioral specialist because of their frustration with the eating behavior of their 4-year-old daughter Penny, their second child. The parents express concern over what they perceive as Penny's eating patterns. This somewhat regimented family "always" eats three meals a day, scheduled at the same time every day. From infancy, Penny has seemed to have had difficulty complying with scheduled meals, and the parents are surprised that this has not changed over time. Even now, Penny does not accommodate to the meal schedule of her family, clearly preferring to eat whenever she is hungry.

A detailed clinical interview reveals that Penny exhibits similar patterns with other behaviors (e.g., sleep, bathroom habits); this is a child who has never responded especially well to scheduling. The clinician explains to the parents that Penny is not being purposefully obstinate; rather, her temperament has not adapted to rigid scheduling. The therapist further explains that problems may arise if the parents do not modify their style to accommodate the child's innate temperamental tendencies.

Think About It

Temperament and Parent Training

Sheeber and Johnson (1994) reported on the results of a parent training program for 20 mothers whose 3- to 5-year-old children were characterized as temperamentally difficult. Half of the mothers were assigned to an 8-week parent training program based on the principles of temperament theory while the others were assigned to a wait-list control group. Both at week 9 and at a 2-month follow-up, those mothers who participated in the temperament-based parent training program reported reductions in their children's behavior problems and fewer disruptions at home. The authors present these data to support a temperament-based parent training approach. What other ways could there be of explaining the results?

Biological Theory

Current research in child and adolescent psychopathology supports the idea that biological factors are involved in psychological disorders. Theories that acknowledge biological predisposition, chemical imbalance, and the like already integrate biological approaches and psychological issues. Adhering to a psychological perspective is not incompatible with the biological approach. Good clinical practice will integrate data obtained from both psychological and biological perspectives. Toward that end, we will briefly review the major biological models of etiology: the physiological approach and the genetic approach.

The Physiological Approach The *physiological approaches* to psychopathology postulate behavior to be a function of specific morphological, biochemical, and/or neurological factors. These models explain both pathological and healthy behaviors as resulting from a combination of various physiological processes transpiring within the body.

To apply this model to the psychopathology of childhood and adolescence, a practitioner presented with some pathological behavior will obtain data (blood tests, hormone assays, etc.) on physiological functioning. Tests may show a hormone imbalance or another form of chemical imbalance. Or, some pathology in neural function may partly or completely explain the presenting behavior. For example, the schizophrenic symptoms of a 15-year-old girl may be caused by a disturbance in brain chemistry. Similarly, the agitation observed in a 10-year-old boy with Attention Deficit Disorder may be caused by a brain abnormality or by genetic factors.

The Genetic Approach Biological theories based on genetics look to inherited traits to explain behavioral phenomena. These models assess the incidence of the target behavior in other family members. The so-called nature/nurture controversy debates whether an organism's characteristics depend primarily on genetic endowment ("nature") or environmental influences ("nurture"). Most practitioners believe that most behaviors represent an interaction between genetic and environmental factors.

Now that the nature/nurture controversy has died down somewhat, most researchers acknowledge that there is a genetic contribution to at least some behavioral phenomena. A question about family history of psychopathology finds its way into virtually every initial clinical interview.

Conclusions

In spite of the obvious differences between the theoretical models, they overlap considerably. From both a clinical and a pedagogical perspective, it is often more productive to focus more on similarities than on differences between the approaches. Most practitioners working with children and adolescents integrate two or more of the various models in their work rather than limit themselves to one theoretical framework. By regarding these theoretical models as overlapping rather than as mutually exclusive, the practitioner can better assess a particular case; looking at psychoanalytic, behavioral, systems, temperament, attachment, and biological issues.

The following questionnaire will help in the clinical conceptualization of the case studies presented in subsequent chapters of the text. Using this instrument as a general framework, questions applicable to each case study in order to formulate a cross-theoretical clinical conceptualization are asked.

I. Psychoanalytic Issues

    A. Of the five psychosexual stages of development, which was the most difficult for the patient? Does the patient manifest any symptoms of being fixated at any particular stage of Freudian development?

    B. What is the patient's relationship with the parent of the same sex? How has this relationship changed over time?

    C. What is the patient's relationship with the parent of the opposite sex? How has this relationship changed over time?

    D. If old enough to articulate meaningfully, how does the patient describe his or her early childhood?

II. Behavioral Issues

    A. Is there a target behavior whose frequency is to be increased, decreased, or extinguished?

    B. What is the frequency of the target behavior?

    C. When did this behavior begin? Has there been any change in the frequency of this behavior since its onset?

    D. What events are currently serving to reinforce this behavior?

III. Interpersonal Issues

    A. What roles do the patient and the patient's current condition play in the functioning of the family? How has this role changed over time?

    B. How do the primary caregivers describe the patient's behavior as a baby and a young child?

    C. At what age did the patient begin to recognize the mother, the father, and other family members?

    D. How does the patient react to separation from the primary caregivers? Has that reaction changed over time?

    E. How does the patient interact with others of his or her age? Has that interaction changed over time?

IV. Biological Issues
   A. When was the patient's last physical exam? Are there any anomalies?
   B. Is the patient currently taking any prescription or nonprescription medication?
   C. Does the patient have any allergies?
   D. Has the patient ever experienced any physical trauma? What are the details?

Summary

This chapter began with a definition of the term *psychopathology* and then discussed the clinical implications of different approaches to psychopathology. Diagnostic decisions may be accurate (true positive, true negative) or inaccurate (false positive, false negative).

We discussed the statistical, cultural, biological, functional, and clinical approaches to psychopathology, describing each model and its advantages and disadvantages.

We explored the major theoretical orientations toward the psychopathology of childhood and adolescence: psychoanalytic theory, learning theory (classical/respondent conditioning theory, operant conditioning theory, cognitive behavioral theory, and social learning theory), interpersonal theory (systems theory, attachment theory, and temperament theory), and biological theory.

The questionnaire at the end of the chapter provides a framework for analyzing the case material presented in later chapters.

References

Abramowitz, A., & O'Leary, S. (1990). Effectiveness of delayed punishment in an applied setting. *Behavior Therapy, 21,* 231–239.

Achenbach, T. M. (1982). *Developmental psychopathology.* New York: Wiley.

Achenbach, T. M., & Edelbrock, C.S. (1982). *Manual for the Child Behavior Checklist and Child Behavior Profile.* Burlington, VT: Child Psychiatry, University of Vermont.

American Psychiatric Association. (1994). *Diagnostic and statistical manual of mental disorders.* Washington, DC: Author.

Ainsworth, M. D. S. (1963). The development of infant-mother interaction among the Ganda. In B. M. Foss (Ed.), *Determinants of infant behavior: Vol. 2.* London: Methuen.

Berger, M. (1977). Learning theories. In M. Rutter & L. Hersov (Eds.), *Child psychiatry— modern approaches.* Oxford: Blackwell Scientific.

Bowlby, J. (1958). The nature of the child's tie to his mother. *International Journal of Psychoanalysis, 39,* 350.

Bowlby, J. (1969). *Attachment and loss: Vol. 1.* New York: Basic Books.

Carson, D. K., & Bittner, M. T. (1994). Temperament and school-aged children's coping abilities and responses to stress. *Journal of Genetic Psychology, 155,* 289–302.

Ellis, A., & Bernard, M. E. (Eds.). (1983). *Rational emotive approaches to the problems of childhood.* New York: Plenum Press.

Erikson, E. H. (1963). *Childhood and society (sec Ed).* New York: Norton.

Erikson, E. H. (1968). *Identity: Youth and crisis*. New York: Norton.

Eysenck, H. J. (1952). The effects of psychotherapy: An evaluation. *Journal of Consulting Psychology, 16*, 319–324.

Eysenck, H. J. (1967). *The biological basis of personality*. Springfield, IL: Thomas.

Freud, A. (1945). Indications for child analysis. *Psychoanalytic Study of the Child, 1*, 127.

Freud, A. (1952). The role of bodily illness in the mental life of children. *Psychoanalytic Study of the Child, 7*, 42.

Freud, A. (1958). Adolescence. *Psychoanalytic Study of the Child, 13*, 255.

Freud, A. (1965). *The writings of Anna Freud: Vol. 6*. New York: International Universities Press.

Freud, S. (1920). Beyond the pleasure principle. In J. Strachey (Ed.), *The standard edition of the complete psychological works of Sigmund Freud*. London: Hogarth Press.

Freud, S. (1940). An outline of psychoanalysis. In J. Strachey (Ed.), *The standard edition of the complete psychological works of Sigmund Freud*. London: Hogarth Press.

Haley, J. (1973). Strategic therapy when a child is presented as the problem. *Journal of Child Psychiatry, 12*, 642–659.

Kanfer F., & Phillips, D. (1970). *Learning foundations of behavior therapy*. New York: Wiley.

Kendall, P. C. (1985). Toward a cognitive-behavioral model of child psychopathology and a critique of related interventions. *Journal of Abnormal Child Psychology, 13*, 357–382.

Klein, M. (1948). *Contributions to psychoanalysis*. London: Hogarth Press.

Klein, M. (1952). *Psychoanalysis of children*. London: Hogarth Press.

Klein, M. (1958). On the development of mental functioning. *International Journal of Psycho-analysis, 39*, 84.

Klein, M. (1984a). *Envy and gratitude and other works: 1946–1969*. London: Hogarth Press.

Klein, M. (1984b). *Love, guilt and reparation and other works*. London: Hogarth Press.

Little, L., & Kelley, M. (1989). The efficacy of response cost procedures for reducing children's noncompliance to parental instructions. *Behavior Therapy, 20*, 525–534.

Marans S. R., & Cohen, D. J. (1991). Child psychoanalytic theories of development. In M. Lewis (Ed.), *Child and adolescent psychiatry: A comprehensive textbook*. Baltimore: Williams & Wilkins.

Marin, M., & Solomon, J. (1986). Discovery of an insecure disorganized/disoriented attachment pattern. In T. B. Brazelton & M. W. Yogman (Eds.), *Affective development in infancy*. Norwood, NJ: Ablex.

Minuchin, S. (1974). *Families and family therapy*. Cambridge, MA: Harvard University Press.

Munsch, J., & Wampler, R. S. (1993). Ethnic differences in early adolescents' coping with school stress. *American Journal of Orthopsychiatry, 63*, 633–646.

Pavlov, I. (1927). *Conditioned reflexes: An investigation of the pysiological activities of the cerebral cortex*. London: Oxford University Press.

Pearson, J. L., Cowan, P. A., Cowan, C. P., & Cohn, D. A. (1993). Adult attachment and adult child–older parent relationships. *American Journal of Orthopsychiatry, 63*, 606–613.

Ravenscroft, K. (1991). Family therapy. In M. Lewis (Ed.), *Child and adolescent psychiatry: A comprehensive textbook.* Baltimore: Williams & Wilkins.

Sheeber, L. B., & Johnson, J. H. (1994). Evaluation of a temperament-focused parent-training program. *Journal of Clinical Child Psychology, 23,* 249–259.

Skinner, B. F. (1953). *Science and human behavior.* New York: Free Press.

Thomas, A., & Chess, S. (1977). *Temperament and development.* New York: Brunner/Mazel.

Thorndike, E. L. (1932). *The fundamentals of learning.* New York: Teachers College Press.

Watson, R., & Rayner, R. (1920). Conditioned emotional reactions. *Journal of Experimental Psychology, 3,* 1–14.

Winnicott, D. W. (1953). Transitional objects and transitional phenomena. *Journal of Psychoanalysis, 34,* 89–93.

Chapter two
Diagnosis and Classification of the Psychopathology of Childhood and Adolescence

"The tracks!" said Pooh. "A third animal has joined the
other two!"

"Pooh!" cried Piglet. "Do you think it is another woozle?"

"No," said Pooh, "because it makes different marks. It is
either two woozles and one, as it might be, wizzle, or
two, as it might be, wizzles and one, if so it is, woozle."

A. A. Milne, *Winnie-the-Pooh*

What Is Diagnosis?

At first the classification and diagnosis of the psychopathologies of childhood and adolescence may sound like utterances from poor, confused Pooh. But after some practice, the system begins to make sense. The introduction to a recent textbook on psychiatric diagnosis states, "Classification in medicine is called diagnosis. . . . Diagnostic categories . . . like roses . . . can be defined explicitly and have a more or less predictable course" (Goodwin & Guze, 1989). Indeed, diagnosis is a vital and informative component of our understanding of psychopathological phenomena. With a reliable diagnostic schema, the process of diagnosis helps us arrive at an understanding of psychopathology.

What is diagnosis? Is it a universally agreed-upon labeling system, or does the process of diagnosis go beyond labeling? The term *diagnosis* comes from a Greek word meaning "to know." More modern etymologists interpret the Greek root into something as broad as "thorough understanding" (see Kessler, 1988). The typical dictionary definition reads something like this:

1. The art or act of identifying a disease from its signs or symptoms
2. A concise technical description or a taxon
3. Investigation or analysis of the cause or nature of a condition, situation, or problems or a statement or conclusion concerning the nature or cause of some phenomenon

This definition incorporates issues of etiology into the concept of diagnosis. We can, in fact, use diagnostic systems not only to identify and label certain disease states but also to provide information about causes.

When we consider the psychopathologies of childhood and adolescence, we want to know whether we can rely on one diagnostic system to provide all the information we need. The field of psychopathological diagnosis is controversial, however. There is no agreement as to the utility or even the need for, diagnostic systems in general. There is some feeling that diagnostic schema have little value with respect to treatment or clinical understanding, and some practitioners go so far as to say that a diagnosis of psychopathology is more harmful than helpful to the patient.

In this chapter, we discuss the advantages and disadvantages of diagnosis, and we present a history of the development of different diagnostic systems for child and adolescent psychopathology. The chapter concludes with a detailed description of the most popular diagnostic systems, with examples of their application.

Advantages of Diagnosis

Diagnostic systems are invaluable. It is difficult to imagine clinical practice without a framework within which psychopathologies can be classified, described, and defined. After all, we need to know precisely what the problem is before it can actually be treated. In order for practitioners, researchers, academicians, and students to rigorously explore the different psychopathologies, we need a uniform language and scheme to describe the phenomena.

One advantage of using a diagnostic system to classify, describe, and define psychopathological categories is that practitioners are "speaking the same language." By providing **operational definitions** for the various disorders, the diagnostic system yields valuable information.

For example, diagnosing a child with Attention Deficit Disorder conveys a significant amount of information. Because the diagnostic system used in the United States is primarily definitional, such a diagnosis makes a statement about the child's symptomatic profile. To be diagnosed with Attention Deficit Disorder, the patient must exhibit a minimum number of symptoms over a 6-month period; onset of symptoms must be prior to age 7; and the patient must not meet the diagnostic criteria for Pervasive Developmental Disorder. In summary, then, a great deal of information is inherent in the diagnosis of Attention Deficit Disorder. Indeed, this is true for all of the psychopathological diagnostic categories. Any given diagnosis carries with it a substantial amount of associated data.

It is appropriate to evaluate diagnostic systems in terms of whether they provide practitioners, researchers, and patients with a solid framework within which to treat, study, and understand the various psychopathological phenomena. Ideally, with uniform operational definitions, diagnostic criteria, and differential diagnostic information, a given diagnostic system should provide a foundation for scientific investigation. Why, then, does controversy exist among clinicians and theoreticians alike with respect to the usefulness of a diagnostic schema? In what way can a diagnosis cause harm?

Disadvantages of Diagnosis

In a review of the process of diagnosis and classification as applied to psychopathology, Klerman (1990) listed five major criticisms that have historically been directed against psychological diagnosis. Such arguments focus on these major points: (1) the medicalization of psychopathology, (2) the reliability of any given diagnostic schema, (3) the stigma associated with the application of a diagnosis to a given individual, (4) the issue of psychopathology being a continuous versus a dichotomous construct, and (5) the external validity of any given diagnostic system. Here we will use these five points as the basis of discussion, focusing on the application of these arguments to the psychopathology of childhood and adolescence.

The first argument against diagnosis questions whether psychopathology is best conceptualized along the same dimensions as physical illness. Because psychopathology is not a physical illness, the argument goes, it is inappropriate to attempt to apply a diagnostic schema to psychological disorders. Proponents of this argument point out that in medical illnesses there is usually a demonstrable organic or physiological anomaly, but this is typically not the case for psychopathologies. In the majority of psychological disorders, it is difficult if not impossible to identify any physical or chemical anomaly and, further, to demonstrate some definitive etiological relationship between the anomaly and the disorder.

This perspective argues that diagnosticians err in attempting to make the fields of psychiatry and psychology more objective and scientific. Labeling theorists and so-called anti-psychiatry writers, such as Thomas Szasz (1972), insist that psychopathology is not comparable to true medical pathology. Some theorists even purport that psychiatry is not part of the field of medicine.

Consider the case of Andrea, a 5-year-old girl who exhibits symptoms of Oppositional Defiant Disorder. Those around her can certainly attest to her annoying behavior patterns, but no objective physiological indicator confirms the existence of a disorder. In other words, aside from observable behavior, there are no objective physiological indicators to confirm the diagnosis of the disorder. Unlike the case in the majority of medical illnesses, no physiological anomalies are associated with Oppositional Defiant Disorder. Opponents of diagnosis in psychopathology argue that this lack of objective physiological indicators is a justification for not applying the same diagnostic approach to psychopathology that is utilized in classification of medical disorders.

The second argument against psychological diagnosis focuses on the perceived lack of reliability among the different diagnostic categories. When considering reliability, we evaluate whether the data contributing to the diagnosis are accurate or in error. That is, how much of the information used in formulating the diagnosis is a function of true clinical symptomatology, and how much is merely a function of artifact?

The issue of reliability also assesses the clinician's confidence that another practitioner would make the same diagnostic decision, given the same data. When the same clinical case is presented to several different professionals who adhere to the same diagnostic system, what is the correlation between their diagnoses? We evaluate the diagnostic schema in terms of its inter-rater and test-retest reliability.

Proponents of this argument against diagnosis contend that if reliability is not high, the criteria utilized to determine diagnostic categories are not sufficiently objective. Further, they argue that no system for diagnosing psychopathology can be acceptably reliable, given current technology.

Consider again the case of Andrea, the 5-year-old diagnosed with Oppositional Defiant Disorder. What proportion of the data utilized in making this diagnostic decision uniquely characterizes Oppositional Defiant Disorder? Conversely, how much of the data depend on environmental factors and actually have little if anything to do with Oppositional Defiant Disorder? And finally, what percentage of diagnosticians would arrive at this same diagnosis for this child?

Andrea's negativistic behavior could indeed be a function of Oppositional Defiant Disorder. However, this behavior pattern could instead be a function of the young child's particular developmental stage. She could also have had a bad day at day care, or she might have been suffering from her parents' recent divorce. This argument against psychopathological diagnosis states that because any number of factors can affect behavior, there is little possibility of a reliable diagnosis. Further, because of the interference of the environment, inter-rater reliability is low; different practitioners would make different diagnoses.

The third argument against psychological diagnosis focuses on the impact that diagnosis itself may have on the patient. This argument points to the stigma that is associated with a diagnosis of psychopathology. This position postulates that simply being diagnosed with a psychopathology can cause a patient to suffer additional difficulties unrelated to the actual psychopathology itself. The diagnosis becomes a kind of self-fulfilling prophecy, and behaviors occur because they are expected to occur.

Think About It

The Effects of Labeling

Labeling is a potentially negative effect of a diagnosis of psychopathology. If a child is characterized by a single label (i.e., the diagnosis), that label can "stick" to the child throughout life, even after development has virtually eliminated the symptoms. Children diagnosed with psychopathologies may be managed more punitively than others, or they may internalize the diagnostic label and define their identity in terms of the diagnostic category. Application of a diagnostic label can result in an overemphasis of the pathology associated with that label, and often strengths and positive attributes of the child are ignored. How can such effects be minimized, if not eliminated?

The fourth argument against using a diagnostic system to classify psychopathological phenomena questions the very nature of psychopathology. According to this viewpoint, psychopathology is not a dichotomous entity that is either present or absent in any given individual. Rather, psychopathology is conceptualized as more continuous; everyone has varying amounts of the different psychopathological disorders. From this position, then, it would not be appropriate to label individuals as belonging or not belonging to any given diagnostic category. Instead, it is more appropriate to conceptualize people as possessing varying amounts of the associated symptoms. Taking this argument to its logical extreme, the act of diagnosis becomes invalid because it forces individuals into categories that have no meaning in the real world. There is no point in classifying a child as having Oppositional Defiant Disorder because all children manifest symptoms of this diagnosis to some degree, and the same is true of the other diagnostic categories.

Think About It

Diagnosis and Third-Party Reimbursement

With the growing importance of financial constraints on treatment for psychopathology, is-sues have arisen with respect to diagnosis. Some insurance companies cover specified diag-nostic categories but not others. Ethically, a clinician cannot radically alter a diagnosis so that a patient can be reimbursed for treatment. How do you think this situation could affect the di-agnostic process?

The fifth argument against a diagnostic system for psychopathology focuses on the issue of **external validity.** That is, how does the diagnostic system apply to cultural contexts beyond the one in which it was created? To what degree can any diagnostic system be generalized to other cultures? If diagnostic systems are bound by cultural specificity, then there can be no diagnostic system that transcends its culture, and the very definition of psychopathology is a function of the culture's conceptualization of normalcy.

Let's use an example to illustrate how each of these five arguments can be applied to a sin-gle clinical situation.

Case Study 2.1

The school psychologist diagnosed 9-year-old Marcos with Developmental Arithmetic Disor-der. This child consistently scores much lower on arithmetic tests than on tests in other sub-jects. Marcos now receives special help daily in the school's resource room as well as from a private tutor.

Argument 1:

Can Developmental Arithmetic Disorder be considered a true diagnostic entity in the medical sense? First, there is no medication that can be prescribed to "cure" the problem. Second, no organic anomaly can be demonstrated via X ray, CAT scan, or the like. These facts demonstrate that Developmental Arithmetic Disorder cannot be conceptualized as a diagnostic entity in the true sense.

Argument 2:

Would the majority of clinicians diagnose Marcos in the same manner? What would the inter-rater reliability be if several clinicians examined this youngster? The reliability coeffi-cient may not be sufficiently high to justify the existence of such a diagnostic category.

Argument 3:

How will the diagnosis of Developmental Aarithmetic Disorder affect Marcos? Now that the youngster is aware that he is diagnosed with Developmental Arithmetic Disorder, he might be inclined to put forth less effort in his arithmetic because he feels it won't matter anyway. What are the implications for his self-esteem, now that Marcos gets special help *on a regular basis from a resource teacher and a private tutor? Finally, how will his class-mates react to the special attention Marcos is receiving, and perhaps more important, how will Marcos react to his classmates' reactions?*

Argument 4:

All of us experience difficulties in various task areas. Some people have problems remembering names; others have difficulties with directions; still others have problems with spelling, and others with balancing their checkbooks. Is it appropriate to diagnose each of these individuals with a "developmental disorder" in each of these areas? At what point is it appropriate to assign a diagnosis of psychopathology?

Argument 5:

Would Marcos be similarly diagnosed if he exhibited the same behavior pattern in another culture? If the answer to this question is not "yes" in virtually all cultures, then the diagnosis of psychopathology is merely a function of the value system in which we live. Is it clinically justified to label an individual with a diagnosis that depends on a cultural value system?

By applying all five arguments to a single case, we can see how they can be used in a clinical situation.

Think About It

Ethnicity and Diagnosis

A recent study of adolescents (Kim & Chun, 1993) looked at psychiatric diagnoses applied to 529 Asian-American boys, 425 Asian-American girls, 576 caucasian boys, and 471 caucasian girls. Overall, the Asian-American adolescents received more nonpsychiatric diagnoses than the caucasians. Asian-American girls were diagnosed with major affective disorders more frequently than caucasian girls. Asian-American boys were diagnosed with affective disorders less often than caucasian boys. Would you interpret these findings as unequivocal support for a cultural difference in the incidence of psychopathology?

History of the Diagnosis of Psychopathology in Childhood and Adolescence

While we discuss the development of classification schemes for the psychopathology of childhood and adolescence in this section, remember to keep in mind the five criticisms of diagnostic systems.

The *DSM* System

Interestingly, the history of the diagnosis and classification of mental disorders is relatively short. The American Medical Association produced the first formal classification of mental disorders in 1928, and the first *Diagnostic and Statistical Manual of Mental Disorders (DSM)* was published in 1952.

The history of the formal classification of psychopathologies in childhood and adolescence is even shorter. Most psychohistorians mark its beginning in the 1930s, with the publication of the first textbook of child psychiatry. This English text referred to all childhood psychopathological disorders as being problems of "personality." There was not any significant improvement with the publication of the first *DSM* in 1952. There were no clinicians on the *DSM* committee with a specific expertise in children or adolescents, so the book had no section addressing these disorders. Child and adolescent psychopathology was limited to four diagnostic categories: (1) chronic brain syndrome associated with birth trauma; (2) schizophrenic reaction, childhood type; (3) special symptoms reactions; and (4) adjustment reactions of infancy, childhood, and adolescence.

It was not until 1965, when the World Health Organization (WHO) proposed an international diagnostic schema, that a formal classification system was introduced for the psychopathologies of childhood and adolescence. Soon after, the Committee on Child Psychiatry of the Group for the Advancement of Psychiatry (GAP) published its own system (Kaplan & Sadock, 1991; Wiener, 1991). Based on a Freudian conceptualization of behavior within a psychosocial and developmental framework, the GAP schema divided the psychopathologies of childhood and adolescence into ten diagnostic categories. The first six categories were arranged in ascending order of severity. (The first category was designated "healthy responses," thereby incorporating nonpathological behaviors in the classification schema.) The seventh, eighth and ninth categories listed disorders considered to be caused by physiological factors. GAP reserved the tenth category for "other disorders."

Diagnostic Categories in the GAP System

1. Healthy responses
2. Reactive disorders
3. Developmental deviations
4. Psychoneurotic disorders
5. Personality disorders
6. Psychotic disorders
7. Psychosomatic disorders
8. Brain syndromes
9. Mental retardation
10. Other disorders

Two years later, the first revision of the *DSM* was published as the *DSM-II*. Although only 2 of 39 individuals on the revision committee claimed expertise in the field of child and/or adolescent psychopathology, the *DSM-II* represented significant improvement over its predecessor with respect to the classification of the disorders of children and adolescents. This edition included a section titled "Behavior Disorders of Childhood and Adolescence" with 11 relevant diagnostic categories.

DSM-II Categories

Behavior Disorders of Childhood and Adolescents

1. Hyperkinetic reaction
2. Withdrawing reaction
3. Overanxious reaction
4. Runaway reaction
5. Undersocialized aggressive reaction
6. Group delinquency reaction
7. Adjustment reactions
8. Learning disturbances
9. Enuresis
10. Feeding disturbances
11. Other reactions of childhood

The *DSM-II* generally avoided implications with respect to etiology, focusing instead on specific symptom profiles. However, because no operational definitions were included for the individual diagnostic categories, reliability and validity of the diagnostic categories could not be tested. Improvement in the classification of the psychopathologies of children and adolescents was still needed (Mattison & Hooper, 1992; Wiener, 1991).

The third edition of the *DSM*, known as the *DSM-III*, was published in 1980. This revision presented major improvements in classification of the childhood and adolescent disorders, and it also reflected major changes in psychological diagnosis in general. First and foremost, operational definitions were included for each diagnostic category, facilitating research on reliability and validity. In addition, the *DSM-III* included decision trees and more detailed descriptions of each diagnostic category in an attempt to ensure more accurate diagnostic decisions. Continuing to emphasize an atheoretical approach to diagnosis, making no reference to etiology, the *DSM-III* focused on symptomatology, providing inclusionary as well as exclusionary criteria for the various diagnoses.

The *DSM-III* classification system is based on a *multiaxial* system. The *DSM-III* includes 18 categories of psychopathological diagnosis incorporating over 200 specific disorders. Every complete formal diagnosis in this system incorporates a separate diagnosis along each of five axes. All diagnoses along four of these five axes have an associated code number. (The codes are especially helpful with respect to confidentiality issues.)

Axis I and Axis II of the *DSM-III* are the axes along which all of the psychopathologies are diagnosed. Axis II is for **Personality Disorders** (i.e., Paranoid, Schizoid, Schizotypal, Antisocial, Borderline, Histrionic, Narcissistic, Avoidant, Dependent, Obsessive-Compulsive, Passive-Aggressive, Personality Disorder Not Otherwise Specified) and **Developmental Disorders** (i.e., Mental Retardation, Pervasive Developmental Disorders, Specific Developmental Disorders, Developmental Disorders Not Otherwise Specified). Axis I is for other disorders that are first evidenced in childhood or adolescence (i.e., Disruptive Behavioral Disorders, Anxiety Disorders of Childhood or Adolescence, Eating Disorders, Gender Identity Disorders, Tic Disorders, Elimination Disorders, Speech Disorders, and Other Disorders of Childhood or Adolescence).

Axis III is for the diagnosis of physical problems, whether or not they are related in any way to the psychopathology in question. Axis III is the only axis that does not use numerical codes.

Axis IV is for rating of the severity of **psychosocial stressors** that contribute directly or indirectly to the psychopathology. Stressors are rated along a 6-point scale: 1, none; 2, mild; 3, moderate; 4, severe; 5, extreme; and 6, catastrophic. A rating of zero is coded if the clinician does not have sufficient data to make a rating. To facilitate inter-rater reliability, the *DSM-III* provides two tables (one for adults, the second for children and adolescents) with examples of stressors and their relevant ratings.

Axis V is for **Global Assessment of Functioning (GAF).** The rating score ranges from 1 (the lowest level) to 90 (optimal level) and was actually designed to be a composite rating of functioning in three areas: social relations, occupational or school functioning, and psychological functioning. The *DSM-III* required that two GAF ratings be given: one representing the patient's current level of functioning, and the second representing the patient's highest level of functioning during the past year. As for Axis IV, *DSM-III* provides a table with examples of different levels of functioning with their corresponding ratings.

The *DSM-III* expanded the number of diagnostic categories to 32. Diagnoses specific to children and adolescents were classified into 9 major categories: (1) Mental Retardation, (2) Attention Deficit Disorder, (3) Conduct Disorder, (4) Anxiety Disorders, (5) Eating Disorders, (6) Stereotyped Movement Disorders, (7) Other Disorders with Physical Manifestations, (8) Pervasive Developmental Disorders, and (9) other. This classification system coded Specific Developmental Disorders on Axis II. It is important to note that this was virtually the first time that developmental constructs were incorporated into the *DSM* diagnostic system.

In addition, the *DSM-III* provided an opportunity for the coding of conditions that are a "focus of attention or treatment" that are "not attributable to a mental disorder." These **V-codes** (whose diagnostic code numbers are all prefaced with a *V*) included several diagnostic categories particularly relevant to children and adolescents (e.g., Academic Problem, Borderline Intellectual Functioning, Malingering, Parent-Child Problem, Other Interpersonal Problem, Other Specified Family Circumstances).

In addition to providing a greater number of diagnostic categories than its predecessors, the *DSM-III* included more descriptive information for each diagnostic category. Finally, a glossary and decision trees were provided to assist in differential diagnosis.

Some seven years after the publication of the *DSM-III*, yet another revision was released. Intended to be an intermediary publication between the *DSM-III* and the *DSM-IV*, this revision was entitled *DSM-III-R* (the *R* stood for "Revised"). It incorporated developments in the field over the preceding seven years, including more empirical validation, and made two major changes in the overall classification schema for childhood/adolescent disorders. First, the *DSM-III-R* combined Attention Deficit Disorder and Conduct Disorder under the overall category of Disruptive Behavior Disorders. The *DSM-III-R* also included Mental Retardation and Pervasive Developmental Disorder among the diagnostic categories to be coded on Axis II. These and other revisions resulted in eight categories to classify the psychopathologies of childhood and adolescence: (1) Disruptive Behavior Disorders, (2) Anxiety Disorders, (3) Eating Disorders, (4) Gender Identity Disorders, (5) Tic Disorders, (6) Elimination Disorders, (7) Specific Developmental Disorders, and (8) other.

In 1994, the American Psychiatric Association saw the need for yet another major revision of the diagnostic system. Designed to coincide with the World Health Organization's *ICD-10* (discussed later), the *DSM-IV* presented several major revisions, especially in the field of child and adolescent psychopathology. This edition retained the multiaxial approach to diagnosis as well as a generally atheoretical perspective with respect to etiology. Tables 2.1 and 2.2 present the criteria for diagnoses along Axis IV and Axis V.

Table 2.1 Axis IV Psychosocial and Environmental Problems

Problems with primary support group
Problems related to the social environment
Educational problems
Occupational problems
Housing problems
Economic problems
Problems with access to health care services
Problems related to interaction with the legal system crime
Other psychosocial and environmental problems

Source: DSM-IV (Washington DC: American Psychiatric Association, 1994)

Table 2.2 Global Assessment of Functioning (GAF) Scale

Consider psychological, social, and occupational functioning on a hypothetical continuum of mental health-illness. Do not include impairment in functioning due to physical (or environmental) limitations.

Code (**Note:** Use intermediate codes when appropriate, e.g., 45, 68–72.)

100 91	**Superior functioning in a wide range of activities, life's problems never seem to get out of hand, is sought out by others because of his or her many positive qualities. No symptoms.**
90 81	**Absent or minimal symptoms** (e.g., mild anxiety before an exam), **good functioning in all areas, interested and involved in a wide range of activities, socially effective, generally satisfied with life, no more than everyday problems or concerns** (e.g., an occasional argument with family members).
80 71	**If symptoms are present, they are transient and expectable reactions to psychosocial stressors** (e.g., difficulty concentrating after family argument); **no more than slight impairment in social, occupational, or school functioning** (e.g., temporarily falling behind in schoolwork).
70 61	**Some mild symptoms** (e.g., depressed mood and mild insomnia) **OR some difficulty in social, occupational, or school functioning** (e.g., occasional truancy, or theft within the household). **but generally functioning pretty well, has some meaningful interpersonal relationships.**
60 51	**Moderate symptoms** (e.g., flat affect and circumstantial speech, occasional panic attacks) **OR moderate difficulty in social, occupational, or school functioning** (e.g., few friends, conflicts with peers or co-workers).
50 41	**Serious symptoms** (e.g., suicidal ideation, severe obsessional rituals, frequent shoplifting) **OR any serious impairment in social, occupational, or school functioning** (e.g., no friends, unable to keep a job).
40 31	**Some impairment in reality testing or communication** (e.g., speech is at times illogical, obscure, or irrelevant) **OR major impairment in several areas, such as work or school, family relations, judgment, thinking, or mood** (e.g., depressed man avoids friends, neglects family, and is unable to work: child frequently beats up younger children, is defiant at home, and is failing at school).
30 21	**Behavior is considerably influenced by delusions or hallucinations OR serious impairment in communication or judgment** (e.g., sometimes incoherent, acts grossly inappropriately, suicidal preoccupation) **OR inability to function in almost all areas** (e.g., stays in bed all day; no job,. home, or friends).
20 11	**Some danger of hurting self or others** (e.g., suicide attempts without clear expectation of death; frequently violent; manic excitement) **OR occasionally fails to maintain minimal personal hygiene** (e.g., smears feces) **OR gross impairment in communication** (e.g., largely incoherent or mute).
10 1	**Persistent danger of severely hurting self or others** (e.g., recurrent violence) **OR persistent inability to maintain minimal personal hygiene OR serious suicidal act with clear expectation of death.**
0	Inadequate information.

Source: DSM-IV (Washington DC: American Psychiatric Association, 1994)

In revising the *DSM-III-R*, the 27-member *DSM-IV* task force and some 13 work groups, each having responsibility for a section of the manual, engaged in a three-component process involving comprehensive literature reviews of the available material on each disorder, alternative analysis on data that had been previously collected, and field trials. The latter two procedures were employed especially when the literature on a subject contained contradictory data or little information. These three approaches allowed for increased empirical support for information presented in the revised edition.

According to the introductory comments in the *DSM-IV*, the criteria for actually making changes to the *DSM-III-R* were significantly more stringent that in previous revisions of the *DSM*. "An attempt was made to strike an optimal balance in *DSM-IV* with respect to historical tradition (as embodied in *DSM-III* and *DSM-III-R*), compatibility with *ICD-10*, evidence from reviews of the literature, analyses of unpublished data sets, results of field trials and consensus of the field. . . . Of course, common sense was necessary, and major changes to solve minor problems required more evidence than minor changes to solve major problems" (American Psychiatric Association, 1994, p. xx).

Unlike the previous revisions to the *DSM*, however, the *DSM-IV* contains fewer diagnostic categories specific to children and adolescents than did its immediate predecessor. The fourth edition incorporates descriptions of psychopathology in children and adolescents within the section on adult disorders. The rationale behind this approach was to increase consistency.

The *DSM-IV* contains ten major categories of psychopathological diagnoses considered to be disorders usually first diagnosed in infancy, childhood, or adolescence. These major categories, along with their subsumed diagnoses, are listed below.

Mental Retardation
    Mild Mental Retardation
    Moderate Retardation
    Severe Mental Retardation
    Profound Mental Retardation
    Mental Retardation, Severity Unspecified
Learning Disorders (Academic Skills Disorder)
    Reading Disorder (Developmental Reading Disorder)
    Mathematics Disorder (Developmental Arithmetic Disorder)
    Disorder of Written Expression (Developmental Expressive Writing Disorder)
    Learning Disorder Not Otherwise Specified
Motor Skills Disorder
    Developmental Coordination Disorder
Pervasive Developmental Disorders
    Autistic Disorder
    Rett's Disorder
    Childhood Disintegrative Disorder
    Asperger's Disorder
    Pervasive Developmental Disorder Not Otherwise Specified (including Atypical Autism)
Attention Deficit and Disruptive Behavior Disorders
    Attention Deficit/Hyperactivity Disorder
        Combined type
        Predominantly inattentive type
        Predominantly hyperactive-impulsive type

Attention Deficit/Hyperactivity Disorder Not Otherwise Specified
Conduct Disorder
Oppositional Defiant Disorder
Disruptive Behavior Not Otherwise Specified
Feeding and Eating Disorders of Infancy or Early Childhood
  Pica
  Rumination Disorder
  Feeding Disorder of Infancy or Early Childhood
Tic Disorders
  Tourette's Disorder
  Chronic Motor or Vocal Tic Disorder
  Transient Tic Disorder
  Tic Disorder Not Otherwise Specified
Communication Disorders
  Expressive Language Disorder (Developmental Expressive Language Disorder)
  Mixed Receptive/Expressive Language Disorder
  Phonological Disorder (Developmental Articulation Disorder)
  Stuttering
  Communication Disorder Not Otherwise Specified
Elimination Disorders
  Encopresis
    With constipation and overflow incontinence
    Without constipation and overflow incontinence
  Enuresis
Other Disorders of Infancy, Childhood, or Adolescence
  Separation Anxiety Disorder
  Selective Mutism (Elective Mutism)
  Reactive Attachment Disorder of Infancy or Early Childhood
  Stereotypic Movement Disorder (Stereotypy/Habit Disorder)
  Disorder of Infancy, Childhood, or Adolescence Not Otherwise Specified

To help lend some clinical realism to the *DSM-IV* classification system, the following clinical case studies are taken from the author's files.

Case Study 2.2

Jeff is a 9-year-old boy who has been diagnosed with Mild Mental Retardation and is now mainstreamed in the local school system. He was brought to a clinical psychologist for problems with Nocturnal Enuresis. The bed-wetting began approximately 3 months ago, coinciding with the divorce of his parents and his father's moving out of the home. Soon after the bed-wetting began, Jeff's mother took the boy to a physician, who determined him to be in excellent physical health. According to his mother, Jeff interacts quite well with his friends and is "almost never" a behavior problem. With the aid of a private tutor, he performs adequately in school. In general, then, aside from the enuresis, Jeff has always functioned quite well and continues to function well.

Axis I Functional Enuresis, Nocturnal

Axis II Mental Retardation—Mild

Axis III None

Axis IV 4 (severe—divorce of parents)

Axis V GAF (present): 85

GAF (past): 90

Case Study 2.3

Brad is a 14-year-old boy who was brought for therapy because of "problems at home." At least three times per week, Brad gets into intense arguments with his stepfather. Although these arguments have never escalated to physical violence, Brad's mother perceives them as being extremely disruptive to the household. Brad is described as having many friends and as a model student, with an "A" average in all his subjects. Brad's mother reports that although she remarried 10 years ago (when Brad was 4 years old), problems between the boy and his stepfather began only within the past several weeks. Aside from occasional bouts of asthma, Brad has no physical problems, and he is a star member on several of his junior high sports teams.

Axis I Parent-Child Problem (a V-code)

Axis II None

Axis III Asthma

Axis IV 2 (mild)

Axis V GAF (present): 80

GAF (past): 90

Case Study 2.4

Tina is a 14-year-old girl who was brought to a psychologist after having attempted suicide by ingesting two bottles of aspirin. She ingested the pills 2 months after her best friend died of cancer. When asked about her own parasuicide, Tina blandly stated "I have nothing left to life for.... Life sucks, it's unfair.... Why bother?" Over the past 3 weeks, Tina's appetite has been poor and she has been unable to sleep through the night. She was previously an honor student, but her schoolwork has deteriorated, and Tina seems to have no interest in any of her usual activities. At this point, she is showing no physical deterioration, although she has been diagnosed with a benign mitral valve prolapse.

Axis I Major Depression, single episode

Axis II None

Axis III Mitral Valve Prolapse

Axis IV 5 (Extreme)

Axis V GAF (present): 35

GAF (past): 85

Other Diagnostic Systems

Although the *DSM* is commonly used in the United States, other classification systems exist.

Some of them were designed specifically for use in child and adolescent psychopathology. Anna Freud, for example, devised a system founded on developmental parameters (1965), and more recently, Spiel devised a triaxial system (1981).

Perhaps the most popular of these alternative systems is the **dimensional approach** of Achenbach and his colleagues (e.g., see Achenbach, Conners, & Quay, 1985). With a history in the literature of some 40 years, this perspective began to be applied to child and adolescent psychopathology in the late 1970s. This empirically based approach employs statistically related clusters of psychopathological behaviors called *dimensions*. Studies are currently being performed to determine relationships between these statistically derived dimensions and the categories in the *DSM* system.

Another diagnostic system, often used in Europe and Great Britain, is the World Health Organization's *International Classification of Diseases (ICD)*. While the *DSM-III-R* was being used in the United States, the ninth version of the *ICD* (the *ICD-9*) was being used in Europe. The *ICD-9*, which was considered to be more conservative than the *DSM-III-R*, based its diagnostic categories on a glossary system rather than on specific diagnostic criteria (Mattison & Hooper, 1992). All the *DSM-III-R* diagnoses were included in the *ICD-9*, but not vice versa. Despite the variations between the *DSM-III-R* and *ICD-9* systems, studies of their reliability have yielded similar results.

WHO designed its next revision of the *ICD* manual to correspond as closely as possible with the *DSM-IV*. The *ICD-10* designates more diagnostic categories specific to children and adolescents than does the *DSM-IV*. The *ICD-10* lists 14 major diagnostic categories (in addition to mental retardation), each with several subcategories. The following categories are relevant to the psychopathology of children and adolescents.

Mental retardation
    Mild mental retardation
    Moderate mental retardation
    Severe mental retardation
    Profound mental retardation
    Other mental retardation
    Unspecified mental retardation
Disorders of psychological development
Specific developmental disorders of speech and language
    Specific speech articulation disorder
    Expressive language disorder
    Receptive language disorder
    Acquired aphasia with epilepsy
    Other developmental disorders of speech and language
Specific developmental disorders of scholastic skills
    Specific reading disorder
    Specific spelling disorder
    Specific disorder of arithmetic skills
    Mixed disorder of scholastic skills
    Other developmental disorders of scholastic skills
    Developmental disorder of scholastic skills, unspecified
Specific developmental disorder of motor function
Mixed specific developmental disorders
Pervasive developmental disorders

Childhood autism
Atypical autism
Rett's syndrome
Other childhood disintegrative disorders
Overactive disorder associated with mental retardation and stereotyped movements
Asperger's syndrome
Other pervasive developmental disorders
Pervasive developmental disorder, unspecified
Other disorders of psychological development
Unspecified disorder of psychological development
Behavioral and emotional disorders with onset usually occurring in childhood and
    Adolescence
Hyperkinetic disorders
Disturbance of activity and attention
Hyperkinetic conduct disorder
Other hyperkinetic disorders
Hyperkinetic disorder, unspecified
Conduct disorders
Conduct disorder, confined to the family context
Unsocialized conduct disorder
Socialized conduct disorder
Oppositional defiant disorder
Other conduct disorders
Conduct disorder, unspecified
Mixed disorders of conduct and emotions
Depressive conduct disorder
Other mixed disorders of conduct and emotions
Mixed disorder of conduct and emotions, unspecified
Emotional disorders with onset specific to childhood
Separation anxiety disorder of childhood
Phobic anxiety disorder of childhood
Sibling rivalry disorder
Other childhood emotional disorders
Childhood emotional disorder, unspecified
Disorders of social functioning with onset specific to childhood and adolescence
Elective mutism
Reactive attachment disorder of childhood
Disinhibited attachment disorder of childhood
Other childhood disorders of social functioning
Childhood disorders of social functioning, unspecified
Tic Disorders
Transient tic disorder
Chronic motor or vocal tic disorder
Combined vocal and multiple motor tic disorders
Other tic disorders
Tic disorder, unspecified
Other Behavioral and Emotional Disorders with Onset Usually Occurring in Childhood
and Adolescence

Nonorganic enuresis
Nonorganic encopresis
Feeding disorder of infancy and childhood
Pica of infancy and childhood
Stereotyped movement disorders
Stuttering
Cluttering
Other specified behavioral and emotional disorders with onset usually occurring in childhood and adolescence
Unspecified behavioral and emotional disorders with onset usually occurring in childhood and adolescence

Reliability and Validity of Diagnostic Systems

The issues of reliability and validity with respect to diagnostic systems have already been introduced. Clinicians are concerned about three major types of reliability in regard to diagnosis: (1) test-retest reliability, (2) inter-rater reliability, (3) internal consistency. Test-retest reliability depends on the specific diagnostic category. Diagnoses of problems that tend to be chronic and long-lasting (e.g., mental retardation) yield higher test-retest reliability coefficients than diagnoses that are more situation-specific or acute (e.g., enuresis). Test-retest reliability is the measure that depends most on the quality of the diagnostic criteria.

Studies investigating the reliability of the *DSM* system have yielded mixed results. Even those that focused on the diagnostic categories for children and adolescents were far from consistent. A major study by Werry, Methven, Fitzpatrick, and Dixon in 1983 found an overall reliability coefficient of 0.71 (as did several subsequent studies), but studies of the inter-rater reliability of specific diagnostic categories were not conclusive.

Different aspects of validity need to be considered in assessment of diagnostic systems. **Face validity** means that the measure or system "looks like" it measures what it intends to measure. **Predictive validity** means that the diagnosis has prognostic value. **Construct validity** means that the diagnosis is consistent with the theoretical concept. **Descriptive validity** is a measure of the extent to which the diagnostic criteria are valid in terms of differential diagnosis.

In general, diagnostic systems for child and adolescent psychopathology have adequate face validity, but their predictive and construct validity tend to be low (see Spitzer & Cantwell, 1980). Recent studies addressing the validity of the *DSM-III* and *DSM-III-R* generally agree that they yielded significant improvements in validity over earlier editions. However, researchers have criticized the actual diagnostic categories (e.g., Rutter & Tuma, 1988), as well as the relevance of the diagnostic system to actual clinical work with children and the scientific validity of the approach itself (e.g., Eysenck, 1986). These issues are now being addressed for the *DSM-IV*.

Conclusions

No diagnostic process should be followed blindly and without question. As we proceed through our study of child and adolescent psychopathology, we will pay special attention to the implications that the diagnostic process itself may bring to clinical management. That is, we must always consider how a particular case would have been managed differently if the diagnostic system had been applied in a different way or if an entirely different diagnostic system had been employed.

Summary

In this chapter we explored the process of diagnosis, both in general and as it is applied to the psychopathology of childhood and adolescence. We discussed the purpose of diagnosis from both theoretical and clinical perspectives, focusing on the advantages of utilizing the diagnostic process. Potential disadvantages of diagnosis include medicalization of psychopathology, questions of inter-rater reliability, the psychological and social effects of the diagnosis, psychopathology as a continuous (as opposed to a discrete) variable, and the external validity of diagnostic categories across different cultures.

A history of psychological diagnosis was presented. We focused on the changes in the different editions of the American Psychiatric Association's *Diagnostic and Statistical Manual (DSM)*, especially as they are relevant to the diagnosis of the psychopathology of childhood and adolescence.

We mentioned other diagnostic systems, including Achenbach's dimensional system and the World Health Organization's *International Classification of Diseases (ICD)*.

Reliability and validity are important issues in regard to any diagnostic system. Test-retest reliability, inter-rater reliability, internal consistency, predictive validity, construct validity, face validity, descriptive validity are considered here.

References

Achenbach, T. M., Conners, C. K., & Qucy, H. C. (1985). *The ACQ Behavior Checklist.* Burlington: University of Vermont.

Akiskal, H. S. (1989). The classification of mental disorders. In H. I. Kaplan & B. J. Sadock, (Eds.), *Comprehensive textbook of psychiatry:* Vol. 5. Baltimore: Williams & Wilkins.

American Psychiatric Association. (1952). *Diagnostic and statistical manual of mental disorders.* Washington, DC: Author.

American Psychiatric Association. (1968). *Diagnostic and statistical manual of mental disorders* (2nd ed.). Washington, DC: Author.

American Psychiatric Association. (1980). *Diagnostic and statistical manual of mental disorders* (3rd ed.). Washington, DC: Author.

American Psychiatric Association. (1987). *Diagnostic and statistical manual of mental disorders* (3rd ed., Rev.). Washington, DC: Author.

American Psychiatric Association. (1994). *Diagnostic and statistical manual of mental disorders* (4th ed.). Washington, DC: Author.

Anderson, J. C., Williams, S., McGee, R., & Silva, P. A. (1987). *DSM-III* disorders in preadolescent children: Prevalence in a large sample from the general population. *Archives of General Psychiatry, 44,* 69–76.

Eysenck, H. J. (1986). A critique of contemporary classifications and diagnosis. In T. Millon & G. L. Klerman (Eds.), *Contemporary directions in psychopathology.* New York: Guilford Press.

Goodwin, O. W., & Guze, S. B. (1980). *Psychiatric diagnosis (4)* New York: Oxford University Press.

Kaplan, H. I., & Sadock, B. (1991). *Synopsis of psychiatry.* Baltimore: Williams & Wilkins.

Kessler, J. (1988). *Psychopathology of childhood.* Englewood Cliffs, NJ: Prentice Hall.

Kim, L., & Chun, C. (1993). Ethnic differences in psychiatric diagnosis among Asian American adolescents. *Journal of Nervous and Mental Disease, 181,* 612–617.

Klerman, G. L. (1990). Paradigm shifts in USA psychiatric epidemiology since World War II. *Social Psychiatry and Psychiatric Epidemiology, 25,* 27–32.

Mattison, R. E., & Hooper, S. R. (1992). The history of modern classification of child and adolescent psychiatric disorders: An overview. In S. R. Hooper, G. W. Hynd, & R. E. Mattison (Eds.), *Child psychophathology: Diagnostic criteria and clinical assessment.* Hillsdale, NJ: Erlbaum.

Rutter, M., & Tuma, A. H. (1988). Diagnosis and classification: Some outstanding issues. In M. Rutter et al. (Eds.), *Assessment and diagnosis in child psychopathology.* New York: Guilford Press.

Spitzer, R. L., & Cantwell, D. P. (1980). The *DSM-III* classification of the psychiatric disorders of infancy, childhood and adolescence. *Journal of the American Academy of Child Psychiatry, 19,* 356–370.

Szasz, T. (1972). *Ideology and insanity.* New York: Doubleday.

Werry, J. S., Methven, R. J., Fitzpatrick, J., & Dixon, H. (1983). The inter-rater reliability of *DSM-III* in children. *Journal of Pediatric Psychology, 11,* 463–479.

Wiener, J. M. (1991). Classification of child and adolescent psychiatric disorders: A historical review. In J. M. Wiener (Ed.), *Textbook of child and adolescent psychiatry.* Washington, DC: American Psychiatric Association.

World Health Organization. (1977). *International classification of diseases* (9th ed.). Geneva: WHO.

World Health Organization. (1992). *The ICD-10 classification of mental and behavioural disorders: Clinical descriptions and Diagnostic Guidelines.* Geneva: World Health Organization.

Chapter three
Assessment of the Psychopathology of Childhood and Adolescence

"There's Pooh," he thought to himself. "Pooh hasn't much brain, but he never comes to any harm. He does silly things and they turn out right. There's Owl. Owl hasn't exactly got brain, but he knows things. He would know the right thing to do when surrounded by water. There's rabbit. He hasn't learnt in books, but he can always think of a clever plan. There's Kanga. She isn't clever, Kanga isn't, but she would be so anxious about Roo that she would know a good thing to do without thinking about it. And then there's Eyore. And Eyore is so miserable anyhow that he wouldn't mind about this. But I wonder what Christopher Robin would do?"

A. A. Milne, *Winnie-the-Pooh*

Introduction

Piglet's assessment of the intelligence of his friends entails little more than simple behavioral observation. Contemplating the way in which each character would respond in certain situations, Piglet estimates the extent to which each one "has brain." Behavior is observed and quantified, and, on that basis, a conclusion is derived with respect to the relative amount of a given characteristic.

Assessment of the psychopathologies of childhood and adolescence involves more formal data collection. Assessment entails the gathering of data in an attempt to come to a conclusion about a clinical issue.

In some cases, assessment involves little more than behavioral observation. In other cases, the process involves complicated testing followed by data analysis and interpretation that can be equally complex. Computer software is designed for the scoring and interpretation of certain psychological assessment instruments that would be difficult to handle in any other way.

Purposes of Assessment

Most children who are referred for assessment are sent for one of two reasons. Often, a parent or teacher becomes concerned regarding some aspect of the child's behavior and requests a psychological evaluation. In other cases, a mental health provider wants to clarify a clinical issue involved in treatment that is already taking place. The referral questions may involve issues of differential diagnosis, level of cognitive functioning, and/or severity of pathology.

Psychological assessment batteries are often classified according to the nature of the referral question. The categories overlap, but they can be divided as follows: *Personality assessments* gather data about an individual's psychological profile. *Behavioral assessments* determine the frequency, nature, and severity of a given behavior pattern. *Cognitive assessments* determine the level of cognitive functioning. *Clinical assessments* collect data on a specific disorder.

The manner in which data are collected can vary, depending on the theoretical orientation of the examiner and the nature of the data to be collected. Assessment instruments may be *objective* (e.g., symptom checklists, questionnaires), *projective* (e.g., drawings, inkblots), *observational* (e.g., family observations), or in interview format.

Qualifications of the Examiner

Although virtually anyone—a parent, teacher, or sibling—could "assess" a given child or adolescent, there are professional and legal restrictions on who can use specific assessment instruments. Some distributors require proof of professional certification and/or training before they sell these instruments. In addition, the Code of Ethics of the American Psychological Association states that a professional who administers a psychological assessment battery must be a licensed psychologist or school psychologist or be working under the supervision of a licensed psychologist.

Some people think these provisions are too restrictive. Clinical social workers, school counselors, teachers, and other professionals who work with children and adolescents may feel that they should be able to administer assessment batteries. They ask why a Ph.D. should be required in order to administer a questionnaire to a 10-year-old child. Why should special training be required in order to follow a test manual, then administer and score the test?

Access to assessment instruments is limited because practitioners need to know how to interpret test data accurately and how to prevent their misuse. Superficial knowledge of the procedural aspects of test administration and scoring is not sufficient. Interpretation of the results requires knowledge of and familiarity with the test's statistical properties, theoretical foundations, standardization procedures, and limitations. Psychologists are trained in testing and assessment to ensure that they will draw only appropriate conclusions from the data.

It is important to remember, however, that assessment is not limited to formal test batteries. Valid assessment data are also obtained via clinical interviews and behavioral observation, and there are no restrictions on the use of these techniques by professionals who are not psychologists.

Theoretical Approaches to Assessment

The theoretical orientation of the clinician affects how an assessment is carried out, and the clinician's experience also plays a role in choice of theoretical orientation. Clinical experience, a graduate school mentor, or the congruence of a theoretical approach with the practitioner's own value system may all affect this choice.

Many clinicians perceive a range of theoretical approaches as acceptable. They may approach different cases in different ways, depending on the specific issues involved. For example, the same practitioner might take a cognitive behavioral assessment approach with a child who has symptoms of school phobia and a completely different approach with a child who has symptoms of gender identity disturbance.

Psychodynamic Approaches

Clinicians who adhere to a psychodynamic orientation often use assessment instruments to evaluate *latent* or unconscious characteristics of personality. Typically, this approach involves the use of **projective tests** that provide a minimal amount of stimulus or structure. The goal of projective tests is to provide the subject with a "blank slate" upon which to project his or her own feelings. The clinician observes how the child or adolescent responds.

The most popular projective tests involve **free association.** The examiner presents some type of visual stimulus and then asks the subject to talk about it. The stimulus may be a vague, unstructured design, as in the Rorschach inkblot test. The patient is simply asked, "What might this be?" and is allowed to freely respond to each of the stimulus cards. Other projective tests offer more structure, using drawings that depict interpersonal interactions. The Thematic Apperception Test (TAT) and the Children's Apperception Test (CAT) take this approach. The child or adolescent is asked to tell the examiner what is happening in each picture. Norms have been established for these tests to assist the clinician in interpreting the child's responses. Scoring can be complicated. The Exnerian scoring system for the Rorschach, for example, involves the calculation of several ratios and percentages, each of which may yield its own interpretive data. Scoring for some projective tests is considerably more subjective, and data interpretation is therefore more subject to criticism.

Other types of projective tests take another approach. They do not ask the child to respond to a pictorial stimulus. Rather, the Rotter Incomplete Sentences Blank, for example, instructs the individual to complete the beginnings of sentences supplying the child or adolescent with the beginnings of a sentence and directing him/her to finish the sentences. Another type of projective test asks the child to draw something specific—most often a self-portrait, a family portrait, a house, tree, a person, or some combination of these things. As in the other methods of projective testing, the child or adolescent is provided with minimal instructions. The clinician analyzes these drawings according to their content, form, color, orientation, and placement on the page. Several interpretive hypotheses have been published with respect to analysis of projective drawing tests. Tests of this nature are prominent in the history of assessment, especially for the psychopathologies of children and adolescents. (e.g., with respect to size, shape placement, and detail of component parts see Ostes and Gould, 1987).

Think About It

Drawing Conclusions from Projective Tests

The use of projective tests in the assessment of psychopathology is controversial because of their low face validity. Many clinicians as well as laypeople do not have a great deal of respect for projective assessment measures. In addition, data from such measures have sometimes been misused; practitioners who misinterpret the data may draw conclusions that are not justified. One interesting article (Ames & Riggio, 1995) reported misuse of the Rotter Incomplete Sentences Blank to determine the incidence of psychological "maladjustment" in a sample of 368 high school students ages 14 to 18). Using the criteria published in the test manual, the examiners classified 55 percent of the students as maladjusted. These results were obtained because the instrument was normed on a college student sample from the late 1940s. What does this study imply about drawbacks of drawing clinical conclusions from other older projective instruments?

Behavioral Approaches

The behavioral approach to assessment of the psychopathologies of childhood and adolescence is not limited to those clinicians who identify themselves as operating from a behavioral theoretical perspective. Clinicians who subscribe to other theoretical perspectives utilize assessment measures that are clearly behavioral, at least in the initial phases of their work.

Behavioral approaches to assessment typically focus on observable behaviors: frequency, precipitating circumstances, and the reactions these behaviors elicit. Behavioral assessment instruments can take various forms: problem checklists (e.g., Child Behavior Checklist, Behavior Problems Checklist), parent rating scales (e.g., Conners' Scales), and self-report scales.

Think About It

Cross-Cultural Validity of Projective Tests

The external validity of behavioral assessment measures—that is, the extent to which results are valid in subjects of different ethnicities and cultures—has long been a concern of clinicians and researchers alike. A recent article (DeGroot, Koot, & Verhulst, 1994) that addressed the cross-cultural validity of the Child Behavior Checklist with U.S. and Dutch children ages 4 to 18 supported the cross-cultural generalizability of this particular instrument across these populations.

Behaviorally oriented clinicians will observe a patient in various situations. These sessions may include visiting the child at home, observing the child in school, and audio- or videotaping interactions with others, as well as observing the child in the office. Clinicians often supplement observation with objective paper-and-pencil personality tests, and the results of these tests are integrated with the behavioral data.

In an introductory chapter of a book describing behavioral assessment of childhood psychological disorders, Marsh and Terdal (1988) list 12 features that characterize this approach. Although other assessment approaches share some of these features, taken as a whole the list is a thorough description of the behavioral approach.

1. *Observed behaviors are taken at face value.* Behavioral approaches are less likely than other assessment approaches to interpret a child's behavior as representative of underlying pathology. Behavioral approaches see behaviors themselves as potential treatment targets.

2. *Behaviors are conceptualized within an idiographic format.* Data are interpreted as characteristic of the individual rather than descriptive of group norms.

3. *Environmental influences on behavior are emphasized.* Situational factors that influence the behavior are taken into account.

4. *Behaviors of children and adolescents are seen as unstable.* The basic premise of the behavioral approach is that the behavior of children and adolescents varies over time.

5. *The behavioral approach is a systems approach.* By definition, behavioral approaches are systems-oriented.

6. *The present situation is emphasized over historical environmental variables.* The emphasis is on current events and phenomena rather than those of the past in connection to the behavior in question.

7. *Behaviors are analyzed at their manifest level.* All behaviors can be studied in and of themselves; they are not merely symbolic representations of underlying pathologies.

8. *Assessment data are directly relevant to treatment.* Data obtained during a behavioral assessment are designed to be directly relevant to the subsequent treatment process.

9. *A variety of methodologies and sources are used in the assessment process.* Behavioral assessments typically employ a variety of techniques and involve contact with significant individuals in the life of the identified patient.

10. *Inference is minimized in interpreting assessment data.* Behavioral data are designed to yield practical information. Little, if any, inference is required to illustrate relevance to the treatment situation.

11. *Behavioral assessments are ongoing.* By definition, all behavioral assessments are ongoing; they do not terminate after the initial data are collected.

12. *Assessment procedures are empirically based.* Behavioral theory bases assessment and treatment upon the current knowledge about the behavior in question.

Systems Approaches

Systems-oriented practitioners address the child's place within the family as well as the roles family members play, both individually and as a group, in maintaining the pathological symptoms. Questionnaires and symptom checklists are often administered to the entire family—both in terms of completing the instruments with respect to the so-called identified patient as well as possibly requesting that family members provide data about themselves.

Systems-oriented practitioners often use input from as many family members as possible to construct a **genogram** as a supplement to the assessment process. The genogram informs both the clinician and the family about the psychiatric history of the family and about psychological and behavioral patterns of family members. Construction of genograms during one of the initial sessions is advantageous for several reasons. First, the process can build therapeutic rapport among family members as they provide information and discuss issues that are not as threatening as the presenting complaint. In addition, the therapist "metacommunicates" the basic premise of the systems approach—that the entire family is the patient.

In conceptualizing the entire family as the identified patient, the practitioner attempts to involve as many family members as are willing in the assessment process. In her book on child psychotherapy, Brems (1993) writes about the goals of the initial family assessment interview. She lists seven points that summarize the major objectives of a systems-oriented assessment:

(1) to gather data about the presenting problem, (2) to overcome any family resistance, (3) to build therapeutic rapport with as many family members as possible, (4) to assess the structure of the family, (5) to assess the overall competence of the family, (6) to assess family processes, and (7) to assess family relating.

Integrative and Eclectic Approaches

It has already been noted that most practitioners who work with children and adolescents use a wide range of approaches. In addition, not all assessment methods are identified with any single theoretical orientation. Rather, these approaches are themselves eclectic, and the theoretical approach of the clinician determines the manner of their administration and interpretation. For example, both structured and unstructured clinical interviews are used by most clinicians. However, the specific questions, the individuals involved in the interview, the data looked for, and the manner in which the data are interpreted all depend on the practitioner's theoretical approach.

In the remainder of this chapter we will discuss the major topics of psychological assessment and instruments used for testing. We will consider: (1) assessments designed to address issues of personality and/or diagnosis and (2) instruments designed to address intellectual and/or cognitive functioning. As is the case with so many issues in the field of child and adolescent psychopathology, these categories are not mutually exclusive.

Think About It

Cross-Cultural Impact on Assessment

A recent study published in the *Journal of Clinical Child Psychology* (Huang, 1994) emphasizes that clinicians must be aware of cultural, sociocontextual, and developmental factors that affect psychological assessments on Asian-American adolescents. Aside from basic issues centering around respect and ethics, can you think of some clinical justification for taking these factors into account?

Assessment Procedures

Before we discuss assessment methods, we need to address procedural issues that are unique to clinical work with children and adolescents.

It is necessary to establish rapport when working with any patient—and this is especially crucial when working with younger individuals. Rapport building entails some unique procedures with this population.

To begin with, the assessment process begins well before the clinician ever has face-to-face contact with the patient. Data collection begins with the first telephone or written contact referring the individual for testing. Analysis of the referral materials, be they formal school reports or reports from other clinicians or a parent's descriptions of the child's behavior, can provide the astute clinician a wealth of assessment data.

Developing Rapport with Children

The waiting area should be "user-friendly." An extremely formal waiting area sends a negative message the moment the family enters. Although a clinician who sees adults as well as young children may not want a waiting room that resembles a playground, it is important to have children's books and magazines, a few toys, perhaps a child-size table and chairs, paper and water-soluble markers, and a few games. This metacommunicates to the family as well as to other patients that the clinician takes his or her work with children seriously and is sensitive to their needs.

For the initial assessment session, the child or adolescent should be accompanied by the parents or primary caretakers. It is necessary for the clinician to establish rapport with both the child and the parents without appearing to "take sides." This building of therapeutic rapport begins with the first greeting by the clinician in the waiting room. The therapist should greet every member of the family individually, attempting to make eye contact with each.

Young children, and often even school-age children, may be reluctant to be alone with the clinician in the consulting room. It is often helpful to have a parent bring the child into the consulting room. Parent and child can tour the area, with the clinician reassuring the child that there is nothing to be afraid of. At this point, the clinician will typically explain to the child what will be transpiring and will encourage and answer any questions. In many cases, the therapist must spend some time dealing with the child's fears. At this stage, the parents can usually return to the waiting room, leaving the child with the clinician without any major anxiety. If the child is still reluctant to separate from the parents and stay with the clinician, it may be best to allow the parents to remain in the consulting room for this initial interview.

Depending on the specific situation and the family dynamics, it can be preferable to meet with the child first so that later, when the clinician meets with the parents, the child does not experience undue concern. Some practitioners prefer to meet alone with the parents first so that they can serve as a model for going into the consulting room.

Valuable information is gained when the clinician observes the way family members react to the initial meeting. Careful observation of these interactions provides information about the child's dependency issues, the family's interaction modalities, and the relationship dynamics between the child and the parents.

Developing Rapport with Adolescents

Adolescents are not likely to be afraid to join the clinician in the consulting room because of stranger anxiety or overdependence on a parent, but dynamics still need to be considered. Although the anxieties and fears of an adolescent are manifest differently—often via anger instead of overt fear—the clinician must always address these issues. It is often advisable to see the adolescent first so that he or she does not get the impression that the parents have somehow prejudiced the clinician against him or her. In other cases, however, the therapist should meet the adolescent together with the parents, in order to observe the manner in which the identified patient interacts with family members. Another advantage of the joint meeting is that the therapist will not get different accounts of the familial situation from the adolescent and the parents.

The therapist must respect the adolescent's feelings, yet maintain necessary limits. It is safe to assume that the adolescent is not especially pleased to be at the session and is even less pleased that this adult's focus is on him or her. When interacting with adolescents, the clinician must try not to infantilize, yet, simultaneously, not to overidentify with his or her characteristics. This will be further explored in the subsequent section on clinical interviews.

The Interview as an Assessment Instrument

Although not a formal test or measurement instrument, the clinical interview is regarded by most clinicians as one of the most useful assessment tools, perhaps especially in the assessing psychopathologies of children and adolescents.

Costello (1991a) points out in a recent review that the clinical interview has gone through several changes. In the early 1900s, the format was loose and nondirective. As the century progressed, so did the degree of structure in the clinical interview with more and more practitioners today taking goal-oriented and structured approaches.

A clinical interview can take many forms. Assessment interviews for children and adolescents are classified according to (1) the relative degree of structure and (2) the individual(s) involved. The first category relates to the manner in which the clinician proceeds with the questioning as well as the content of the questions asked; the second addresses whether other people significant in the child's life participate in the interview process. Clearly, whereas these are the two dimensions most often utilized in the classification of clinical interviews, these dimensions are not at all mutually exclusive in that (as will be discussed below) there can be considerable overlap among categories and within dimensions.

Content of the Clinical Interview

Certain areas are covered in virtually all interviews, regardless of structure. (See Table 3.1.) The approach is adjusted to the developmental level of the patient.

In addition to addressing these basic data points, the interviewer needs to consider why the child is being assessed. Ideally, the clinician will address all pertinent topics at an age-appropriate level with the child as well as with each family member present. Thus, the clinician will typically begin with questions about the presenting symptoms, determining their history and nature and attempting to elicit information about reinforcement. It is usual to begin with questions that are least likely to be threatening or anxiety-provoking to the interviewee.

Interview Techniques

Interviewing the School-Age Child Most practitioners allow 45 to 90 minutes for the initial clinical interview of a school-age child, but it is important to be flexible when working with this age group. Factors such as the development of therapeutic rapport and the child's attention span, anxiety level, and overall developmental level will affect the amount of clinical interviewing the child will be able to tolerate.

With a school-age child, the clinical interview itself is often multimodal; that is, it typically extends beyond the usual question-and-answer format. The child's developmental level, cognitive level, and ability to use language affect the usefulness of interview data, so other approaches must be used as well. The therapist may, for example, observe the child playing with toys in the consulting room. Other assessment measures, such as projective drawings, "make-believe" questions, asking the child to make up a story, and "what if" scenarios can also be informative. With the older school-age child, the clinician can add more verbally oriented projective approaches. For example, 10- or 12-year-old children can be asked to list three good things about themselves and three things they would want to change, or to tell how friends would describe them, or to say which famous person they would like to be (Fletcher, Levin, & Satz, 1989; Kestenbaum, 1991). These exercises can be used as springboards for more in-depth discussions of issues that may be foci of the therapy.

It is important to note that timing is crucial in interviews. Some children may need two or more sessions before the therapist will be able to delve into clinical issues. Two points are im-

Table 3.1 Topics Covered in Assessment Interviews

Developmental history
    Prenatal factors
    Developmental milestones
    Childhood illnesses
Environmental issues
    Home environment
        Family structure
        Substance use or abuse
        Psychosocial stressors
    School performance and behavior
        Academic performance
        Achievement as compared
        with ability
        School behavior and conduct
Interpersonal behavior
    Parents
        Nature of marital relationship
        Psychosocial stressors affecting
        parents
        Psychological status of parents
    Siblings and other family members
        Birth-order issues
        Sibling relationships
        Psychological status of siblings
    Peers
        Quality and quantity of
        peer relationships

Interview behavior
    Affect
        Appropriateness of affect
        Quality of affect
    Cooperation
        Attitude toward therapy process
        Rapport with clinician
        Approach to answering questions
    Anxiety
        Spontaneous anxiety
        Defenses against anxiety
        Reaction to clinician-induced anxiety
    Reality orientation
        Orientation to person, place, time
        Evidence of psychotic process
    Self-concept
        Opinion of self
        Perception of how others perceive
        him or her
    Developmental cognitive level
        Degree of age-appropriateness

portant here: First, the clinician must be careful not to trivialize the significance of the content of the early part of the interview(s). What could be considered unimportant and irrelevant if verbalized by an adult may be valuable clinical data coming from a child. Second, the therapist must not allow a personal desire to be "clinically productive" or "timely" to drive the interview process. The clinician should match pace so as not to intimidate the child from freely providing information.

Interviewing the Adolescent Clinical interactions with adolescents are especially difficult because of the developmental stage of these patients. Although they are not yet adult by society's standards, most adolescents resent being conceptualized as children. Thus, the clinician needs to balance a fine line in approaching adolescent patients. Equally important is that the clinician be aware of the developmental issues confronting adolescents, as these issues have a direct bearing on the patient's presentation. In a review chapter on the clinical interview, Schowalter and King (1991) list five developmental issues most adolescents are dealing with:

1. A desire for autonomy as well as a feeling of vulnerability
2. Hypersensitivity regarding perceived criticism, attempts at control, and/or dependency
3. Narcissistic vulnerability that leads to the perception that problems have purely external sources
4. Affective lability and a short-term perspective
5. Perception of thought as omnipotent

A clinician who keeps these developmental issues in mind is likely to establish an empathetically based relationship with an adolescent patient rather than getting bogged down in a relationship marked by anger, power struggles, and frustration.

Many issues pertinent to interviewing the school-age child are also relevant to interviewing the adolescent. These issues, however, manifest themselves differently in adolescents and must be addressed in a developmentally appropriate manner. In as many ways as possible, the therapist should clearly communicate that he or she is interested in hearing the patient's view of the situation. Although this should be done within a context of respect and empathic listening, it is important that the clinician not "overidentify" with the adolescent and that role boundaries are not blurred. When an adolescent is recalcitrant, anger and silence should be acknowledged and addressed. This direct approach metacommunicates to the adolescent that the therapist respects his or her right to be angry and is not afraid of that anger. Further, it sets the tone for future sessions. The clinician should always encourage the adolescent to feel safe in communicating openly.

Like the clinical interview with a school-age child an interview with an adolescent should not be exclusively symptom-focused. The interview should not resemble a cross-examination. By inquiring about the adolescent's strengths, goals, accomplishments, hobbies, friends, pets, and so on, the therapist metacommunicates the attitude that the adolescent is a human being, not just a problem-ridden "clinical case." In addition, this approach gives the adolescent the opportunity to talk about his or her positive qualities and can boost good feelings about the self. In the long run, there may be some improvement in self-esteem.

Interviewing the Parents and Other Family Members Involving the parents and other members of the family in the interview process has two primary functions. First, by involving others in the interview process, the clinician obtains data from sources other than the patient. This information can increase the reliability and validity of the data by alerting the clinician to distortions in the perception of either the patient or a family member.* Second, family involvement allows the clinician to observe firsthand the role the child or adolescent plays in the family system. This information is invaluable, especially with respect to understanding the presenting psychopathology.

The child and other family members can participate in a **conjoint interview,** or the therapist can interview family members one at a time. Conjoint interviews with parents or other family members expose the dynamics of familial interactions. The therapist can observe how members of the family deal with affect, conflicts, and control issues. This type of interview also reveals the family attitude toward authority, generational boundaries, family rules and rigidity, defense mechanisms, and any subgroups within the family. Conjoint sessions can also serve a beneficial function for the child or adolescent: they allow the youngster to see how

---

*Kashani and colleagues (1985) reported a consistent bias between the reports of psychopathology symptoms from parents and children. Children reported more anxiety and depressive symptoms, and parents reported more behavioral symptoms.

others in the family system perceive them as well as the impact their behavior has on others (Fletcher, Levin, & Satz, 1989; Levanthal & Conroy, 1991; Sholevar, 1991).

Think About It

Comparing Interview Data from Different Sources

Although it is intuitively obvious that there are advantages to obtaining interview data from multiple sources, the clinician must assess the degree to which data from the various sources are in agreement. The strength of the correlations depends on the degree and type of psychopathology within the child as well as within the family system.

Researchers have looked at the correlations between the responses of 299 children ages 6 to 18 and their parents on the highly structured Diagnostic Interview Schedule for Children (DISC) (Costello et al., 1984; Edelbrock, Costello, Dulcan, Conover, & Kalas, 1985). No parent and child were interviewed by the same individual, and 60 percent of the interviewers were clinically trained personnel. Overall, the highest levels of agreement were found for symptoms relevant to oppositionalism, substance abuse, nonaggressive conduct disorder, and combined problems of behavior and conduct. Lower levels of agreement were found for responses regarding symptoms characteristic of psychosis, anxiety disorders, and affective disorders. Parent-child agreement was consistently higher for adolescents than for young children.

How would you explain these results?

Assessment Instruments

Most clinicians design their own interviews to conform with their particular clinical style. Even when the interview format is structured, clinicians often modify the questions.

Published formats are available for structured interviews with children and adolescents of different ages and for assessment interviews with parents and other family members. Clinicians who prefer a more unstructured format for their interviewing often use questions from formal interview protocols. Others who opt for a more structured approach often use the standardized interview schedules to obtain assessment data. Two of the most commonly utilized assessment interview formats are the Child Assessment Schedule, designed for ages 7 to 16 (Hodges & Saunders, 1989), and the Diagnostic Interview Schedule for Children and Adolescents, designed for ages 6 to 17 (Herjanc & Reich, 1982).

Behavior Assessment

Virtually all psychological assessments of children and adolescents focus on behavior to some degree. Some assessment approaches focus on observable behavior, and some behavioral assessment instruments involve direct behavioral observation; others ask either the child or an adult family member to rate the presence and/or frequency of certain behavioral patterns. Behavioral ratings are usually done within the framework of a checklist or a **Likert scale.**

Some behavioral scales focus on a single diagnostic category, so the items on the scale refer to behavioral traits characteristic of that diagnosis. These instruments are used primarily when the referral for assessment is intended to resolve a question of differential diagnosis. They may also be used when the clinician wants to determine whether a patient meets the clinical criteria for a given diagnosis or to determine the severity of given condition.

Other, more generic behavioral rating scales touch on several different diagnostic areas, with the goal of determining which of the diagnostic categories would be the most relevant for the child or adolescent. These scales contain items relevant to different diagnostic categories, so the clinician can assess how much each diagnostic entity contributes to the pathological profile. Some instruments provide data about the severity of the symptoms; others simply determine the presence or absence of symptoms and therefore the appropriateness of a given diagnosis.

Behavioral scales also differ in terms of who is to provide the data. Some are constructed in a **self-report** format that asks the child to complete the scale; if the individual is too young or otherwise unable to read, the clinician reads the questions aloud. Other scales are designed to obtain data from a parent, teacher, clinician, or other significant individual in the child or adolescent's life. Many newer scales contain multiple components to be completed by different individuals so that data obtained via self-report can be compared with those obtained from other sources (see Kotsopoulos, Walker, Copping, & Cote, 1994, for a study examining the reliability of parent ratings of adolescents). Similarly, data obtained from parents can be compared with information obtained from school personnel, other clinicians, and so on in order to check inter-rater reliability. In comparing data from different sources, the clinician becomes aware that these "objective measures" are actually subjective. Some of these generic behavioral measures are the Children's Behavior Checklist (9 general scales, with behavior ratings along a 3-point scale), the Behavior Problems Checklist (55 items rated on a 3-point scale), and the Conners Scales (self-report scales for children and adolescents of different ages as well as scales to be completed by parents and school personnel).

Personality Assessment

Although the different categories of assessment instruments overlap considerably, one distinguishing feature separates the majority of the behavioral scales from the personality scales. This characteristic is the "observableness" of the traits measured. Behavioral assessment instruments typically focus on more *overt* aspects of psychology. Personality inventories, in contrast, focus on more *covert* aspects of the patient's psychology, asking for information regarding thoughts, affect, anxiety, interpersonal style, coping, and defense mechanisms. Some personality inventories, however, do assess observable behaviors, and some behavioral inventories also address covert aspects of personality.

Most objective personality inventories designed for children and adolescents use the self-report format. In the past, many instruments designed for adults were administered to children with little if any modification. Many newer instruments were designed specifically to assess personality in children and adolescents. Most of these are paper-and-pencil questionnaires that ask the child to respond to true/false questions or along a Likert scale.

Think About It

Gender and Race in Personality Assessment

The issue of bias, familiar in regard to intelligence tests, is also relevant to tests that purport to assess personality. Researchers have attempted to evaluate bias in tests designed for adults (see Dahlstrom, Lachar, & Dahlstrom, 1986). Research on bias in personality testing for children and adolescents is beginning to appear in journals.

One such study (Lachar & Godowski, 1979) investigated the effects of the child's age, sex, and race on the results of the Personality Inventory for Children (Wirt, Lachar, Klinedinst, & Seat, 1977). This objective, paper-and-pencil parent report assesses the child's cognitive, affective, and behavioral symptoms. Ratings can be provided by the child's teacher as well as the clinician. Except for symptom patterns that vary with developmental level, the Personality Inventory for Children did not appear biased in regard to gender or race. What elements would make an assessment instrument more or less susceptible to gender and racial biases?

Projective measures are also used in the assessment of personality in children and adolescents. Again, instruments originally designed for adults have been administered to younger individuals, but a substantial number of projective assessment regimens have been designed for children. Many of the projective tests are described in the section of this chapter on psychodynamic approaches.

Think About It

The Draw-A-Person Test

Machover's Draw-A-Person Test (D-A-P) is over 45 years old, but it is one of the ten most frequently utilized tests (see Piotrowski, Sherry, & Keller, 1985). Despite its clinical popularity, its face validity is somewhat low, and its true reliability and validity are often questioned. An investigation was undertaken by Yama (1990) at the University of Idaho to assess the relationship of the D-A-P to psychological adjustment. Using 61 Vietnamese refugee children ranging in age from 6 to 17 as subjects, Yama chose the number of foster care placements over the next 5 years as his dependent variable. Analyzing the results of the D-A-P on its measures Overall Artistic Quality, Overall Bizarreness, Estimated Adjustment of the Client, and Emotional Indicators, the study reported that all four of these measures were adequate predictors of overall adjustment. Further, Yama reported that the single measure Overall Bizarreness was an adequate predictive criterion. Would these data be generalizable to U.S. children?

Cognitive Assessment

The third major group of assessments is designed to evaluate some aspect of the child's cognitive functioning. Instruments have been designed to assess academic achievement, developmental level, intelligence quotient (IQ), or deficits in neuropsychological functioning. Most testing instruments in the first three categories are designed and administered according to the age of the child. Tests of neuropsychological functioning are more or less generic with respect to age.

A referral for cognitive assessment may address questions about developmental level, intellectual capacity, academic achievement, differential diagnosis, and cognitive strengths and weaknesses. In interpreting data from cognitive tests, however, the clinician must consider the child's psychological status, especially as it may affect test results. It is often advisable to administer one or more assessment instruments from the personality or behavior categories in conjunction with the cognitive battery.

Personality can affect tests of cognitive or intellectual functioning, and vice versa. Tests designed to assess intelligence in children and adolescents include the Wechsler Intelligence Scale for Children—Revised (WISC-3); the Woodcock-Johnson Psychoeducational Battery (WJPEB), designed to assess academic achievement; the Wide-Range Achievement Test (WRAT), designed to assess knowledge in several academic areas from preschool age through adulthood; and the Kaufman Assessment Battery Test For Children (Kaufman & Kaufman 1983), designed to assess arithmetic, reading, and functional academic skills from age 15 to 90. Intelligence testing is discussed in detail in subsequent chapters of this text.

The primary purpose of neuropsychological assessment is to analyze the relationship between overt behavior and brain functioning. During its early history, neuropsychological assessment focused on organicity, deterioration, and deficits in brain functioning. Neuropsychological tests are now able to discriminate between different types of brain damage and can determine what area of the brain is affected.

The two most common neuropsychological batteries were designed for use with adult populations. Developed over 40 years ago, the Halstead-Reitan Battery incorporates subtests designed to detect brain damage and, in some cases, to determine the nature of the pathology. Although the Reitan is an extremely lengthy test to administer, it is often accompanied by either a partial or complete age-appropriate WISC-3 as well as the Minnesota Multiphasic Personality Inventory (MMPI-2). The Luria-Nebraska Neuropsychological Battery (LNNB) incorporates several subscales scored on 14 different dimensions. Included among these scales are the Left Hemisphere Scale, the Right Hemisphere Scale, and the Pathognomonic Scale, which is made up of 31 items designed to identify brain damage.

Research on the reliability and validity of these scales has produced contradictory data. Several early studies find the Halstead-Reitan useful in diagnosing brain damage (e.g., Reitan, 1955; Russell, Neuringer, & Goldstein, 1970), but later studies criticize it for lack of specificity and find it unable to distinguish between brain-damaged subjects and those who suffer from some form of schizophrenia (see Goldstein, 1986). Similarly, research on the reliability and validity of the LNNB has yielded contradictory results. Some researchers (e.g., Purisch &

Sbordone, 1986) find that the Luria-Nebraska can distinguish between brain-damaged patients and those who are psychotic, but other investigators report difficulties in replicating such findings.

Reliability and Validity Issues in Assessment

Reliability

We discussed reliability in Chapter 2, defining it as the degree to which a test measures true variance (as opposed to error). There are several different types of reliability. Assessing **test-retest reliability** involves administering the same test twice, then measuring the correlation between the two scores obtained. The more reliable the measure, the higher the correlation.

Practice effects can interfere with measures of test-retest reliability. The test taker's memory and increased skill may affect performance on the second test. The researchers might simply wait longer between tests, but reliability could still suffer because the behavior being measured could change within that time span.

Parallel-forms reliability is assessed through use of two or more forms of the same instrument. The tests are theoretically identical in content, yet with different items. One group of subjects is administered one form, then the alternative version a few days later. A second group is administered the alternative form first, then the other form. The correlation coefficient serves as the reliability estimate.

Think About It

Reliability and Behavioral Assessment Instruments

Behavioral assessment instruments are notorious for faring poorly when their reliability is measured via either the test-retest or parallel-forms methods. Why do you think this is true?

Partially as a response to some of the inadequacies of the test-retest and parallel-forms methods, three new methods were developed for assessing test reliability. Focusing on their internal consistency, researchers categorize these methods as the *split-half* and the *odd/even* approaches. Split-half reliability involves obtaining two half scores for each measure (one based on the first half, the other on the second half of the test). The reliability coefficient is based on the correlation between the two scores.

An obvious difficulty with the split-half method emerges when performance changes as the test progresses. Thus, in these cases odd/even reliability (or other types of half-score methods) coefficients are calculated. Here, the odd-numbered items make up half the test and the even-numbered items the other half. Such approaches are especially useful if fatigue or some other factor might influence the test taker's performance.

Validity

Validity is defined as the degree to which a test actually measures what it is that it is supposed to measure. (See Chapter 2.) Worded more simply, validity is a measure of how "good" a test is—of whether it does what it is designed to do. There are several different types of validity that depend on what the test is supposed to accomplish. Table 3.2 lists the major kinds of validity.

Table 3.2 Types of Validity

Concurrent validity	Does the test provide an accurate estimate of an established criterion for the concept being measured?
Construct validity	Does the test accurately measure a given theoretical construct?
Content validity	Do test items adequately sample the pool of potential item?
Convergent validity	When two or more tests are constructed to measure the same thing, do their results correlate positively?
Discriminant validity	When two or more tests are constructed to measure different things, do their results correlate negatively?
Face validity	Does test appear to measure what it is supposed to measure?

Conclusions

Assessment is seldom an isolated process. Rather, it is a means toward optimizing clinical treatment. One goal of the assessment process is to obtain data that will be useful in the clinical management of a given case.

It is imperative to remember that assessment is a *process*. No single test instrument can fulfill the goals of an assessment. A complete assessment consists of more than a test battery; the clinician integrates data obtained from testing, clinical interviews, and structured and unstructured observation. Finally, assessment is an ongoing process. Data continue to be collected well after the initial assessment, throughout all therapeutic interaction thereafter.

Summary

This chapter began with a broad definition of assessment presented in terms of the most common purposes for which the process is used. The major assessment questions fall into four categories: differential diagnosis, personality assessment, behavior assessment, and cognitive assessment. The four major assessment modalities are objective testing, projective testing, observation, and interviewing. Each of these four formats has advantages and disadvantages. Anyone who administers psychological tests should be trained in their interpretation.

Different approaches to psychological assessment can be taken, depending on the theoretical orientation of the clinician. Different practitioners may adopt psychodynamic or projective approaches, a behavioral approach, or an eclectic approach to different diagnostic categories.

Procedures in assessment interviews vary, depending on who will participate in the interview. School-age children, adolescents, and parents and families may be approached differently.

Assessment instruments have been developed to study behavior, personality, and cognitive functioning. The reliability and validity of these instruments can be checked by measuring test-retest correlations, using parallel forms, or using internal measures of consistency. Practice effects may interfere with test-retest reliability.

References

Ames, P. C., & Riggio, R. E. (1995). Use of the Rotter Incomplete Sentence Blank with adolescent populations: Implications for determining maladjustment. *Journal of Personality Assessment, 64,* 159–67.

Brems, C. (1993). *A comprehensive guide to child psychotherapy.* Needham Heights, MA: Allyn & Bacon.

Costello, A. J. (1991a). Structured interviewing. In M. Lewis (Ed.), *Child and adolescent psychiatry: A comprehensive textbook.* Baltimore: Williams & Wilkins.

Costello, A. J., Edelbrock, C. S., Dulcan, M. K., & Kolas, R. (1984). *Testing of the NIMH DISC in a clinical population.* Final Report. Rockville MD: Center for Epidemiological Studies, NIMH.

Dahlstrom, W. G., Hacher, D., Dahlstrom, L. E. (1986). *MMPI patterns of American minorities.* Minneapolis: University of Minnesota Press.

DeGroot, A., Koot, H. M., & Verhulst, F. C. (1994). Cross-cultural generalizability of the Child Behavior Checklist cross-informant syndromes. *Psychological Assessment, 6,* 225–230.

Edelbrock, C., Costello, A. J., Duken, M. K., Kales, R., & Conover, N. C. (1985). Age differences in the reliability of the psychiatric interview of the child. *Child Development, 56,* 265–275.

Fletcher, J. M., Levin, H. S., & Satz, P. (1989). Neurological and intellectual assessment of children. In H. I. Kaplan & B. J. Sadock (Eds.), *Comprehensive textbook of psychiatry: Vol 5.* Baltimore: Williams & Wilkins.

Goldstein, G. (1986). The neuropsychology of schizophrenia. In I. Grant & K. M. Adams (Eds.), *Neuropsychological assessment of psychiatric disorders* New York: Oxford University Press.

Herjanc, B., & Reich, W. (1982). Development of a structured psychiatric interview for children: Agreement between child and parent on individual symptoms. *Journal of Abnormal Child Psychology, 10,* 307–324.

Hodges, K., Saunders, W. B., Kashani, J., Hamlett, K., & Thompson, R. J. (1990). Internal consistency of DSM-III diagnoses using the symptom scales of the CAS. *Journal of the American Academy of Child and Adolescent Psychiatry, 29,* 635–641.

Huang, L. N. (1994). An integrative approach to clinical assessment and intervention with Asian-American adolescents. *Clinical Child Psychology, 23,* 21–31.

Kashani, J. H., Orvasschel, H., Burk, J. P., & Reid, J. C. (1985). Informant variance: The issue of parent-child disagreement. *Journal of the American Academy of Child and Adolescent Psychiatry, 29,* 635–641.

Kaufman, A., & Kaufman, N. (1983). *Kaufman assessment battery for children.* Circle Pines, MN: American Guidance Services.

Kestenbaum, C. J. (1991). The clinical interview of the child. In J. M. Weiner (Ed.), *Textbook of child and adolescent psychiatry.* Washington, DC: American Psychiatric Press.

Kotsopoulos, S., Walker, S., Copping, W., & Cote, A. (1994). Parent-rating and self-report measures in the psychiatric assessment of adolescents. *Adolescence, 29,* 653–663.

Lachar, P., & Godowski, C. L. (1979). *Actuarial assessment of child and adolescent personality: An interpretive guide for the PIC profile.* Los Angeles: Western Psychological Services.

Levanthal, B. L., & Conroy, L. M. (1991). The parent interview. In J. M. Weiner (Ed.), *Textbook of child and adolescent psychiatry.* Washington, DC: American Psychiatric Press.

Marsh, E. J., & Terdal, L. G. (1988). Behavioral assessment of child and family disturbance. In E. J. Marsh & L. G. Terdal (Eds.), *Behavioral assessment of childhood disorders* (2nd ed.). New York: Guilford Press.

Oster, G. D., & Gould, P. (1987). *Using drawings in assessment and therapy.* New York: Brunner/Mazel.

Piotrowski, C., Sherry, P., & Keller, J. W. (1985). Psychodiagnostic test usage: A survey of the society for personality assessment. *Journal of Personality Assessment, 49,* 115–119.

Purisch, A. D., Golden, C. J., & Hammeke, T. A. (1978). Discrimination between schizophrenic and brain injured patients by a standard version of Luria's neuropsychological tests. *Journal of Consulting & Clinical Psychology, 46,* 1266–1273.

Reitan, R. M. (1955). *Manual for the administration of neuropsychological batteries for adults and children.* Seattle: Privately Published.

Russell, E. W., Neuringer, C., & Goldsten, G. (1970). *Assessment of brain damage: A neuropsychological key approach.* New York: Wiley.

Schowalter, J. E., & King, R. A. (1991). The clinical interview of the adolescent. In J. M. Weiner (Ed.), *Textbook of child and adolescents psychiatry.* Washington, DC: American Psychiatric Press.

Sholevar, G. P. (1991). The family interview. In M. Lewis (Ed.), *Child and adolescent psychiatry: A comprehensive textbook.* Baltimore: Williams & Wilkins.

Wirt, R. D., Lachar, D., Klinedinst, J. K., & Seat, P. D. (1977). *Multidimensional description of child personality: A manual for the Personality Inventory for Children.* Los Angeles: Western Psychological Services.

Yama, M. F. (1990). The usefulness of human figure drawings as an index of overall adjustment. *Journal of Personality Assessment, 54,* 78–86.

Chapter four
Treatment Approaches to the Psychopathology of Childhood and Adolescence

```
"Well?"

"Exactly," said Owl. "Precisely." And he added, after a
little thought, "If you had not come to me, I should have
come to you."

"Why?" asked Rabbit.

"For that very reason," said Owl, "hoping that something
helpful would happen soon."
```

A. A. Milne, *The House at Pooh Corner*

Introduction

Treatment for the psychopathologies of childhood and adolescence is approached in much the same way as treatment for the adult disorders. Procedures are often modified to make them more relevant to the needs of younger patients.

In this chapter we will explore ethical issues in treatment of psychopathology. Next we will discuss variations of the psychopharmacological, psychotherapeutic, and behavioral therapy approaches. We will discuss each approach in terms of its application to children and adolescents, noting differences from treatment of adults. Clinical case studies are provided to illustrate successful and unsuccessful application of treatment approaches. Finally, we consider empirical studies that discuss and/or evaluate the application of therapeutic techniques.

A new type of treatment approach has recently come into its own. These preventive therapies can be applied to either the general population or to identified high-risk populations in an attempt to reduce the incidence of more severe psychopathology. Some of the best-known preventive treatments are early identification programs and other programs designed to enhance interpersonal, academic, and cognitive skills. These primary/secondary programs are compatible with the tertiery treatment modalities we will explore in the remainder of this chapter.

Ethical Issues in the Treatment of Children and Adolescents

Formal ethical standards for the professional practice of psychology are relatively new. *Ethical Standards for Psychologists* was first published in 1953. The standards have been revised several times as psychology has emerged as a professional discipline; the goal is for the standards to ensure patients' safety. The most recent revision was published in 1992, titled *Ethical Principles of Psychologists and Code of Conduct.*

The APA's ethical standards address issues pertinent to the practice of psychotherapy, the teaching of psychology, the supervision of students, and the conduct of psychological research. Topics include competence, integrity, professional and scientific responsibility, respect for people's rights and dignity, concern for others' welfare, and social responsibility. A section on ethical standards addresses evaluation, assessment or intervention, advertising and other public statements, privacy and confidentiality, teaching, training, supervision, research and publishing, forensic activities, and the resolving of ethical issues.

Ethical principles that are straightforward in regard to adults become slightly more involved in the case of individuals younger than the age of legal consent. The American Psychological Association's *Ethical Principles* specifically addresses clinical work with children and adolescents in principle 2.04, on use of assessment; Principle 2.04, on informed consent; Principle 4.02, on couple and family relationships; and Principle 4.03, on confidentiality. Each of these principles is discussed in the following section.

Evaluation, Assessment, and Intervention

The APA's *Ethical Principles* emphasizes that clinicians often need to modify assessment protocols and interpretations when they work with different patients.

> *Psychologists attempt to identify situations in which particular interventions or assessment techniques or norms may not be applicable or may require adjustment in administration or interpretation because of factors such as individuals' gender, age, race, ethnicity, national origin, religion, sexual orientation, disability, language or socioeconomic status.* (APA, 1992, Standard 2.04)

The clinician must consider the patient's developmental level when performing any type of psychological intervention. It is inappropriate to apply adult clinical norms to children or adolescents. Rather, children and adolescents are clinical populations in their own right. Therapeutic and assessment procedures should be designed especially for use with the population in question or should be modified appropriately for the patient's developmental level.

Case Study 4.1

Nine-year-old Zara was brought to a private psychologist who specializes in anxiety disorders. The parents perceived the girl as being "nervous all the time" and a "chronic worrier," but they were unsure whether she needed professional treatment. The clinician was familiar with several instruments used to diagnose anxiety disorders in adults, but recognized that they were not appropriate for Zara. Instead, the psychologist administered the Behavior Assessment System for Children (1992) inventories to Zara, her parents, and her teacher. By integrating the results of the three instruments with data obtained from clinical interviews with Zara and her parents, the psychologist was able to make an accurate diagnosis.

Informed Consent to Therapy

Informed consent is a crucial element of all professional psychological interactions. But how is the practitioner to obtain informed consent from children and adolescents? The APA's *Ethical Principles* stresses the necessity of the patient's ability to fully understand the procedure: information must be worded so that the patient is able to understand. When psychological or developmental factors prevent the patient from giving informed consent, the psychologist must ensure that any treatment is in the patient's best interest. The principle reads as follows:

A. *Psychologists obtain appropriate informed consent to therapy or related procedures, using language that is reasonably understandable to participants. The content of informed consent will vary depending on many circumstances; however, informed consent generally implies that the person (1) has the capacity to consent, (2) has been informed of significant information concerning the procedure, (3) has freely and without undue influence expressed consent, and (4) consent has been appropriately documented.*

B. *When persons are legally incapable of giving informed consent, psychologists obtain informed permission from a legally authorized person, if such substitute consent is permitted by law.*

C. *In addition, psychologists (1) inform those persons who are legally incapable of giving informed consent about the proposed interventions in a manner commensurate with the persons' psychological capacities, (2) seek their assent to those interventions, and (3) consider such persons' preferences and best interests. (APA, 1992, Standard 4.02)*

The psychologist must offer patients an explanation of all services, whether therapeutic or diagnostic in nature. When working with children or adolescents, the clinician explains the assessment or therapeutic procedures in a manner appropriate to the patients' developmental level. When such an explanation is not feasible, the therapist may obtain informed consent from a representative of the child—a parent, a teacher, or another responsible party. (It is important to note that in virtually all cases, a child or adolescent cannot be seen for assessment or therapy without the consent of his or her parent or guardian.) The psychologist must always act in the best interest of the patient.

Case Study 4.2

Six-year-old Daniel was referred for intelligence testing by his school counselor. He has been slow in accomplishing some tasks in kindergarten, and the school counselor recommended that he be evaluated for special classes. In explaining the testing to the child, the psychologist said, "You are here to answer some questions, play some games, and do some puzzles. After I see the way you do these things, I'll be able to help your teacher help you do better in school." Although this is a simplistic explanation of intelligence testing, nothing included in this statement is false, and the explanation is worded in a manner that the child can comprehend.

Couple and Family Relationships

The APA ethical standards address problematic situations in which the psychologist has a therapeutic relationship with a married couple or with a parent and child. The psychologist's ethical obligations to both patients may present an ethical dilemma. The *Ethical Principles* requires the psychologist to define his or her roles and their limitations with each person at the onset of therapy.

> When a psychologist agrees to provide services to several persons who have a relationship (such as husband and wife or parents and children), the psychologist attempts to clarify at the outset (1) which of the individuals are patients or clients and (2) the relationship the psychologist will have with each person. This clarification includes the role of the psychologist and the probable uses of the services provided or the information obtained. (APA, 1992, Standard 4.03)

Case studies relevant to this issue follow in the next section, which discusses confidentiality.

Confidentiality

The fifth principle of the ethical standards addresses the confidentiality of the therapeutic relationship. Specific issues include the boundaries of confidentiality with respect to psychotherapy and the sharing of assessment data.

Discussing the Limits of Confidentiality

> A. Psychologists discuss with persons and organizations with whom they establish a scientific or professional relationship (including, to the extent feasible, minors and their legal representatives) (1) the relevant limitations on confidentiality, including limitations where applicable in group, marital, and family therapy or in organizational consulting, and (2) the forseeable uses of the information generated through their services.
> B. Unless it is not feasible or is contraindicated, the discussion of confidentiality occurs at the outset of the relationship and thereafter as new circumstances may warrant.
> C. Permission for electronic recording of interviews is secured from clients and patients. (APA, 1992, Principle 5.01)

Maintaining Confidentiality

> Psychologists have a primary obligation and take reasonable precautions to respect the confidentiality rights of those with whom they work or consult, recognizing that confidentiality may be established by law, institutional rules, or professional or scientific relationships. (APA, 1992, Principle 5.02)

It is not uncommon for confidentiality issues to be ambiguous in clinical work with children and adolescents. Although confidentiality applies regardless of the age of the patient, some clinicians interpret the principle as applying only to the parents when the patient is a young child. In either case, it is imperative that therapists recognize that issues of confidentiality change as children grow through childhood and adolescence.

When working with children and adolescents, the clinician may not share information with any individual(s) not "clearly concerned with the case." This issue can become complicated; as it is a rather subjective decision as to precisely who is to be considered "involved with the case." Most clinicians agree that it is prudent to inform parents as to the progress and content of therapy sessions with young children. But how should the clinician approach the situation if the child's parents are not living together? The parents may be divorced or separated, or they may never have married. Is the parent who is not living with the child entitled to the same amount of information as the parent with whom the child lives? And what about stepparents who live with the child? The permutations can seem infinite.

After the clinician has decided whether to share any information with a parent, the question remains as to precisely what information will be shared, and in how much detail. The APA's ethical standards state that in any situation in which "not to do so [reveal information] would result in clear danger to the person or others," the information in question must be shared. More ambiguous however, are those situations in which no actual or potential danger is involved; here, the decision about sharing information with the parents will depend on the clinician's conceptualization of the case.

The following case studies illustrate some situations in which questions of confidentiality and disclosure of information need to be confronted by the clinician. There is not an unequivocally correct manner in which the clinician should proceed, so these case studies are presented without answers. Rather, the reader is encouraged to consider the advantages and disadvantages of several options and make a decision based upon his or her own judgment.

Case Study 4.3

Eight-year-old Torrance was brought to a psychologist by his mother, who says Torrance has been "depressed" and has performed poorly in school over the past 6 or 8 months. She thinks that Torrance is upset because she and her husband are involved in hostile divorce proceedings and Torrance's custody is a primary area of disagreement. The judge has granted custody to Torrance's mother, and Torrance's father is allowed overnight visitation every second weekend.

After the child's fifth session, the psychologist received a telephone message from Torrance's father, who had learned that his son was seeing a therapist. The father expressed concern as to the content of these sessions. Before the psychologist had the opportunity to return the call, Torrance's mother called. Torrance told his mother that he had mentioned his visits to the psychologist to his father, and the mother wanted to be sure that the psychologist would not give the boy's father "any information whatsoever."

Option A: Do not give any information to the father.
Option B: Invite the father to attend a session with the child and the mother.
Option C: Give the father only information the mother has approved in advance.
Option D: Invite the father to attend a session with the child.

Case Study 4.4

Thirteen-year-old Jesse was brought to a psychologist by his extremely frustrated mother. When scheduling the initial appointment, the mother explained that she had taken Jesse to four different psychologists in 5 months. After one visit with each psychologist, however, Jesse had announced to his mother that he needed to see someone else. Jesse's mother gently stated that she hoped that this psychologist would be different.

At the first meeting, Jesse appeared well-groomed and not anxious. Jesse willingly went into the consulting room, and then he announced to the psychologist that he would agree to work with her if, and only if, the psychologist would agree not to share any information with Jesse's mother. "I am not nor will I be a danger to myself or others," the boy said. "I know my rights." Jesse went on to say that the four other psychologists would not agree to these terms.

Option A: Tell Jesse that no information will be shared with his mother unless he gives some indication of becoming a danger to himself or others.
Option B: Tell Jesse that all information will be shared with his mother because a therapist cannot make a confidentiality agreement with a child.
Option C: Tell Jesse that no information will be shared with mother unless he is told in advance.

Think About It

Ethics in Today's World: Child Abuse and the Therapist

When a clinician suspects that a child or adolescent patient is being abused or neglected, the clinician is legally obligated to report this suspicion to a child protection agency as soon as possible. Many states require that clinicians—physicians, psychologists, and so on—attend a mandatory class in abuse reporting prior to license renewal. As a professional, what conflicts would you have around this issue and how would you deal with them? Failure to make a report can result in a loss of license. Nonetheless, therapists worry about the impact such reporting might have on rapport with the family. Studies reveal a considerable amount of noncompliance with these laws (see Kalichman, Craig, & Follingstad, 1990).

Think About It

When Should Confidential Information Be Disclosed?

A recent study (Thelen, Rodriguez, Manuel, & Sprengelmeyer, 1994) surveyed 1,000 practicing psychologists, to determine under what conditions they would breach confidentiality in cases of suicide threats, homicide threats, and child abuse. Although only 33 percent of the sample actually responded, 24 percent of respondents expressed a belief in absolute confidentiality regardless of the situation. If you were a practicing psychologist, under what situations, if any, would you find it appropriate to breach confidentiality?

Exchange of Information

Closely related to confidentiality issues are those issues which result in the exchange of clinical information with other professionals. Especially frequent when doing clinical work with children and adolescents is the need to interface with other professionals who interact regularly with the patient. Often one of these professionals made the initial referral to the psychologist.

Such a situation can present an ethical dilemma. For example, the clinician is placed in a difficult situation if school personnel refer a child for therapy and the parents request information. It is not always prudent to share details of the therapeutic process with the parents. The therapist is obligated to act in the best interest of the child or adolescent, and this often means withholding information from the parents.

Case Study 4.5

Thirteen-year-old Marissa has been having trouble in junior high. Previously an exceptional student, she barely received a passing average this quarter. Several teachers have seen her break out in tears in the middle of classes. In addition, she isolates herself during free periods, although in the past Marissa was one of the more social girls in the school. When the teacher referred her for outside counseling, her mother gave consent for treatment.

Marissa revealed that for several months her father had been verbally abusive during their weekend contacts. Although the problem did not seem sufficiently intense to warrant a report to the state child abuse hotline, Marissa was in considerable distress.

After learning that Marissa was seeing a psychologist, her father called the psychologist and demanded to be fully informed about the content of the therapy sessions.

Option A: Inform the father about the content of the sessions.
Option B: Do not provide any information to the father.
Option C: Invite the father to attend a joint session with Marissa.
Option D: Discuss the father's call with Marissa's mother.

Conclusions

Confidentiality can be a difficult issue in clinical work with children and adolescents. It can be difficult to define boundaries and limitations with respect to sharing clinical information. Although the clinician is ethically—and in most states, legally—obligated to maintain the confidentiality of every patient, when the patient is a child or adolescent, there can be ambiguity. In cases where there is obvious danger to the patient or to others, the Code of Ethics provides for sharing of relevant clinical data. In other situations, it is not always clear to whom the clinician's confidentiality obligations lie, or when it is in the best interest of the child or adolescent to exchange information with parents, family members, school personnel, or other professionals.

Many factors must be weighed in coming to a decision. These issues often involve the clinician's own psychological response to the patient, the child's emotional response to the clinician, and the way these responses affect each other. These interpersonal dynamics not only affect decisions regarding ethical issues but also influence the entire course of therapy.

Therapeutic Modalities

The therapeutic modalities utilized to treat children and adolescents are classified according to the type of intervention employed. The therapeutic modality may be primarily biological (somatic) or psychological. That is, treatment can be aimed at biological targets (using drug interventions) or psychological targets (using psychotherapy as the primary intervention). The efficacy of each type of treatment depends on the diagnostic category for which it is used; we will discuss efficacy in later chapters on specific disorders.

Formats Used in Psychotherapy

For our purposes, we will classify all treatment approaches that are *not* psychopharmacological as psychotherapy. Psychotherapeutic approaches are classified according to their theoretical basis as psychodynamic, behavioral, cognitive-behavioral, or humanistic. Psychotherapeutic modalities are also classified according to format—that is, according to the individuals involved in the therapeutic interaction. For example, some clinical situations involve interaction between only the therapist and the patient; others involve the child or adolescent and the parents; others involve the entire family system; and other formats treat patients in groups. Each of the theoretical approaches can be used in each of the formats. We will discuss the advantages and disadvantages of the different formats as they are applied in the different theoretical approaches.

Individual Psychotherapy Individual treatment is the most common approach taken with adults as well as with children and adolescents. In most if not all sessions, the primary interaction is between the clinician and the patient. When taking this approach, the clinician treats the child or adolescent as the patient and assumes that clinical progress can take place with the primary contact limited to the identified patient. Clinicians who take this approach do not deny the importance of obtaining data from parents, other family members, or school personnel. However, the child or adolescent is conceptualized as the patient, and, the primary clinical interactions are with him/her.

This approach has the advantage of metacommunicating to the child that he or she deserves the clinician's sole attention. It also allows the child to privately share information with the clinician. A disadvantage of this format is that the clinician has little opportunity to observe interaction patterns between the child and the parents. Another drawback is that the therapist has less opportunity to validate information the child provides.

Family Therapy The roots of family therapy date back to the child guidance movement of the early twentieth century, but this approach has only recently been used in the treatment of children and adolescents. An article published in the mid-1970s (McDermott & Char, 1974) actually discussed the "war" between child psychiatry and family therapy, and a survey of child psychiatrists a decade later (Silver & Silver, 1983) reported that practicing child psychiatrists spent little time in family therapy. A more recent review (Malone, 1991) blamed the slow acceptance of family therapy on its systems-oriented, adiagnostic approach; the lack of a single theoretical framework; and the absence of an agreed-upon diagnostic schema. As empirical data accumulate in support of the efficacy of family therapy, this modality is gaining acceptance within the clinical community.

Family therapists initially assumed an **environmentalist perspective,** minimizing the importance of focusing on an identified patient and instead looking at the family as a dynamic system. As practitioners integrated their own theoretical perspectives into their work, however, the practice of family therapy incorporated a multitude of clinical orientations. Nonetheless, the focus remains on dynamic interactions among and between family members and subgroups within the family. According to a recent psychiatry textbook, "The family perspective is, first and foremost, an internal clinical stance rendering the therapist open to all biopsycho-social levels within the family-therapist system. In effect, this new orientation reorganizes and reintegrates individual and biological perspectives into a more holistic, reciprocally interactional framework, doing away with the individual-family dichotomy" (Ravenscroft, 1991, p. 851).

The process of family therapy involves an assessment of the overall functioning of the family as a unit. The family unit itself is conceptualized as the identified patient; the child or adolescent is not deemed to be the only problem. Family assessment, however, has as one of its major goals the determination of how the child's difficulties relate to the family's overall level of function. The clinician analyzes the family dynamics and, in turn, the influence this family system has on the symptomatic patterns being observed.

Malone's review of family therapy with children and adolescents (1991) presents three major therapeutic models, each of which is influenced by the theoretical orientation of the clinician. The **multigenerational model** focuses on issues of enmeshment and individuation with respect to the various generations involved in the therapeutic process. The therapist focuses on the degree to which members of the family have achieved **individuation** as opposed to remaining enmeshed in the often pathological dynamics of the family system.

Case Study 4.6

Thirteen-year-old Gloria was brought to family therapy because of depression. She had begun to exhibit symptoms 6 weeks earlier, when her brother announced his decision to attend college in another state. Her parents said that Gloria and her brother had never been especially close; in fact, Gloria had always been unusually close to her mother. Taking a multigenerational approach, the clinician ascertained that Gloria's mother was unusually close to both children—so close, in fact, that the mother had been acting "strangely" since her son's acceptance to college. Clinical interviewing revealed that Gloria's mother was manifesting the signs and symptoms of a reactive depression. Because of Gloria's enmeshed relationship with her mother, the adolescent had "assimilated" her mother's symptoms and therefore appeared to be depressed.

The **structural approach** to family therapy conceptualizes the family in terms of its structural characteristics, especially as they relate to issues of authority, power, boundaries, and overall balance. Clinicians taking this approach look at the relationships between family members in terms of their power structure, paying particular attention to any ways in which a **pathognomic** power structure may support pathology.

Case Study 4.7

A mother of three children came for a psychological consultation for some family therapy. She reports that her son Randy, age 12, is physically abusive toward his siblings, a sister age 14 and a younger brother age 8, seemingly "for no reason." If the mother intervenes,

Randy becomes physically aggressive toward her. When the clinician inquired about the father's role in the family, the mother responded that her husband works a lot and feels that the children are her responsibility. The clinician used the structural model to analyze the situation. She determined that Randy's behavior reflects a pathognomic power structure and poor boundary management within the family.

The third model conceptualizes psychopathology as being a function of maladaptive problem-solving techniques. This **strategic model of family therapy** also assesses the familial forces that resist significant change, particularly in the face of developmental transitions of family members. Psychopathology is viewed as caused by an inability to confront the problems inherent in living and life. Rather than make the transition, the family relies on dysfunctional interaction patterns.

Case Study 4.8

A young family with two children consulted a psychologist for what they perceived as "odd" behavior manifested by their oldest son, Kent, age 5. Both parents describe Kent as a "model child . . . the center of our lives since he was born . . . never any problem." However, the couple had a new baby boy 9 weeks ago, and over the past 4 weeks, Kent has wet the bed almost every night. In addition, he carries his old "blankie," which he had willingly relinquished over a year ago. The clinician took a structural perspective and explained Kent's behavior as caused by failure to adjust to presence of the new baby, whom he perceived as usurping his role in the family system.

No single approach to family therapy has been demonstrated to be empirically superior to others. However, one review (Gurman, Kniskern, & Pinof, 1986) concludes that family approaches are superior to no-treatment controls. Family approaches obtain "positive outcomes" in approximately two-thirds of cases and are as effective as traditional therapies offered for family conflicts. Other researchers, however, describe the results of family therapy as "respectable but not outstanding" (Henggeler & Borduin, 1990).

Szykyula, Sayger, Morris, and Sudweels (1987) looked at the relative efficacy of the strategic and behavioral approaches to family therapy used at an outpatient clinic for patients in different diagnostic categories. Using patient satisfaction, side effects, and change in target behavior as the measures of success, this study found the two approaches virtually equal in efficacy.

One advantage of family therapy is that the amount of clinical data available to the therapist increases. Another is that involvement of other individuals significant in the child's life allows the clinician to observe interaction patterns and to validate data obtained from the child.

There are some disadvantages to family approaches. First, the presence of other individuals can inhibit the spontaneity of the child's interactions with the therapist. The child might share information with the clinician in a private session that he or she would never reveal in the presence of the parents or siblings. Second, because the presence of other individuals prevents the clinician from focusing solely upon the child or adolescent, the therapeutic value of the situation may be lower than the case in which the child is the sole focus of the clinician's attention.

Parent Training Closely related to the family therapy approaches are the relatively new therapeutic formats that purport to train the parents as cotherapists for the child or adolescent. A therapy session takes up a relatively small proportion of an individual's waking hours, so these approaches attempt to work with the family to train the parents in behaviors that address the treatment objectives. This therapeutic approach typically involves individual work with the identified patient (i.e., the child or adolescent), instructional sessions with the parents (including some explanation of the target symptom and behavioral principles as well as the role the parents may play in reinforcing the behavior pattern), and family sessions. Although parent training is behavioral in approach, a behavioral orientation is not a prerequisite for this modality.

The procedures used in this approach depend on both the presenting complaint and the theoretical orientation of the clinician. A major advantage of this approach is that treatment can take place outside the scheduled therapy sessions. By directly involving parents in the use of therapeutic techniques, the therapist recognizes the parents' role in the intervention. In addition, the family will be more likely to follow through on treatment recommendations. This approach empowers the family unit as a pivotal factor in the treatment process, thereby reducing dependence on the therapist. Finally, when the parents are directly involved in the treatment process in a cotherapist role, the family is not projecting an "It's your problem" attitude toward the child.

Parent training interventions do, however, have disadvantages. There are parents who, because of their own psychopathology, use their influence consciously or unconsciously to sabotage treatment. Whether they are unable or simply unwilling to do the psychological "work" necessary to fully comprehend the child's situation, some parents will not cooperate in therapy. In addition, for some children and adolescents, the presence of the parents can be a hindering factor, especially when the parent-child relationship is already badly damaged. In this situation, it is often advisable to meet with the parents and the child separately for the initial sessions, prior to actively involving the parents in treatment as cotherapists.

A classic set of studies evaluated the efficacy of parent training methods (Forehand & McMahon, 1981). Unusual in its research quality and methodology, this set of studies looked at an outpatient program designed to treat child noncompliance with parental rules and demands. Based on operant conditioning theory and utilizing contingency management, the training program consisted of two phases. The first phase instructed the participating parents in ways to increase positive reinforcing experiences for the child while decreasing parental negative verbalizations; the second phase instructed the parents in a time-out procedure. In order for parents to participate, they had to identify target behaviors as well as precipitating events. Outcome was evaluated on the basis of data from parent interviews as well as clinical observations.

Group Therapy Group therapy has long been used as a clinical intervention with children and adolescents. Group therapy as we know it today, however, was not utilized with children or adolescents to any significant degree in the United States until 20 years ago. Since that time, this modality has been employed to treat children and adolescents diagnosed with a wide variety of psychopathologies (Schamess, 1993). Group therapy is currently one of the most popular therapeutic interventions for psychopathologies of adolescents (Kymiss, 1993).

Like individual therapy, group therapy can give the clinician insight into the manner in which the patient interacts with the world. Group therapy reveals how the child or adolescent interacts with the therapist as well as with peers. Equally important is that in the presence of peers, a child or adolescent may feel less inhibited about sharing information that could be awkward in a one-on-one situation with an adult. Of course, as for adults, group therapy provides the child or adolescent the opportunity to recognize that his or her problems are not unique (Cramer-Azima, 1991) and that they do not reflect an innate "weirdness."

The actual group therapy process depends on the therapeutic orientation of the clinician. Thus, group therapy sessions may be psychoanalytic, behavioral, cognitive-behavioral, and so on.

"Specialized" or "special interest" groups, which can assume any of the theoretical perspectives, are designed for children or adolescents who are experiencing similar problems. For example, a group can be made up of children of alcoholic parents, adolescents who have experienced a serious loss, or children manifesting certain symptoms. There are weight control groups, anger management groups, attention deficit disorder groups, social anxiety groups, and so on. Specialized groups are homogeneous along at least one dimension (e.g., the situation, the symptoms and/or diagnostic category, the treatment medium), yet they may vary along others. Special **Psychoeducation** groups provide specified information or teach certain skills to the participants.

Group therapy can be combined with family therapy and parent training. Typically, these combinations take one of three basic formats: **Parallel groups** involve parent groups that meet separately from the child or adolescent groups. **Merged groups** usually involve children in early and middle childhood. The parents, usually the mothers, meet together and with the same therapists. The third, less commonly used approach entails working with two or more families together in a single group.

Like the other therapeutic modalities, group therapy has its disadvantages. First, there are some patients and some problems that do not lend themselves to group treatment. Whereas most diagnostic categories as well as most children and adolescents can, at some time during their treatment, benefit from group interventions, group therapy is not always the optimal intervention. Many children are too easily intimidated or too disturbed to participate meaningfully in group therapy. In some cases, group therapy can even hinder the optimal progression of treatment. For such cases, individual treatment is usually indicated at the outset; group therapy can be added at a later date, if clinically indicated.

Think About It

Predicting Premature Termination of Therapy

How can a clinician ensure that a child and his or her family will remain in therapy long enough to obtain maximum benefit? The psychotherapy literature is replete with studies attempting to identify factors that predict either positive or negative therapeutic outcome. One recent study (Kazdin & Mazurick, 1994) looked for factors that predict premature termination of the therapy process. The authors found three sets of factors to be related to premature termination from therapy. Family factors were low socioeconomic status and adverse child-rearing practices; parent factors included stressors, adverse life events, and a history of antisocial behavior; and child factors were low IQ, poor peer relations, and chronicity and severity of antisocial behavior. How would you explain the relationship between these factors and premature termination of therapy?

Techniques Used in Psychotherapy

Psychodynamic Approaches

The use of psychodynamic approaches in the treatment of the psychopathologies of children and adolescents dates back to the almost legendary work of Sigmund Freud in his treatment of Little Hans (1909) and to the work of Melanie Klein and Anna Freud some 20 years later. Interestingly, Klein's and Anna Freud's work proceeded in somewhat different directions; Anna Freud's approach is more commonly used in the United States. We will review the work of each of these pioneers to set the framework for our discussion of psychodynamic approaches.

The basic premise behind the psychotherapy of Melanie Klein is that children use play to prepare for their roles as adults. They reveal through their play the same kinds of things adults reveal through free association. Conceptualizing play as the child's primary expressive modality, Klein interpreted the child's ability to play as indicative of the level of his or her psychological functioning. Klein used the concept of transference in her work with children in much the same way as it had been utilized in the past with adults. (See the discussion of transference that follows.) Klein wrote that even the youngest children are capable of transferential reactions, most often transferring feelings for their parents onto the therapist. The role of the psychoanalyst is strictly neutral—the therapist provides interpretations of the child's play, drawings, and so on. Klein stated that the purpose of therapy is to have the child clarify his or her unconscious fantasies in order to attain better adjustment in daily interactions (Klein, 1932).

The therapeutic approach of Anna Freud also has as its goal the exploration of the unconscious to "improve" the conscious, but her theoretical framework differs from that of Melanie Klein. Freud emphasized developmental factors that make psychoanalytic work with children different from work with adults. Most important, Freud questioned whether children are universally capable of free association, and she did not consider play an adequate substitute for free association. Thus, Freud did not recommend this form of treatment for young children who had not mastered verbal skills. Finally, Anna Freud conceptualized transference differently from Klein. Freud believed that the child can develop more functional ways of relating with others by working through transference issues with the therapist (A. Freud, 1965).

Current approaches to child and adolescent psychoanalysis combine the two schools of thought. Most clinicians use a variation of the traditional psychoanalytic approach called either **psychoanalytic psychotherapy** or **psychodynamic psychotherapy.** Therapy of this type is conceptualized as divided into three major stages, each with specific goals and objectives. These three stages parallel the "stage" concept of child development—each stage of therapy presenting tasks that the child must be accomplish prior to moving to the subsequent stage.

During the *initial phase* of psychodynamic therapy, the **therapeutic alliance** is formed between the therapist and child. The therapist puts the child at ease by telling the child what will happen in the therapy sessions, explaining how these sessions will focus on the content and process of the child's verbalizations and behaviors.

Most of the serious work involved in therapy is accomplished in the *middle phase*. It is during this stage that the process of **working through** occurs, when the therapist offers interpretations of the child's behaviors and the transferential relationship is processed. This process of working through is considered to be the corrective element in this therapeutic modality. The therapist must remember, however, that the patient's relationship with the parents is typically current and active and is likely to have a significant effect on this process.

The third and final phase of therapy is the **termination phase.** Progression into this phase is indicated by accomplishment of several of the initial goals of therapy, although the termination is intended to be therapeutic itself. Ranging in length from 6 to 30 weeks, this phase of therapy focuses on issues of separation, loss, and dependence. It is not uncommon for the child or adolescent to manifest some **regression,** but this, too, is interpreted and processed and is used as clinical content.

Both proponents and opponents of psychodynamic theory agree that there is a lack of empirical research evaluating the efficacy of this approach. A recent article (Fonagy & Moran, 1990) cites two major reasons for the lack of research in this area. First, the stated goals of this type of therapy are rather general and ambiguous. In other words, psychodynamic psychotherapy does not lend itself to easily measurable behavioral goals, so its efficacy can be difficult to assess. Second, according to Fonagy and Moran, psychodynamic therapists tend to be reluctant to submit their work for investigation. The most likely reason for this reluctance is that their theoretical orientation does not place a high premium on empirically derived results.

Investigators agree that more research should be aimed at evaluating the efficacy of psychodynamic intervention with children and adolescents. A chapter on psychotherapy with children (Freedheim & Russ, 1992) presents a list of suggestions for research topics in this area. Researchers need to clearly describe the treatment modality and the way it is used; they need to use multiple **outcome criteria** as dependent measures; and they need to assess the validity of the way outcomes are measured, developmental factors affecting outcome, and the relationship between the treatment interventions and the targeted symptomatology.

Transference and Countertransference

The idea that psychological issues influence the process of therapy is acknowledged in virtually all theoretical approaches. The term **transference** refers to the way a patient's unresolved psychological issues are actually *transferred* onto the therapist. This phenomenon affects the process of therapy. Similarly, the term **countertransference** refers to the way a clinician's unresolved psychological issues are transferred onto the patient, again affecting therapy. These concepts were originally derived from clinical work with adults, but current literature acknowledges that they also apply to work with children and adolescents.

As would be expected in work with children and adolescents, transferential issues involve unresolved issues with parental figures. In the majority of cases in which transference becomes an issue in therapy with young people, the therapist reminds the patient of a parent, teacher, grandparent, or another adult. The patient then transfers whatever feelings he or she has toward that adult, whether positive or negative, onto the therapist and reacts to the therapist accordingly.

Case Study 4.9

Five-year-old Beverly was brought to therapy by her father shortly after the accidental death of the child's mother. Both the therapist and Beverly's father were surprised when, at their first meeting, Beverly ran to the psychologist and tried to kiss her. The psychologist had some physical resemblance to Beverly's deceased mother. The child's reaction was an example of transference, in which strong feelings about one person are transferred onto another individual.

Transference is not always positive in nature, as it was for Beverly. Frequently transferential reactions involve feelings that are highly negative. Even negative transference can be useful in treatment, as a considerable proportion of the "unfinished business" in therapy centers on negative feelings. When a child or adolescent has experienced traumatic incidents, for example, he or she may transfer feelings retained toward the perpetrator onto the therapist.

Case Study 4.10

Thirteen-year-old Tanya was brought to a psychologist by her mother because of the girl's "weird behavior." For the past 3 months, Tanya has been extremely withdrawn and quiet. Her eating habits have changed; she either eats virtually nothing or binges compulsively. When her mother was interviewed in some detail, she reported that Tanya's aberrant behavior began shortly after a visit to her father in another state.

When Tanya was introduced to the male psychologist, she seemed to "freeze." She began to breathe rapidly and manifested many of the symptoms of an anxiety attack. After some exploration, the psychologist realized that Tanya had experienced a transference reaction—she had transferred her feelings toward her father onto the male therapist.

As already mentioned, transferential reactions are not limited to the patient. Therapists are human, and they too experience transferential reactions. This phenomenon of countertransference can be as potent as transference, especially in therapy with children and adolescents. Clinicians must therefore be aware of specific issues that stimulate their own countertransferential reactions. They should seek consultation when countertransference occurs.

A recent chapter on the psychiatric assessment of infants, children, and adolescents (Lewis, 1991) summarizes signs of countertransference. The following list presents the major categories of warning signs indicating ways that the clinician's own countertransferential issues could negatively affect the treatment process.

1. *Failure to appropriately apply developmental issues to the treatment process.* The clinician may conceptualize the child or adolescent as being less or more mature than he or she is in reality. Such a distortion can severely compromise therapeutic process.
2. *Interaction of the clinician's own issues with those presented by the patient.* Issues presented by the patient may resonate with the clinician's own psychology. This can appear in therapy as an overidentification with the patient, in repeated power struggles, or in arguments with the patient during sessions. The clinician may inadvertently reinforce inappropriate acting-out behavior outside of sessions. More subtly, the clinician may become overly intense when interacting with the patient, feeling an excessive need for approval. The clinician may also have "blind spots" that interfere with understanding of the patient's psychology.
3. *Violation of therapeutic boundaries.* Sometimes a patient develops the role of being "special" in the eyes of the therapist and is given privileges not allowed other patients—for example, extended therapy sessions, rearrangement of meeting times, exchanging of gifts, and activities outside the therapeutic realm.
4. *Grandiosity on the part of the therapist.* The therapist may feel that he or she is extremely well suited to provide a particular patient with all that he or she was deprived of. Acting on this feeling can lead the therapist to overstep therapeutic boundaries and to establish unrealistic expectations for the therapy process.

In the majority of situations in which countertransference affects therapy, the therapist acts without malevolent intent. Rather, countertransference typically occurs at an unconscious level, characteristically with a well-meaning therapist. For that reason, it is essential that therapists be alert to and aware of issues that evoke their own countertransferential reactions. Although these will vary from clinician to clinician and from patient to patient, self-aware therapists will therefore take appropriate action to limit the impact of countertransference on therapy. Such action may consist of consultation with a trusted colleague or a more formal approach such as a peer group supervisory session, individual supervision, or individual psychotherapy.

Behavioral Approaches

In contrast to the psychodynamic approaches discussed in the previous section, behavioral techniques emphasize the importance of obtaining measurable, reliable, valid, and replicable results. A survey in the early 1980s (O'Leary, 1984) reported that about half of all child psychologists considered themselves behaviorists. Until 30 years ago, however, the literature on behavioral approaches with children and adolescents was sparse (Powers & Rickard, 1992). Behavioral therapists later recognized that the child's developmental level must be taken into consideration in the design of therapy. The child must have the skills required to meaningfully participate in a behavioral therapy regimen (Harris & Ferrari, 1983).

As mentioned in the discussion of theoretical perspectives offered in Chapter 1, behavioral interventions can assume a variety of formats. Behavioral approaches have been developed from many perspectives. The classical or respondent conditioning paradigm has led to the systematic desensitization method and to relaxation training. Operant conditioning theory has produced reinforcement methods, and social learning theory has also produced behavioral models. Cognitive-behavioral therapy is another variation on behavioral therapy. In this section we will consider the application of these paradigms in therapy for children and adolescents. Further discussion of behavioral therapies is included in later chapters on specific diagnostic categories.

Classical Conditioning Models Techniques based on classical conditioning are most often employed with children and adolescents as treatments for pathological anxiety and/or fear reactions. Simple phobias (or monophobias) are most often approached through systematic desensitization and implosive therapy. Both procedures involve pairing exposure to the phobic stimulus with a behavior that is inherently incompatible with the pathological response. For example, for a snake phobia, exposure to the phobic situation be paired with a response such as relaxation, which is incompatible with anxiety. Ideally, the target phobic situation will become classically conditioned with the preferred behavior, and the pathological response will be extinguished.

Systematic desensitization, whether via imagery or actual exposure, involves a *gradual* introduction of the phobic stimulus while the patient focuses on the newly learned incompatible behavior. **Implosive therapy,** in contrast, involves a rapid, intense exposure to the phobic stimulus while the patient is encouraged to cope with the anxiety through more adaptive measures. Both of these methodologies have been researched extensively with adult patients, but research with child and adolescent patients is sparse.

Case Study 4.11

Thirteen-year-old Rosemary was brought to a psychologist because of her fear of injections, especially those associated with dental procedures. Rosemary needs some dental work, but at the mention of going to the dentist she has an intense panic reaction. She reports no other phobic reactions, so the psychologist decided to treat her anxiety via systematic desensitization. After three sessions of relaxation training to provide Rosemary with a response incompatible with the pathological anxiety reaction, the psychologist spent the next session constructing an anxiety hierarchy with respect to the phobic response. Rosemary would first see the word *needle* on a piece of paper, then a drawing of a needle, then a photograph of a needle. Eventually a needle would be placed in her mouth. The therapist instructed Rosemary to practice her relaxation-inducing exercises as she was exposed to the different items in the hierarchy. After eight sessions, as well as homework assignments to practice the material covered in the sessions, Rosemary was able to begin her dental treatment.

Case Study 4.12

Fifteen-year-old Gary came to the school psychologist because of what he described as a "phobia of cats." Gary suffered from a true cat phobia that dated back to his early childhood. Gary agreed to participate in an implosive therapy regimen with a trusted colleague of the school psychologist. Gary first learned some anxiety management techniques, then met with the therapist for a 3-hour session in which he was exposed to a cat and "coached" by the therapist in the use of anxiety management techniques.

Operant Conditioning Models Of all the forms of behavioral therapy in use today in the treatment of children and adolescents, those interventions based on operant conditioning models are by far the most widely employed. These techniques focus on the modification of a behavior or behavior pattern by manipulating either the environmental precipitating event or the reinforcement that follows the event. Behaviors whose frequency the clinician wishes to increase are reinforced through the addition of a positive stimulus or the removal of a negative stimulus; behaviors whose frequency the clinician wishes to decrease are followed by punishment (the addition of a negative stimulus or the removal of a positive stimulus). These techniques often involve the parents as cotherapists (see Schaefer & Briesmeister, 1989); in school or in inpatient situations, school or facility personnel act as cotherapists.

Think About It

The Use of Punishment in Behavior Modification

There has been considerable controversy over the years regarding the use of punishment in the modification of behavior. Some of the controversy has centered around ethical issues, while some has focused more on the relative efficacy of punishment when compared with reinforcement. Research has determined that punishment is most effective when it immediately follows the undesirable behavior, proceeds on a continuous schedule, and has a clear beginning and ending (O'Leary & Wilson, 1975). For certain behaviors, however, interventions that were designed to be punishments may actually serve as reinforcers. Temper tantrums and anxiety responses, for example, are often inadvertently reinforced. When a child or adolescent is so disturbed that he or she engages in self-injurious behaviors, a clinician may decide to employ aversive stimuli, such as mild electrical shock, slapping, vile-tasting mouthwash, or obnoxious noises. Many people who read about such interventions cringe at their apparent cruelty and the resemblance of these procedures to physical abuse. Defenders of this practice claim that these interventions, albeit unpleasant, inflict discomfort that is mild compared to what the patient inflicts on himself or herself. What do you think about the use of physical punishment in the treatment of disturbed children and adolescents?

Contingency management—the regulated removal or addition of reinforcing stimuli— varies in format and can involve a variety of techniques. Procedures such as "time out" (removing the child from the reinforcing situation), **response cost** ("fining" the child for undesirable behavior), and **overcorrection** (requiring the child to perform extreme variations of corrective behaviors to "right" undesirable behavior) are all used in operant models.

Case Study 4.13

Six-year-old Francine has recently acquired the habit of spilling her drinks whenever she does not get her own way. When she becomes frustrated and it is not mealtime, she goes to the refrigerator and pours any liquid she can find onto the floor. Her parents have tried various disciplinary techniques, but to no avail.

As a "last resort," Francine's parents consulted a psychologist, who recommended the technique of overcorrection. Every time Francine spills a liquid, she not only has to mop up the spill—she has to mop the entire room with disinfectant. At first Francine's spilling behavior increased slightly (she was "testing" her parents to see if they would follow through). Within 3 weeks, however, the spilling behavior ceased completely.

Social Learning Models Therapeutic approaches classified as social learning models are, in many ways, a combination of the techniques utilized in the classical and operant conditioning approaches (Werry & Wollersheim, 1989). As the name indicates, social learning models are used primarily to improve the patient's interpersonal interaction skills. These approaches can use either group or individual formats, and actual modalities and the content of sessions are variable. Treatment modalities range from didactic teaching sessions to role-playing, problem-solving instruction, and modeling procedures. The skills taught in social learning sessions, regardless of modality, also vary. Virtually any form of interactionary skill an individual needs in order to function optimally can be considered a clinically appropriate target for social learning interventions. Treatment may seek to improve skills for interacting with teachers, peers, and/or parents; to help the child cope with anxieties; to teach anger management techniques; and so on.

Case Study 4.14

Eleven-year-old Matt has been having severe difficulty relating with his peers at school. He feels extremely anxious around children his own age, and he does not know what to say to them. If a peer approaches him, Matt becomes so anxious that he begins to stutter and stammer. He is unable to speak coherently, let alone carry on a conversation. The psychologist recommended that Matt's treatment include role playing, audiotaping, and videotaping. After eight such sessions, Matt agreed to participate in a socialization group for 9- to 12-year-old children. After attending this time-limited 6-week group therapy course, Matt was able to interact comfortably with his peers.

Cognitive-Behavioral Methods In a recent review, cognitive-behavioral approaches with children and adolescents were defined as "a purposeful attempt to preserve the demonstrated positive effects of behavioral therapy within a less doctrinaire context and to incorporate the cognitive activities of the client into the efforts to produce therapeutic change. Accordingly, cognitive-behavioral strategies with children and adolescents use active, performance-based procedures as well as cognitive interventions to produce changes in thinking, feeling and behavior" (Kendall, 1993, 235). This modality integrates the cognitive, behavioral, affective, social, and contextual strategies for therapeutic intervention. The role of the cognitive behavioral therapist is to act as a consultant, diagnostician, and educator.

As one of the newer psychotherapeutic modalities, the cognitive-behavioral perspective prides itself on the active involvement of the patient. By assigning homework and encouraging the child to assume responsibility for his or her behavior, and therefore for any improvement, the therapist gets the patient to take an active role in treatment. This approach metacommunicates the therapist's confidence in the patient's ability to change his or her behavior.

Although the cognitive-behavioral approach integrates components of several other therapeutic approaches, it is unique in integrating the more "affectively focused" therapies with behavioral techniques. Further, its focus on the "thinking" and "feeling" aspects of the target behavior links this modality and the more psychodynamic models. Cognitive-behavioral therapists attempt to work at the cognitive level of the child to explore, confront, challenge, and change beliefs about a given situation in order to encourage behavior change.

The cognitive-behavioral approach is based on three postulates: (1) Cognitions mediate behavior; (2) a predictable relationship exists between cognition and the individual's experience of affect; and (3) maladaptive cognitive styles are associated with the development of specific psychopathologies (Zarb, 1992). The first goal of cognitive-behavioral therapy is to arrive at an operational definition of the target behavior. The next is to identify the child's mediating cognitions (i.e., beliefs, values, and causal attributions). After explaining the rationale at a level appropriate to the child's level of cognitive functioning, the therapist initiates intervention techniques to modulate these cognitions. The patient practices newly learned skills during the session and often has assignments to practice at home.

Case Study 4.15

Thirteen-year-old Susan is having difficulty dealing with the recent separation and imminent divorce of her parents. A major factor contributing to her difficulties is that one reason for the divorce is her father's abuse of cocaine. When her father's arrest for drug possession was reported in the local newspaper, things worsened for Susan. An "A" student, she refuses to attend school. Further, Susan avoided contact with her friends, her peers, or family members. She reluctantly agreed to discuss her problems with a local psychologist after being reassured that the session would be confidential.

The psychologist began a regimen of cognitive-behavioral therapy. Susan's beliefs regarding her parents' situation were explored in detail. The therapist began to explore with Susan the meaning of each of these beliefs in her system as well as the affect they evoked. Finally, the two worked together challenging the rationality of each belief as well as the logic in the connection between each belief and the feeling it evoked.

Play Therapy

Although play therapy is typically considered a psychodynamic approach, its use is not restricted to practitioners who adhere to that theoretical orientation. Brems (1993) delineates three general goals of play therapy: (1) establishment of a trusting, special relationship; (2) disclosure: facilitating diagnosis, and assessment, allowing the expression of feelings, the acting out of fears and unconscious material, allowing the expression of forbidden affects, and needs, allowing the expression of conflicts, and allowing reconstruction of conflict, and other experiences; and (3) healing: providing an arena for therapeutic intervention and a sense of direction, dealing with defense mechanisms, resolving resistances, relieving tensions, facilitating catharsis, providing corrective emotional experiences, teaching of more adaptive coping skills, and experimenting with new behaviors.

A wide range of definitions of play is offered in the clinical literature. Thompson and Rudolph (1992) believe that play therapy should meet the following criteria: facilitation of an improved therapeutic rapport between child and clinician, facilitation of the child's expressing his or her feelings, facilitation of the clinician's understanding of the child's world, facilitation of the child's testing of reality, and provision of an appropriate modality for expression of otherwise "inappropriate" feelings and thoughts. Commonly employed mediums for play therapy, depending on the developmental level of the child, include crayons, markers, drawing paper, puppets (often nonhuman figures, as they can be less threatening to the child), dolls, stuffed animals, carefully chosen books, sand, clay, tubs of water, dollhouses, army figures, and board games at various levels. The specific choices depend as much on the therapist's preferences as on the clinical presentation of the child.

Because play is one of the natural developmental tasks of childhood, it is a modality through which children can express themselves easily. It is not uncommon for a child who is uncomfortable verbalizing feelings to clearly express these feelings through play. Play represents how the child interacts in the outside world. The child's approach toward dolls, army figures, puppets, and so on reveals to the therapist the quality of the child's interpersonal interactions. Finally, it is important to note that the play modality, with its varying amount of the component of "let's pretend," allows the child to work with threatening psychological issues without taking responsibility for them.

Case Study 4.16

Five-year-old Kayla enjoys coming to the psychologist's office every week. She calls the clinician her "play doctor." Because of Kayla's age, most of each session is spent in play therapy. The psychologist sits on the office floor and either observes Kayla in independent play or joins the little girl in her play activities. At almost every session, Kayla spends some time playing with the dollhouse and its figurines. While observing Kayla play with the doll house, the therapist obtains pertinent clinical data. For example, the unusually large amount of conflict between the mother and father in Kayla's play family mirrors events in the child's home. The therapist pays special attention to verbalizations that Kayla ascribes to the figurine she identifies as the "little girl." Occasionally the therapist interrupts Kayla's play to ask her some projective questions, such as "How do you think the little girl feels when the mother and father do that?" or "What would be a better way for the little girl to act?"

Erik Erikson summarizes play therapy as follows:

> Modern play therapy is based on the observation that a child made insecure by a secret hate or fear of the natural protectors of his play in the family and neighborhood seems able to use the protective sanction of an understanding adult to regain some play peace. Grandmothers and favorite aunts may have played that role in the past; its professional elaboration of today is the play therapist. The most obvious condition is that the child has the toys and adult for himself, and that sibling rivalry, parental nagging, or any kind of sudden interruption does not disturb the unfolding of his play intentions. (Erikson, 1994)

Psychopharmacological Treatment

Introduction

Most children have been treated with prescription drugs for ear infections, strep throat, or other physical maladies by the time they have reached adolescence. The opposite is true for psychopharmacological interventions. Even the most disturbed children may not be treated with psychopharmacological intervention. Most pediatric clinicians regard psychopharmacological interventions as adjuncts to psychotherapy. Practitioners consider drugs only when the symptomatology is chronic or when the symptom profile is likely to be recurrent.

Few empirical studies have investigated the use of medications to treat the psychopathologies of childhood and adolescence. A study published in 1937 evaluated the efficacy of amphetamines on a diagnostically heterogeneous sample of children, but no similar studies were published until the 1970s. A review of the literature reveals that even then, only a few empirically sound studies were published. These primarily focused on children with Attention Deficit Hyperactivity Disorder (Campbell, 1991). One reason for this paucity of information is that pharmaceutical companies rarely fund investigation of the use of their products with children. In spite of the multitude of recent research articles, books, professional presentations, and advertisements in psychiatric journals, and book chapters, problems with research protocol preclude the formulation of valid, definitive conclusions.

Dosages for psychopharmacological interventions are not as well established for children and adolescents as they are for adults. Even the well-known *Physicians' Desk Reference (PDR)* cannot be utilized with as much assurance for young people as it is for adults. This is a problem because all pharmacological interventions carry the risk of **developmental toxicity.** Medications can interfere with developmental processes, in the physical, cognitive, psychological, behavioral, or growth spheres.

Pharmacokinetics—the manner in which a drug is metabolized by the various systems of the body—are difficult to anticipate when dealing with children and adolescents. Drug therapy is age-dependent because growing tissue may metabolize the drug in unexpected ways. It is often difficult to determine an optimal dosage and regimen (Dulcan & Popper, 1991). The clinician must keep in mind that children often require larger dosages in proportion to body weight than would adults, because children have a more rapid metabolism (Green, 1991a). Thus, although an initial dosage is often too low to be effective, any increases must be gradual, and the clinician must watch for negative side effects as well as positive responses. Behavioral problems are often the first sign of drug toxicity. Failure of the child or adolescent to respond positively to medication is a contraindication for continuing that drug (Campbell, 1991).

Clinical and Psychotherapeutic Considerations

Behavioral therapies and psychotherapies are usually recommended as the first modalities to try when treating the psychopathologies of childhood and adolescence. Drug treatment is typically considered *only in conjunction* with one of the psychosocial treatments; it seldom is utilized as a sole intervention. The decision to employ psychopharmacological intervention must be made thoughtfully, with careful clinical consideration to the diagnosis and the target symptoms.

If the clinician has decided that psychopharmacological intervention is appropriate, both the child and his or her family must be involved in the planning for treatment. The therapist should explain the need for drug therapy in a manner consistent with the child's developmental level, explaining the rationale for the prescription, the medication schedule, and the results expected from this treatment. Considering the child as a partner in treatment has multiple clinical advantages, not the least of which are increased compliance and the metacommunication that the patient plays a role in his or her treatment. The clinician will need to decide whether to explain potential side effects to the child. This decision should be made on an individual basis. Sometimes an explanation of side effects decreases anxiety by letting the patient know what to expect; in other cases, anticipatory anxiety can lead to non-compliance with treatment.

When the parents are involved in the initial decision to prescribe medication, compliance generally improves. Parents who are acknowledged as active participants in their child's treatment, rather than passive observers, are likely to give more support to the identified patient. Of course, in cases with younger children, the explanations given to parents may differ dramatically in complexity from those given to the young patient. However, often with patients of young or middle childhood age, the potential for positive parental influence with respect to compliance is greater than that with the adolescents or preteens.

Think About It

"Needing" Medicine

In addition to considering undesirable physical effects of psychopharmacological treatment, the clinician must be aware of the psychological ramifications of drug intervention. No generic rule applies to all children and adolescents, but the clinician must try to determine what it means to the patient to be on psychiatric medication. What are the implications to a child of feeling a need to take medication to control his or her behavior? Does drug treatment imply that the individual is not responsible for his or her actions? With the association in our society between taking medications and being sick, what message does drug treatment convey to the child? Finally, how does the need to take psychiatric medication affect the patient's sense of self-worth?

Psychotherapeutic Drugs

A wide array of medications are used in treating psychopathologies of childhood and adolescence, including antihistamines, alpha-adrenergic antagonists, opiate antagonists, beta-blockers, and antiepileptic drugs. Here we will discuss five major categories: stimulants, antidepressants, lithium, antipsychotics, and anxiolytics.

Stimulants Of all the psychopharmacological treatments for psychopathology in children and adolescents, stimulants are by far the most frequently used, as well as the most frequently researched.

Currently, stimulants are used most often as a treatment for children with Attention Deficit Hyperactivity Disorder (ADHD). The empirical literature documents that stimulants increase attention span and decrease hyperactivity in these children. Stimulants are also prescribed as adjunct treatments for inattention and hyperactivity in children and adolescents suffering from Conduct Disorders, Oppositional Defiant Disorder in conjunction with ADHD, Mental Retardation, and Pervasive Developmental Disorders. Stimulants used in treatment of child and adolescent psychopathologies include methylphenidate (Ritalin) for children 6 and older, dextroamphetamine sulfate (Dexedrine) for children 3 and older (it is the only stimulant approved for children under age 6); pemoline (Cylert) for children 6 and older; and fenfluramine (Pondimin), recommended as a short-term treatment for exogenous obesity for individuals 12 and older. All these drugs are partially metabolized by the liver and are excreted via the kidneys.

Many of the side effects associated with stimulant treatment will typically disappear within 14 to 21 days. Dosage-related side effects include abdominal pain, weight loss, irritability, mild dysphoria, and anorexia. At higher dosages, there may be some impairment in cognitive performance. More serious side effects of stimulants include slowed growth, slowed weight gain, psychotic symptoms, manic symptoms, the inducement or aggravation of tics, and cardiovascular problems. **Rebound effects** are also reported, in which the child manifests an exacerbation of symptomatology, usually about 5 hours after a dose.

The most common side effect of stimulant medication is insomnia, which is reported to occur in over 50 percent of ADHD children taking methylphenidate (see Barkley, Anastopoulos, & Guevremont, 1991). Anorexia and weight loss are also commonly observed with stimulant treatment. These side effects, however, are typically short term (Rosenberg, Holttum, & Gershon, 1994).

Antidepressants The tricyclic antidepressants are the most commonly used in treatment of children and adolescents. The tricyclics are the only antidepressants approved by the FDA for treatment of depression in individuals as young as 12. Tricyclics have also been used in the treatment of children as young as 10 diagnosed with Obsessive-Compulsive Disorder, Sleep Disorders, ADHD, Tourette's Disorder, Separation Anxiety Disorder or School Phobia, and Enuresis.

Antidepressant medications are metabolized differently in children and adults. First, children have a lower fat-to-muscle ratio, so there is greater potential for toxicity. Second, children have a proportionately larger liver and they metabolize drugs more quickly, so the effective dose is in proportion to their body weight.

The most worrisome side effect of tricyclic antidepressants is the risk of cardiovascular problems. Although this is an issue in adults as well, antidepressants are especially risky in children and adolescents because of children's more rapid metabolism of the drug into cardiotoxic substances. To reduce the likelihood of such side effects, these drugs are often administered in divided doses (Dugas, Zarifan, & Lehevzey, 1980). Other potential side effects include anticholinergic symptoms (dry mouth, constipation, blurred vision), drowsiness, anxiety, insomnia and nightmares (uncommon), agitation, aggression and anger, rashes, mild tremors, and worsening of psychotic symptoms (uncommon). Most of these symptoms are transitory, and they respond to a decrease in dosage. Upon withdrawal of antidepressant medication, some children experience flu-like symptoms such as nausea, headache, and gastrointestinal distress.

Tricyclic antidepressant medications used in the treatment of child and adolescent psychopathology include imipramine (Tofranil) for Depressive Disorders, Enuresis, ADHD, School Phobia, and sleep problems; nortriptyline (Pamelor) for Depressive Disorders; amitriptyline (Elavil) for Depressive Disorders; desipramine (Norpramin) for Enuresis, ADHD, and Tic Disorders; and clomipramine (Anafranil) for Obsessive-Compulsive Disorder, Enuresis, Depressive Disorders, ADHD, and school phobia. Other antidepressants used with children and adolescents include the monoamine oxidase inhibitors for Depressive Disorders; fluoxetine (Prozac) for Depressive Disorders, Obsessive-Compulsive Disorders, and Tic Disorders; and bupropion (Wellbutrin) for ADHD.

Lithium Carbonate Currently, lithium is approved only for the treatment of individuals over age 12 who suffer from manic episodes of Bipolar Disorder. Research is currently under way to investigate lithium treatment for children with severe behavioral symptomatology, especially those who manifest aggressive behavior toward themselves or others (see Campbell, Green, & Deutsch, 1985). Because of the way lithium is metabolized, the drug reaches therapeutic levels more quickly in children than in adults. Interestingly, the dosage required to treat even young children does not differ considerably from that used to treat older adolescents and adults.

One problem with lithium is that it reaches toxicity at levels not very different from those which are therapeutic. There is no established treatment for lithium toxicity, so patients must be carefully monitored. If symptoms of toxicity appear, the drug should be withheld until the lithium level in the blood is checked. The drug can be resumed at a revised dosage within 1 to

2 days. Symptoms of lithium toxicity include gastrointestinal distress, ataxia (loss of coordination), tremor, sedation, slurred speech, and impaired coordination. If allowed to progress, lithium toxicity can be fatal.

Common side effects of lithium treatment in children and adolescents include gastrointestinal distress and a fine tremor, both of which usually subside as treatment progresses. Because lithium metabolism affects the kidneys, the patient's kidney functioning should be monitored throughout treatment (Rosenberg et al., 1994).

Antipsychotics When they were introduced, antipsychotics, also known as *neuroleptics,* were used in the treatment of several disorders of childhood and adolescence that were not classified as psychotic. As research, time, and experience have yielded more data, the usage of this class of drugs in children has expanded further. Currently, antipsychotic medication is prescribed for Childhood Schizophrenia, Autistic Disorder, certain Tic Disorders, severe cases of Conduct Disorder, and severe behavioral symptoms in the mentally retarded.

The liberal use of antipsychotics is a problem because their potential for dangerous side effects is high. Adverse effects include extrapyramidal side effects similar to those seen in Parkinson's disease (tremor, rigidity, drooling, loss of muscle tone); tardive dyskinesia; lowering of the seizure threshold; neuroleptic malignant syndrome (which can be potentially fatal); and overall behavioral toxicity. The most common side effects are seen even with short-term usage, especially with high-potency agents. They include the extrapyramidal symptoms and the dystonic reactions. Abnormal movement disorders are the most common side effect associated with long-term usage (Rosenberg et al., 1994).

The following drugs are approved for treatment of the psychopathologies of childhood and adolescence: chlorpromazine (Thorazine), prescribed for psychotic disorders and for severe behavior problems in children over 6 months old; thioridazine (Mellaril), for psychotic disorders, severe behavior problems, and short-term treatment of ADHD accompanied by Conduct Disorder; trifluoperazine (Stelazine) for psychotic disorders and for short-term treatment of certain anxiety disorders in children over 6; haloperidol (Haldol) for psychotic disorders, Tourette's disorder, and extreme cases of certain behavioral disorders in children over 3; thiothixene (Navane) for psychotic disorders in children over 12; and fluphenazine (Prolixin) for psychotic disorders in individuals over 12.

Anxiolytics Anxiolytics or antianxiety drugs, specifically the benzodiazepines, were the most frequently prescribed class of drugs from 1968 until 1980. As their potential for abuse and addiction became known, however, their use declined. There is no current indication that anxiolytics should play a primary role in the treatment of child and adolescent psychopathology, with the possible exception of certain sleep disorders.

Summary

In this chapter, we discussed different approaches to the treatment of psychopathology in childhood and adolescence. In some cases, "at risk" children and adolescents can be targeted for preventive interventions that seek to decrease the incidence of psychopathology. The *Ethical Principles* of the American Psychological Association governs clinical work with children and adolescents. We discussed ethical concerns about the use of assessment instruments, informed consent, clinical work with couples and families, and confidentiality. Case studies presented ethical dilemmas common in clinical practice.

Therapeutic modalities are divided into two major classifications: psychotherapeutic and psychopharmacological interventions. These two modalities are often employed at the same time. Psychotherapy can involve individual treatment, family sessions, parent training, and group settings.

Each clinician tends to favor particular psychotherapeutic techniques, but most practitioners adjust their approach for patients with different problems. The age of the child is always a consideration. Transference and countertransference affect work with children and adolescents. Behavioral or learning theory has given rise to techniques that apply classical conditioning, operant conditioning, social learning, and cognitive-behavioral models. Psychotherapeutic interventions may involve the theory and applications of play therapy.

Psychopharmacological interventions are used less often than psychotherapy in the treatment of children and adolescents. Dosage is a concern in prescribing psychiatric medication to young people because of physiological, psychological, and compliance issues. Stimulants, antidepressants, lithium, antipsychotics, and antianxiety are all used in treating young people. These medications are discussed in greater detail in chapters on specific psychopathologies.

References

American Guidance Service. (1992). *Behavior assessment system for children.* Circle Pines, Minnesota.

American Psychological Association. (1992). *Ethical principles of psychologists and code of conduct.*

Barkley, R. A., Anastopoulos, D. C., & Guevremont, D. C. (1991). Adolescents with ADHD: Patterns of behavioral adjustment, academic functioning, and treatment utilization. *Journal of the American Academy of Child and Adolescent Psychiatry, 27,* 336–341.

Brems, C. (1993). *A comprehensive guide to child psychotherapy.* Boston: Allyn & Bacon.

Campbell, M. (1991). Pharmacotherapy. In H. I. Kaplan & B. J. Sadock (Eds.), *Comprehensive textbook of psychiatry: Vol. 5.* Baltimore: Williams & Wilkins.

Campbell, M., Godfrey, K. A., & Magee, H. J. (1992). Pharmacotherapy. In C. E. Walker & M. C. Roberts (Eds.), *Handbook of clinical child psychology* (2nd ed.).New York: Wiley.

Campbell, M., Green, W. H., & Deutsch, S. I. (1985). *Child and adolescent psychopharmacology.* Beverly Hills, CA: Sage.

Dugas, M., Zarifan, E., & Lehevzey, M. F. (1980). Preliminary observations of the significance of monitoring tricyclic antidepressant plasma levels in the pediatric patient. *Therapeutic Drug Monitoring, 2,* 307–314.

Dulcan, M. K., & Popper, C. W. (1991). *Child and adolescent psychiatry.* Washington, DC: American Psychiatric Press.

Erikson, E. (1994). In C. Schaefer & H. Kaduson (Eds.), *The quotable play therapist* (p. 246). Northvale, NJ: J. Aronson.

Fonagy, P., & Moran, G. S. (1990). Studies on the efficacy of child psychoanalysis. *Journal of Consulting and Clinical Psychology, 58,* 684–695.

Forehand, R. L., & McMahon, R. J. (1981). *Helping the noncompliant child: A clinician's guide to parent training.* New York: Guilford Press.

Freedheim, D. K., & Russ, S. W. (1992). Psychotherapy with children. In C. E. Walker & M. C. Roberts, *Handbook of clinical child psychology* (2nd ed.). New York: Wiley.

Freud, A. (1965). *Normality and pathology in childhood: Assessments and development.* New York: International Universities Press.

Green, W. H. (1991b). Principles of psychopharmacotherapy and specific drug treatments. In M. Lewis (Ed.), *Child and adolescent psychiatry: A comprehensive textbook.* Baltimore: Williams & Wilkins.

Gurman, A. S., Kniskern, D. P., & Pinsof, W. (1986). Research on the process and outcome of marital and family therapy. In S. L. Garfield, & A. E. Bergin (Eds.), *Handbook of psychotherapy and behavior change.* New York: Wiley.

Harris, S. L., & Ferrari, M. (1983). Developmental factors in child behavior therapy. *Behavior Therapy, 14,* 54–72.

Henggeler, S. W., & Borduin, C. M. (1990). *Family therapy and beyond: A multisystemic approach to treating the behavior problems of children and adolescents.* Pacific Grove, CA: Brooks/Cole.

Kalichman, S. C., Craig, M. E., & Follingstad, D. R. (1990). Professionals' adherence to mandatory child abuse reporting laws: Effects of responsibility attribution, confidence ratings and situational factors. *Child Abuse and Neglect, 14,* 69–77.

Kazdin, A. E., & Mazurick, J. L. (1994). Dropping out of child psychotherapy: Distinguishing early and late dropouts over the course of treatment. *Journal of Consulting and Clinical Psychology, 62,* 1069–1074.

Kendall, P. C. (1993). Cognitive-behavioral therapies with youth: Guiding theory, current status, and emerging developments. *Journal of Consulting and Clinical Psychology, 61,* 235–247.

Klein, M. (1932). *Psychoanalysis of children.* London: Hogarth Press.

Kymiss, P. (1993). Group psychotherapy with adolescents. In H. I. Kaplan & B. J. Sadock (Eds.), *Comprehensive group psychotherapy.* Baltimore: Williams & Wilkins.

Lewis, M. L. (1991). Intensive individual psychodynamic psychotherapy: The therapeutic relationship and the technique of interpretation. In M. Lewis (Ed.), *Child and adolescent psychiatry: A comprehensive textbook.* Baltimore: Williams & Wilkins.

Malone, C. A. (1991). Family therapy. In J. M. Wiener (Ed.), *Textbook of child and adolescent psychiatry.* Washington, DC: American Psychiatric Press.

McDermott, J. F., & Char, W. F. (1974). The undeclared war between child and family therapy. *Journal of the American Academy of Child Psychiatry, 13,* 422–436.

O'Leary, K. D. (1984). The image of behavior therapy: It's time to take a stand. *Behavior Therapy, 15,* 219–233.

O'Leary, K. D., & Wilson, G. T. (1975). *Behavior therapy: Application and outcome.* Englewood Cliffs, NJ: Prentice Hall.

Powers, S. W., & Rickard, H. C. (1992). Behavior therapy with children. In C. E., Walker & M. C. Roberts (Eds.), *Handbook of clinical child psychology* (2nd ed.). New York: Wiley.

Rosenberg, D. R., Holttum, J., & Gershon, S. (1994). *Textbook of pharmacotherapy for child and adolescent psychiatric disorders.* New York: Brunner/Mazel.

Schaefer, C. E., & Briesmeister, J. M. (1989). *Handbook of parent training: Parents as cotherapists for children's behavior problems.* New York: Wiley.

Schaefer, C., & Kaduson, H. (Eds.). (1994). *The quotable play therapist.* Northvale, NJ: Aronson.

Schamess, G. (1993). Group psychotherapy with children. In H. I. Kaplan & B. J. Sadock (Eds.), *Comprehensive group therapy.* Baltimore: Williams & Wilkins.

Silver, L. B., & Silver, B. J. (1983). Clinical practice of child psychiatry: A survey. *Journal of the American Academy of Child Psychiatry, 22,* 573–579.

Szykula, S. A., Sayger, T. V., Morris, S. B., & Sudweeks, C. (1987). Child-focused behavior and strategic therapies: Outcome comparisons. *Psychotherapy, 24,* 546–551.

Thelen, M. H., Rodriguez, M. D., & Sprengelmeyer, P. (1994). Psychologists' beliefs concerning confidentiality with suicide, homicide and child abuse. *American Journal of Psychotherapy, 48,* 363–379.

Thompson, C. L., & Rudolph, L. B. (1992). *Counseling children* (3rd ed.). Pacific Grove, CA: Brooks/Cole.

Werry, J. S., & Wollersheim, J. P. (1989). Behavior therapy with children and adolescents: A twenty-year overview. *Journal of the American Academy of Child and Adolescent Psychiatry, 28,* 1–18.

Williams, D. T. (1991). Hypnosis. In J. M. Wiener (Ed.), *Textbook of child and adolescent psychiatry.* Washington, DC: American Psychiatric Press.

Woolston, J. L. (1991). Psychiatric inpatient services for children. In M. Lewis (Ed.), *Child and adolescent psychiatry: A comprehensive textbook.* Baltimore: Williams & Wilkins.

Zarb, J. M. (1992). *Cognitive-behavioral assessment and therapy with adolescents.* New York: Brunner/Mazel.

Chapter five
Mood Disorders of Childhood and Adolescence

Eeyore, the old grey donkey, stood by the side of the
stream, and looked at himself in the water.

"Pathetic," he said. "That's what it is. Pathetic." He
turned and walked slowly down the stream for twenty
yards, splashed across it, and walked slowly back on the
other side. Then he looked at himself in the water
again.

"As I thought," he said. "No better from this side. But
nobody minds. Nobody cares. Pathetic. That's what it is.
Pathetic."

A. A. Milne, *Winnie-the-Pooh*

Introduction

Although clinical reports of mood disorders in children and adolescents date back as far as the mid-nineteenth century (see Esquirol, 1845), it was not until 20 years ago that the clinical community acknowledged this form of psychopathology in young people. We do not need to look very far back in the psychiatric and psychological literature to find clinicians writing that childhood depression is impossible because children have immature superegos and are therefore unable to experience the consequences of loss. In more practical terms, this ignorance and apparent denial of the existence of mood disorders in young people could be caused by the difficulty of identifying affective symptoms in this age group, especially in the very young. Because of their stage of verbal development, some young children are unable to articulate their feelings. In addition, depression often manifests itself somewhat differently in the young than in the adult population, so clinical cases of childhood depression have often been ignored or misdiagnosed.

The National Institute of Mental Health recognized depression as a valid diagnosis for children and adolescents in the mid-1970s. Bipolar disorders were similarly acknowledged in the 1980s. The clinical literature now presents abundant case studies, empirical investigations, and review articles on the phenomenology, epidemiology, etiology, and treatment of mood disorders in children and adolescents. A review article published in the late 1980s made three major points. First, there is a consensus that depression exists as a clinical entity in children and that the feelings accompanying depression in children are similar to those accompanying depression in adults. Second, depressed children and adolescents may manifest symptoms that have traditionally been considered more characteristic of other diagnostic categories (e.g., somatic symptoms, conduct disorders). Finally, anxiety and depression may be encountered concurrently as well as independently (Kotsopoulos, 1989).

Terminology

Before we begin a discussion of the manifestation, etiology, and treatment of mood disorders in childhood and adolescence, we need to define some terms used in current diagnostic schemata (the *DSM-IV* and the *ICD-10*) and contemporary clinical literature. Clinical examples are presented in the chapter sections focusing on such specific diagnoses.

Perhaps the most generic term is **affect.** Closely related to *mood,* the term *affect* describes the patient's external (or overt) manifestation of emotional status. Clinicians evaluate affect by observing the patient's facial expression, overall body posture, and tone of voice, as well as the patient's ability to react appropriately to an emotionally charged situation.

Affect is rated along a continuum according to the degree to which the patient manifests an appropriate range of expression. Those patients who demonstrate a wide range of affective expression relevant to the current external situation are classified as having a **normal range of affect.** Patients whose range of affect is reduced somewhat are classified as having a **constricted affect.** If the range of affective expression is further limited, the patient is classified as having **blunted affect.** When the patient appears unable to manifest any variation in affective expression, the appropriate descriptive term is **flat affect.** Patients whose affective expression changes frequently and rapidly, often without any stimulus, are referred to as manifesting **affective liability** or *liability of affect.* And patients who manifest affective responses that are the opposite of what would normally be expected are referred to as having **inappropriate** or **incongruent affect.** Constricted affect, blunted affect, and flat affect are characteristic of depressive disorders, and affective lability and incongruent affect tend to be more characteristic of the bipolar or manic disorders. These terms are useful in describing the depth with which the patient appears to express his or her emotions.

It is beyond the scope of this chapter to describe every mood that a patient could possibly experience. Here we will limit our discussion to those terms used to describe pathological expressions of mood.

Three terms are used to describe a mood that has some degree of sadness, or **dysphoria. Dysthymia** describes the mildest manifestation, and **depression** describes the most severe cases. Depressive symptoms can be described as sadness carried to a pathological extreme. Typically, dysthymia tends to be shorter in duration and is characterized by fewer and less severe symptoms than depression. Thus, both *dysthymia* and *depression* refer to the same syndrome, differing only in the degree of severity of the symptoms they describe.

Cyclothymic disorder is diagnosed in patients whose affective symptomatology fluctuates from dysthymia or depression to the other extreme of *hypomania* or *mania.* Manic symptoms are the polar opposite of depressive symptoms. They can be characterized as happiness carried to a pathological extreme. Manic individuals typically manifest expansive affect and **overproductive speech** (also called *pressured speech*). They tend to overestimate their powers and abilities and underestimate the impact of their actions. Those individuals diagnosed as hypomanic exhibit similar symptomatology, but to a less severe degree.

Table 5.1 Range of Mood in Children and Adolescents

1. Clinical depression
2. Dysphoric affect
3. Nonpathological affect
4. Hypomania
5. Mania

Mood Disorders of Childhood and Adolescence

Depressive Disorders

Diagnostic Criteria Neither the *Diagnostic and Statistical Manual of Mental Disorders (DSM-IV)* nor the *International Statistical Classification of Diseases and Related Health Problems (ICD-10)* have a specific diagnostic category for mood disorders of childhood and adolescence. The *DSM-IV* uses the adult diagnostic criteria for depressive disorders in childhood and adolescence. The three categories include *Major Depressive Disorder, Dysthymic Disorder,* and *Depressive Disorder Not Otherwise Specified.* Diagnostic criteria for depression are listed in Box 5.1.

box**5.1**

Diagnostic Criteria for Depression

A. Five (or more) of the following symptoms have been present during the same 2-week period and represent a change from previous functioning; at least one of the symptoms is either (1) depressed mood or (2) loss of interest or pleasure.

   1. Depressed mood most of the day, nearly every day, as indicated by either subjective report (e.g., feels sad or empty) or observation made by others (e.g., appears tearful).... *Note:* In children and adolescents, can be irritable mood.

   2. Markedly diminished interest or pleasure in all, or almost all, activities most of the day, nearly every day (as indicated by subjective account or observation made by others)

   3. Significant weight loss when not dieting or weight gain (e.g., a change of more than 5% of body weight in a month), or decrease or increase in appetite nearly every day. *Note:* In children, consider failure to make expected weight gains.

   4. Insomnia or hypersomnia almost every day

5. Psychomotor agitation or retardation nearly every day (observable by others, not merely subjective feelings of restlessness or being slowed down)

6. Fatigue or loss of energy nearly every day

7. Feelings of worthlessness or excessive or inappropriate guilt (which may be delusional) nearly every day (not merely self-reproach or guilt about being sick)

8. Diminished ability to think or concentrate, or indecisiveness, nearly every day (either by subjective account or as observed by others)

9. Recurrent thoughts of death (not just fear of dying), recurrent suicidal ideation without a specific plan, or a suicide attempt or a specific plan for committing suicide

B. The symptoms cause clinically significant distress or impairment in social, occupational, or other important areas of functioning.

C. The symptoms are not due to the direct effects of a substance (e.g., a drug of abuse, a medication) or a general medical condition (e.g., hypothyroidism).

D. The symptoms are not better accounted for by bereavement, i.e., after the loss of a loved one, the symptoms persist for longer than 2 months or are characterized by marked functional impairment, morbid preoccupation with worthlessness, suicidal ideation, psychotic symptoms, or psychomotor retardation.

Source: American Psychiatric Association, *DSM-IV*, p. 327. Reprinted with permission from the *Diagnostic and Statistical Manual of Mental Disorders,* Fourth Edition. Copyright © 1994 American Psychiatric Association.

A less severe diagnosis than would be Major Depression, the *DSM-IV* diagnostic criteria for Dysthymic Disorder are listed in Box 5.2. The diagnosis of dysthymia is characterized as having an early onset before age 21, a late onset after age 21.

box **5.2**

DSM-IV Diagnostic Criteria for Dysthymic Disorder

A. Depressed mood for most of the day, for more days than not, as indicated either by subjective account or observation made by others, for at least 2 years. *Note:* In children and adolescents, mood can be irritable and duration must be at least 1 year.

B. Presence, when depressed, of two (or more) of the following:

1. Low self-esteem or low self-confidence, or feelings of inadequacy.

2. Feelings of pessimism, despair, or hopelessness.

3. Generalized loss of interest or pleasure.

4. Social withdrawal.

5. Chronic fatigue or tiredness.

6. Feelings of guilt, or brooding about the past.

7. Subjective feelings of irritability or excessive anger.

8. Decreased activity, effectiveness, or productivity.

9. Difficulty in thinking, reflected by poor concentration, poor memory, or indecisiveness.

C. During the 2-year period (1 year for children or adolescents) of the disturbance, the person has never been without the symptoms in Criteria A and B for more than 2 months at a time.

D. No Major Depressive Episode . . . during the first 2 years of the disturbance (1 year for children and adolescents); i.e., the disturbance is not better accounted for by chronic Major Depressive Disorder or Major Depressive Disorder, In Partial Remission. *Note:* There may have been a previous Major Depressive Episode provided there was a full remission (no significant signs or symptoms for 2 months) before development of the Dysthymic Disorder. In addition, after the initial 2 years (1 year in children and adolescents) of Dysthymic Disorder, there may be superimposed episodes of Major Depressive Disorder in which cases both diagnoses may be given. . . .

E. There has never been a Manic Episode . . . a mixed Episode . . . or a Hypomanic Episode. . . .

F. The disturbance does not occur exclusively during the course of a chronic Psychotic Disorder, such as Schizophrenia or Delusional Disorder.

G. The symptoms are not due to the direct effects of a substance (e.g., a drug of abuse, a medication) or a general medical condition (e.g., hypothyroidism).

Source: American Psychiatric Association, *DSM-IV*, p. 349. Reprinted with permission from the *Diagnostic and Statistical Manual of Mental Disorders,* Fourth Edition. Copyright © 1994 American Psychiatric Association.

The diagnosis of Depressive Disorder Not Otherwise Specified is described by the *DSM-IV* as including disorders "that do not meet the criteria for any specific Depressive Disorder, Dysthymic Disorder, Adjustment Disorder with Depressed Mood . . . or Adjustment Disorder with Mixed Anxiety and Depressed Mood" (p. 530). Disorders that meet the criteria for this diagnostic category include the following:

1. Premenstrual dysphoric disorder
2. Minor Depressive Disorder
3. Recurrent Brief Depressive Disorder
4. Postpsychotic Depressive Disorder of Schizophrenia
5. A major depressive episode superimposed upon delusional disorder, psychotic disorder not otherwise specified, or the active phase of schizophrenia
6. Depressive disorder of uncertain etiology (may be primary, due to a general medical condition, or substance-induced (APA, *DSM-IV*, p. 350)

Clinical Presentation Here we will discuss the way depressive disorders manifest themselves in children and adolescents. Symptoms vary, depending on the developmental stage of the child.

> The criteria for making a clinical diagnosis of depression during childhood are based on the clinical appearance of the child (his sad, unhappy physiognomy), presenting symptoms (that include feelings of inferiority, of badness, of worthlessness), and on his general reactions of withdrawal, boredom, disinterest, apathy, discontentment and anhedonia. He looks and feels and is a miserable child. He feels rejected and unloved and yet is unwilling to accept comfort. (Anthony, 1994, p. 249)

Research on depression in adults has been a starting point for the investigation of depression in younger individuals. Although the major diagnostic systems do not address developmental issues in detail, recent investigations have yielded valuable information about symptomatology in children of different ages. Data indicate that the frequency as well as the patterning of symptom presentations depends on developmental level (Achenbach, 1982).

Even infants can suffer from depression. Classic studies of **anaclitic depression** describe the symptoms of babies born in a penal home for adolescent mothers (Spitz, 1946). These babies suffered from **emotional deprivation** and showed pathological symptoms by the age of 6 months. Symptoms included weight loss, insomnia, problems with human interaction, weepy and withdrawn behavior eventually replaced by a chronic blank stare, retardation and regression in developmental milestones, and increased susceptibility to infection. Spitz reported that the longer the babies suffered from maternal deprivation, the worse their symptoms became.

Depression in infants is recognized in the clinical literature. It can be manifest via a collection of symptoms. One such syndrome is **failure to thrive.** These infants show evidence of poor care, delay in psychosocial development, and poor weight gain. A short-term problem is labeled **sensory-motor depression.** These babies have a sad, flat facial expression and an irritable tone to the cry. They make prolonged eye contact without the usual "brightness." Language development is delayed, and social smiling disappears. Pathological eating behaviors, an increase in the amount of sleep, a lack of curiosity, an increased number of physical illnesses, and delayed cognitive development are also seen. Depression is typically first noticed by the primary caretakers; the initial symptoms are apathetic attitude, weight loss, sleep problems, and social withdrawal.

The symptomatic pattern begins to change if depression continues as the infant matures into a young child. Between the ages of 1 and 3 years, the depressive syndrome affects achievement of developmental milestones expected during this period. Clinicians observe **developmental arrest** or **developmental regression.** Depression can cause delay or regression in language skills, gross motor skills, and/or toilet-training skills; an increase in self-stimulating behaviors, often replacing interest in age-appropriate play; delay in cognitive development; and sleep disturbances. In addition, there is often an obvious increase in negativism and oppositional behavior, which can manifest itself in what appears to be an intense distrust of parents or other caretakers.

Preschoolers suffering from depressive disorders manifest their own developmentally specific symptom patterns. In 3- to 5-year-olds, depression is exhibited as sadness, **anhedonia,** affective lability, and a preoccupation with negative or punitive themes. Play involvement with peers decreases noticeably. The child shows lessened interest in newly acquired motor skills and does not seem to have a feeling of accomplishment. Possible manifestations of depression in this age group include disturbed eating and sleeping behaviors, decline in cognitive abilities, and even expression of suicidal ideas.

PEANUTS reprinted by permission of United Feature Syndicate, Inc.

Case Study 5.1

Four-year-old Scott was brought to a child psychologist by his mother at the recommendation of his preschool teacher. Over the past 2 months, Scott's behavior has changed dramatically. Previously one of the most sociable, outgoing children in his play group, Scott now refuses to play with other children. Instead, he sits alone in a corner of the room, looking sullen.
With urging from the teacher, he participates in activities involving the entire class, but only
passively. When the class breaks up into smaller play groups, Scott returns to his corner and
draws. Scott describes his own drawings, done entirely in black crayon, as "the inside of my
heart" or "the inside of my head."

Presentation of depressive symptomatology in the school-age child (6 through 12 years)
closely resembles that in the adult. Most data on childhood depression have been obtained
through work with schoolchildren. Because most children this age can verbalize their feelings,
clinicians can elicit direct reports of dysphoric affect, anhedonia, problems with psychosocial
functioning, sleep problems, and suicidal ideation. In addition to the symptoms typical of adult
depression, school-age children manifest morbid fantasies, difficulties in peer relationships,
decline in academic performance, agitation, motor clumsiness, self-criticism, excessive guilt,
and suicidal ideation or intent that some clinicians interpret as repressed anger turned inward.

Case Study 5.2

Seven-year-old Dana was referred to the school psychologist by her teacher. The teacher was
unable to explain exactly what was wrong, except that Dana's behavior appeared to be "different" and "changing." Dana was formerly a top student but is now barely receiving passing
grades. In addition, she initiates arguments and physical fights with her peers. When repri-
manded for her poor academic performance or her aggressive behavior, Dana says, "I guess
I'm just no good at all—maybe somebody should shoot my head off with a shotgun."

A review examined the manner in which childhood depression has been diagnosed over
the years (Angold, 1988). Key symptomatic patterns include a general anhedonia, often accompanied by a total inability to experience pleasure (see the 1991 study by Wierzbicki and

Sayler, which reports the tendency of depressed children to engage in unpleasant activities). Other symptoms are a "downcast" mood of some duration, self-deprecation, increased tiredness, poor concentration, and overall restlessness. The most important diagnostic criteria, however, is the concurrent appearance of two or more symptoms.

Along the same lines, a review of assessment approaches for depression in children and adolescents (Kendall, Cantwell, & Kazdin, 1989) lists the following "related constructs" the clinician should be alert for in a potentially depressed child or adolescent: distortion in perceived control over life events, low self-esteem or poor evaluation of personal worth, helplessness, hopelessness, loneliness or perceived isolation from peers, deficiencies in social behavior, stressful life events, and a paucity of reinforcing events and activities in the child's life.

A more recent study reported epidemiological data on comorbidity with depression and other disorders (Angold & Costello, 1993). The study found that depression coexists with the conduct disorders approximately 21 to 83 percent of the time—admittedly a wide range. It may also coexist with anxiety disorders (30 to 75 percent) and with Attention Deficit Disorder (0 to 57 percent). A later article concludes that with depressive disorders in children and adolescents, "Co-morbidity is the rule rather than the exception, and thus much of what is thought to be known about the disorder may be shaped by its co-occurrence with other disorders and symptoms" (Hammen & Compas, 1994, p. 602).

Interestingly, despite the cultural lore about the misery of adolescence, depression is not a characteristic of adolescence itself. Clinical literature indicates that adolescent depression is usually a continuation of a depressive process initiated earlier in childhood. Indeed, a recent study (Weiss, Weisz, Politano, Carey, Nelson, & Finch, 1992) reports that the symptoms of depression in children and adolescents differ only slightly.

It can be difficult to differentiate between clinical depression and the normal mood swings of adolescence. Data indicate that adolescent depression has been significantly underdiagnosed, so we can infer that epidemiological figures underestimate its actual occurrence. Symptoms common in clinically depressed adolescents include an intensification of the usual adolescent lability; an increase in emotional outbursts; a delay in puberty; acute cognitive pathology; low self-esteem; substance use or abuse; antisocial behavior; negative cognitive patterns (see Garber, Weiss, & Shanley, 1993); weight gain or loss; somatic problems; and expression of suicidal ideation or intent.

Think About It

Adolescent Moodiness or Depression?

When you read the description of depressive symptomatology in adolescents, did you ask yourself, "Isn't this just adolescence?" How can a parent or a clinician distinguish between "normal adolescent mood swings" and true clinical depression? Using the discussion of abnormality in Chapter 1 as a conceptual framework, what other factors would you consider in making such a decision?

Adolescents suffering from depressive disorders are more likely than younger children to present with an acute onset. Research indicates that one out of every five adolescents suffering from a mood disorder also has a substance abuse problem. An article written in the 1980s (Carlson & Kashani, 1988) classifies adolescent depression as being either primary or secondary. Primary depression means there is no preexisting psychopathology, a secondary case is associated with another psychiatric or psychological diagnosis. Those adolescents who suffer from secondary depressive disorders are more aggressive, irritable, and somatically preoccupied. They also have more conduct and academic problems as well as an increased risk of suicide.

Case Study 5.3

Fifteen-year-old Tricia made an appointment with her school guidance counselor "just to talk." Tricia described herself as feeling "bummed out all the time lately" and feeling as if she wants to "leave the planet." Tricia has been having difficulty sleeping at night, but during the weekends she sleeps until mid-afternoon. When the counselor asked Tricia what she meant by wanting to "leave the planet," Tricia responded that if she could think of a way to kill herself that "would work and wouldn't hurt too bad," she would do it.

Epidemiology Although the published figures must be taken with caution, the generally accepted figure for the incidence of Major Depression in prepubertal children ranges from 1.7 to 2 percent. There is a considerable increase in adolescence, with a rate of 4.7 percent. Similarly, the rate of dysthymic disorders in adolescence is 3.3 percent. The incidence rate for all mood disorders in adolescents has been quoted as approximately 15 percent (Dulcan & Popper, 1991; Kaplan & Sadock, 1985).

Unlike the case in adults, female children and adolescents do not appear to suffer from clinical depression more frequently than males. Only in late adolescence does the increased tendency in females become evident. African-American adolescents seem to exhibit more depression than Caucasians. It must be noted, however, that this observation was made in groups of mixed socioeconomic status, and lower socioeconomic status is itself associated with depression (Stavrakaki & Gaudet, 1989).

Assessment of Depression in Children and Adolescents

Ideally, the assessment of depressive disorders in children and adolescents should be multimodal. As discussed in Chapter 3, diagnostic decisions should not be based solely upon data obtained from a single source, whether an objective instrument, projective test, or a clinical interview. Information obtained from others in the patient's life is valuable. Studies indicate that 25 percent of the cases of depressive disorders in children and adolescents can be accurately diagnosed from reports by the patient and parent. A 25 percent false positive rate is reported when data are obtained only from the child and a 50 percent false positive rate when data are obtained only from the parents (see Akiskal & Weller, 1991).

Think About It

Who Should Be Believed?

How should a clinician proceed when data obtained from a parent conflict with data obtained from a child or adolescent patient? Is it safe to assume that an adult is more likely to provide accurate information (and that a child or adolescent will have a distorted perception)? In fact, parental reports of symptomatology may be less than accurate. The clinician must consider all data in the light of the family dynamics. What factors must the clinician consider, and how will he or she use this material in assessment and therapy?

Modalities used to assess depressive disorders in children and adolescents fall into three major categories: (1) clinical interviews, with varying degrees of structure; (2) generic assessment instruments that place cases of depression into one of several diagnostic categories; and (3) instruments designed to assess the presence and/or intensity of clinical depression. The second and third categories can be subdivided into instruments constructed for, and therefore normed on, child or adolescent populations, and those designed for adults. Here we will focus on assessment measures designed for children and adolescents.

Interview Formats Structured and semistructured interviews have been developed for evaluation of depressive symptoms in children and adolescents, largely because of dissatisfaction with the more traditional methods (Roberts, Vargo, & Ferguson, 1989).

As described in Chapter 3, different semistructured diagnostic interviews have been designed to provide diagnostic data on child and adolescent patients. All of these include depressive disorders as one of their many diagnostic categories, but none is designed primarily to assess depressive disorders. The Diagnostic Interview for Children and Adolescents (DICA) includes mood disorders as one of 18 diagnostic categories for which data are collected. The Diagnostic Interview Schedule for Children (DISC) addresses depressive and other mood disorders in addition to 25 other diagnostic categories. The Child Assessment Schedule (CAS) includes mood and affect with 11 other content areas. Clinical cutoff scores assist the clinician in determining whether a diagnosis of depression is indicated.

One semistructured interview focuses more specifically on depressive and mood disorders in children and adolescents. The Schedule for Affective Disorders and Schizophrenia—Children's Version (K-SADS) was published in the mid-1980s. The interview consists of some 100 items addressing approximately 50 content areas, although the major focus is on the mood disorders. Requiring anywhere from 45 to 120 minutes to complete, the K-SADS consists of three parts: an unstructured interview; a section with questions that address depressive and other mood disorders; and a section requiring observation by the clinician, primarily with respect to the child's overall level of functioning.

Another semistructured interview that was constructed for the diagnosis of childhood depression is the Interview Schedule for Children (ISC). This interview was designed primarily for research rather than clinical practice. The ISC is administered separately to the parent and the child. Each component typically lasts an hour. Designed to be used with individuals from 8 to 17 years of age, the assessment procedure consists of two parts. The first part of the ISC is relatively unstructured. Its goal is to ascertain the general nature of the difficulty the child or adolescent is experiencing. The more structured second part of the ISC is a collection of questions addressing the frequency and severity of 43 depressive symptoms rated on a 9-point scale.

Other interview formats are designed to assess depressive symptom patterns in children and adolescents. The two most popular measures are the Bellevue Index of Depression and the Children's Depression Rating Scale—Revised. Both are semistructured and have interviews that allow the clinician to obtain data that might be missed in a self-report inventory or checklist.

The Bellevue Index of Depression (BID; see Petti, 1978) is composed of 40 items, which are rated by a clinician on the basis of a semistructured interview. As each item is presented, the child is asked whether he or she perceives this area as a problem in his/her life. If the interviewee responds in the affirmative, the clinician probes further with respect to the intensity and severity of the problem. The items themselves comprise 10 symptom areas associated with childhood and adolescent depression: loss of energy, change in appetite or weight, sleep problems, aggressive behavior, dysphoric mood, self-deprecatory ideation, difficulties with academic performance, difficulties with attitude toward school, social withdrawal, and somatic complaints. A version of the BID is available for use by parents and teachers.

The Children's Depression Rating Scale—Revised (CDRS; see Poznarski, Cook, & Carroll, 1979) consists of 17 items that can be used with the child or the parents. Each item is rated by the clinician on a 5- or 7-point scale based on the responses of the interviewee to questions regarding depressive symptomatology. Three of the items focus on the clinician's observation of nonverbal behaviors of the child during the interview process, and the remaining 14 address ability to experience pleasure, school performance, somatic complaints, fatigue, self-esteem, guilt, morbid ideation, social withdrawal, suicidal ideation, eating patterns, irritability, and crying behavior.

Think About It

Self-Reported Depression in Adolescents

When utilizing self-report measures as a means of assessing depression in children and adolescents, how can a clinician evaluate the accuracy of the data collected? This has been the topic of many research publications. One study looked at self-reported depressive symptoms in inner-city adolescents seeking routine health care services (Schichor, Bernstein, & King, 1994). With a sample of 966 adolescents (mean age 15.5 years), the authors report that girls were twice as likely to acknowledge dysthymic or depressive symptoms as were boys. Do you think that this means that inner-city girls, in general, are more frequently depressed than boys, or could there be another explanation?

Generic Rating Scales Those checklists and rating scales which are classified as "generic" are not designed to focus on depression or other mood disorders. Rather, generic measures obtain data on symptoms from several diagnostic categories. The most commonly used are the Child Behavior Checklist, the Brief Psychiatric Rating Scale for Children, and the Behavior Assessment System for Children.

The Child Behavior Checklist (CBCL) is designed for use with individuals ranging from 4 to 16 years of age (Achenbach & Edelbrock, 1983). Separate versions are completed by parents as well as by teachers. Each individual responds to 112 statements rated on a Likert scale. School behaviors are rated on a 5-point scale, behavior problems on a 3-point scale, and adaptive functioning on a 7-point scale. The presence or degree of depressive disorder is decided based upon established cutoff scores for the measure. Each version takes less than 30 minutes to complete.

The Brief Psychiatric Rating Scale for Children (BPRSC) (Overall & Hollister, 1979) is a rating scale designed to be completed by the clinician. Modeled after an adult-version predecessor, the BPRSC consists of a list of items rated on a 7-point Likert scale. Major content areas in addition to depressive disorders include anxiety, cognitive distortion, behavior problems, organicity, withdrawal, and psychomotor excitation.

The Behavior Assessment System for Children (BASC) (Reynolds & Kamphaus, 1992) is a series of objective measures for the child or adolescent, the parent, and the teacher. The version of the form used depends on the age of the identified patient. The BASC presents a series of statements that the respondents rate on a 4-point scale in terms of frequency of occurrence. Raw scores are summed, providing a rating for each of 12 diagnostic categories.

Depression Rating Scales Several measures have been designed to assess depression in children and adolescents. The four tests described here are self-reports administered and interpreted by a trained clinician. Among the most popular of such assessment instruments are the Children's Depression Inventory, the Depression Self-Rating Scale, Children's Depression Scale, and the Dimension of Depression Profile for Children and Adolescents.

The Children's Depression Inventory (CDI; see Kovacs, 1985) is one of the most widely utilized measures to assess depressive disorders in children and adolescents. This extensively researched scale consists of 27 items designed to assess the multiple dimensions of Depressive Disorder (i.e., behavioral, affective, motivational, and cognitive). Each item is rated on a 3-point scale.

The Depression Self-Rating Scale (DSRS; see Birleson, 1981) used in children is patterned on the Zung Depression Scale used in adults. The DSRS is a self-report measure that asks the child or adolescent to respond to 18 statements. The respondent is asked to indicate how often during the past week they have felt the way the statement describes. Responses indicate the severity of the depressive symptomatology. A revised version of the DSRS (Asarnow & Carlson, 1985) incorporates items addressing feelings of hopelessness and the respondent's capacity to experience empathy.

The Children's Depression Scale (CDS; see Tisher & Lang, 1983) is modeled after a statistical procedure. Each of 66 items is written on a separate card, and the respondent rates each item by placing the card on a pile indicating the applicability of the item to the child's current situation. Of these 66 items, 48 address depressive symptomatology, focusing on guilt, self-esteem, somatic preoccupation, affective response, and social problems. The CDS covers ages 9 through 16, with a comparable form for parents, teachers, or other significant adults.

The Dimension of Depression Profile for Children and Adolescents (DPCA) is one of the newer scales designed to measure depressive disorders in children and adolescents (Harter 1990). It is divided into subscales, each made up of six items, designed to address the five major symptomatic areas of depression: energy and interest, suicidal ideation, depressed affect, global self-worth, and self-blame. Each subscale receives its own score, and the six scores are summed to provide a global rating. Thus, the DPCA not only provides an overall depression score but also provides data about the contribution of each component factor.

Think About It

Reliability and Validity of the Depression Adjective Check Lists

Lubin, VanWhitlock, McCollum, and Thummel (1994) conducted two studies to determine the reliability and validity of the Depression Adjective Check Lists (DACL) as an assessment tool for depression in adolescents. Results indicate that the measure is both reliable and valid for the assessment of transient mood or affect. If we accept this interpretation, under what clinical situations would the DACL be a useful measure to employ?

Etiology of Depression in Children and Adolescents

The theories of the etiology of childhood/adolescent depression are classified into two major categories: biological and psychological. Again, the biological and psychological approaches need not be considered mutually exclusive.

One of the primary biological theories to explain the etiology of depression focuses on genetic contributions to the disorder. Studies have found evidence of increased concordance rates in monozygotic twins, genetic clusters in family units, and a higher rate of depressive diagnoses in close relatives of depressed individuals. Data on bipolar diagnoses are often interpreted as supporting a strong genetic contribution. Such data are inconclusive; they give correlational rather than causal information.

Some researchers explain the etiology of depressive disorders by focusing on neurochemical systems. Research on neurotransmitters has yielded mixed results. Further, because the majority of these empirical investigations have utilized adult samples, their external validity with respect to children and adolescents is yet to be determined. Among the neurotransmitters that may play an etiological role in depressive disorders are serotonin, norepinephrine, dopamine, and acetylcholine. One theory attempts to integrate conflicting research data on neurotransmitters and depression by hypothesizing that different subtypes of depressive disorders vary in their neurochemical etiology. Other research studies have evaluated the influence of cortisol (e.g., Roy, Pickar, DeJone, Karoum, & Linnoila, 1988), growth hormone (e.g., Gold, Goodwin, & Chrousos, 1988), and melatonin (e.g., Cavallo, Holt, Hejazi, Richards, & Meyer, 1987) in depressive disorders in children and adolescents.

In recent years, there has also been some empirical investigation of the impact of temperament on the development of depressive symptoms. One such study (Goodyer, Ashby, Altham, & Vize, 1993) looked at the relationship between temperament and mental status in 193 adolescents ages 11 to 16. Using a temperament scale completed by teachers and parents and a modified version of the DISC, results supported a relationship between high (negative) emotionality and development of major depression. Although this trend was found to be stronger in female subjects, it was also evidenced in the male subjects tested.

Other theories regard depression in childhood and adolescence as due to nonbiological causes. The now classic book *Why Isn't Johnny Crying: Coping with Depression in Children* (McKnew, Cytryn, & Yahraes, 1983) conceptualizes the nonbiological causes of depression as being a function of "stress." The authors discuss factors that can cause stress in the life of a child. A list of these psychosocial factors is presented in Table 5.2.

The cognitive-behavioral and **learned helplessness** theories of the etiology of depression in children and adolescents can both be easily integrated with psychosocial factors. These closely related theories focus on attributions that depressed individuals use to explain environmental events. The cognitive-behavioral approach emphasizes a maladaptive cognitive triad: (1) negative perceptions of the self, the world, and the future; (2) stable cognitive patterns; and (3) cognitive errors (Eelen & Van Den Bergh, 1986). It is the incorporation of this way of looking at the world into one's day-to-day life which results in depressive symptoms.

Table 5.2 Psychosocial Factors in Childhood Depression

Familial events
Separation from significant persons or places
Loss of a strong attachment
Depreciation and/or rejection from significant figures
Depressive disorders in parents or significant others
Sudden loss
Various interpersonal and social factors

Similarly, the learned helplessness theory originated by McKinney (1984), was revised to explain the etiology of depressive symptoms, explains the onset of depression as the result of the causal attributions an individual makes to explain negative life events.

Think About It

Cognitive Understanding of Depression

A recent paper (Lennings, 1994) presents a cognitive understanding of suicidal behavior in adolescents. After reviewing the cognitions believed to be associated with suicide attempts, the authors present a model of adolescent suicidal behavior. Included among the cognitive factors investigated were covert suicide rehearsal, development of a suicide schema, cognitive rigidity, and distortion in time perspective. The model presents suicide as being on an individual's continuum of escape or noncoping behaviors. Specifically, the paper focuses on distorted time perspective and conceptualizes it as a major variable in the assessment of suicide risk in adolescents. How would a distorted perception of time relate to suicide ideation and suicide risk in this population?

Treatment of Depression in Children and Adolescents

The treatment of depressive disorders in children and adolescents is not unlike the treatment of many of the other psychopathologies of childhood and adolescence. Most clinicians recommend some combination of pharmacological and psychotherapeutic approaches. Here we will discuss the various therapeutic interventions as well as their advantages and disadvantages.

Psychotherapeutic Approaches The psychotherapeutic approaches used to treat depressive disorders in children and adolescents are somewhat limited in their range. This is not surprising, however, when we consider how recently depressive disorders were recognized as valid diagnostic entities in young people. Treatment approaches used with children and adolescents were developed from those used with depressed adults. The majority of outcome studies focus on the pharmacological interventions. A few empirical studies have investigated the behavioral (e.g., social skills training) and cognitive-behavioral approaches. These two modalities are useful in treating adult depressive disorders, and they are considered the most efficacious of the nonpharmacological approaches (Milling & Martin, 1992).

Any theoretical approach can be superimposed on any number of different therapy formats. Behavioral, cognitive behavioral, and other approaches can be applied in individual, family, or group formats, depending on the needs of the child or adolescent and on the preferences of the therapist. Similarly, play therapy, supportive interventions, and psychodynamic approaches can be used.

Even though many different therapeutic approaches have been directed at depressive disorders in children and adolescents, the cognitive-behavioral methods have received most of the attention in the empirical literature. The efficacy of social skills therapies as well as purely supportive modalities has also been investigated in controlled studies. A recent study (Tarnowski, Simonian, Bekeny, & Park, 1992) indicates that both patients and their parents prefer behavioral and cognitive behavioral modalities over the social skills approaches, and they prefer all three psychological interventions over the psychopharmacological modalities.

Derived from cognitive-behavioral work with adults, cognitive-behavioral approaches for children and adolescents focus on modification of identified maladaptive thoughts that are associated with the child's perception of the world. Cognitive-behavioral approaches for depressive disorders address issues of characteristic coping patterns, maladaptive attributions for failure and lack of accomplishment, overall negative thinking, the **imaginary audience** phenomenon, and self-blaming and self-deprecation tendencies (Weiner, 1992; Garber et al., 1993).

Although cognitive-behavioral therapies have been found to be effective interventions in the treatment of adult depressive disorders, there are problems in applying the methodology to children and adolescents. A recent article (Weisz, Rudolph, Granger, & Sweeney, 1992) emphasizes the necessity of considering child's developmental level, especially with respect to cognitive functioning. If maladaptive cognitions have a role in depressive disorders, the developmental stage at which these cognitions are formed may have an effect on treatment. The therapist should proceed in an informed manner with respect to age-related cognitive changes, specifically in terms of attributional styles, self-regulatory styles, and self-deprecatory attributions.

The integration of developmental stage is equally significant regardless of the therapeutic intervention employed. Indeed, any attempt at modifying behavior via operant methods must incorporate contingencies the child or adolescent will find reinforcing. Further, the child's ability to delay gratification must also be taken into consideration in any type of behavioral program. A therapist planning a purely supportive intervention must also consider the child's developmental stage so that the patient will not feel lectured to, "not heard," or patronized.

Psychopharmacological Approaches The use of antidepressant medication for the treatment of depressive disorders in children is surprisingly limited. The two FDA-approved drugs for the treatment of depression in children age 12 and over are imipramine (Tofranil) and nortriptyline (Pamelor). Treatment of depression in adolescents may also employ amitriptyline (Elavil) and fluoxetine (Prozac).

Few studies have investigated the efficacy of pharmacological treatment for depressive disorders in children and adolescents. These have been limited to **open-label studies;** few if any true **double-blind placebo studies** are available. It is interesting to note a consistent pattern: the open-label studies report that psychopharmacological medication is superior to placebo, and the few double-blind studies show much more equivocal results. Research data are similarly faulty in work with adolescents as well (Green, 1991; Pliszka, 1991; Ryan, 1992).

Whereas this is not to imply that tricyclic pharmacological treatment of depressive disorders in children and adolescents is not effective, it is imperative that one is acutely aware of the limitations of the available research studies, and, therefore, the conclusions that can be drawn from them. While the tricyclic pharmacological treatment of depressive disorders in children and adolescents may be effective, it is imperative to be aware of the limitations of the available research studies and the conclusions which can be drawn from them.

Another class of antidepressant medications, the monoamine oxidase inhibitors (MAOIs), are usually prescribed for adults whose depression does not respond to the tricyclic medications. Patients must be informed of dietary restrictions to prevent a potentially fatal hypertensive crisis. These drugs are approved by the FDA for administration only to individuals 16 years of age and older.

Other Mood Disorders of Childhood and Adolescence

Before addressing the other mood disorders of childhood and adolescence, we need to explore the concepts of mania and hypomania. Clinical reports of mania occurring in children and adolescents date back as far as the mid-nineteenth century. Kraeplin (1915) wrote that although mania was relatively rare in children, 0.5 percent of his manic patients had their first episode before age 10. Many clinicians today, however, doubt that mania and hypomania occur in childhood or adolescence. Others apply the adult diagnostic criteria to younger patients. Problems arise, however, because manic symptoms overlap with other childhood diagnostic classifications, obscuring the differential diagnosis.

Clinical Presentation The *DSM-IV* does not provide specific diagnostic criteria for manic or hypomanic episodes in children and adolescents. Thus, practitioners are forced to apply the adult criteria listed in Box 5.3.

box **5.3**

Diagnostic Criteria for Manic Episodes

A. A distinct period of abnormally and persistently elevated, expansive, or irritable mood, lasting at least 1 week (or any duration if hospitalization is necessary).

B. During the period of mood disturbance, three (or more) of the following symptoms (four if the mood is only irritable) and have been present to a significant degree:

  1. Inflated self-esteem or grandiosity

  2. Decreased need for sleep (e.g., feels rested after only 3 hours of sleep)

  3. More talkative than usual or pressure to keep talking

  4. Flight of ideas or subjective experience that thoughts are racing

  5. Distractibility (i.e., attention too easily drawn to unimportant or irrelevant external stimuli)

  6. Increase in goal-directed activity (either socially, at work or school, or sexually) or psychomotor agitation

  7. Excessive involvement in pleasurable activities that have a high potential for

    painful consequences (e.g., engaging in unrestrained buying sprees, sexual indiscretions, or foolish business investments)

C. The mood disturbance is sufficiently severe to cause marked impairment in occupational functioning or in usual social activities or relationships with others, or to necessitate hospitalization to prevent harm to self or others. . . .

D. The symptoms are not due to the direct physiological effects of a substance (e.g., drugs of abuse, a medication, or other treatment) or a general medical condition (e.g., hyperthyroidism).

Source: American Psychiatric Association, *DSM-IV,* p. 332. Reprinted with permission from the *Diagnostic and Statistical Manual of Mental Disorders,* Fourth Edition. Copyright © 1994 American Psychiatric Association.

The diagnostic criteria for a hypomanic episode are listed in Box 5.4.

box **5.4**

Diagnostic Criteria for Hypomanic Episodes

A. A distinct period of sustained elevated, expansive, or irritable mood, lasting throughout at least 4 days, that is clearly different from the usual nondepressed mood.

B. During the period of mood disturbance, three (or more) of the following symptoms have persisted (four if the mood is only irritable) and have been present to a significant degree:

    1. Inflated self-esteem or grandiosity

    2. Decreased need for sleep (e.g., feels rested after only 3 hours of sleep)

    3. More talkative than usual or pressure to keep talking

    4. Flight of ideas or subjective experience that thoughts are racing

    5. Distractibility (i.e., attention too easily drawn to unimportant or irrelevant external stimuli)

    6. Increase in goal-directed activity (either socially, at work or school, or sexually) or psychomotor agitation

    7. Excessive involvement in pleasurable activities that have a high potential for painful consequences (e.g., the person engages in unrestrained buying sprees, sexual indiscretions, or foolish business investments)

C. The episode is associated with an unequivocal change in functioning that is uncharacteristic of the person when not symptomatic.

D. The disturbance in mood and the change in functioning are observable by others.

E. The symptoms are not due to the direct effects of a substance (e.g., a drug of abuse, a medication, or other treatment) or a general medical condition (e.g., hyperthyroidism).

Source: American Psychiatric Association, *DSM-IV*, p. 338. Reprinted with permission from the *Diagnostic and Statistical Manual of Mental Disorders,* Fourth Edition. Copyright © 1994 American Psychiatric Association.

The clinical presentation of manic episodes depends on the age of the child. Children age 9 or younger tend to be irritable and show affective lability, whereas older children tend to be more paranoid or euphoric or to have grandiose ideas (Carlson & Kashani, 1988). Manic symptoms in adolescents closely resemble those observed in adults, although the extreme mood fluctuations characteristic of adult bipolar disorder are observed more frequently in adolescents.

Especially when working with the preadolescent cases, clinicians must consider issues of differential diagnosis. Other diagnostic categories, such as Attention Deficit Hyperactivity Disorder (ADHD), Conduct Disorder, and Childhood Schizophrenia can be misdiagnosed or confused with manic episodes or can coexist with mania. Children experiencing a manic episode tend to manifest more affect, usually euphoric or irritable in nature, and children with ADHD often exhibit deficits in self-esteem. In addition, age of onset differs. ADHD appears considerably earlier (at toddler age) than mania. For differential diagnosis with respect to Conduct Disorder, the clinician should look for pressured speech, flight of ideas, and grandiosity, which are characteristic of manic and hypomanic episodes and not of Conduct Disorder. In order to differentiate between manic episodes and schizophrenic disorders, the clinician should evaluate information about the child's premorbid personality. Premorbid symptoms of ADHD, Conduct Disorder, or other affective problems are likely to be more indicative of manic and hypomanic cases, while bizarre behaviors and/or schizoid traits are more likely to be characteristic of a schizophrenic process (Weller & Weller, 1991).

The actual diagnosis depends on the manner in which the manic hypomanic episode presents itself. There are four possible diagnoses. A diagnosis of *Bipolar I Disorder (Manic or mixed)* is given when the child presents an alternating mixture of both manic and depressive symptoms, with the depressive symptoms present for at least a 24-hour period. A diagnosis of *Bipolar II Disorder* is given when the child manifests symptoms consistent with a depressive diagnosis, yet has experienced one or more hypomanic episodes previously. A diagnosis of *Cyclothymic Disorder* is used when there have been several hypomanic episodes over a 1-year period in addition to several episodes of depressive affect that did not meet all the criteria for a diagnosis of depressive disorder. The diagnosis of *Bipolar Disorder Not Otherwise Specified* is employed when manic or hypomanic features are manifested, yet the criteria for another diagnosis are not met.

Epidemiology Little information is available on the epidemiology of bipolar disorders in children and adolescents. There are virtually no studies in any age group younger than adolescence, partly because bipolar disorders are rare in young children. A single study (Carlson & Kahshani, 1988) reports an incidence rate of 0.6 percent in a sample of 14- to 16-year-olds, and another (Robins et al., 1984) reports lifetime prevalence of up to 1.1 percent.

Treatment Psychopharmacological treatments are used for the bipolar disorders. Problems arise, however, because antidepressants may precipitate a manic or hypomanic episode. Further, antidepressant medication may increase the rate of affective cycling in the bipolar patient. Thus, when a bipolar disorder is suspected, clinicians often recommend treatment with lithium for the manic or hypomanic symptoms. Another regimen combines lithium and antidepressant therapy (Pataki, Carlson, Rapport, & Biancaniello, 1993). Antidepressants are discussed in the previous section.

Although children and adolescents tend to tolerate lithium better than adults, the drug has not been approved by the FDA for individuals under age 12. In spite of this, lithium has often been used in children as young as age 5, and the recommended dosage is almost the same as for adults. Studies investigating the use of lithium in prepubertal children report success rates as high as 82 percent within a period of several days, but not all of these studies were well-controlled, double-blind protocols (Green, 1991). A relatively recent study (Strober et al., 1981) reports a relapse rate of 92 percent for adolescents who discontinued their lithium therapy prematurely, compared with a 21 percent relapse rate for those who took the medication for a longer period of time.

Because of the danger of lithium toxicity, blood tests and physical exams are a necessity before and during the treatment regimen. Possible side effects and premorbid indicators of lithium toxicity include nausea, vomiting, slurred speech, incoordination, diarrhea, excessive urination, weight gain, sedation, and excessive thirst (Pataki & Carlson, 1992).

Summary

Mood disorders of childhood were first described in the nineteenth century, but childhood depression was not an accepted diagnosis until the mid-1970s.

Patients may exhibit a normal range of affect, a constricted affect, or blunted or flat affect. Some demonstrate affective lability or incongruent affect. Sadness is expressed as dysphoria, dysthymia, or depression. Patients with cyclothymic disorder fluctuate between dysthymic or depressed moods and hypomania or mania.

The *DSM-IV* presents diagnostic criteria for depression, dysthymic disorder, and other depressive disorders. Clinical presentation in children will vary, depending on their developmental stage. Even infants can suffer from depression. Young children may show developmental arrest or regression. Language and motor skills as well as social skills may be affected. Problems in academic achievement are not unusual among depressed schoolchildren. Depression often coexists with the conduct disorders. Adolescent depression is usually a continuation of a preexisting condition rather than a particular problem of this developmental stage.

A diagnosis of depression can often be reached using a clinical interview. Formal assessment instruments have been designed to diagnose depression and rate its severity.

The etiology of depression may involve genetics and/or brain chemistry. Psychosocial factors may also be involved.

Depression in children and adolescents can be treated with drugs. Behavioral and cognitive-behavioral approaches are also employed.

DSM-IV criteria for diagnosis of manic and hypermanic episodes are the same for adults and children. Young children may be irritable rather than showing adult symptoms. For differential diagnosis, clinicians need to consider conduct disorders, schizophrenia, and Attention Ddeficit Hyperactivity Disorder. Treatment for bipolar disorders usually includes antidepressants and/or lithium.

References

Achenbach, T. M. (1982). *Developmental psychopathology* (2nd ed.). New York: Wiley.

Achenbach, T. M., & Edelbrock, C. S. (1983). *Manual for the child behavior checklist revised behavior profile.* Burlington, VT: TM Achenbach.

Akiskal, H. S., & Weller, E. B. (1991). Mood disorders and suicide in children and adolescents. In H. I. Kaplan & B. J. Sadock (Eds.), *Comprehensive textbook of psychiatry: Vol. 5.* Baltimore: Williams & Wilkins.

American Psychiatric Association. (1994). *Diagnostic and statistical manual of mental disorders* (4th ed.). Washington, DC: Author.

Angold, A. (1988). Childhood and adolescent depression: Research in clinical populations. *British Journal of Psychiatry, 153,* 476–492.

Angold, A., & Costello, E. J. (1993). Depressive comorbidity in children and adolescents: Empirical, theoretical and methodological issues. *American Journal of Psychiatry, 150,* 1779–1791.

Anthony, E. J., & Gilpin, D. C. (Eds.). *Clinical faces of childhood.* Northvale, NJ: Jason Aronson.

Asarnow, J. R., & Carlson, G. A. (1985). Depression self rating scale: Utility with child psychiatric in patients. *Journal of Consulting and Clinical Psychology. 53,* 491–499.

Birleson, P. (1981). The validity of depressive disorders in childhood and the development of a self rating scale: A research report. *Journal of Child Psychology and Psychiatry, 22,* 73–88.

Carlson, G., & Kashani, J. (1988). Phenomenology of major depression from childhood through adulthood: Analysis of three studies. *American Journal of Psychiatry, 145,* 1222–1225.

Cavallo, A., Holt, K., Hejazi, M., Richards, G. E., & Meyer, W. J. (1987). Melatonin circadian rhythm in childhood depression, *Journal of the American Academy of Child & Adolescent Psychiatry. 26,* 395–399.

Dulcan, M. K., & Popper, C. W. (1991). *Concise guide to child and adolescent psychiatry.* Washington, DC: American Psychiatric Press.

Eelen, P., & Van Den Bergh, O. (1986). Cognitive behavioral models of depression. *Acta Psychiatrica Belgica, 86,* 748–59.

Esquirol, E. (1845). *Mental maladies.* Philadelphia: Lea & Blanchard.

Garber, J., Weiss, B., & Shanley, N. (1993). Cognitions, depressive symptoms, and development in adolescents. *Journal of Abnormal Psychology, 102,* 47–57.

Gold, P., Goodwin, F., & Chrousos, G. (1988). Clinical and biochemical manifestations of depression; Second of two parts. *New England Journal of Medicine, 319, 7.*

Goodyer, I. M., Ashby, L., Altham, P. M., & Vize, C. (1993). Temperament and major depression in 11 to 16 year olds. *Journal of Child Psychology and Psychiatry and Allied Disciplines, 34,* 1409–1423.

Green, W. H. (1991). *Child and adolescent clinical psychopharmacology.* Baltimore: Williams & Wilkins.

Hammen, C., & Compas, B. E. (1994). Unmasking unmasked depression in children and adolescents: The problem of comorbidity. *Clinical Psychology Review, 14*, 585–603.

Harter, S. (1990). Issues in the assessment of the self concept of children and adolescents. In A La Green (Ed.), *Through the eyes of a child* (pp. 292–325). Boston: Allyn & Bacon.

Kaplan, H., & Sadock, B. (1985). *Modern synopsis of comprehensive textbook of psychiatry—IV,* Baltimore: Williams & Wilkins.

Kendall, P. C., Cantwell, D. P., & Kazdin, A. E. (1989). Depression in children and adolescents: Assessment issues and recommendations. *Cognitive Therapy and Research, 13*, 109–46.

Kotsopoulos, S. (1989). Phenomenology of anxiety and depressive disorders in children and adolescents. *Psychiatric Clinics of North America, 12*, 803–814.

Kovacs, M. (1985). The interview schedule for children. *Psychopharmacology Bulletin, 21*, 991–994.

Kraepelin, E. (1915). *Compendium der psychiatric.*

Lennings, C. J. (1994). A cognitive understanding of adolescent suicide. *Genetic, Social and General Psychology Monographs, 120*, 287–307.

Lubin, B., VanWhitlock, R., McCollum, K. L., & Thummel, H. (1994). Measuring the short-term mood of adolescents: Reliability and validity of the state form of the Depression Adjective Check Lists. *Adolescence, 29*, 591–604.

McKinney, W. (1984). Animal models of depression: An overview. *Psychiatric Development, 2*, 77–96.

McKnew, D. H., Cytryn, L., & Yahraes, H. C. (1983). *Why isn't Johnny crying?* New York: Norton.

Milling, L., & Martin, B. (1992). Depression and suicidal behavior in preadolescent children. In C. E. Walker & M. C. Roberts (Eds.), *Handbook of clinical child psychology* (2nd ed.). New York: Wiley.

Overall, J. E., & Hollister, L. E. (1979). Comparative evaluation of research diagnostic criteria for schizophrenia, *Archives of General Psychiatry, 36*, 1198–1205.

Pataki, C. S., Carlson, G. A., Rapport, M. D., & Biancaniello, T. M. (1993). Side effects of methylphenidate and desimpramine alone and in combination in children, *Journal of the American Academy of Child and Adolescent Psychiatry, 32*, 1065–1072.

Petti, T. A. (1978). Depression in hospitalized child psychiatry patients: Approaches to measuring depression. *Journal of the American Academy of Child Psychiatry, 17*, 49–59.

Pliszka, S. R. (1991). Antidepressants in the treatment of child and adolescent psychopathology. *Journal of Clinical Child Psychology, 20*, 313–320.

Poznarski, E., Cook, S., & Carroll, B. (1979). A depression rating scale for children. *Pediatrics, 64*, 442–450.

Reynolds, C. R., & Kamphaus, R. W. (1992). *Behavior assessment system for children.* Circle Pines, MN: American Guidance Services.

Roberts, N., Vargo, B., & Ferguson, H. B. (1989). Measurement of anxiety and depression in children and adolescents. *Psychiatric Clinics of North America, 12*, 837–860.

Robins, L., Helzer, J., Weissman, M. Overaschel, H., Gruenberg, E., Burke, J., & Reginer, D. (1984). Lifetime prevalence of specific psychiatric disorders in three sites. *Archives of General Psychiatry, 41,* 949–958.

Roy, A., Pickar, D., DeJons, J., Karoum, F., & Linnoila, M. (1988). Norepinephrine and its metabolites in cerebrospinal fluid, plasma and urine. *Archives of General Psychiatry, 45,* 849–857.

Ryan, N. D. (1992). The pharmacological treatment of child and adolescent depression. *Psychiatric Clinics of North America, 15,* 29–40.

Schichor, A., Bernstein, B., & King, S. (1994). Self-reported depressive symptoms in inner-city adolescents seeking routine health care. *Adolescence, 29,* 379–388.

Spitz, R. A. (1946). Anaclitic depression. *Psychoanalytic study of the child,* Vol. 2. New York: International Universities Press.

Seligman, M. E. P. (1975). *Helplessness: On depression, development, and death.* San Francisco: Freeman.

Stavrakaki, C., & Gaudet, M. (1989). Epidemiology of affective and anxiety disorders in children and adolescents. *Psychiatric Clinics of North America, 12,* 791–802.

Strober, M., Green, J., & Carlson, G. (1981). Phenomenology and subtypes of major depressive disorder in adolescence. *Journal of Affective Disorders, 3,* 281–290.

Tarnowski, K. J., Simonian, S. J., Bekeny, P., & Park, A. (1992). Acceptability of interventions for childhood depression. *Behavior Modification, 16,* 103–117.

Tisher, M., & Lans, M. (1983). The children's Depression Scale: Review and further developments. In D. P. Cantwell & G. A. Carlson (Eds.), *Affective disorders in childhood and adolescence* (pp. 181–205). New York: Spectrum.

Weiner, J. M. (1992). *Textbook of child and adolescent psychiatry.* Washington, DC: American Psychiatric Association.

Weiss, B., Weisz, J. R., Politano, M., Carey, M., Nelson, W. M., & Finch, A. J. (1992). Relations among self-reported depressive symptoms in clinic-referred children versus adolescents. *Journal of Abnormal Psychology, 101,* 391–397.

Weisz, J. R., Rudolph, K. D., Granger, D. A., & Sweeney, L. (1992). Cognition, competence and coping in child and adolescent depression: Research findings, developmental concerns, therapeutic implications. *Development and Psychopathology, 4,* 627–653.

Weller, E. B., & Weller, R. A. (1991). Mood disorders. In M. Lewis (Ed.), *Child and adolescent psychiatry: A comprehensive textbook.* Baltimore: Williams & Wilkins.

Wierzbicki, M., & Sayler, M. K. (1991). Depression and engagement in pleasant and unpleasant activities in normal children. *Journal of Clinical Psychology, 47,* 499–505.

Chapter six
Anxiety Disorders of Childhood and Adolescence

"Piglet," said Rabbit, taking out a pencil, and licking
the end of it, "you haven't any pluck."
"It's hard to be brave," said Piglet, sniffing slightly,
"when you're only a very small animal."

A. A. Milne, *Winnie-the-Pooh*

Introduction

Anxiety can be sufficiently intense to affect a person's day-to-day functioning. Yet anxiety is actually a normal, nonpathological phenomenon that serves a necessary purpose. Before we explore the nature of the anxiety disorders of childhood and adolescence, we need to look at the characteristics of anxiety itself.

The Biological Basis of Anxiety

In order to provide a framework for the biological conceptualization of anxiety, it is necessary to understand the structure of the human **nervous system.** The nervous system consists of the **central nervous system,** which includes all **neurons** found in the brain and the spinal cord, and the **peripheral nervous system,** which consists of all neurons functioning outside of the brain and spinal cord. The peripheral system is subdivided into the **somatic** and **autonomic** nervous systems; the latter of which is further subdivided into the **sympathetic** and **parasympathetic** divisions. The brain is directly involved in the experience of anxiety with the peripheral nervous system (particularly portions of the limbic system) most directly related to the experience of anxiety. The sympathetic component of the peripheral nervous system prepares the body to react appropriately in times of perceived danger. When a stimulus that is experienced as potentially dangerous is coded by the brain, the sympathetic division triggers a release by the adrenal glands of the neurotransmitters epinephrine and norepineph-

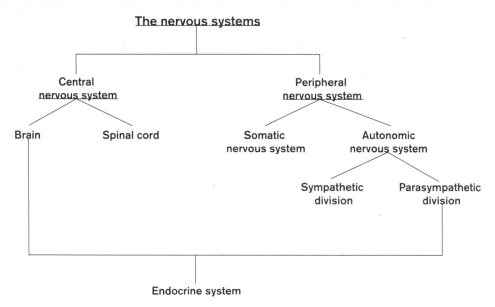

The nervous systems

- Central nervous system
  - Brain
  - Spinal cord
- Peripheral nervous system
  - Somatic nervous system
  - Autonomic nervous system
    - Sympathetic division
    - Parasympathetic division

Endocrine system

figure 6.1

rine (formerly called adrenaline and noradrenaline). These chemicals induce the **flight-or-fight reaction,** which is a series of physical reactions that were designed to prepare the body to react in times of danger. (In contrast, it is the parasympathetic component that returns the body to a more status-quo, relaxed state once the threat of danger is perceived to be gone.)

An increase in heart rate, dry mouth, sweating, a threatening feeling in the pit of the stomach, an overall feeling of impending doom and necessity to escape can all be (at least partially) attributed to the increased secretion of epinephrine and norepinephrine caused by the perception of approaching danger.

Case Study 6.1

Thirteen-year-old Carla usually rides the school bus, but her home is close enough for her to walk. One Friday Carla stayed after school for a play rehearsal. She missed the bus, so she had to walk home. A group of five older boys began to follow her. At first they taunted her; then the taunts escalated into threats, and one of the boys bumped into her. She saw that two of the boys had weapons. Her heart began to beat fast, and she started sweating. Afraid that the boys had violent intentions, Carla ran faster than she had ever run in her life to a shopping mall across the street. Carla's perception of danger had triggered a fight-or-flight reaction.

Sometimes the perception of danger leads to an opposite reaction. Instead of moving at unusual speed and operating with unusual strength, an organism will become immobile. One name for this is "playing possum." Sometimes people, too, are paralyzed by fear—they feel as if they cannot move. The clinical literature describes anxiety sufferers who are physically immobilized by anxiety.

Both of these responses can enable people to cope with threats, but they can also be pathological if they are triggered at inappropriate times. If an individual perceives danger when there is none, the fight-or-flight response pattern may be triggered inappropriately. An intense physiological reaction that is out of proportion to the actual danger can lead to subjective experiences of intense anxiety.

Cognitive components associated with these physiological processes contribute to the subjective experience of anxiety. The physical reactions will be associated with **catastrophic cognitions.** Anxiety is often accompanied by fear of embarrassment or disaster—a heart attack, fainting, passing out, losing control of bodily functions, or even dying.

It is the combination of physiological responses and catastrophic cognitions that characterizes the experience of pathological anxiety. The physiological reactions can trigger the catastrophic cognitions, which in turn produce anxiety and intensify the physiological reactions. This feedback can create a cyclical pattern in which the physiological responses and the cognitive components engage in an interactive relationship, gaining strength from each other.

Anxiety: Disorder or Age-Appropriate Response?

Anxiety is a natural part of life, and in many circumstances it can even be adaptive. In certain situations, however, the intensity of the anxiety or the situations that elicit it can interfere with daily life. How can the clinician distinguish between a valid response to threatening environmental stimuli and an anxious response that is out of proportion to the actual danger?

When evaluating the anxious responses of children and adolescents, the clinician must always consider developmental stage. Responses that would be diagnosed as full-blown anxiety disorders at certain ages are perfectly appropriate at other developmental stages. For example, 5-year-old Juan would be very anxious if his mother left him at home alone while she ran an errand, and his response would be normal. We would not however, expect 11-year-old Ryan to manifest the same behavior. Juan's behavior is age-appropriate and not pathological, but the same behavior in Ryan might warrant a diagnosis of Separation Anxiety Disorder.

As we discuss the anxiety disorders of childhood and adolescence, we will address the developmental issues involved in making diagnoses. We will consider symptoms within the context of developmental stages, drawing a distinction between so-called normal anxiety and the true anxiety disorders. Although fear and anxiety are normal components of the developmental process, children's fears and anxieties are often perceived as unrealistic by adults.

Classification Schema for Anxiety Disorders

Anxiety neurosis, cardiac neurosis, Da Costa's syndrome, disordered action of the heart, irritable heart, nervous exhaustion, nervous tachycardia, neurocirculatory asthenia, soldier's heart, vasomotor neurosis, vasoregulatory asthenia . . . (Uhde & Nemiah, 1989, p. 952)

These terms have been used as synonyms for anxiety over the past century. Psychiatry and psychology have matured in their classification of anxiety disorders, but the connection between these outdated phrases and many current diagnostic categories is still clear.

The original *Diagnostic and Statistical Manual (DSM)* published in 1952 grouped all anxiety disorders under the heading "psychoneurotic disorders." Not addressing anxiety disorders specific to childhood and adolescence at all, this manual classified all anxiety disorders into four groupings: (1) anxiety reactions, (2) phobic reactions, (3) obsessive-compulsive reactions, and (4) psychoneurotic and other reactions. The *DSM-II* (1968) retained the four primary categories but relabeled the disorder as "neuroses." In addition, the *DSM-II* included three categories for anxiety under the global heading "behavior disorders of childhood and adolescence": withdrawing reaction, overanxious reaction, and other (Adams, 1989).

The *DSM-III* represented a major departure from the previous editions. Division of the manual into sections focusing on the presenting psychopathology, and moving the section on the psychopathologies of childhood and adolescence from the end to the beginning of the manual, the *DSM-III* clearly represented a substantive revision. Rather than grouping anxiety disorders under the generic heading "neuroses," the *DSM-III* created a new category labeled "anxiety disorders" with seven major diagnostic categories: (1) phobic disorders (previously labeled phobic neuroses), (2) panic, (3) generalized anxiety disorder, (4) obsessive-compulsive disorder, (5) posttraumatic stress disorder, (6) atypical anxiety disorder, and (7) adjustment disorder with anxious mood. Further, the *DSM-III* created a specific category for anxiety disorders of childhood or adolescence: (1) separation anxiety disorder, (2) avoidant disorder of childhood or adolescence, and (3) overanxious disorder.

In 1987, the *DSM-III-R* contained further revisions in the classification of anxiety disorders in general (most blatantly, conceptualizing Panic Disorder as primary over Agoraphobia when they occur simultaneously). No major changes occurred in this revision in the classification of the anxiety disorders of childhood and adolescence.

The *DSM-IV* substantially revises the classification of anxiety disorders in children and adolescents. In this revision, the only anxiety diagnosis specific to children and adolescents is Separation Anxiety Disorder; criteria for the other anxiety disorders experienced by children and adolescents are listed in the section addressing anxiety disorders in adults. Overanxious Disorder is subsumed under the more generic category of Generalized Anxiety Disorder, and Avoidant Disorder of Childhood has been eliminated. The manner in which the other anxiety disorders—phobias, Panic Disorder, Obsessive-Compulsive Disorder—manifest themselves in childhood and adolescence is addressed in the generic anxiety disorders section (American Psychiatric Association, 1993).

Assessment of Anxiety in Children and Adolescents

Therapists take a multimodal approach to assessment of anxiety disorders in children and adolescents. Assessment instruments used to address physiological, behavioral, and/or cognitive components of anxiety can be classified along two major dimensions: (1) the format utilized to measure the phenomenon, and (2) the aspect of anxiety being assessed or measured. In this section we will discuss the major modalities for anxiety assessment in children and adolescents, providing examples of each type. In addition, we will explore the relative advantages and disadvantages of each against the backdrop of empirically and clinically relevant concerns.

A written format is used in many objective personality tests, symptom checklists, and self-report measures and in some anxiety scales. Behavioral assessment may involve observations by teachers, therapists, parents, and other family members. Interview formats may be structured or unstructured. Physiological measurements (e.g., polygraph studies) may also be made.

Measurement of anxiety itself depends on the way anxiety is defined. Some measures focus on the psychophysiological components of anxiety; others (e.g., anxiety scales, symptom checklists) focus on specific symptoms or symptom constellations exclusive to anxiety disorders; others (e.g., personality inventories, intelligence tests) focus on certain aspects of the individual's psychology that correlate with the presence of anxiety disorders.

Anxiety Scales

The typical anxiety scale calculates the number of symptoms (or symptom constellations) present that are considered to be characteristic of an anxiety disorder. A symptom checklist or self-report inventory is completed by either the child or a parent or teacher. Different scales vary in their focus on somatic, cognitive, avoidant, behavioral (or some combination of the above) manifestations of anxiety. For the most part, however, the content of anxiety scales is limited to items that assess the presence and intensity of fears, phobias, and worries (Barios, Harmant, & Shigetomi, 1981; Klein, 1988). Responses on the scales are converted to numerical data. For each measure, norms are established for cutoff scores that define clinical levels of anxiety.

The first measure that was designed to assess anxiety symptoms in children was a revision of the Taylor Manifest Anxiety State scale for adults. First published in the mid-1950s, the Children's Manifest Anxiety Scale (CMAS) included 42 true/false and yes/no items that detected anxiety symptoms and assessed the validity of the responses. The CMAS obtained an anxiety score by summing the items answered "true" or "yes." In 1984, the CMAS was revised and renamed "What I Think and Feel." Written at the third-grade reading level, this revised version (also referred to as the CMAS-R) consists of 37 items, 25 of them from the original scale, and is based on norms obtained from several hundred children and adolescents from age 5 through 18. Physiological indicators of anxiety, worry and oversensitivity, and cognitive anxiety are measured on this scale (Reynolds & Richmond, 1984).

A commonly used self-report measure was modeled after the classic Wolpe-Lang Fear Survey. Consisting of 80 items, the Fear Survey Scale for Children (Scherer & Nakamura, 1968) asks the child to rate his or her fear of specific situations along a 5-point Likert scale, ranging from "no fear" to "very much" fear. The version in use today is the Fear Survey Scale for Children—Revised (Ollendick, 1983).

Two other prominent self-report scales devised to assess anxiety in children are the State-Trait Anxiety Inventory for Children (STAIC; Spielberger, 1973) and the Institute of Personality and Ability Testing Anxiety Scale (IPAT) (Cattell & Cattell, 1979). The STAIC asks the child to respond to scale items according to how he or she feels both at the time of taking the test and in general. The IPAT, which consists of 40 items, was modified from a similar scale normed on high school students.

The Childhood Anxiety Sensitivity Index (CASI; Peterson & Reiss, 1987) is a self-report measure that asks the child to indicate how negatively he or she views various symptoms of anxiety. Thus, rather than measuring the frequency or intensity of the anxiety symptoms themselves, the CASI assesses the child's affective and cognitive associations to the symptoms. Based on the "fear of fear" concept proposed in the early 1980s (Chambless, 1985), the CASI correlates with some of the more traditional anxiety measures discussed above (Silverman, Fleisig, Rabian, & Peterson, 1991). Two other scales that focus on the cognitions of anxious children and adolescents are the Worry Scale (Francis, 1988) and the Children's Anxious Self-statement Questionnaire (Kendall & Ronan, 1990).

Clinical Interviews

In assessing anxiety in children and adolescents, the therapist typically interviews both the patient and the parents. Besides validating data obtained from each source, this method also allows the clinician to obtain different information from them. Structured and unstructured interview protocols have been developed. The more structured interviews focus on symptom presentation or symptom constellations; the less structured interviews generally address a broader range of data, often including developmental history, familial interaction patterns, psychiatric history, and so on.

The use of structured interviews in children and adolescents dates back to the late 1960s with the publication developed by Rutter and Graham (Rutter & Graham, 1968). This interview was rather global in its content since it was designed to assess the presence of psychopathology in general, rather than specific anxiety symptoms. The specific measurement of anxiety disorders, however, was addressed by a subscore.

As the *DSM* was revised, many structured interviews were developed to assess anxiety disorders as well as other psychopathologies. Interview protocols that were designed to address overall psychopathology yet included specific sections for anxiety disorders include the Kiddie Schedule for Affective Disorders and Schizophrenia (K-SADS; Chambers, 1985); the Diagnostic Interview for Children (Costello, 1984, Edelbrock et al.); and the Diagnostic Interview for Children and Adolescents (Reich, 1982). Two semistructured interview protocols designed to assess anxiety are the Children's Anxiety Evaluation Form (Hoehn-Saric, Maisami, & Wiegand, 1987) and the Anxiety Disorders Interview Schedule for Children (Silverman, 1987, 1991).

The K-SADS was originally designed to assess childhood depression. Appropriate for children from ages 6 through 17, the instrument contains both structured and unstructured segments. The unstructured component obtains information regarding history and current symptom presentation, and the more structured component rates the occurrence and severity of symptoms grouped according to disorders. There is also an observational component to this instrument.

Both the Diagnostic Interview for Children and Adolescents (DICA) and the Diagnostic Interview for Children (DISC) were designed as research instruments. The DICA is made up of three sections: a 19-question interview administered conjointly to parent and child, a 247-item section administered to the child, and an observational component. Like the DICA, the DISC includes over 200 items that cover all the major diagnostic categories.

The Anxiety Disorders Scale for Children (ADIS) is composed of two parts. Parents complete the ADIS-P, and the child completes the ADIS-C. Each consists mostly of yes/no questions relevant to the child's anxiety symptoms. The ADIS items are grouped according to disorder (Silverman & Nelles, 1988). One portion of the Children's Anxiety Evaluation Form (CAEF) is similar; this instrument also allows the clinician to incorporate a general history, observations during the interview, a review of the clinical record, and the patient's subjective assessment (Hoehn-Saric, Maisami, & Wiegand, 1987).

Personality Tests

Personality tests provide data relevant to the assessment of anxiety disorders in the child or adolescent. Clearly, these measures overlap with those described in the previous section. Many of the general measures of child and adolescent psychopathology that have relevance to the diagnosis of anxiety symptoms can also be classified as personality tests.

Some personality tests useful in the assessment of anxiety disorders are projective tests (e.g., the Rorschach inkblot test, the Thematic Apperception Test (TAT), the Bender-Gestalt Test, and the Draw-A-Person test). Other measures require the child to provide data in the form of self-reports (e.g., the Minnesota Multiphasic Personality Inventory, the BASC scales, and the California Tests of Personality) or a daily journal or diary (Beidel, Neal, & Lederer, 1991). Others take the form of a symptom checklist to be completed by parents or teachers (e.g., Conners' Rating Scales, Child Behavior Checklist).

Behavioral Assessment Measures

Although virtually all of the measures described up until now could technically be characterized as being behavioral in nature, those assessment modalities that are truly considered to be behavioral usually involve some type of direct behavioral observation. This observation can focus either on global behaviors or on psychophysiological measures.

The clinician can observe the more overt aspects of anxious behavior in the patient's school, home or in the office. Observations often follow a rating protocol. Structured observation strategies such as the Behavioral Profile Rating Scale or the Observer Rating Scale of Anxiety may be used. In other situations, the clinician may assign the child a task designed to evoke an anxious reaction. Standardized behavioral avoidance tasks determine the degree to which the child manifests anxiety in prescribed situations (Kendall et al., 1992).

Although there is not a major body of empirical literature addressing the psychophysiology of children or adolescents with anxiety disorders, there is reason to believe that participation in anxiety-evoking experiences affects psychophysiological responses. Studies that place a child in an anxiety-provoking situation and then measure the psychophysiological response indicate that there is a relationship between individual responses to anxiety and measurable changes in physiology (Beidel, 1989). Physiological responses can be measured in the cardiovascular system (heart rate, blood pressure, peripheral blood flow); via skin conductance; and as electrical activity in the skin muscles (Kendall et al., 1992).

Anxiety Disorders of Childhood and Adolescence

Anxiety disorders fall into two categories: (1) those conceptualized by the *DSM-IV* as exclusive to children and adolescents, and (2) those experienced by adults as well as children and adolescents. In this section we will discuss each of the diagnostic categories in detail, addressing clinical presentation, diagnosis, treatment, and etiology. Following the discussion of each specific disorder will be an exploration of etiological theories relevant to the child/adolescent anxiety disorders in general.

Separation Anxiety Disorder

Clinical Presentation Separation Anxiety Disorder is the only diagnostic category listed in the *DSM-IV* as exclusive to children and adolescents. Box 6.1 lists the diagnostic criteria for Separation Anxiety Disorder.

---

box **6.1**

Diagnostic Criteria for Separation Anxiety Disorder

A. Developmentally inappropriate and excessive anxiety concerning separation from home or from those to whom the child is attached, as evidenced by at least three of the following:

1. Persistent and excessive worry about losing, or possible harm befalling, major attachment figures

2. Persistent and excessive worry that an untoward event will lead to separation from a major attachment figure (e.g., getting lost or being kidnapped)

3. Persistent reluctance or refusal to go to school or elsewhere because of fear of separation

4. Persistently and excessively scared or reluctant to be alone or without major attachment figures at home or without significant adults in other settings

5. Persistent reluctance or refusal to go to sleep without being near a major attachment figure or to sleep away from home

6. Repeated nightmares involving the theme of separation

7. Repeated complaints of physical symptoms (such as headaches, stomach aches, nausea or vomiting) when separation from major attachment figures is anticipated or involved

8. Recurrent excessive distress when separation from home or major attachment figures is anticipated or involved

B. Duration of the disturbance of at least four weeks.

C. Onset before age 18.

D. The disturbance causes clinically significant distress or impairment in social, academic (occupational), or other important areas of functioning.

E. Does not occur exclusively during the course of a Pervasive Developmental Disorder, Schizophrenia, or other Psychotic Disorder.

(Specify if: Early onset if onset occurs before age 6)

Source: American Psychiatric Association, *DSM-IV*, p. 113. Reprinted with permission from the *Diagnostic and Statistical Manual of Mental Disorders*, Fourth Edition. Copyright © 1994 American Psychiatric Association.

Separation Anxiety Disorder is characterized by anxious distress precipitated by separation from key (usually parental) figures. This distress often leads to a resistance to being apart from these key figures. When separation occurs, the child will typically manifest anxiety in tantrum behavior, insistence on resumption of contact with the key figure, an inability to pursue expected activities, and/or somatic symptoms. Children who suffer from Separation Anxiety Disorder often have persistent unrealistic worries about harm or disaster occurring to the key figures and/or an almost phobic level of fear that they will be kidnapped, murdered, or in some other fashion violently removed from the key figure. These children often have trouble sleeping alone, and have nightmares and night terrors. They require repeated reassurance of the presence of the attachment figure. A child or adolescent may find "reasons" for unusually frequent contact (e.g., needing to ask a question, requesting help performing a simple task; Leonard & Rapoport, 1991; Livingston, 1991).

When considering a diagnosis of Separation Anxiety Disorder, the clinician takes the developmental stage of the child into account. Indeed, at certain developmental stages, it is appropriate for a child to manifest anxiety upon separation from a key attachment figure. For example, a 3-year-old who cries intensely when left with a babysitter for the first time will not be diagnosed with this disorder. In contrast, a 6-year-old who cries every time he is left with a sitter may be a prime candidate for such a diagnosis.

Epidemiologically, 3 percent is the generally accepted figure for incidence in the general population (Anderson, Williams, & McGee, 1987). However, data on the symptomatic profile of Separation Anxiety Disorder are not consistent. Although some studies report that more girls than boys suffer from this disorder, other reports have not borne this out. Symptom presentation does vary with the age of the child. Young children ages 5 to 8 years and adolescents show the greatest number of symptoms. Children ages 5 to 8 worry about catastrophic events befalling the attachment figures; children ages 9 to 12 have more negative symptoms, such as withdrawal, poor concentration, apathy, and overall dysphoric affect; and adolescents present with more somatically oriented complaints coupled with school refusal (Francis, Last, & Strauss, 1987; Last, Francis, Hersen, Kazdin, & Strauss, 1987).

Case Study 6.2

Reggie, a 12-year-old boy, was brought to a psychologist because of an unusual problem. For his spring birthday, his parents gave him an enrollment to a 4-day summer baseball camp. Reggie loves going to baseball games with his father and also enjoys watching professional teams play on television, so his parents thought that this camp would be a special present for him. Much to their surprise, however, Reggie became extremely anxious and started to cry when they told him the plan. When his parents asked him what the problem was, he screamed, "Don't make me go! I don't want to go! This isn't a present, this is the worst thing in the world." Reggie's parents did not know how to interpret this behavior, so they changed the subject. Over the next several weeks, however, every time the prospect of baseball camp was discussed, Reggie manifested the same behavior. The only other times Reggie has reacted this way were when he was invited to a classmate's sleepover birthday party 6 months ago and when his grandparents asked him to spend a 3-day weekend at their home in the country.

Etiology As with all of the anxiety disorders of childhood and adolescence to be discussed, theories regarding the etiology of Separation Anxiety Disorders are both psychosocial and biological in nature. The majority of theories around etiology of Separation Anxiety Disorder, however, focus on the more psychosocial aspects. Specifically, these psychosocially based theories can be divided into those which focus on psychodynamic factors, sociological factors, and behavioral factors.

Although psychodynamic theories of anxiety date back to Sigmund Freud's work in the early 1900s, few clinicians today view Separation Anxiety Disorder within the psychoanalytic framework of expression of unconscious sexual and/or aggressive drives. Rather, clinicians with a psychodynamic orientation focus on attachment issues as well as difficulties with separation and individuation. These more modern psychodynamic formulations interpret the development of Separation Anxiety Disorder as a reflection of the psychological distress inherent the child's conflict between fear of separating from the mother and fear of being engulfed by the mother (Bowlby, 1973; Mahler, Pine, & Bergman, 1975).

Another group of theories focuses on the child's relationship with the parents. Theories of *parent-induced anxious attachment* integrate psychodynamic formulations regarding attachment with the notion of behavior reinforcement. The premise behind this approach is that either consciously or unconsciously, parents encourage the child to exhibit behaviors that reflect a pathological attachment. The parents may have unresolved issues of separation and individuation or may be suffering from an anxiety disorder.

The cognitive-behavioral explanation of Separation Anxiety Disorder focuses on maladaptive cognitions as well as pathogenic interpretation of environmental stimuli. In a 1985 paper, Kendall postulated that children and adolescents suffering from anxiety disorders also suffer from cognitive distortions. These young people attend to environmental stimuli, but process these stimuli in a dysfunctional manner. Their misperceptions induce anxiety as they interpret innocuous stimuli as threatening. Thus, a child may perceive a temporary separation from an attachment figure as permanent. A permanent separation would evoke panic in most children.

Familial trauma may also be a factor in the development of Separation Anxiety Disorder. Children who have experienced traumatic separation (e.g., because of illness, divorce, or death) are more likely to manifest signs and symptoms of Separation Anxiety Disorder.

Biological explanations of separation anxiety focus on genetics and/or temperament. Children with Separation Anxiety Disorder are statistically more likely to have parents with an anxiety disorder or some other form of psychopathology, and this fact is often interpreted as evidence for a genetic influence in the etiology of Separation Anxiety Disorder. Temperament theories hypothesize that certain children are born with a biological predisposition to react to environmental stimuli in particular ways. These children with certain biological predispositions will manifest separation anxiety.

Differential Diagnosis The symptom presentation of Separation Anxiety Disorder often overlaps with that of other psychopathologies of children and adolescents. Three categories must be considered in addressing differential diagnosis: Depression, Panic Disorder, and Phobic Disorders (most often School Phobia).

Quite often, the dysphoric affect and somatic symptoms associated with Separation Anxiety Disorder are virtually identical to symptoms observed in Depressive Disorders of childhood and adolescence. Affective disorders are discussed in Chapter 5. Here we will briefly address the differential diagnosis of Separation Anxiety Disorder and Depression.

First, although the symptoms present in a similar manner, the clinical course is different for the two disorders. In cases of Separation Anxiety Disorder, the symptoms are reliably elicited when the child perceives that the "required" proximity to an attachment figure is threatened. The child can be reassured that the attachment figure is safe and will return. In cases of Depressive Disorder, these symptoms are not as easily alleviated by simple reassurance or reunion with an attachment figure.

Issues of differential diagnosis are rather similar in distinguishing between Panic Disorder and Separation Anxiety Disorder. Although many of the intense panic and anxiety symptoms characteristic of Separation Anxiety Disorder are similar in presentation to those observed during a panic attack, again, the trigger events and the environment in which the symptoms are observed can help in clarifying differential diagnosis. In Separation Anxiety Disorder, panic symptoms are elicited only in situations that the child perceives as threatening separation from the key attachment figure. Symptoms are seldom observed when the key attachment figure is present and there is no perceived threat of separation. In contrast, a child or adolescent suffering from Panic Disorder may appear to exhibit intense anxiety spontaneously, and reassurance that the key attachment figure is safe or will return provide no apparent relief.

Another study (Perugi, Deltitio, Soriani, Musetti, Petracca, Nisita, Maremmani, & Cassano, 1988) reports that Panic Disorder with Agoraphobia is statistically associated with

Childhood Separation Anxiety. These authors also report that Separation Anxiety in Childhood is a **premorbid marker** or risk factor for the development of Panic Disorder with Agoraphobia later in life.

Phobic disorders are discussed in detail later in this chapter. Here we will focus on differential diagnosis of Separation Anxiety and phobias. Because one characteristic of phobic disorders is anxious avoidance of specific situations, the withdrawal and avoidance that so often play a major role in the symptom constellation of Separation Anxiety Disorder can complicate the differential diagnosis. Bowlby (1973) addresses this issue in his work on attachment and loss, explaining that phobias (specifically school phobias) that are secondary to Separation Anxiety Disorder involve the active searching and reaching out for the key attachment figure as part of the anxious reaction. This search for reassurance is not as common in the classic cases of pure School Phobia, in which the absence of the key attachment figure does not play as pivotal a role in the panic reaction. In addition, in clinical cases of pure School Phobia, the phobic anxiety and avoidance are limited to school attendance, while in cases of Separation Anxiety Disorder, the symptoms can be triggered by any situation involving separation from the key attachment figure.

Treatment Although psychopharmacological treatment is employed in some severe cases, for the most part Separation Anxiety Disorder is treated by psychotherapeutic interventions. Treatment may involve the child, the parents, or the entire family.

Psychopharmacological treatment typically involves one of the tricyclic antidepressants, most often imipramine (Tofranil) (Adams, 1989; Dulcan & Popper, 1991). Drug treatment is almost always accompanied by psychotherapy or behavioral therapy.

Treatment regimens for Separation Anxiety Disorder commonly apply behavior therapy as the major intervention. Therapy typically involves graduated in vivo exposure to separation experiences, reciprocal inhibition, differential reinforcement, cognitive-behavioral therapy, or some combination of these methods. Most reports evaluating the efficacy of these modalities for the treatment of Separation Anxiety Disorder are individual case studies; clinical experience and data on treatment of disorders with similar symptom profiles support the superiority of behavioral modalities (Thyer & Sowers-Hoag, 1988).

Treatments involving graduated in vivo exposure entail placing the child in situations that involve varying degrees of separation from the key attachment figure and therefore evoke varying degrees of anxiety. This is carried out in a systematic, hierarchial format in which the child works with the therapist and sometimes the parents to compose a list of situations involving varying degrees of separation. The items on this list are arranged to reflect the degree of anxiety the child anticipates they would elicit. Either during a therapy session or as homework, the child engages in these experiences repeatedly until only minimal anxiety is produced. This procedure is repeated until the entire list is completed.

Before using this procedure, the clinician must develop a trusting relationship with the child. The therapist conveys awareness of the difficulties entailed in complying with this procedure, but insists that it is necessary to cure the problem. The rationale behind the procedure should be explained to the child. The child should be empowered with as much control as possible in carrying out graduated in vivo exposure.

Case Study 6.3

Five-year-old Debbie is manifesting the signs and symptoms of Separation Anxiety Disorder with respect to attending her half-day kindergarten. The night before each school day, she

has tantrums and cries, and she does not fall asleep until past midnight. In the morning, her parents have to carry her to the car, and they leave her screaming in the kindergarten classroom. Debbie's teacher reports that the child cries almost incessantly until nap time, then collapses from exhaustion. A clinical history reveals that Debbie demonstrates the same behaviors whenever the idea of being away from her mother is suggested. Her parents have not been able to leave Debbie with sitters and have not been away from her for any period of time.

The therapist worked with the parents to compose a list of separation experiences. First, Debbie played in a room while her mother stayed in an adjacent room. Later Debbie stayed and played while her mother went to another floor of the building. Debbie was separated from her mother for increasing periods of time. Eventually she was able to stay while her mother left the building. These exercises were initially supervised by the therapist via videotapes and a one-way mirror. Eventually, the parents proceeded along the list on their own. Within 10 weeks, Debbie was able to participate in activities separate from her mother without undue anxiety.

The principles of **reciprocal inhibition** are often used in graduated in vivo exposure. The premise of reciprocal inhibition is that if the individual experiences feelings incompatible with anxiety during the exposure, the connection between anxiety and the behavior in question will be extinguished. With adults, programmed relaxation is typically utilized as the incompatible response. With children, however, eating is often employed as the response behavior incompatible with anxiety (see Montenegro, 1968). In Case Study 6.3, for example, the in vivo procedure could have been accelerated by providing Debbie with food treats during the exercises.

To use differential reinforcement, the parents, teachers, or others provide positive reinforcement for increasing degrees of separation. Children are rewarded for anxiety-free experiences of separation. Positive reinforcement can be material (e.g., a new toy for a week of tantrum-free behavior at school), verbal (e.g., a compliment for "grown-up" behavior), or some combination (e.g., "special" time with the key figure after a certain amount of anxiety-free separate time). Of course, differential reinforcement is used informally in virtually all behavioral treatment modalities. The formal, consistent application of differential reinforcement principles leads to noticeable therapeutic benefits.

Cognitive-behavioral approaches are useful with older children and adolescents, who have more developed verbal and reasoning skills. These approaches involve restructuring or reframing the beliefs of the parents and the child regarding separation. This cognitive restructuring can be done in individual or family sessions and is often accompanied by instruction in the use of **self-statements** to facilitate coping (Mansdorf & Lukens, 1987).

Case Study 6.4

Eleven-year-old Antonia is an only child who has never been away from her parents overnight. She is about to begin a new school that has scheduled a weekend orientation for all new students. When Antonia refused to go, her parents brought her to a psychologist for a consultation. Antonia explained that she is afraid of what might happen if she is not in the same building with her parents at night. She fears being kidnapped or murdered by strangers. After talking with the parents, the psychologist concluded that they reinforced Antonia's fear with an overprotective attitude and constant warnings about strangers. The psychologist employed a cognitive-behavioral approach with Antonia and her parents, separately at first, confronting the irrationality of their beliefs, doing some cognitive reframing with respect to their views of the world, and providing Antonia with some self-talk statements. In joint family sessions, Antonia and her parents discussed how they could integrate their cognitive modifications into separation experiences. Beginning with one-night stays at homes of family members, Antonia was able to increase her tolerance of sleeping away from her parents' home.

Generalized Anxiety Disorder

Clinical Presentation Because of the obvious overlap between Generalized Anxiety Disorder in adults and Overanxious Disorder in children, the *DSM-IV* combines both in the broader, more generic diagnostic category Generalized Anxiety Disorder (see Box 6.2). The revised diagnostic criteria for Generalized Anxiety Disorder address issues which were formerly addressed in the category of Overanxious Disorder.

---

box **6.2**

Diagnostic Criteria for Generalized Anxiety Disorder

    A. Excessive anxiety and worry (apprehensive expectation), occurring more days than not for at least six months, about a number of events or activities (such as work or school performance).

    B. The person finds it difficult to control the worry.

    C. The anxiety and worry are associated with at least three of the following six symptoms (with at least some symptoms present for more days than not for the past six months):

        1. Restlessness or feeling keyed up or on edge

        2. Being easily fatigued

        3. Difficulty concentrating or mind going blank

        4. Irritability

        5. Muscle tension

        6. Sleep disturbance (difficulty falling or staying asleep, or restlessness unsatisfying sleep)

    D. The focus of the anxiety and worry is not confined to features of an Axis I disorder, e.g., the anxiety or worry is not about having a panic attack (as in Panic Disorder), being embarrassed in public (as in Social Phobia), being contaminated (as in Obsessive-

Compulsive Disorder), being away from home or close relatives (as in Separation Anxiety Disorder), gaining weight (as in Anorexia Nervosa), or having a serious illness (as in Hypochondriasis), and is not part of Posttraumatic Stress Disorder.

E. The anxiety, worry, or physical symptoms cause clinically significant distress or impairment in social, occupational, or other important areas of functioning.

F. Not due to the direct effects of a substance (e.g., drugs of abuse, medication) or a general medical condition (e.g., hyperthyroidism) and does not occur exclusively during a Mood Disorder, Psychotic Disorder, or a Pervasive Developmental Disorder.

Source: American Psychiatric Association, *DSM-IV*, pp. 435–436. Reprinted with permission from the *Diagnostic and Statistical Manual of Mental Disorders*, Fourth Edition. Copyright © 1994 American Psychiatric Association.

Children and adolescents with Generalized Anxiety Disorder tend to seek constant reassurance of positive outcomes and of their own abilities and worth. Such individuals also have a tendency to project a pseudomaturity and compliance with authority in an attempt to defend against their own insecurity. Children and adolescents with this disorder often perceive authority figures as hypercritical and are often reluctant to participate spontaneously in social and competitive events for fear that they will not succeed. Hypersensitive to criticism and feeling as if their performance is never "good enough," these children and adolescents go through life in a state of constant tension.

Children and adolescents with Generalized Anxiety Disorder are described as constant worriers and as unusually serious in their approach toward life. They often ask questions about their environment and subsequent events in an attempt to assuage their anxiety about any unpredictability. The pervasiveness and apparent constancy of the symptomatic presentation is largely a result of the fact that there is no specific stimulus that triggers the anxiety of these individuals; rather, they experience a pervasive sense of intense concern, self-doubt, and impending doom (Dulcan & Popper, 1991; Husain & Kashani, 1992; Leonard & Rapoport, 1991).

A recent study addressing issues of comorbidity of ADHD and Generalized Anxiety Disorder in children and adolescents (at that time referred to as Overanxious Disorder) outlines a structured interview with seven major categories: (1) excessive or unrealistic worry about future events, (2) excessive or unrealistic worry about past behavior, (3) excessive or unrealistic concern about competence, (4) somatic complaints, (5) marked self-consciousness, (6) excessive need for reassurance about a variety of concerns, and (7) marked feelings of tenseness or inability to relax. Each category contains one or more questions the child or adolescent responds to along a 3-point scale. Provisions are made in the structured interview for the clinician to prove any response to gain more information (Pliszka, Maas, Javors, Rogueness, & Baker, 1994).

Epidemiologically, Generalized Anxiety Disorder does not appear to be more common in one sex. It does appear to be more common among firstborn children, especially in small, achievement-oriented families (Livingston, 1991). A study performed in the late 1980s reported that 7 percent of adolescents experience symptoms of what was then referred to as Overanxious Disorder (Kashani & Devaschel, 1988).

Symptomatic presentation differs as a function of age. Children between the ages of 5 and 11 more often manifest concomitant symptoms of Separation Anxiety Disorder or Attention

Deficit Disorder, and adolescents between the ages of 12 and 19 more often manifest symptoms of Major Depression or a Simple Phobia. Further, the adolescents present with a larger number of anxiety symptoms than do younger children (Strauss, Lease, Last, & Francis, 1988).

Case Study 6.5

Twelve-year-old Jodi was brought to the school psychologist at the recommendation of both her teachers and her parents. Jodi is sometimes unable to complete her schoolwork because of her intense feelings of anxiety. She occasionally experiences full-blown panic attacks, but more often she is worried about doing well, and she is unable to work productively. When she is not at her seat worrying, she is at the teacher's desk seeking reassurance that the small steps she has made in her work are correct. Jodi's parents report similar behavior at home. Although she is unusually well-behaved, Jodi constantly asks for reassurance regarding her behavior. Her nights are restless, especially before school days. She has few friends her own age, and she prefers to sit by herself, "thinking," or to "help" adults.

Etiology Generalized Anxiety Disorder is a new diagnosis as applied to children and adolescents, and little information about the etiology of this disorder is available for this age group. The discussion here is based on theories of etiology relevant to Overanxious Disorder, a diagnosis subsumed under the new category.

The large majority of the theories explaining Overanxious Disorder in children and adolescents focus on psychosocial factors, especially familial interaction patterns. Two situations are proposed to be related to the development of Generalized Anxiety Disorder (Overanxious Disorder) in children and adolescents: (1) the familial expectations for the child are excessive, and (2) the parents are unable to establish consistent limits with the child.

Biological theories to explain Generalized Anxiety Disorder in children and adolescents focus on family histories of anxiety disorders and/or other psychopathologies as well as the presence of **neurological soft signs,** which often indicate a deficit in sensory integration capabilities.

Differential Diagnosis Generalized Anxiety Disorder shares some features of other anxiety disorders and depressive disorders. Some behavioral components are similar to those shown in Separation Anxiety Disorder and in many of the Phobic Disorders. In Separation Anxiety Disorder and the Phobic Disorders, however, the anxiety is less pervasive and less constant. As discussed in the previous section, the symptoms of Separation Anxiety can reliably be alleviated by the presence of the key attachment figure and are specific to the perceived threat of separation from that individual. The phobic disorders also involve anxiety specific to a single stimulus or set of stimuli that will evoke the response.

Although some of the somatic symptoms of Generalized Anxiety Disorder are also present in Depressive Disorders, depression is not typically characterized by anxiety.

Treatment Generalized Anxiety Disorder is treated through some combination of behavioral therapy, individual psychotherapy, family therapy, and pharmacotherapy. Treatments are often modified from adult approaches.

Many of the behavioral treatments employed to treat this disorder in children and adolescents are geared toward direct reduction of the anxious experience. Relaxation training seeks to help the patient relax. Sensory imagery or progressive muscle relaxation, systematic desensitization to anxiety-provoking situations (as described above), and various operant methods are also utilized. In cognitive-behavioral therapy, the patient is instructed in use of self-statement and cognitive control techniques (Strauss, 1988).

Individual and family psychotherapy is designed to increase the child's tolerance of day-to-day situations that elicit anxiety, as well as to modify the child's psychological framework to increase assertiveness, alter self-defeating attitudes, and modify perfectionistic attitudes (Dulcan & Popper, 1991). Therapy directed at the parents often focuses on reducing their anxiety. Parents can also receive instruction in behavioral techniques so they can serve as cotherapists.

There is little information about the use of psychopharmacological methods in treatment of children and adolescents with Generalized Anxiety Disorder or the older diagnosis of Overanxious Disorder. Anxiolytics, especially diazepam (Valium), may be prescribed in low doses to be taken at bedtime. Pharmacological treatments are typically used in conjunction with other therapeutic methods.

Case Study 6.6

The parents of 10-year-old Victor have noticed some problems over the past few months. Although Victor has always been a worrier and a perfectionist, lately he seems unable to relax or to enjoy life. Victor appears to be in a constant state of intense anxiety. There is no obvious stimulus that precipitates his anxiety. Victor is very concerned about pleasing his parents and teachers, doing well in school (he has always been an A student), and being liked by others. Unfortunately, Victor's intense anxiety sabotages him. He becomes nervous, asks for reassurance constantly, and is so tense that others do not want to be around him. A psychologist began individual therapy with Victor, applying behavioral training in relaxation methods as well as some cognitive restructuring with respect to his perfectionism. The psychologist worked with the parents as well, using a cognitive-behavioral approach focusing on their insistence on perfection from Victor. The psychologist instructed the parents on reinforcing Victor for positive interpersonal behaviors as well as achievement- and goal-oriented ones.

Obsessive-Compulsive Disorder

Clinical Presentation Clinical documentation of Obsessive-Compulsive Disorder in children dates back to the early 1900s (Janet, 1903). The disorder in children and adolescents is virtually identical to its presentation in adults. The symptomatology includes two major components: intrusive, **ego-dystonic** thoughts referred to as **obsessions;** and repetitive, often ritualistic behaviors referred to as **compulsions** that are performed in an attempt to attenuate the obsessive thought. Box 6.3 lists the diagnostic criteria for a diagnosis of Obsessive-Compulsive Disorder.

box **6.3**

Diagnostic Criteria for Obsessive-Compulsive Disorder

A. Either obsessions or compulsions:

Obsessions as defined by (1), (2), (3), and (4):

1. Recurrent and persistent thoughts, impulses, or images that are experienced, at some time during the disturbance, as intrusive and inappropriate, and caused marked anxiety or distress

2. The thoughts, impulses, or images are not simply excessive worries about real-life problems

3. The person attempts to ignore or suppress such thoughts or impulses or to neutralize them with some other thought or action

4. The person recognizes that the obsessional thoughts, impulses, or images are a product of his or her own mind (not imposed from without as in thought insertion)

Compulsions as defined by (1) and (2):

1. Repetitive behaviors (e.g., handwashing, ordering, checking) or mental acts (e.g., praying, counting, repeating words silently) that the person feels driven to perform in response to an obsession, or according to rules that must be applied rigidly

2. The behaviors or mental acts are aimed at preventing or reducing distress or preventing some dreaded event or situation; however, these behaviors or mental acts either are not connected in a realistic way with what they are designed to neutralize or prevent, or are clearly excessive

B. At some point during the course of the disorder, the person has recognized that the obsessions or compulsions are excessive or unreasonable. *Note:* This does not apply to children.

C. The obsessions or compulsions cause marked distress; are time-consuming (take more than a half hour a day); or significantly interfere with the person's normal routine, occupational functioning, or usual social activities or relationships with others.

D. If another Axis I disorder is present, the content of the obsessions or compulsions is not restricted to it (e.g., preoccupation with food in the presence of an Eating Disorder; hair pulling in the presence of Trichotillomania; concern with appearance in the presence of Body Dysmorphic Disorder; preoccupation with drugs in the presence of a Substance Use Disorder; preoccupation with having a serious illness in the presence of Hypochondriasis; or guilty ruminations in the presence of Major Depressive Disorder).

E. Not due to the direct effects of a substance (e.g., drugs of abuse, medication) or a general medical condition.

Source: American Psychiatric Association, *DSM-IV*, pp. 422–423. Reprinted with permission from the *Diagnostic and Statistical Manual of Mental Disorders,* Fourth Edition. Copyright © 1994 American Psychiatric Association.

There is also a provision in the diagnostic criteria for the distinguishing of "poor insight type" when the patient does not realize that the obsessions are unreasonable or excessive. Many of the criteria considered to be diagnostically significant for Obsessive-Compulsive Disorder are relatively common at various developmental stages of childhood. Indeed, by age 2, many children demand that rituals be carried out, especially around issues of eating, bedtime, bathing, and separation from parents. By the time the child reaches age 4, many of these rituals have lessened, but bedtime rituals tend to remain or even intensify. Through the school years, ritualized play with elaborate rules, superstitious behaviors, hobbies involving "collections," or intense preoccupations with certain activities or idols predominate at various stages. From some perspectives, these are considered to be normal developmental progressions indicative of maturing levels of cognitive skill. These developmental "obsessive-compulsive-like" behaviors tend to differ in content and intensity from true obsessive-compulsive behaviors. Further, most simple childhood rituals lessen or disappear by age 8, but true Obsessive-Compulsive disorder tends to intensify after age 7. Finally, the rituals of normal development generally enhance socialization, whereas the symptoms of true Obsessive-Compulsive Disorder impede social interaction (Judd, 1965; Leonard, Goldberger, Rapoport, Cheslow, & Swedo, 1990). Table 6.2 illustrates how developmentally appropriate superstitions and rituals fit into the obsessive-compulsive syndrome.

Another study performed over 20 years ago (Adams, 1973) explored personality characteristics of children and adolescents suffering from Obsessive-Compulsive Disorder: (1) a tendency to internalize; (2) "loving one's IQ" (i.e., placing inappropriate emphasis on intellectual or academic excellence); (3) a view of life as a power struggle; (4) a preoccupation with death; (5) attempts to gain constant reassurance with respect to self-preservation and safety; and (6) some immaturity in cognitive style despite superficial appearances of adult-like behavior. Typically, these children have significant problems with peer relationships—either they prefer to be alone, or they are frequently the target of their peers' taunts.

The most common foci of obsessive-compulsive sufferers are thoughts of violence (at times with sexual themes), cleaning, checking and/or counting, exactness or symmetry, religious themes, and bodily functions (Swedo, Rapoport, Leonard, Lennie, & Chesklow, 1989; Twobin & Riddle, 1991). The typical age of onset is between 3 and 5 years, but the child's embarrassment and shame and adults' tendency to consider the symptoms as part of a developmental stage typically delay the diagnosis until the symptoms can no longer be hidden or dismissed.

Epidemiologically, Obsessive-Compulsive Disorder is twice as common in boys as in girls. Boys also show an earlier age of onset. Incidence is estimated at 0.2 percent of all clinical populations, 1 percent of all child psychiatric inpatients, but this condition is probably underreported. Most sufferers of Obsessive-Compulsive Disorder are aware that their symptoms are bizarre, and they tend to hide their symptoms. Studies indicate that one-third to one-half of adult obsessive-compulsive sufferers report onset prior to age 15 (Husain & Kashani, 1992).

Table 6.2 The Obsessive Child Spectrum

1. Ritualized collective play, as in games with repetitive chanting or rigidly repetitive, ritualized behavior
2. Phase-appropriate rituals, such as seen in 2- or 3-year-olds and again in pubescent children, needing everything "just so"
3. Ritualized solitary play—for example, compulsive play with string figures, cards, and mechanical toys
4. Obsessive collecting
5. Circumscribed interests, such as being "nuts" about rockets, meteorology, or television call letters to the exclusion of all other concerns
6. Obsessive character
7. Secondary obsessions
8. Obsessions related to or combined with other disorders
9. Obsessive-compulsive neurosis (primary OCD)
    a. Compulsive rituals: cleaning (akin to phobics)
    b. Compulsive rituals: checking
    c. Obsessions driven by fear
    d. Obsessions driven by guilt
    e. Obsessions driven by shame

Source: Adams, 1985, p. 309.

Case Study 6.7

Twelve-year-old Marlene was brought for therapy because her "weird habits" have begun to interfere with her life functioning. At first, her mother interpreted these behaviors as typical childhood superstitions, but they have intensified. Marlene explains that there are basically two types of people in the world: those who call her Marlene and those who call her by some nickname (e.g., Mar or Marly). Whenever anyone addresses Marlene by anything other than her full name, the young girl imagines herself being completely covered with feces. In order to rid herself of that intrusive image, Marlene immediately rushes to a water source, drinks three full glasses of water, and then runs water over her hands for three minutes. Although Marlene is aware of the "weirdness" of her habit, the images are so anxiety-provoking that she feels she must engage in the water rituals to rid herself of the intrusive visions.

Etiology Most etiological theories explain Obsessive-Compulsive Disorder in children and adolescents as biological in nature. Traditional psychoanalytic conceptualizations regard Obsessive-Compulsive symptoms as representing an inability to deal with angry anal impulses, but the current approaches explain Obsessive-Compulsive Disorder more in terms of neurological, neurochemical, or genetic mechanisms. The more psychosocially oriented theories focusing on parenting practices and/or modeling have been dismissed.

Neurological studies of Obsessive-Compulsive subjects support some involvement of the frontal lobes of the brain in the etiology of this disorder (Baxter, Phelps, & Mazzota, 1987, 1988; Garber, Ananth, & Chin, 1989; Swedo, Schapiro, & Grady, 1989). Electroencephalogram (EEG) results are abnormal in 11 to 65 percent of obsessive-compulsive sufferers (Rappoport, 1986).

Obsessive-Compulsive Disorder in children and adolescents is thought to involve the neurotransmitter serotonin. Psychopharmacological interventions (e.g., Anafranil) that block the body's reuptake of serotonin are useful in many cases of Obsessive-Compulsive Disorder. Empirical and clinical investigations of the role of serotonin in the etiology of this disorder have yielded conflicting results, but obsessive-compulsive patients may have an increased sensitivity to serotonin, and other, undetermined mechanisms may be involved as well (Twobin & Riddle, 1991).

One-fourth of patients have a family history of Obsessive-Compulsive disorder. Because the specific symptoms exhibited by the child and the parent or other relatives are different, the condition is more likely to be due to genetics than to modeling of the behavior (Lenane, Swedo, & Lenane, 1990). Other studies reported concordance in 81 percent of monozygotic twins and 47 percent in dizygotic twins (Carey & Gottesman, 1981). The current literature supports a genetic transmission of vulnerability to Obsessive-Compulsive Disorder, with the concept of direct genetic inheritance being less well confirmed.

Differential Diagnosis Issues of differential diagnosis have a minor role in Obsessive-Compulsive Disorder. As mentioned in the *DSM-IV*, when the clinician can determine that the obsessive and compulsive behavior is not secondary to another disorder, differential diagnosis is not a major concern. Although there may be some superficial similarities to Phobic Disorders in terms of avoidance of certain stimuli or to Tourette's disorder in terms of ritualistic behaviors, careful clinical examination typically differentiates these cases.

The obsessive-compulsive patient's beliefs associating the intrusive thoughts and their corresponding rituals can resemble those observed in psychotic delusional processes. In most cases, however, the two disorders can be distinguished by two factors: (1) the greater generalization of the irrational beliefs in psychotic disorders, in contrast to the relatively limited nature of the irrational beliefs in Obsessive-Compulsive Disorder; and (2) the intense ego-dystonic component evidenced in virtually all cases of Obsessive-Compulsive Disorder, in contrast to the more ego-syntonic aspect of psychotic delusions.

Treatment Both pharmacological and behavioral modalities are used to treat Obsessive-Compulsive Disorder. Behavioral treatments often incorporate cognitive-behavioral elements, and insight-oriented psychotherapy is used with both individuals and families.

Drug treatment is designed to inhibit the reuptake of the neurotransmitter serotonin. The serotonin reuptake inhibitors most often prescribed are clomipramine (Anafranil) and desipramine (Norpramin). Other drug regimens include fluoxetine (Prozac) and alprazolam (Xanax). With the exception of Anafranil, these medications are new for the treatment of Obsessive-Compulsive Disorder in children and adolescents. Regular and informed monitoring of all side effects is imperative (Dulcan & Popper, 1991; Flament, Rapoport, Berg, Sceery, Kilts, Mellstrom & Linnoila, 1985; Kaplan & Sadock, 1993).

Although psychodynamic, insight-oriented approaches are still occasionally employed, their utility in the treatment of Obsessive-Compulsive Disorder in children is questionable. They are best utilized as a supplement to behavioral approaches. The three most common behavioral modalities are response prevention, thought-stopping procedures, and differential reinforcement of other responses (DRO). The involvement of parents, teachers, and family members is often crucial. These significant others act both as cotherapists and as sources of primary support for the child (Wolff & Rapoport, 1988).

Response prevention involves working with the patient to eliminate the compulsive component—the ritualistic behavior—from the response repertoire. The patient is exposed to the obsessive images within the controlled context of the therapy session and is not allowed to act out the behavioral rituals. The procedure elicits significant anxiety from the patient, but in the controlled setting of the therapy session, the patient can learn other methods for dealing with the anxiety precipitated by the obsessive images.

Where response prevention focuses on the compulsive rituals of Obsessive-Compulsive Disorder, the behavioral procedure known as **thought stopping** focuses on the intrusive obsessive thoughts. The procedure is based on classical conditioning principles. The patient is asked to elicit the intrusive thoughts and then signal to the therapist, who yells "Stop!" extremely loudly. This sequence is repeated until the patient has learned to associate the aversive experience of the loud noise with the unwanted thoughts. Eventually, the patient is given homework to practice the same technique.

Differential reinforcement of other behavior (DRO) can be utilized either on an individual basis or with the parents or other significant adults as cotherapists. Based on operant conditioning principles, this procedure provides the patient with reinforcing experiences whenever he or she engages in behaviors that are incompatible with the compulsive ritual or does not engage in the compulsive ritual for a given time period. These reinforcers can be either self-regulated or controlled by the parents or other authority figures.

These behavioral methods are often accompanied by cognitive-behavioral techniques involving direct confrontation of the "magical thinking" involved in the obsessive-compulsive cycle. This procedure is most effective with older children. The patient must be verbal and able to reason productively. Another cognitive-behavioral method involves the use of self-statements, which take the form of self-control affirmations and/or reinforcement of principles initiated in the therapy sessions.

Case Study 6.8

Fifteen-year-old Andrew has been suffering from Obsessive-Compulsive Disorder for the past year and a half. Having vivid images in his mind of members of his family being mutilated, Andrew believes he can prevent these catastrophes from occurring only by never saying their full names. Thus, he will say only the first syllable of any family member's first name. If he is forced to say the entire name, Andrew immediately touches his left ear three times in succession.

The therapist treating Andrew worked with him initially within a cognitive-behavioral format attempting to confront the irrationality behind his beliefs. Next, the therapist used response prevention, having Andrew repeat the names of family members without touching his ear. This in-session practice was followed by daily homework assignments supervised by Andrew's parents.

Phobic Disorders

Clinical Presentation Fears are a normal developmental feature of childhood and adolescence. In fact, certain fears are characteristic at different ages (Dulcan & Popper, 1991). Loss of physical support, loud noises, and large rapidly approaching objects frighten infants from birth to 6 months of age. Strangers frighten babies from 7 to 12 months old. Storms, animals, darkness, and separation from parents frighten children from age 1 to 5. Monsters and ghosts are the fears from age 3 to 5. Fears of bodily injury, burglars, being punished, poor academic achievement, and social embarrassment are characteristic of the teen years.

Whenever anxiety or the avoidant component of fear interferes with the individual's optimal functioning, and whenever fear is out of proportion to the danger and not developmentally appropriate, the diagnosis of a phobic disorder must be considered. The *DSM-IV* lists two general types of phobic disorders. A *specific phobia* is diagnosed when the individual exhibits phobic symptoms in response to a specific stimulus, and a *social phobia* or *social anxiety disorder* is diagnosed when the individual manifests phobic symptoms in one or more social situations. Diagnostic criteria for each of the categories are listed in Box 6.4.

box**6.4**

Diagnostic Criteria for Phobia

Specific Phobia

A. Marked and persistent fear that is excessive or unreasonable, cued by the presence or anticipation of a specific object or situation (e.g., flying, heights, animals, receiving an injection, seeing blood).

B. Exposure to the phobic stimulus almost invariably provokes an immediate anxiety response, which may take the form of a situationally bound or situationally predisposed panic attack. *Note:* In children, the anxiety may be expressed by crying, tantrums, freezing or clinging.

C. The person recognizes that the fear is excessive or unreasonable. *Note:* In children, this may be absent.

D. The phobic situation(s) is avoided, or else endured with intense anxiety or distress.

E. The avoidance, anxious anticipation, or distress in the feared situations interferes significantly with the person's normal routine, occupational (academic) functioning, or with social activities or relationships with others, or there is marked distress about having the phobia.

F. The anxiety, panic attacks or phobic avoidance associated with the specific object or situation are not better accounted for by another mental disorder, such as Obsessive-Compulsive Disorder (e.g., fear of contamination), Post-traumatic Stress Disorder (e.g., avoidance of stimuli associated with a severe stressor), Separation Anxiety Disorder (e.g., avoidance of school), Social Phobia (e.g., avoidance of social situations because of fear or embarrassment), Panic Disorder with Agoraphobia, or Agoraphobia Without History of Panic Disorder.

Social Phobia

A. A marked and persistent fear of one or more social or performance situations in which the person is exposed to unfamiliar people or to possible scrutiny by others.

The individual fears that he or she will act in a way (or show anxiety symptoms) that will be humiliating or embarrassing. *Note:* In children, there must be evidence of capacity for social relationships with familiar people and the anxiety must occur in peer settings, not just in interactions with adults.

B. Exposure to the feared social situation almost invariably provokes anxiety, which may take the form of a situationally predisposed panic attack. *Note:* In children, the anxiety may be expressed by crying, tantrums, freezing or withdrawal from the social situation.

C. The person recognizes that the fear is excessive or unreasonable. *Note:* In children, this feature may be absent.

D. The feared social or performance situations are avoided, or else endured with intense anxiety or distress.

E. The avoidance, anxious anticipation, or distress in the feared social or performance situation(s) interferes significantly with the person's normal routine, occupational (academic) functioning, or with social activities or relationships with others, or there is marked distress about having the phobia.

F. The fear or avoidance is not due to the direct effects of a substance (e.g., drugs of abuse, medication) or a general medical condition, and is not better accounted for by Panic Disorder With or Without Agoraphobia, Separation Anxiety Disorder, Body Dysmorphic Disorder, a Pervasive Developmental Disorder, or a Schizoid Personality Disorder.

G. If a general medical condition or other mental disorder is present, the fear in (A) is unrelated to it, e.g., the fear is not of stuttering, trembling (in Parkinson's disease) or exhibiting abnormal eating behavior (in Anorexia Nervosa or Bulimia Nervosa).

Source: American Psychiatric Association, *DSM-IV*, pp. 410–411; 416–417. Reprinted with permission from the *Diagnostic and Statistical Manual of Mental Disorders,* Fourth Edition. Copyright © 1994 American Psychiatric Association.

Many research studies on the nature of the fears of children and adolescents address issues of epidemiology as well as developmental changes in the content of fears as the child matures into adolescence. Estimates of incidence range from 0.3 to 4.5 percent for cases of specific phobia, with a similarly wide range for cases of social phobia (previously referred to in the literature as *avoidant disorder of childhood and adolescence*). In general, however, developmental fears are consistent in content across gender and socioeconomic class, and true phobic reactions are similar across various samples (Bamber, 1974; Bauer, 1976; Eme & Schmidt, 1978; Miller, Barrett, Hampe, & Noble, 1972; Ollendick, Matson & Helsel, 1985; Orton, 1982). Although studies report a greater prevalence of phobic disorders in girls than in boys, it is unclear as to whether this is a valid finding or an artifact because girls are more willing than boys to acknowledge fear (Francis, 1992).

The term *school refusal behavior* distinguishes children with a true school phobia from those who refuse to attend school for some reason other than pathological fear or anxiety directed toward some school-related stimulus. In a 1995 review of school refusal behavior, Christopher A. Kearney, a clinician affiliated with the School Refusal Clinic of the University of Nevada, describes school refusal behavior as a "largely unpredictable blend of internalizing and externalizing behavior"; he lists fear, general and social anxiety, low self-esteem, and depression as internalizing symptoms, and running away from school, general noncompliance, and conduct behavior problems among the externalizing symptoms. The *DSM-IV* does not include a diagnostic category for school refusal, so children who exhibit school refusal symptoms are typically diagnosed with School Phobia, Depression, or a Conduct Disorder. Treatment protocols often follow from diagnosis, so treatment for school refusal evolves from the primary source of the symptomatology.

Case Study 6.9

Twelve-year-old Meredith was brought to a psychologist for a consultation because of her intense fear of doctors and dentists. Her mother had not taken the child for a medical or dental check-up for over 5 years. If her parents tried to insist that she needed an appointment, Meredith screamed, hyperventilated, and sweated profusely. Meredith told the psychologist that it was not the visit to the physician or dentist that bothered her, but the thought of receiving an injection. Meredith's anxiety and avoidance met the criteria for a diagnosis of a specific phobia.

Case Study 6.10

Eight-year-old Megan moved to a new neighborhood with her family 6 months ago. She has been invited to several birthday parties. Although Megan likes these girls, she refuses to attend any of the birthday parties. Her parents say that Megan would not attend parties in her previous neighborhood either. They feel it would be inappropriate to "force" their daughter to attend social functions, but they are concerned about the intensity of Megan's refusal. The psychologist determined that Megan is suffering from Social Phobia.

Etiology Theories of the etiology of phobic disorders in children and adolescents can be divided into four major categories: (1) psychodynamic perspectives; (2) behavioral perspectives, including classical conditioning as well as modeling approaches; (3) genetic perspectives; and (4) psychophysiological perspectives. The first three theoretical modalities are applied to phobic disorders of children and adolescents in much the same way as they are to the other anxiety disorders.

Psychodynamic perspectives explain the development of phobic disorders in Freudian terms, as the result of "displaced" sexual or aggressive energies. They regard the phobic stimulus as relatively innocuous and the unconscious fear as the true problem. Based almost exclusively on clinical case studies, the psychodynamic perspective expands the traditional interpretation of displaced sexual conflicts to encompass displaced feelings of aggression, separation anxiety, and non-oedipal issues.

According to the behavioral perspectives, children acquire classically conditioned fear reactions to given stimuli, and they model phobic behavior observed in other family members. Theories derived from Watson's classic Little Albert experiment (Watson & Raynor, 1920) and those based on classical conditioning have received limited empirical support, however; the majority of phobias cannot be traced to traumatic life events. Operant theories focus on reinforcements (e.g., attention, special treatment) often extended to the phobic child.

Genetic perspectives are supported by evidence that children with phobic disorders often have phobic parents. This fact can also be explained by phenomena other than genetics (i.e., modeling, psychodynamic factors).

The psychophysiological approach conceptualizes individuals with phobic disorders as being high in **autonomic lability.** That is, in certain individuals the autonomic nervous system is triggered and activated at a lower threshold. This theory implies that some children and adolescents experience the phenomenon of anxiety because of activation of the autonomic nervous system in nonthreatening circumstances which ordinarily would not evoke a fearful response. Thus, this hyperarousal condition leads to a classically conditioned response to situations that then become phobic stimuli.

Differential Diagnosis Differential diagnosis of Phobic Disorders is most often a concern in relation to some of the other anxiety disorders. Separation Anxiety Disorder may have some similarities in clinical presentation; however, there is no specific phobic stimulus, and the perceived or actual absence of the key attachment figure triggers the anxiety. Similarly, some of the avoidance and preoccupation evidenced in Obsessive-Compulsive Disorder and Eating Disorders may appear similar to that observed in Phobic Disorders. However, in Obsessive-Compulsive Disorder there is often a ritual accompanying the avoidance; in eating disorders, the phobic stimulus is not food itself but rather a fear of gaining weight.

Differential diagnosis may be a concern in regard to Panic Disorders. Anxious reactions manifested by sufferers of Phobic Disorders occurs only in response to the phobic stimulus. In Panic Disorder, the precipitant for the panic attack is less clear-cut. Panic may "come out of the blue." It should also be noted that there is current controversy in the clinical and empirical literature as to the existence of Panic Disorder in children and adolescents (see Alessi & Magen, 1988; Moreau & Weissman, 1992; Nelles & Barlow, 1988).

CURIOUS AVENUE copyright © 1992, 1993 TOLES. Reprinted with permission of Universal Press Syndicate. All rights reserved.

Treatment Unlike the case in many of the other Anxiety Disorders of Childhood and Adolescence, the most effective treatments for phobic disorders are behavioral or cognitive-behavioral. These treatments fall into four major modalities: (1) systematic desensitization, (2) modeling, (3) operant models, and (4) cognitive-behavioral therapies (Ollendick & Francis, 1988).

Systematic Desensitization is used in treating phobic disorders much as it is applied in other cases. The patient is first trained in relaxation methods and is then taught to pair the newly learned relaxation response with phobic images and eventually with in vivo exposure to the phobic stimulus. This approach is most useful with Specific Phobic Disorders as opposed to cases in which there are multiple phobic triggers.

Modeling entails having the patient view other individuals confronting the phobic stimulus in a calm, nonanxious manner. The more similar the model is to the patient, the more effective the treatment. Modeling evolves into role playing or rehearsal, in which the patient confronts the phobic stimulus in controlled conditions, usually during a therapy session or in the presence of the therapist.

Operant and Cognitive-Behavioral models are applied to the treatment of Phobic Disorders as they are in the treatment of anxiety disorders. Parents and other family members learn to reinforce the patient for confronting the phobic stimulus and for coping with anxious responses. Similarly, Cognitive-Behavioral Models work by helping the patient to reframe thoughts about the phobic stimulus in order to gain a more realistic view of the danger. These techniques are especially useful in the treatment of Social Phobias.

Case Study 6.11

Six-year-old Jenny presented with a phobia of dogs. Her phobic disorder was so intense that she could not even watch television for fear that a commercial might show a dog. The therapist utilized systematic desensitization and modeling. Jenny learned some relaxation procedures and then worked with her therapist, pairing the relaxation response with dog imagery. After Jenny worked through a hierarchy of dog images, the therapist showed her videotapes of other young children (mostly girls) interacting with dogs in a calm manner. In the final part of the treatment regimen, Jenny was gradually exposed to dogs within a controlled setting.

CURIOUS AVENUE copyright © 1992, 1993 TOLES. Reprinted with permission of Universal Press Syndicate. All rights reserved.

Summary

Anxiety is a natural, evolutionarily based component of the human experience. When anxiety is too intense or too frequent, however, the diagnosis of an anxiety disorder must be considered. Assessment and diagnosis of these anxiety disorders can take various formats. Assessment instruments may focus on anxiety symptoms or take a more global approach.

Classification of the anxiety disorders experienced by children and adolescents has gone through substantial revisions. Under the current diagnostic system, only one anxiety disorder is considered to be exclusive to children and adolescents: Separation Anxiety Disorder. Other diagnostic categories have been subsumed under the adult category of Anxiety Disorders (Generalized Anxiety Disorder, Obsessive-Compulsive Disorder, and the Phobic Disorders).

Treatment of the anxiety disorders may include psychosocial as well as biological methods. Psychotherapeutic approaches are predominantly systems-oriented and/or behavioral in nature, and family members are often involved. Pharmacological treatment may be used in conjunction with psychotherapeutic modalities.

References

Adams, P. L. (1973). *Obsessive children: A sociopsychiatric study.* New York: Brunner/Mazel.

Adams, P. L. (1985). The obsessive child: A therapy update. *American Journal of Psychotherapy, 39,* 301–313.

Adams, P. L. (1989). Anxiety disorders. In H. I. Kaplan & B. J. Sadock (Eds.), *Comprehensive textbook of psychiatry: Vol. 5.* Baltimore: Williams & Wilkins.

Alessi, N. E., & Magen, J. (1988). Panic disorder in psychiatrically hospitalized children. *American Journal of Psychiatry, 145,* 1450–1452.

American Psychiatric Association. (1994). *Diagnostic and statistical manual of mental disorders.* (4th ed.). Washington, DC: Author.

Anderson, J. C., Williams, S., & McGee, R. (1987). DSM-III disorders in preadolescent children: Prevalence in a large sample from the general population. *Archives of General Psychiatry, 44,* 69–76.

Bamber, J. H. (1974). The fears of adolescents. *Journal of Genetic Psychology, 125,* 127–140.

Barios, B. A., Hermann, D. P., & Shigetomi, C. (1981). Fears and anxieties in children. In E. J. Marsh & L. G. Terdel (Eds.), *Behavior assessment of childhood disorders* (pp. 259–304). New York: Guilford Press.

Bauer, D. H. (1976). An exploratory study of developmental changes in children's fears. *Journal of Child Psychology and Psychiatry, 17,* 69–74.

Baxter, L. R., Phelps, M. E., & Mazziota, J. C. (1987). Local cerebral glucose metabolic rates in obsessive-compulsive disorder. *Archives General Psychiatry, 44,* 211–219.

Beidel, D. C. (1989). Assessing anxious emotion: A review of psychophysiological assessment in children. *Clinical Psychology Review, 9,* 717–736.

Beidel, D. C., Neal, A. M., & Ledere, A. S. (1991). The feasibility and validity of a daily diary for the assessment of anxiety in children. *Behavior Therapy, 22,* 505–517.

Bowlby, J. (1973). *Attachment and loss: Vol. 2.* New York: Basic Books.

Carey, G., & Gottesman, I. (1981). Twin and family studies of anxiety, phobic, and obsessive disorders. In D. F. Klein & J. Rabkin (Eds.), *Anxiety: New research and changing concepts* (pp. 117–133). New York: Raven Press.

Cattell, R. B., & Cattell, M. D. (1979). The High School Personality Questionnaire. Champaign, IL: Institute for Personality and Ability Testing.

Chambers, W. J., Puig-Antich, J., & Hirsch, M. (1985). The assessment of affective disorders in children and adolescents by semistructured interview. *Archives of General Psychiatry, 42,* 696–702.

Chambless, D. (1985). The relationship of severity of agoraphobia to associated psychopathology. *Behavior Research and Therapy, 23,* 305–310.

Costello, A. J., Edelbrock, C. S., Dulcan, M. K., Kales, R., & Kleric, S. H. (1984), *Report to the NIMH on the NIMH Diagnostic Interview for Children (DISC).* Washington, DC: National Institute of Mental Health.

Dulcan, M. K., & Popper, C. W. (1991). *Concise guide to child and adolescent psychiatry.* Washington DC: American Psychiatric Press.

Eme, R., & Schmidt, D. (1978). The stability of children's fears. *Child Development, 49,* 1277–1279.

Flament, M. F., Rapoport, J. L., Berg, C. J., Sceery, W., Kilts, C., Mellstrom, B., & Linnoila, M. (1985). Clomipramine treatment of childhood obsessive compulsive disorder. *Archives of General Psychiatry, 42,* 977–983.

Francis, G. (1992). Behavioral treatment of childhood anxiety disorders. In S. M. Turner, K. S. Calhoun, & H. E. Adams (Eds.), *Handbook of clinical behavioral therapy* (2nd ed.). New York: Wiley.

Francis, G., Last, C., & Strauss, C. (1987). Expression of separation anxiety disorder: The roles of age and gender. *Child Psychiatry & Human Development, 18,* 82–89.

Garber, H. J., Ananth, J. V., & Chin, L. C. (1989). Nuclear magnetic resonance study of obsessive compulsive disorder. *American Journal of Psychiatry, 146,* 1001–1005.

Graham, P., & Rutter, M. (1965). The reliability and validity of the psychiatric assessment of the child. *British Journal of Psychiatry, 114,* 381–392.

Hoehn-Saric, E., Maisami, M., & Wiegand, D. (1987). Measurement of anxiety in children and adolescents using semi-structured interviews. *Journal of the American Academy of Child and Adolescent Psychiatry, 26,* 541–545.

Husain, S. A., & Kashani, J. H. (1992). *Anxiety disorders in children and adolescents.* Washington, DC: American Psychiatric Press.

Janet, P. (1903). *Les obsessions et la psychiastrcinic, Vol 1.* Paris: Felix Alean.

Judd, L. J. (1965). Obsessive compulsive disorders in children. *Archives of General Psychiatry, 12,* 136–143.

Kaplan, H. I., & Sadock, B. J. (1993). *Pocket handbook of psychiatric drug treatment.* Baltimore: Williams & Wilkins.

Kashani, J. H., & Devaschel, H. (1988). Anxiety disorders in mid-adolescence: A community sample. *American Journal of Psychiatry, 44,* 69–76.

Kearney, C. A. (1995). School refusal behavior. In A. R. Eisen, C. A. Kearney, & C. E. Schaefer (Eds.), *Clinical handbook of anxiety disorders in children and adolescents.* Northvale, NJ: Jason Aronson.

Kendall, P. C. (1985). Toward a cognitive-behavioral model of child psychopathology and a critique of related interventions. *Journal of Abnormal Child Psychology, 13,* 357–372.

Kendall, P. C., Chansky, T. E., Kane, M. T., Kim, R. S., Kontlander, E., Ronen, K. R., Sessa, F. M., & Siqueland, L. (1992). *Anxiety disorders in youth: Cognitive-behavioral interventions.* Boston: Allyn & Bacon.

Kendall, P. C., & Ronan, K. R. (1990). Assessment of children's anxieties, fears and phobias: Cognitive behavioral models and methods. In C. R. Reynolds & R. W. Kamphaus (Eds.), *Handbook of psychological and educational assessment of children.* New York: Guiliford Press.

Klein, R. G. (1988) Childhood anxiety disorders. In C. J. Kestenbaum & D. T. Williams (Eds.), *Handbook of clinical assessment of children and adolescents.* New York: New York University Press.

Last, C. G., Francis, G., Hersen, M., Kazdin, A. E., & Strauss, C. C. (1987). Separation anxiety and school phobia: A comparison using DSM-III criteria. *American Journal of Psychiatry, 144,* 653–657.

Lenane, M. C., Swedo, S. E., & Leonard, H. (1990). Psychiatric disorders in first degree relatives of children and adolescents with obsessive compulsive disorder. *Journal of American Academy of Child & Adolescent Psychiatry, 29,* 407–412.

Leonard, H. L., Goldberger, E. L., Rapoport, J. L., Cheslow, D. I., & Swedo, S. E. (1990). Childhood rituals: Normal development or obsessive-compulsive symptoms? *Journal of the American Academy of Child & Adolescent Psychiatry, 29,* 17–23.

Leonard, H. L., & Rapoport, J. L. (1991). Simple phobia, social phobia and panic disorders. In J. M. Wiener (Ed.), *Textbook of child and adolescent psychiatry* (pp. 330–338). Washington DC: American Psychiatric Press.

Livingston, R. (1991). Anxiety disorders. In M. Lewis (Ed.)., *Child and adolescent psychiatry: A comprehensive textbook* (pp. 673–685). Baltimore: Williams & Wilkins.

Mahler, M. S., Pine, F., & Bergman, A. (1975). *The psychological birth of the human infant.* New York: Basic Books.

Mansdorf, I. J., & Lukens, E. (1987). Cognitive-behavioral psychotherapy for separation anxious children exhibiting school phobia. *Journal of the American Academy of Child & Adolescent Psychiatry, 26,* 222–225.

Miller, L. C., Barrett, C. L., Hampe, E., & Noble, H. (1972). Factor structure of childhood fears. *Journal of Consulting and Clinical Psychology, 39,* 264–268.

Montenegro, H. (1968). Severe separation anxiety in two preschool children: Successfully treated by reciprocal inhibition. *Journal of Child Psychology and Psychiatry, 9,* 93–103.

Moreau, D., & Weissman, M. M. (1992). Panic disorder in children and adolescents: A review. *American Journal of Psychiatry, 149,* 1306–1314.

Nelles, W. B., & Barlow, D. H. (1988). Do children panic? *Clinical Psychology Review, 8,* 359–372.

Ollendick, T. H. (1983). Reliability and validity of the revised Fear Survey Schedule for Children (FSSC-R). *Behavior Research and Therapy, 21,* 685–692.

Ollendick, T. H., & Francis, G. (1988). Behavioral assessment and treatment of childhood phobias. *Behavior Modification, 12,* 165–204.

Ollendick, T. H., Matson, J. L., & Helsel, W. J. (1985). Fears in children and adolescents: Normative data. *Behavior Research and Therapy, 23,* 465–467.

Orton, G. L. (1982). A comparative study of children's worries. *Journal of Psychology, 110,* 153–162.

Perugi, G., Deltitio, J., Soriani, A., Musetti, L., Petracca, A. Nisita, C., Maremmani, I., & Cassano, G. B. (1988). Relationship between panic disorder and separation anxiety with school phobia. *Comprehensive Psychiatry, 29,* 98–107.

Peterson, R. A., & Reiss, S. (1987). *Test manual for the anxiety sensitivity index.* Orland Park, IL: International Diagnostic Systems.

Pliszka, S. R. Maas, J. W., Javors, M. A., Rogueness, G. A., & Baker, J. (1994). Urinary catecholamines in ADHD with and without comorbid anxiety. *Journal of the American Academy of Child & Adolescent Psychiatry, 33,* 1165–1173.

Reich, O. (1982). Development of a structured psychiatric interview for children. *Journal of Abnormal Child Psychology.* pp. 325–336.

Reynolds, C. R., & Richmond, B. O. (1984). Revised Children's Manifest Anxiety Scale. Los Angeles: Western Psychological Services.

Rutter, M., & Graham, P. (1968). The reliability and validity of the psychiatric assessment of the child: I Interview of the child. *British Journal of Psychiatry, 114,* 563–579.

Scherer, M. W., & Nakamura, C. Y. (1968). A fear survey schedule for children (FSS-FC): A factor analytic comparison with manifest anxiety (CMAS). *Behavior Research and Therapy, 6,* 173–182.

Silverman, W. K. (1987). Anxiety Disorders Interview Schedule for Children (unpublished manuscript).

Silverman, W. K. (1991). *Anxiety Disorders Interview Schedule for Children.* Albany, NY: Graywind.

Silverman, W. K., Flesig, W., Rabian, B., & Peterson, R. A. (1991). Childhood anxiety sensitivity index. *Journal of Clinical Child Psychology, 20,* 162–168.

Silverman, W. K., & Nelles, W. B. (1988). The Anxiety Disorders Interview Schedule for Children. *Journal of the American Academy of Child and Adolescent Psychiatry, 27,* 772–778.

Spielberger, C. (1973). *Manual for Stait-Trait Anxiety Inventory for Children,* Palo Alto, CA: Consulting Psychologists Press.

Strauss, C. C. (1988). Behavioral assessment and treatment of overanxious disorder in children and adolescents. *Behavior Modification, 12,* 234–251.

Strauss, C. C., Lease, C. A., Last, C. G., & Francis, G. (1988). Overanxious disorder. An examination of developmental differences. *Journal of Abnormal Child Psychology, 16,* 433–443.

Swedo, S. E., Rapoport, J. L., Leonard, H., Lenarie, M., & Cheskow, D. (1989). Obsessive-compulsive disorder in children and adolescents. *Archives of General Psychiatry, 46,* 335–341.

Swedo, S. E., Schapiro, M. B., & Grady, C. L. (1989). Cerebral glucose metabolism in childhood onset obsessive-compulsive disorder. *Archives of General Psychiatry, 46,* 518–527.

Thyer, B. A., & Sowers-Hoag, K. M. (1988). Behavior therapy for separation anxiety disorder. *Behavior Modification, 12,* 205–233.

Twobin, K. E., & Riddle, M. A. (1991). Obsessive compulsive disorder. In M. Lewis (Ed.), *Child and adolescent psychiatry: A comprehensive textbook.* Baltimore: Williams & Wilkins.

Uhde, T. W., & Nemiah, J. C. (1989). Anxiety disorders. In H. I. Kaplan & B. J. Sadock, (Eds.), *Comprehensive textbook of psychiatry: Vol. 5.* Baltimore: Williams & Wilkins.

Watson, J. B., & Raynor, R. (1920). Conditioned emotional reactions. *Journal of Experimental Psychology, 3,* 1–14.

Wolff, R., & Rapoport, J. (1988). Behavioral treatment of childhood obsessive-compulsive disorder. *Behavior Modification, 12,* 252–266.

Chapter seven
Schizophrenic Disorders of Childhood and Adolescence

```
Halfway up the stairs
Isn't up,
And isn't down.
It isn't in the nursery,
It isn't in the town.
And all sorts of funny thoughts
Run round my head:
"It isn't really
Anywhere!
It's somewhere else
Instead!"
```

A. A. Milne, *When We Were Very Young*

Introduction

The study of childhood schizophrenic disorders is in a state of confusion. Of all of the diagnostic categories pertinent to the psychopathologies of childhood and adolescence, these are among the most controversial, complicated, and potentially confusing childhood psychopathologies. Diagnostic criteria, definitions of terms, differential diagnosis, symptomatology, and even the existence of schizophrenic disorders in this age group are controversial. The field is continuing to evolve as clinical and empirical data accumulate.

Part of the problem is that clinicians do not even agree about the schizophrenic disorders as they manifest themselves in the adult population. Rather than a single disorder with a prescribed set of symptoms, schizophrenia presents in several variations. Although there is some commonality among patients diagnosed as schizophrenic, symptoms cover a wide range, affecting thought processes, sensory experiences, accuracy of perceptions, affect, and functional level. The intensity of the specific symptoms can vary widely in different schizophrenic patients or even in the same patient at different times.

A recent discussion (Russell, 1992) summarizes unanswered questions and current controversy with respect to the schizophrenic disorders in young people, reducing the debate to five basic issues: (1) the heterogeneity of the group of children and adolescents who meet the criteria for a schizophrenic diagnosis; (2) the degree of overlap between schizophrenic and autistic disorders; (3) the degree of overlap with the positive symptoms characteristic of adult manifestations of the disorder; (4) the interface of developmental processes with the disorder; and (5) the possibility that schizophrenic symptoms may represent a continuum, and Schizophrenia Spectrum Disorder may incorporate Schizotypal Personality Disorder. We will discuss these issues in this chapter.

Historical Background

Overall, the schizophrenic disorders of childhood and adolescence are conceptualized along the same continuum as are the schizophrenic disorders of adulthood. It seems appropriate to begin this description of historical background with an exploration of schizophrenia as a more generic clinical entity before discussing the application of this clinical concept to children and adolescents.

One of the earliest references to schizophrenic illness dates to the mid-1800s. Benedict Morel, a psychiatrist, (see Grebb & Cancro, 1989), reported a clinical case of an adolescent whose condition deteriorated from "bright and active" to "gloomy and withdrawn." Morel called this condition *demence precoce* in 1856. Emil Kraepelin translated this term into Latin as *dementia praecox* some 40 years later. Kraeplin's work described this disorder as being organic in etiology and being characterized by a deteriorating course. His descriptions of the nature of the symptoms are surprisingly similar to descriptions being written today (Grebb & Cancro, 1989).

Eugen Bleuler coined the term *schizophrenia*, translated literally as "splitting of the mind," in 1911. Bleuler listed the "four A's," four fundamental symptom patterns manifested in schizophrenics: fragmented and discontinuous *a*ssociations in thinking, *a*utistic behavior and thinking (self-absorption, poor reality contact), *a*bnormal affect, and *a*mbivalence. The manifestation of these symptoms is discussed in the section of this chapter on clinical presentation. Bleuler specified that these symptoms are often shown by nonschizophrenic individuals in certain situations. Thus, it is not the presence of these symptoms but their intensity that distinguishes the schizophrenic process.

Since the time of Bleuler, the study of the schizophrenic disorders in young people has followed a varied and tumultuous course. The terminology itself has changed—some of the terms that have been applied to these disorders include *childhood psychosis, dementia praecocissima, childhood schizophrenia, schizophrenia—childhood type,* and *autism.*

Psychohistorians divide the field of study into several eras. The first half of the twentieth century is called the *continuum period.* Until the early 1940s, the schizophrenic disorders of childhood and adolescence were conceptualized as being an early stage of psychopathology. Kraepelin wrote that 3.5 percent of schizophrenic cases had their onset prior to age 10, with another 2.7 percent between the ages of 10 and 15. Similarly, Bleuler wrote that there was childhood onset in some 5 percent of his cases.

Publication of Bradley's classic *Schizophrenia in Childhood* (see Bradley & Bowen, 1941) marked the beginning of what was to be known as the *unitary stage* in this field. Until the 1970s, schizophrenic disorders in childhood were considered synonymous with autism and other childhood psychoses. Throughout the 1940s and 1950s, there was considerable controversy as to the overlap of these three diagnostic classifications. Two major publications helped clarify the issue. The *DSM-II* included a diagnostic category of Schizophrenia, Childhood Type. The Group for the Advancement of Psychiatry (GAP) published *Psychopathic Disorders of Childhood* (1966), which differentiated between Schizophrenia and Psychotic Disorders of Childhood and Infancy. In the GAP classification system, the term *Schizophreniform Psychotic Disorder* was applied instead of *Childhood Schizophrenia*.

Even today, schizophrenic children who are either nonverbal or preverbal may initially be diagnosed as autistic. Only after the child begins to verbalize and some of the positive symptoms of schizophrenia are present is the diagnosis changed to schizophrenia. This pattern has led to the misconception that autistic children "grow up" to be schizophrenic (Dulcan & Popper, 1991).

The third historical period in the clinical study of the schizophrenic disorders of young people began in the late 1970s. It was marked by the publication of the ninth edition of the *International Classification of Diseases* in 1977. The *ICD-9* was the first diagnostic system to differentiate between Autism and Childhood-Onset Schizophrenia. The *DSM-III* and *DSM-III-R* supported this trend by providing different diagnostic criteria for the two conditions. A further discussion of the differential diagnostic issues relevant to Autistic Disorder and Schizophrenia is presented in Chapter 9.

Diagnosis

Diagnosis of schizophrenic disorders has never been simple. Currently, well over a dozen different diagnostic systems are in use for the disorder: Some of them are the Kraepelin system, the Bleuler system, the *ICD-10*, the St. Louis/Feighner Criteria (Feighner, Robin, & Guze, 1972), the New Haven Schizophrenic Index (1972), Carpenter's Flexible System (Carpenter, Bartko, Strauss, & Hawk, 1978), Wing's Present State Examination (1974), and the Taylor and Abrams system. All of these systems were designed to be used with adults (see Grebb & Cancro, 1989).

In the United States the *DSM* system is the most commonly used for schizophrenic disorders in childhood and adolescence. As the *DSM* diagnostic system has been revised, the manner in which it has conceptualized the Schizophrenic Disorders of Children and Adolescents has changed as well. The first edition of the *DSM* had an entry for Schizophrenic Reaction—Childhood Type, and the *DSM-II* changed its terminology to Schizophrenia—Childhood Type. Autism was included under this heading as well.

The *DSM-III* did not provide a separate diagnostic category for diagnosing Schizophrenic Disorders in Children and Adolescents. Instead, it applied the same set of diagnostic criteria to preadolescent children, adolescents, and adults. The *DSM-III-R* again incorporated the diagnostic criteria for schizophrenia in children and adolescents with those for adults, although it did state that one criterion was the "failure of a child or adolescent to reach an expected developmental level." The *DSM-III-R* also specified that a diagnosis of Autism with Schizophrenia could be applied only if both hallucinations and delusions were present.

The *DSM-IV* lists "lack of achievement of developmental level" as the only diagnostic criterion specific to children and adolescents; the remaining criteria are identical to those for adults. The diagnostic criteria for Schizophrenia presented in the *DSM-IV* are divided into several sections on characteristic symptoms, social and occupational dysfunction, duration, and exclusionary criteria. Box 7.1 lists the diagnostic criteria for Schizophrenia.

box **7.1**

Diagnostic Criteria for Schizophrenia

A. Characteristic symptoms: At least two of the following, each present for a significant portion of time during a one month period (or less if successfully treated):

1. Delusions
2. Hallucinations
3. Disorganized speech (e.g., frequent derailment or incoherence)
4. Grossly disorganized or catatonic behavior
5. Negative symptoms (i.e., affective flattening, alogia or avolition)

Note: Only one criterion: A symptom is required if delusions are bizarre or hallucination consists of a voice keeping up a running commentary on the person's behavior or thoughts, or two or more voices conversing with each other.

B. Social/Occupational Dysfunction: For a significant period of time since the onset of the disturbance, one or more major areas of functioning such as work, interpersonal relations or self-care is markedly below the level achieved prior to the onset (or when the onset is in childhood or adolescence, failure to achieve expected level of interpersonal, academic, or occupational achievement).

C. Duration: Continuous signs of the disturbance persist for at least 6 months. This 6-month period must include at least one month of symptoms that meet Criterion A (i.e., active phase symptoms), and may include periods of prodromal or residual symptoms. During these prodromal or residual periods, the signs of the disturbance may be manifested only by negative symptoms or two or more symptoms listed in Criterion A present in an attenuated form (e.g, odd beliefs, unusual perceptual experiences).

D. Schizoaffective and Mood Disorder exclusion: Schizoaffective Disorder and Mood Disorder with Psychotic Features have been ruled out because either (1) no major depressive or manic episodes have occurred concurrently with the active phase symptoms; or (2) if mood episodes have occurred during active phase symptoms, their total duration has been brief relative to the duration of the active and residual periods.

E. Substance/General Medical Condition Exclusion: The disturbance is not due to the direct effects of a substance (e.g., drugs of abuse, medication) or a general medical condition.

Source: American Psychiatric Association, *DSM-IV,* pp. 285–286. Reprinted with permission from the *Diagnostic and Statistical Manual of Mental Disorders,* Fourth Edition. Copyright © 1994 American Psychiatric Association.

Differential Diagnosis

Five other categories must be considered when addressing issues of differential diagnosis with respect to Schizophrenic Disorders in Children and Adolescents. The first and most prominent is the Pervasive Developmental Disorders, and the remaining four are Schizophreniform Disorder, Schizotypal Personality Disorder, Mood Disorder (see Chapter 5), and Organic Mood Disorder.

Because of the historical association between Pervasive Developmental Disorders (especially Autism) and Childhood Schizophrenic Disorders, the issue of differential diagnosis is significant. In the majority of cases, however, the two diagnostic categories are truly mutually exclusive. Age of onset is typically later in schizophrenic disorders (usually after age 6) than in autism. In addition, children with schizophrenic disorders are more likely to have a positive family history for the disorder. With respect to epidemiological issues, there is a greater sex-ratio discrepancy in autistic disorders (favoring males), and autistic children are mentally retarded while schizophrenic children are usually of average intelligence. Autistic patients tend to exhibit gaze-avoidant behavior and echolalia (repetition of other people's speech), and they manifest little if any interest in other people. In contrast, schizophrenic children are more likely to manifest perceptual disturbances, problems of thought content, and incongruent affect. Finally, there is a pronounced difference in clinical course of the two disorders: schizophrenic patients manifest a gradual deterioration in functional level, whereas patients with developmental disorders manifest a delay in functional development.

Differential diagnosis between the schizophrenic disorders and Schizophreniform Disorder and/or schizotypal personality disorder largely depends on the degree of severity and/or duration of specified symptoms. Schizophreniform Disorder can be considered a somewhat less chronic form of Schizophrenia. Symptoms are of shorter duration, more acute, and related to external factors. Similarly, symptoms in Schizotypal Personality Disorder are well within the schizophrenic continuum, yet are not severe enough (especially with respect to thought disorders) to warrant a diagnosis of Schizophrenia.

Chapter 5 addressed differential diagnostic issues in regard to the Major Mood Disorders and Schizophrenia. Manic or hypomanic episodes often involve delusions, but depression rarely does (see Puig-Antich, Ryan, & Rabinovich, 1985). When present in older children with depressive or other mood disorders, delusions are less systematized and organized than those in true schizophrenic disorders.

Age, clinical presentation and course, and environmental situations surrounding onset are the major crucial factors in differentiating Organic Delusional Syndrome from schizophrenic disorders. In addition, as with the mood disorders, there is a difference in the quality of the delusional ideation, with the delusions being less systematized and consistent than those typically seen in the schizophrenic disorders.

Clinical Presentation

Schizophrenic disorders in childhood and adolescence typically present in one of three ways: acute onset not involving premorbid signs or symptoms; insidious onset involving a gradual deterioration in functioning; and acute exacerbation involving exacerbation of preexisting symptoms (Volkmar, 1991).

Older children manifest insidious onset of schizophrenic disorders more frequently than do younger children. The actual diagnosis of Schizophrenia is rarely made in children under 5. In prepubertal children, typical premorbid symptoms include ritualistic or stereotypal behavior, problems with attention span, impairment of language or cognitive function, and various conduct disorders (Dulcan & Popper, 1991; Green, 1989). A study of 35 schizophrenic children between the ages of 4 and 13 (Russell, Bott, & Sammons, 1989) reports that nonpsychotic premorbid symptoms characteristically last between 3 and 9 years. This study reported premorbid manifestations such as attention problems, aggression, truancy, fire setting, echolalia, and ritualistic behavior. Watkins, Asarnow, and Tangucy (1988) report "a broad spectrum" of premorbid symptoms affecting the sensory, motor, cognitive, and social spheres. A more recent study (Grimes & Walker, 1994) investigated the correlation between preschizophrenic emotional expression and age of onset. Data from this study indicated that preschizophrenic children who showed lower rates of negative emotion during late childhood and in adolescence had a younger age of onset.

The symptomatic presentation of schizophrenic disorders in children and adolescents, which is not dissimilar to that seen in adults, can be divided into five major categories: (1) hallucinations, (2) delusions, (3) thought process disorders, (4) affective symptoms, and (5) motor symptoms. The limited clinical and empirical data available indicate that visual and auditory hallucinations are the most common symptoms, persecutory and somatic delusions the next most common.

Hallucinations A **hallucination** is a distortion in sensory experience that is severe enough to alter the individual's perception of reality. However, prior to diagnosing the presence of hallucinations in children, the clinician must consider developmental stage. It is neither pathological nor uncommon for children to experience ideas that could, at other stages of life, be interpreted as hallucinations. Imaginary companions, **night terrors, pseudohallucinations, eidetic imagery** (extremely vivid memories), and hypnagogic experiences (mental images perceived at the moment of falling asleep) may be either developmentally appropriate or evidence of pathology, depending on the developmental level of the child. True hallucinations are also evident in other psychopathologies of childhood and adolescence (e.g., Mania, Conduct Disorders, Multiple Personality Disorder), so the mere presence of hallucinations is not diagnostic of the schizophrenic disorders (Russell, 1992).

As they present in children and adolescents, true hallucinations include several different types; more than one such type able to be experienced by a single child. The most common type of hallucination is the auditory hallucination, colloquially referred to as "hearing voices." These hallucinations reportedly occur in 80 percent of children and adolescents diagnosed with schizophrenia. Auditory hallucinations can take the form of *conversing* (hearing one or more voices talking to a being other than the child), *command* (hearing one or more voices telling the child to behave in a certain manner), *persecutory* (hearing one or more voices verbally threatening or attacking the child), or *commenting* (hearing one or more voices engaging in a running commentary on the child's behavior). Schizophrenic children and adolescents can also experience visual, tactile, and somatic hallucinations.

Case Study 7.1

Eight-year-old Mamie is experiencing hallucinations as a major symptom of her schizophrenic disorder. These hallucinations are so intense and real to the child that she talks out loud. Her hallucinations are both auditory and visual. Voices tell her that she is "a bad girl, a bad girl, a really bad girl." Mamie's visual hallucinations occur primarily at night. She believes she sees a huge man who is threatening her.

Delusions Delusions, the second most common of the positive symptoms of schizophrenia, are experienced by approximately 50 percent of schizophrenic children and adolescents. Whereas hallucinations involve a perceptual distortion of sensory processes, **delusions** involve a distortion of thought processes, severe enough to alter the individual's perception of reality. Delusions seem to be related to the age of the patient. After age 10, children manifest delusional thought patterns similar to those manifested by adults, although adults' delusions are more organized and systematic. In children younger than 10, the content varies somewhat according to age. Older children exhibit more paranoid, somatically focused delusions, and younger children exhibit more delusions focusing on identity issues, parents, and animals.

Different types of delusional thinking are experienced by children and adolescents suffering from schizophrenic disorders. The most common are paranoid and persecutory delusions—the child believes that something or somebody intends to cause harm. Somatic delusions involve an unusual belief about the child's body. *Ideas of reference* is a term meaning that the child believes that the behavior of others is caused by or has a direct impact on him or her. Grandiose delusions involve the belief that the child has some special power or abilities. Bizarre beliefs are blatantly impossible and irrational. Again, a patient may experience more than one type of delusional thought pattern.

Case Study 7.2

Twelve-year-old Davis was diagnosed with schizophrenia 2 years ago. Among his other symptoms, he experiences grandiose delusions. He believes that he owns the school district and therefore can fire any teacher or administrator at will. He suffers from delusional ideas of reference and becomes violently upset when a television news announcer wears the color navy blue. Davis believes that when an announcer wears that color, he or she can read his mind.

Think About It

Imaginary Friends

It is not at all uncommon for young children to have imaginary friends. Some researchers report that nearly half of children between the ages of 3 and 10 years have had imaginary companions at one time or another (Kaplan & Sadock, 1991). These "companions" may talk to the child, play with the child, join the child at family meals, and even have opinions on certain issues. Technically, this type of behavior is delusional and possibly hallucinatory. When is such behavior symptomatic of schizophrenia rather than a typical developmental stage?

Thought Process Disorders Other schizophrenic symptoms reflect the manner in which the child or adolescent makes connections between components of thought. Several different types of disorders of thought process are evident in adults with schizophrenic disorders, but those reported to occur in young people are somewhat more limited in range. Three disorders of thought process are typical among child and adolescent sufferers of schizophrenia. **Loose associations** are smooth connections varying topics that in reality have little or no relationship to each other. **Thought blocking** involves the sudden cessation of speech. **Poverty of content** refers to the patient's conversation. A schizophrenic patient may talk for a considerable period of time without imparting any information. Again, process disorders that involve speech content and cognitive level need to be considered in terms of the patient's developmental level.

Case Study 7.3

Ten-year-old Greg has been diagnosed with Schizophrenia. One of his symptoms is that although he will talk with his parents for hours at a time, his conversation contains little if any meaningful content. In addition, in the middle of these conversations, Greg periodically stops in mid-sentence or even in the middle of a word and remains silent for 15 to 20 seconds, seemingly unable to express or remember what he was saying. Following the several seconds of silence, he continues his conversation as if he had never ceased speaking.

Affect Affective symptoms manifested by children and adolescents with schizophrenic disorders include incongruent affect, blunted affect, flat affect, spontaneous giggling, and explosive rages of varying degrees of violence.

Case Study 7.4

Thirteen-year-old Leslie was diagnosed with Schizophrenia 3 years ago. In addition to her delusional ideation, which is usually persecutory in content, she exhibits incongruent affect. For example, several times a day she retells a story about her beloved dog being run over by an automobile, and every time she tells the story, she begins to giggle and then escalates into hysterical laughter.

Movement Movement-related symptoms of the schizophrenic disorders of children and adolescents include **catatonia,** ritualistic or stereotyped movements, bizarre facial gestures, and stilted movements.

Case Study 7.5

Thirteen-year-old Lisa is hospitalized at a private inpatient psychiatric center for children and adolescents. Diagnosed with Schizophrenia at age 11, she has been hospitalized more or less continuously for over 2 years. Because of annoying side effects, Lisa is resistant to taking her medication. She will "cheek" her medications at least a third of the time, so they are not as effective as they could be. Many of her symptoms are alarming in their severity. About once a week, Lisa lapses into a state of catatonia; she appears virtually frozen, glassy-eyed, and immobile. If someone attempts to move her limbs, Lisa manifests a waxy flexibility: the limb simply drops, seemingly automatically.

An interesting article by Tsianatis, Marci, and Maratos (1986) reviewed European data on Schizophrenia in children and adolescents. Included in this review was a description of how schizophrenic disorders present themselves symptomatically as a function of the age of the young person. The descriptions grouped children from birth to 9 years and from 10 to 12 years.

Schizophrenic disorders in children age 9 and under have an *episodic progressive* course with a combination of continuous and intermittent symptoms. Onset is subacute, with the schizophrenic symptoms appearing at the same time as certain personality abnormalities. These children manifest some obsessive and phobic traits along with some motor and speech pathologies. Delusions and hallucinations are relatively rare during this stage, and symptom presentation is typically acute.

From age 10 through 12, Schizophrenia assumes a *continuous sluggish* course. The symptoms develop gradually, without any indications of clear exacerbation or remission. Most obvious at this time is a change in the child's self-perception, accompanied by paranoid delusions that take a *continuous progressive* course.

A longitudinal study (Cawthorn, James, Dell, & Seagroatt, 1994) on adolescent-onset psychosis reports a poor prognosis, with 78 percent of the subjects remaining ill and "socially handicapped" (i.e., manifesting impairment in interpersonal skills).

Think About It

Grief in Parents of Schizophrenic Children

As the clinical symptomatology of Schizophrenia in children is examined, we may overlook the impact that the disorder has on those close to the child. A recent study (Atkinson, 1994) investigated the psychological effects on parents of having a schizophrenic child. Using several objective assessment instruments, the study reports that parents of schizophrenic children manifested a more severe ongoing grief reaction, while parents of children with head injuries manifested a greater initial grief reaction. How does the type of parental grief reaction relate to the child's diagnosis?

Epidemiology

Epidemiological data on schizophrenic disorders in children and adolescents are limited. With this caveat in mind note that estimates of prevalence range from 1.75 to 4 per 10,000 children under age 12. When incorporating children and adolescents into the sample, estimates of prevalence range from 0.5 to 1.0 percent (Eggers, 1978; Green, 1991).

Studies of gender distribution report that twice as many boys as girls have onset prior to age 12. After age 12, the sex ratio becomes close to equal (Eggers, 1978; Kydd & Werry, 1982).

Assessment

Assessment is more difficult with respect to childhood-onset schizophrenic disorders than for some of the other diagnostic categories. A very limited number of assessment instruments have been designed specifically for assessment of these disorders, especially in children. Some of the more generic instruments (e.g., the Weschler Intelligence Scales, the Minnesota Multiphasic Personality Inventory, the Rorschach inkblot test) yield data or scores that address the presence and/or intensity of schizophrenic symptoms, but the diagnosis of schizophrenic disorders in children and adolescents is largely dependent on data obtained during clinical interviews.

Volkmar (1991) presents an assessment protocol with four components: (1) historical information on developmental history, clinical course of the illness, and medical and family history; (2) psychological and communicative examination assessing cognitive functioning and adaptive behavior, interpreting projective tests, and assessing communication skills; (3) psychiatric evaluation of thought disturbance, hallucinations, delusions, and affective pathology as well as new developments in the course of the illness; and (4) medical examination to assess health and neurological condition and substance abuse.

The Weschler Intelligence Scale for Children (WISC) typically used to evaluate intelligence, has some utility in identifying psychotic process. Projective testing for this purpose characteristically includes some combination of the Rorschach inkblot tests, the Children's Thematic Apperception Test, and the Family Kinetic Drawings. The adolescent version of the Minnesota Multiphasic Personality Inventory (MMPI-A) has utility for patients over age 14.

Several of the structured and semistructured diagnostic interviews discussed in Chapter 3 are used frequently in the diagnosis of schizophrenic disorders in children and adolescents (e.g., the Diagnostic Interview for Children and Adolescents (DICA; Herjanic & Reich, 1982), the Diagnostic Interview Schedule for Children (DISC; Costello, Edelbroch, & Costello, 1985), K-SADS-P the (Kiddie-Schizophrenic & Affective Disorder Scale) (Chambers, Puig-Antich, Hirsch, Paez, Ambrosini, Tabrizi, & Davies, 1985).

Etiology

Issues of etiology with respect to schizophrenic disorders in general continue to be fraught with controversy and uncertainty. When the range of consideration is limited to Schizophrenia in children and adolescents, the clinical literature is even less conclusive. Indeed, although several theories have been proposed to explain the etiology of Schizophrenia in young people, none has found significant empirical support. Virtually all of the supportive data have been obtained solely from correlational studies.

Etiological explanations prevalent in the 1940s and 1950s focused on psychosocial influences. Schizophrenia was blamed on a pathological mothering style. The so-called *schizophrenogenic mother* was described as self-centered, unfeeling, and generally incapable of adequate nurturing (see Rank, 1949). Psychosocial theories stimulated subsequent comparative studies evaluating the parenting styles of mothers of children with various psychopathologies. Consistent with the schizophrenogenic theories, these early studies suggested a correlation between pathological parenting and pathological familial dynamics and psychopathology in the offspring, but this conclusion has not been supported by more recent, methodologically rigorous reports.

Other theories based on correlational data support a genetic influence in the etiology of schizophrenic disorders in adults. There is a higher incidence of the disorder among parents and other relatives of schizophrenic children (see Asarnow, Asarnow, Hornstein, & Russell, 1991; Fish, 1984).

Twin studies have investigated the influence of genetic factors in the etiology of Schizophrenia. By comparing concordance rates between identical and fraternal twins, researchers infer conclusions with respect to the influence of heredity. Studies of adopted children (e.g.,

Kety, Rosenthal, Wender, Schulsinger, & Jacobsen, 1978) as well as of foster children (e.g., Heston, 1966) utilize the same conceptual framework.

Taking another approach, researchers are attempting to investigate the etiological basis for Childhood Schizophrenia through the longitudinal study of children who are assumed to be at a high risk for development of the disorder. These children, who have at least one schizophrenic parent, are followed over time to compare those who do indeed become schizophrenic and those who do not.

Neurological testing methods, including computed tomography (CT), magnetic resonance imaging (MRI), and positron-emission tomography (PET), are being utilized to investigate the possibility that a neurochemical or another biological factor is responsible for Schizophrenia in adults. Such studies have reported altered information processing mechanisms, brain/spinal chord dysfunctions and EEG abnormalities. In preliminary studies of children, these methods have provided evidence of morphological abnormalities (e.g., enlarged brain ventricles, atrophy of the left cerebellum), but their relevance to the etiology of Schizophrenia remains to be established.

Biochemical theories attempting to explain the etiology of schizophrenic disorders began to proliferate with the advent of the neuroleptic medications. Because many antipsychotic medications work by blocking the action of the neurotransmitter dopamine, several theories propose that an excess of dopamine is at the root of the schizophrenic process.

Treatment

Both psychotherapeutic and psychopharmacological interventions are used in the treatment of Schizophrenia, but the literature on treatment of schizophrenic children and/or adolescents is disappointingly sparse. The documented treatments apply either one or both of the two treatment major modalities.

Psychotherapeutic Approaches The particular psychotherapeutic approach employed in the treatment of Schizophrenia depends on the theoretical orientation of the clinician. The large majority of interventions take place in an inpatient setting. Psychoanalytic, cognitive, and behavioral approaches have all been utilized with varying levels of efficacy. Less traditional methods, such as art therapy and play therapy, are also used at times.

Some general points apply to any therapeutic technique for working with this population. In all cases, emotional involvement and consistency on the part of the therapist are required. Another prerequisite is parental support (Ajuriaguerra, 1970). The clinician must pay attention to developmental level, especially with respect to ego boundaries (Cantor & Kestenbaum, 1986), and may have to proceed through the primitive stages of emotional development with the child (Kestenbaum, 1978). Development and/or strengthening of appropriate ego functions may be necessary (Green, 1991). Integration of all aspects of the patient's care is essential, especially in an inpatient setting.

Although disparaged by many as being of little or no use, psychoanalytic therapy has maintained its place among treatments for Schizophrenia. Emphasizing the relationship between the young patient and the therapist, with some clinicians promoting the therapist's involvement in virtually all aspects of the patient's day-to-day care, the focus is most often on reestablishment of ego functioning. The therapist works with the child to establish more adaptive defense mechanisms and to decrease perceptual distortions and thereby facilitate more accurate reality testing. In some cases, the therapist assumes the role of the child's auxiliary ego. Modalities of the psychoanalytic approach range from the traditional "talk therapy" formats to play therapies and art therapies. Dolls and stuffed animals help the young child deal with issues around fearful beings. Other toys and games (e.g., building blocks) are used to help the child develop more realistic and adaptive manners of coping with the realities of the world (Cantor & Kestenbaum, 1986).

Cognitive-behavioral approaches can also be taken with children and adolescents with schizophrenic disorders. Clinically appropriate only for the more highly functioning schizophrenics whose developmental level allows meaningful participation, cognitive approaches have as their goal the teaching of self-monitoring techniques to increase the patient's sense of control over his or her environment. A secondary goal of such cognitive interventions is to provide competing responses for some of the stereotypal thoughts and behaviors characteristic of some cases of Schizophrenia (Green, 1991).

Behavioral approaches focus on the overt manifestations of the schizophrenic process. Like the cognitive-behavioral approaches, behavioral therapies for schizophrenic disorders in children and adolescents require awareness of the patient's developmental, functional, and cognitive levels as well as reinforcement potential in order to be effective. Primarily utilizing operant approaches, behavioral therapies work with reinforcements of many types, including food or candy, tokens, and social approval.

Parental and/or familial involvement is often integrated within each of the theoretical approaches described above. Weiner (1992) emphasizes the necessity of using family members as cotherapists who can reinforce corrective behaviors that are developed in individual therapy sessions. Family members can work at selectively reinforcing and punishing certain behaviors, or they can act as models for more appropriate communication patterns. Involvement of significant others is encouraged by most therapists.

Psychopharmacological Approaches The neuroleptic or antipsychotic medications are considered to be the treatment of first choice in the schizophrenic disorders of childhood and adolescence. They are often necessary to stabilize the patient so that he or she can benefit from psychotherapeutic treatment. But these drugs are not as effective in children as they are in adults. Further, few methodologically sound studies have evaluated the efficacy of drugs for the treatment of Schizophrenia in children (Campbell, Spencer, Kowalik, & Erlenmeyer-Kimling, 1991).

Neuroleptics generally have some efficacy on the schizophrenic's positive symptoms (hallucinations and delusions). Typical schedules begin with divided doses three or four times per day, moving to twice per day after the optimal dose is determined.

Among the most commonly prescribed neuroleptic medications for schizophrenic children are chlorpromazine (Thorazine), approved for children over age 5; thioridazine (Mellaril), approved for children age 2 and older; trifluoperazine (Stelazine) approved for children age 6 and older; haloperidol (Haldol) approved for children age 3 and older; thiothixene (Navane), approved for patients age 12 and older; fluphenazine (Prolixin) approved for children age 12 and older; and loxapine succinate (Loxitane), approved for patients age 16 and older.

As in adult patients, the issue of side effects is crucial. Side effects are classified into three categories: agranulocytosis, cognitive effects, and extrapyramidal symptoms. Agranulocytosis appears early and is marked by symptoms of infection. Cognitive side effects involve sedation, which typically attenuates as the patient becomes more accustomed to the medication regime. Extrapyramidal symptoms, which are more common with high-potency neuroleptics, include pseudoparkinsonism, loss of muscle tone, and extreme restlessness. In addition, prolonged use of the neuroleptic medications presents a risk of tardive dyskinesia and/or "rabbit syndrome" (perioral tremor) (Green, 1991).

Summary

The study of schizophrenic disorders in childhood and adolescence has a relatively lengthy history in the clinical literature and lore. The field has undergone continual change and controversy. It can be said to have its own developmental history, with changes in the conceptualization of the disorder occurring throughout the years. At different times, schizophrenic disorders of childhood and adolescence have been regarded as an early stage of the adult disorder, as manifestations of Autism, and as a distinct diagnostic entity.

Schizophrenia manifests itself in much the same way in children, adolescents, and adults. Hallucinations and delusions are the primary symptoms; their content varying with the child's developmental level. The clinician must be aware that childhood fantasies (e.g., imaginary friends) are often developmentally appropriate and do not indicate psychopathology.

Assessment of schizophrenic disorders in children and adolescents is approached through the clinical interview. Several formal assessment instruments have subscales or provide other data to analyze schizophrenic symptoms, but no single assessment instrument can be utilized alone to assess the presence of Schizophrenia in children or adolescents. Subsequent research may identify neurological or biochemical factors involved in the etiology of Schizophrenia.

Treatment of Schizophrenia in childhood and adolescence can be either psychotherapeutic or psychopharmacological in nature. Psychotherapeutic approaches include psychodynamic, behavioral, and cognitive-behavioral methods. Family members are often involved as cotherapists. Psychopharmacological interventions primarily employ the various neuroleptics or antipsychotic drugs that are utilized for treatment of Schizophrenia in adults.

References

American Psychiatric Association (1968). *Diagnostic and statistical manual of mental disorders* (2nd ed.) *(DSM-II)*. Washington, DC: Author.

American Psychiatric Association. (1980). *Diagnostic and statistical manual of mental disorders* (3rd ed.) *(DSM-III)*. Washington, DC: Author.

American Psychiatric Association. (1987). *Diagnostic and statistical manual of mental disorders* (3rd ed. rev.) *(DSM-III-R)*. Washington, DC: Author.

American Psychiatric Association. (1994). *Diagnostic and statistical manual of mental disorders* (4th ed.) *(DSM-IV)*. Washington, DC: Author.

Asarnow, J. R., Asarnow, R. F., Hornstein, N., & Russell, A. (1991). Childhood-onset schizophrenia: Developmental perspectives on schizophrenic disorders. In E. F. Walker (Ed.), *Schizophrenia: A life-course developmental perspective* (pp. 95–121). San Diego: Academic Press.

Atkinson, S. D. (1994). Grieving and loss in parents with a schizophrenic child. *American Journal of Psychiatry, 151,* 1137–1139.

Bleuler, E. (1911). *Dementia praecox or the group of schizophrenias.* New York: International Universities Press.

Bradley, C., & Bowen, M. (1941). Behavior characteristics of schizophrenic children. *Psychiatric Quarterly, 15,* 298–315.

Campbell, M., Spencer, E. K., Kowalik, S. C., & Erlenmeyer-Kimling, L. (1991). Schizo-phrenic and psychotic disorders. In J. M. Wiener (Ed.), *Textbook of child and adolescent psychiatry.* Washington, DC: American Psychiatric Press.

Cantor, S., & Kestenbaum, C. (1986). Psychotherapy with schizophrenic children. *Journal of the American Academy of Child Psychiatry, 25,* 623–630.

Carpenter, W., Bartko, J., Strauss, J., & Hawk, A. (1978). Signs and symptoms as predictors of outcome: A report from the international pilot study of schizophrenia. *American Journal of Psychiatry, 35,* 340–345.

Cawthorn, P., James, A., Dell, J., & Seagroatt, V. (1994). Adolescent onset psychosis: A clinical and outcome study. *Journal of Child Psychology and Psychiatry and Allied Disciplines, 35,* 1321–1332.

Chambers, W. J., Puig-Antich, J., Hirsch, M., Paez, P., Ambrosini, P. J., Tabrizi, M. A., & Davies, M. (1985). The assessment of affective disorders in children and adolescents by semistructured interview: Test-retest reliability. *Archives of General Psychiatry, 43,* 696–702.

Costello, A. J., Edelbrock, C. S., & Costello, A. J. (1985). Validity of the NIMH DISC: A comparison between psychiatric and pediatric referral. *Journal of Abnormality in Child Psychiatry, 13,* 579–595.

Dulcan, M. K., & Popper, C. W. (1991). *Concise guide to child and adolescent psychiatry.* Washington, DC: American Psychiatric Press.

Eggers, C. (1978). Course and prognosis of childhood schizophrenia. *Journal of Autism and Childhood Schizophrenia, 8,* 21–36.

Feighner, J. P., Robins, E., & Guze, S. B. (1972). Diagnostic criteria for use in psychiatric research. *Archives of General Psychiatry, 26,* 57–63.

Fish, B. (1984). Characteristics and sequelae of the neurointegrative disorder in infants at risk for schizophrenia: 1952–1982. In N. F. Watt, E. J. Anthony, L. C. Wynne, & J. E. Rolf (Eds.), *Children at risk for schizophrenia: A longitudinal perspective* (pp. 423–439). Cambridge: Cambridge University Press.

Grebb, J. A., & Cancro, R. (1989). Schizophrenia: Clinical features. In H. I. Kaplan and B. J. Sadock (Eds.), *Comprehensive textbook of psychiatry* (5th ed.). Baltimore: Williams & Wilkins.

Green, W. H. (1989). Schizophrenia with childhood onset. In H. I. Kaplan & B. J. Sadock (Eds.), *Comprehensive textbook of psychiatry: Vol. 5.* Baltimore: Williams & Wilkins.

Green, W. H. (1991). *Child and adolescent clinical psychopharmacology.* Baltimore: Williams & Wilkins.

Grimes, K., & Walker, E. F. (1994). Childhood emotional expressions, educational attainment, and age at onset of illness in schizophrenia. *Journal of Abnormal Psychology, 103,* 784–790.

Group for the Advancement of Psychiatry. (1966). *Psychopathological disorders in childhood: Theoretical considerations and a proposed classification.*

Herjanic, B., & Reich, W. (1982). Development of a structured psychiatric interview for children: Agreement between child and parent on individual symptoms. *Journal of Abnormal Child Psychology, 10,* 307–324.

Heston, L. L. (1966). Psychiatric disorders in foster home reared children of schizophrenic mothers. *British Journal of Psychiatry, 112,* 819–825.

Kaplan, H. I., & Sadock, B. J. (1991). *Synopsis of psychiatry—Behavioral sciences/Clinical psychiatry* (6th ed.). Baltimore: Williams & Wilkins.

Kestenbaum, C. J. (1978). Child psychosis: Psychotherapy. In B. B. Wolman, J. Egan, & A. O. Ross (Eds.), *Handbook of treatment of mental disorders in childhood and adolescence* (pp. 354–384). Englewood Cliffs, NJ: Prentice Hall.

Kety, S. S., Rosenthal, D., Wender, P. H., Schulsinger, F., & Jacobsen, B. (1978). The biologic and adoptive families of adopted individuals who became schizophenic: Prevalence of mental illness and other characteristics. In L. C. Wynne, R. L. Cromwell, & S. Matthysse (Eds.), *The nature of schizophrenia: New approaches to research and treatment.* New York: Wiley.

Kraepelin, E. (1899). *Compendium der psychiatrie.* Leipzig: Abel.

Kydd, R. R., & Werry, J. S. (1982). Schizophrenia in children under 16 years. *Journal of Autism and Developmental Disorders, 12,* 343–357.

Puig-Antich, J., Ryan, N., & Rabinovich, H. (1985). Affective disorders in childhood and adolescence. In J. Wiener (Ed.), *Diagnosis and psychopharmacology of childhood and adolescent disorders.* New York: Wiley.

Rank, B. (1949). Adaptation of the psychoanalytic technique for the treatment of young children with atypical development. *American Journal of Orthopsychiatry, 19,* 130–139.

Russell, A. T. (1992). Schizophrenia. In S. R. Hooper, G. W. Hynd, & R. E. Mattison (Eds.), *Child psychopathology: Diagnostic criteria and clinical assessment.* Hillsdale, NJ: Erlbaum.

Russell, A. T., Bott, L., & Sammons, C. (1989). The phenomenology of schizophrenia occurring in childhood. *Journal of the American Academy of Child and Adolescent Psychiatry, 28,* 399–407.

Tsiantis, J., Macri, I., & Maratos, O. (1986). Schizophrenia in children: A review of European research. *Schizophrenia Bulletin, 12,* 101–119.

Volkmar, F. R. (1991). Childhood schizophrenia. In M. Lewis (Ed.), *Child and adolescent psychiatry: A comprehensive textbook.* Baltimore: Williams & Wilkins.

Watkins, J. M., Asarnow, R. F., & Tanguay, P. E. (1988). Symptom development in childhood onset schizophrenia. *Journal of Child Psychology and Psychiatry, 29,* 865–878.

Weiner, I. B. (1992). *Psychological disturbances in adolescence.* New York: Wiley.

World Health Organization (1977). *International classification of diseases* (9th ed.) (ICD-9). Geneva: World Health Organization.

World Health Organization (1992). *International classification of diseases* (10th ed.) (ICD-10). Geneva: Author.

Chapter eight
Disorders of Identity in Childhood and Adolescence

"Hallo, Rabbit," he said. "Is that you?"
"Let's pretend it isn't," said Rabbit, "and see what happens."

A. A. Milne, *Winnie-the-Pooh*

Introduction

Children and adolescents diagnosed with the psychopathologies discussed in this chapter manifest symptoms indicative of a disturbance in their own sense of who they are and/or who they are developing to be. The overt symptom profile may not involve direct verbalization regarding identity confusion, or even an awareness that difficulties with identity exist, but the nature of the pathology reflects identity issues. The *DSM-III-R* described identity disorders as resulting from an inability to integrate various aspects of the sense of self. The two diagnostic categories discussed in this chapter are Borderline Personality Disorder and Gender Identity Disorder. Only the second appears in the *DSM-IV* as a diagnosis specific to children and adolescents. The borderline diagnosis has only recently been acknowledged as a psychopathology of childhood and adolescence. Gender Identity Disorder, placed in the *DSM-IV* in a separate section immediately following the section on Sexual Disorders, is classified separately from Gender Identity Disorder in Adolescents and Adults.

Borderline Disorders of Childhood and Adolescence

Historical Background

Although the clinical literature has been replete with descriptions of borderline children and adolescents for some period of time (e.g., Freud, 1916), the earliest descriptions of this syndrome in children and adolescents did not use the term *borderline*. Instead, these symptoms were conceptualized as a mild form of schizophrenic disorder. As more data were obtained on schizophrenic disorders, it became clear that schizophrenic children and adolescents represented a different diagnostic category than those who would now carry a borderline diagnosis.

In the mid-1940s, children and adolescents manifesting symptoms that would today be characterized as borderline were diagnosed with some type of preschizophrenic condition (see Chapter 7). By the late 1940s, the clinical literature referred to children who suffered from a "more benign" case of psychotic disorder with "neurosis-like defense mechanisms." Weil (1953) was the first to compare the symptom profile of these young people to that of adult borderline sufferers. Ekstein and Wallerstein (1954) first used the term *borderline children.*

Probably among the most familiar of the psychoanalytic writings on the topic is the work of Anna Freud (1965). Conceptualizing this pathology as deriving from difficulties with respect to establishing a sense of identity, Freud wrote that these children exhibited symptoms of intense anxiety seemingly related to fears of annihilation and/or extreme loneliness. Also included in her list of childhood borderline symptomatology were difficulties in interpersonal interactions, marked by an inability to receive comfort from others; poor reality testing; inadequate development of age-appropriate defense mechanisms; indications of deep levels of regression; and an internally directed focus, to the exclusion of the child's external world.

By the 1950s and 1960s, the diagnosis of Borderline Disorder had been supplanted by the diagnosis of *Adjustment Disorder.* Follow-up studies of this population revealed that the pathology was more severe than that which would be seen in an Adjustment Disorder; furthermore, the majority of these patients were more accurately diagnosed as borderline or schizophrenic.

As clinical knowledge progressed, the continuity between Borderline Disorders of adulthood and those of childhood and adolescence began to come into question. Even now, research has not established whether there is a continuous process through which the borderline disorders of childhood and adolescence develop into those of adulthood. In the following section the current conceptualization of borderline pathology in young people is summarized and compared with the clinical presentation seen in adults.

Clinical Presentation

The clinical presentation of borderline disorders is indeed variable. Partly because the diagnostic criteria are ambiguous, and partly because of the disorder's questionable association with the corresponding diagnosis for adults, the descriptions of the clinical manifestation of Borderline Disorder are far from uniform. Rather than attempt to condense all of the different conceptual approaches to this diagnostic category, we will review the major syntheses in this area.

The most definitive work in this field over the past two decades is a chapter on the classification of borderline disorders in a book titled *The Borderline Child* (Pine, 1983). This classic work classifies the symptoms of the borderline child into seven categories. Pine views these different symptom patterns as sufficiently distinctive to form the basis for differentiating between subgroups of children and adolescents with the borderline diagnosis. Pine's seven subtypes have the following characteristics: (1) shifting levels of ego organization, with fluctuation between a compensated (virtually free of flagrant pathology) state and disordered thought patterns and affective withdrawal; (2) internal disorganization in response to environmental disorganizers, with differential levels of pathology as a function of the structure and/or stress level of the environment (a severely symptomatic individual will rapidly compensate in a structured milieu); (3) chronic ego deviance, with ongoing pathological symptoms that tend to worsen when the patient is involved in a personal relationship; (4) incomplete internalization of psychosis, with pathological symptoms that worsen on separation from an attachment figure; (5) ego limitation, whereby patients show intense deprivation through various symptoms of developmental impairment; (6) schizoid personality, which involves withdrawal from affective interpersonal relationships and a preoccupation with a fantasy life; and (7) splitting of good and bad conceptions of the self and others.

Andrulonis (1990) compared 45 borderline children with controls, finding 16 symptoms that differentiate the two groups: (1) temper tantrums; (2) primitive or aggressive responses to projective tests; (3) excessive fantasy life; (4) mother with depressive disorder; (5) impulsivity; (6) aggressive acting out toward others; (7) difficulty with peer relationships; (8) symptoms of attention deficit hyperactivity disorder; (9) early or premature separation from attachment figures; (10) mother with borderline diagnosis; (11) use of phenothiazines (e.g., Thorazine); (12) problems with speech; (13) adoption; (14) depressive symptoms; (15) chronic wish to be killed; and (16) excessive anxiety.

Bemporad, Smith, Hanson, and Cicchetti (1982) perceive five areas of general pathology as characteristic of borderline children: (1) fluctuation in functioning, with a tendency for the level of psychopathology to become more severe, and even psychotic, under environmental stress; (2) an inability to cope with anxiety at a developmentally appropriate level; (3) impairment in cognitive processes, typified by fluidity and problems with differentiation between reality and fantasy; (4) difficulties in interpersonal relationships; (5) problems in controlling anger and delaying gratification; and (6) miscellaneous associated symptoms.

These heterogeneous descriptions of symptoms characterize the study of Borderline Disorder in young people. Often contradictory collections of "characteristic" symptoms can appear to be almost meaningless. Why, then, is the diagnosis of borderline pathology discussed in a chapter on the identity disorders? Toward the goal of clarifying these points, the next section presents a brief clinical conceptualization of the disorder, attempting to integrate the current knowledge in the field into a more coherent picture.

Clinical Conceptualization

Borderline pathology in children and adolescents is best conceptualized as a severe impairment in the individual's sense of who he or she is as a person. The patient has never developed a sense of identity and therefore requires the input of others to determine and maintain one. This dependence is typically focused on one or a few significant others in the individual's immediate environment. When the borderline individual believes that these others fail to provide sufficient input with respect to his/her identity, the sense of well-being is threatened. A child with this disorder may even feel that his or her existence is imperiled.

It is the intense anxiety precipitated by the lack of interpersonal feedback the child requires that results in the symptom pattern characteristic of the borderline individual. The overt manifestation of borderline symptoms is variable. The same patient may react differently at different times.

Case Study 8.1

Twelve-year-old Evelyn was diagnosed with Borderline Personality Disorder at age 10, after she had seen several professionals and had been treated for various disorders, including schizophrenia. Her mother had first noticed that Evelyn was different from her other children when the girl started school. Evelyn's relationships with her peers were unusual; she seemed to "use" her friends for her own purposes. In fact, Evelyn appeared to have a "using" relationship with most people in her life, except with her mother.

Evelyn's periodic emotional outbursts and mood swings did not greatly worry her parents and teachers, who assumed that she was simply a "difficult child" and that she would probably "outgrow" these behavioral problems. However, when Evelyn was 8 years old, her mother was hospitalized for several days, and the child's reaction to the separation motivated her family to seek professional help.

Evelyn's anxiety was extremely intense. After the second day of the separation from her mother, Evelyn began to exhibit delusional ideation and hallucinations. For example, she believed that television announcers were communicating to her about her mother's impending death, and she heard voices telling her that her mother would never come home. The clinician who was working with Evelyn prescribed antipsychotic medication, but severe side effects of the medication prompted Evelyn's family to look elsewhere for help. The parents eventually contacted a psychologist who specialized in child and adolescent disorders. Evelyn was then rediagnosed as suffering from Borderline Personality Disorder, and she was treated with intense psychotherapy.

Diagnosis

As mentioned earlier in this chapter, the *DSM-IV* does not list specific diagnostic criteria for Borderline Personality Disorder in childhood or adolescence. In fact, no qualifying criteria are listed to make the diagnostic criteria more relevant to younger people. For the most part, then, clinicians apply this diagnosis to children or adolescents by integrating criteria put forth in the clinical literature with the *DSM-IV* criteria for adults.

In the reality of clinical work, these criteria are quite relevant. The majority of studies utilize the criteria for adult disorder listed in the *DSM-IV*. Studies that attempt to validate various assessment instruments or to emphasize the validity of their sample refer to the *DSM* system as evidence of construct validity (see Bentivegna, Ward, & Bentivegna, 1985; Kavoussi, Coccaro, Klar, Bernstein, & Siever, 1990; Lofgren, Bemporad, King, Lindem, & O'Driscoll, 1991; and Ludolph, Westen, Misle, Jackson, Wixom, & Wiss, 1990) for their diagnostic conceptualizations.

The diagnostic criteria for Borderline Personality Disorder as presented in the *DSM-IV* are listed in Box 8.1.

box**8.1**

Diagnostic Criteria for Borderline Disorder

   A. A pervasive pattern or instability of interpersonal relationships, self-image, affects and control over impulses beginning by early adulthood and present in a variety of contexts, as indicated by at least five of the following:

       1. Frantic efforts to avoid real or imagined abandonment. (*Note:* Do not include suicidal or self-mutilating behavior covered in criterion 5.)

       2. A pattern of unstable and intense interpersonal relationships characterized by alternating between extremes of idealization and devaluation

3. Identity disturbance: persistent and markedly disturbed, distorted, or unstable self-image or sense of self

4. Impulsivity in at least two areas that are potentially self-damaging (e.g., spending, sex, substance abuse, reckless driving, binge eating). *Note:* Do not include suicidal or self-mutilating behavior covered in Criterion 5.

5. Recurrent suicidal behavior, gestures, or threats, or self-mutilating behavior

6. Affective instability due to marked reactivity of mood (e.g., intense episodic dysphoria, irritability, or anxiety usually lasting a few hours and only rarely more than a few days)

7. Chronic feelings of emptiness

8. Inappropriate, intense anger or lack of control of anger (e.g., frequent displays of temper, constant anger, recurrent physical fights)

9. Transient, stress-related paranoid ideation or severe dissociative symptoms

Source: American Psychiatric Association, *DSM-IV*, p. 654. Reprinted with permission from the *Diagnostic and Statistical Manual of Mental Disorders,* Fourth Edition. Copyright © 1994 American Psychiatric Association.

Differential Diagnosis

Issues of differential diagnosis with respect to Borderline Disorder in children and adolescents are significantly more involved than they are with respect to many of the other diagnostic categories. For Borderline Disorder, differential diagnostic questions are more in-depth. Usually, a careful examination of the presenting symptoms can often discover a pattern of clinical presentation that differentiates one disorder from another, but in borderline disorders of childhood and adolescence, the diagnostic criteria are ambiguous, making differential diagnosis considerably more involved.

Until the 1980s, there were virtually no objective criteria for the diagnosis of Borderline Disorder in children or adolescents. Diagnostic criteria were drawn from a base of clinical studies that proposed overlapping criteria. It remains to be determined whether these criteria, or a subset of them, have predictive validity for borderline children and/or adolescents. The clinician must not only evaluate the presence of the key clinical symptoms in a given patient, but also evaluate the validity of each criterion. As pointed out by Bemporad and his colleagues (1982), the current trend to apply adult diagnostic criteria to children and adolescents, with only minimal modifications for developmental differences, has important clinical implications.

Therapists must consider the potential negative ramifications of imposing a diagnosis of Borderline Disorder early in a person's life. Any psychiatric or psychological diagnosis can be stigmatizing, but this is especially true of the borderline diagnosis. First, because the borderline diagnosis is classified as a personality or characterological pathology, there is an overriding assumption that the symptoms will be resistant to treatment. That is, the disorder is conceptualized less as an acute reaction to environmental circumstances and more as a general approach to facing life's day-to-day stressors. Thus, most clinicians assume that individuals with personality disorders can, at best, reach a point where they are able to manage the intensity of the symptoms and that these people are destined to operate within the dynamics of the personality disorder for life.

The second negative effect of a Borderline diagnosis is that many clinicians are reluctant to take on these patients. Typically, the compensated borderline individual has an engaging nature which soon transforms into one which evokes intense problems in treatment. The borderline's need to derive a sense of identity from the therapist leads inevitably to disappointment and some degree of acting out behavior.

Assessment

The majority of current research on the topic of Borderline Disorder in children and adolescents acknowledges that the primary source of information on Borderline Disorders in young people is the clinical interview. Clinical intuition is applied to data obtained from clinical interviews with varying degrees of structure. Clearly, such an approach is highly subjective.

The available instruments include the Diagnostic Interview for Borderline Patients, the Schedule for Interviewing Borderlines, and the Structured Interview for Personality Disorders. All were designed for assessing borderline symptomatology, with the adult diagnostic criteria in mind. Studies with adult patients report that these instruments have respectable levels of reliability. However, the applicability of these instruments to the assessment of borderline disorders in young people is in question.

One possible exception is the Structured Interview for DSM-III Personality Disorders. A relatively recent study (Brent, Zelenak, Bukstein, & Brown, 1990) attempted to assess the reliability and validity of this structured interview for the diagnosis of personality disorders in adolescents. The researchers administered the instrument to a sample of 23 young people and their parents. This investigation concluded that the interview had only "modest reliability for personality diagnoses in adolescent patients." Another empirical study (Cornell, Silk, Ludolph, & Lohr, 1983) reports problems with test-retest and interrater reliability with the Diagnostic Interview for Borderline Patients as a function of the experience level of the clinician.

A review of the treatment of borderline children (Smith, Bemporad, & Hanson, 1982) noted the lack of clinical criteria developmentally appropriate for application to younger patients. After reviewing the clinical literature available at the time, the authors described five areas of functioning they perceived as crucial in the evaluation of borderline disorders in children: (1) capacity for consistent functioning, (2) nature and extent of anxiety, (3) thought content and process, (4) relationships with others, and (5) capacity for control.

Epidemiology

Meaningful data on epidemiology of Borderline Disorder in children and adolescents are sparse. The available studies suffer from ambiguities with respect to diagnostic criteria, and none meet rigorous epidemiological standards.

Etiology

Little information is available with respect to the etiology of Borderline Personality Disorder in children and adolescents. A recent textbook on child and adolescent psychiatry makes the following statement:

> It is fruitless, of course, to suggest plausible etiologic influences and pathogenic processes for a concept/syndrome as blurred as borderline disorder of childhood. The population of children that meet an agreed-upon definition with exclusion criteria does not exist. (Robson, 1991, p. 733)

Despite Robson's admonitions, it is important to be aware of the major theories currently proposed as etiological explanations of borderline pathology. These can be conceptualized as biological, psychoanalytic, and familial or systems theories.

Biological explanations of borderline pathology in children and adolescents propose factors such as chemical imbalances, neurological dysfunction, brain dysfunction, and genetic influences. Psychoanalytic approaches focus on a failure to develop adequate mental representations of objects (in particular, the mother) and the concomitant frustrations associated with this developmental defect. Currently, the most popular explanations for Borderline Disorder center around some type of major familial dysfunction, often involving a significant trauma (e.g., sexual abuse, maternal abandonment, parental disruption).

Treatment

Approaches to the treatment of Borderline Disorder in children and adolescents are generally multimodal in format. Smith and colleagues (1982) recommend a comprehensive treatment plan that incorporates psychotherapy, drug interventions, family therapy, and environmental support. They emphasize the involvement of school personnel and as many other people in the child's life as possible. Psychotherapy sessions are divided into three phases that employ each of the above modalities. The first stage focuses on development of the therapeutic alliance and on work with the anxiety; the second stage focuses on the promotion of ego development; and the third stage addresses internalization.

Other approaches are less psychoanalytic in orientation. Behavioral therapy techniques, partial hospitalization (e.g., day treatment), and intensive residential treatment may be integrated with psychopharmacological approaches. All approaches to treatment have the same primary objectives: (1) reduction of impulsive behaviors, (2) improvement of reality testing, (3) reduction of cognitive distortions, and (4) reduction of interpersonal conflicts.

Interventions with family members of the borderline patient typically prove necessary as well as therapeutically beneficial. The transference and countertransference reactions can be intense in working with this diagnostic group, and therapists often find that direct involvement of the family helps to attenuate these reactions. The presence of the family can help the patient express feelings of helplessness and may modify his or her manifestation of splitting behavior (i.e., seeing people as all good or all bad), as well as the therapist's concomitant reaction to these processes.

Psychopharmacological interventions with the borderline child or adolescent cover virtually the entire range of possible medications. In young people with borderline disorders, psychopharmacological treatment is used mostly to address symptomatology that is either too severe for or simply not amenable to psychological interventions. Medications are prescribed to attenuate affective symptomatology (e.g., antidepressants, lithium), attention deficit (Ritalin, imipramine), seizure disorders (e.g., Tegretol), and conduct disorders (e.g., lithium, haldol).

Gender Identity Disorders of Childhood and Adolescence

Although technically classified as a psychosexual disorder, Gender Identity Disorder of Childhood and Adolescence is more accurately conceptualized as a disorder of identity. Its primary distinguishing feature is a clinical pathology associated with the young person's sense of being male or female. Although the disorder is often considered to be a precursor of either adult transsexualism or homosexuality, the empirical literature on this issue is not conclusive (see Davenport, 1986). Gender identity, sexual preference, and sexual orientation are separate entities. Children or adolescents who suffer from Gender Identity Disorder have the potential for the full range of outcomes with respect to their adult sexuality; some will have unremarkable heterosexual lives, and others will manifest homosexuality, transsexualism, or various anomalies in sexual preferences.

In *Behavioral Assessment of Childhood Disorders,* Reekers (1981) emphasizes the distinction between Gender Identity Disorder and Gender Behavior Disorder (which is not an official diagnostic category). The former diagnosis is to be applied to those individuals who are convinced that they are wrongly labeled with respect to gender. This belief causes such children psychological distress and is therefore classified as ego-dystonic. In contrast, the young person diagnosed with Gender Behavior Disorder manifests either androgynous or cross-gender behavior in an ego-syntonic context. In this case, psychological distress is limited to that precipitated by negative feedback from those in the individual's environment.

Clinical Presentation

Clinical symptoms of Gender Identity Disorder of Childhood typically first manifest during the preschool years. Both boys and girls usually begin to show cross-gender preferences around age 3 or 4, but such behavior has been reported to evidence itself around age 2 (Green, 1976). In a young boy, the first signs of Gender Identity pathology are usually cross-dressing, a strong preference for traditionally feminine toys, or an insistence that he is in fact a girl. In a girl, the first symptoms typically involve a preference for rough-and-tumble play, an aversion to traditional feminine clothing, and an insistence that she receive (or that she has) a penis (Bradley & Zucker, 1990).

Over time, a child with Gender Identity Disorder identifies increasingly with the characteristics of the opposite sex. Although the majority of such children are intellectually aware of their true gender (i.e., whether he or she is a boy or a girl), this knowledge of gender can be unstable in certain cases. Ambiguity about gender permanence can transcend expected developmental limitations and can achieve clinically pathological severity.

Girls with Gender Identity Disorder work hard to appear as masculine as possible, both outwardly and in their behavior. They express an intense dislike for traditional feminine clothing; they attempt to involve themselves in play activities considered typical of boys; and they may even alter their walk, voice, and other aspects of their demeanor. Some girls with Gender Identity Disorder will even attempt to urinate standing up or insert objects into their undergarments to give the appearance of having a penis.

Boys with Gender Identity Disorder often wear feminine clothing and engage in feminine fantasies (especially in play); they prefer girls as play companions and prefer to engage in traditionally feminine forms of behavior; and they may attempt to feminize their walk, voice, and other aspects of their demeanor. Some attempt to hide their penis (Zucker & Green, 1992).

By middle childhood or preadolescence, the child's cross-gender behavior leads to conflict in relationships with peers (see Coates & Person, 1985). Since masculinity in girls is tolerated more readily than femininity in boys, peer conflicts are likely to be considerably more severe for boys.

Once fully developed, Gender Identity Disorder in boys includes eight major characteristics: (1) expressed desire for or insistence on being a girl, (2) verbal or behavioral expressions of anatomic dysphoria (dissatisfaction with sexual anatomy), (3) frequent dressing in women's clothing, (4) preference for female roles in fantasy play, (5) preference for stereotypical female play and activities, (6) display of effeminate mannerisms, (7) preference for girls as playmates, and (8) avoidance of rough-and-tumble play.

Case Study 8.2

Seven-year-old James has been a source of concern to his parents and family since he turned 3. He seems "different" from the other boys in the neighborhood. Although James was

his parents' first child and they were inexperienced in parenting, they had an uncomfortable sense about some of his behaviors. The boy was never interested in playing ball or other sports activities; he preferred to go shopping with his mother or an older female cousin to "help" them buy new clothing. When he was outside playing with the other children, there was seldom a problem with conduct. However, James would always be found playing "house" or "school" with the little girls. No amount of taunting, name-calling, or teasing from the other little boys in the neighborhood seemed to make any difference. James's parents wishfully attributed his behavior to a "phase" he was going through and didn't share their concerns with many of their friends. However, just last week, James's first-grade teacher called home. During dismissal, James was found in the corner of the coatroom at school, trying on whatever garments of clothing the little girls in his class were willing to share. As he was putting on the various dresses, skirts, jewelry, and jackets, James announced, "I am really a girl. People just don't know it yet."

In girls, a fully developed case of Gender Identity Disorder is marked by comparable symptoms: (1) expressed desire for or insistence on being a boy; (2) verbal or behavioral expressions of anatomic dysphoria; (3) aversion to traditional feminine clothing, especially skirts and dresses; (4) preference for male roles in fantasy play; (5) preference for stereotypical male play and activities; (6) behavioral display of masculine mannerisms; (7) preference for boys as playmates; and (8) strong interest in rough-and-tumble play (Zucker & Green, 1991b).

Case Study 8.3

Five-year-old Patti has always been perceived as a tomboy. Her family is a bit concerned that she has no female friends, but they attribute this to the fact that Patti "is no sissy" and "just likes to move around more than the other little girls do." Her parents report that ever since Patti has been able to express preferences she has refused to wear dresses or skirts. Again, they perceived her behavior as reasonable because, as her father proudly states, "Those kinds of clothes get in the way."

Patti's family saw no need for professional help until they received a call from Patti's kindergarten teacher, who says the child insists on using the boy's bathroom and urinates standing up. This was brought to the teacher's attention by the little boys in Patti's class, who were upset that "a girl" was using their lavatory facilities.

Diagnosis

The *DSM-IV* places Gender Identity Disorders in a section with the other psychosexual dysfunctions and does not list separate diagnostic criteria for children and adolescents who manifest this disorder. Rather, the *DSM-IV* incorporates the diagnostic criteria for children and adolescents into a more generic listing with adult criteria, making mention of specific criteria that are to be applied when working with young people. The *DSM-IV* diagnostic criteria for Gender Identity Disorder are presented in Box 8.2.

box **8.2**

Diagnostic Criteria for Gender Identity Disorder

A. A strong and persistent cross-gender identification (not merely a desire for any perceived cultural advantages of being the other sex).

In children, manifested by at least four of the following:

1. Repeatedly stated desire to be, or insistence that he or she is, the other sex

2. In boys, preference for cross-dressing or simulating female attire; in girls, insistence on wearing only stereotypical masculine clothing

3. Strong and persistent preferences for cross-sex roles in make-believe play or persistent fantasies of being the other sex

4. Intense desire to participate in the stereotypical games and pastimes of the other sex

5. Strong preference for playmates of the other sex

In adolescents and adults, manifested by symptoms such as stated desire to be the other sex, frequent passing as the other sex, desire to live or be treated as the other sex, or the conviction that one has the typical feelings and reactions of the other sex.

B. Persistent discomfort with one's sex or sense of inappropriateness in the gender of that sex.

In children, manifested by any of the following: in boys, assertion that his penis or testes are disgusting or will disappear or assertion that it would be better not to have a penis, or aversion toward rough-and-tumble play and rejection of male stereotypical toys, games and activities; in girls, rejection of urinating in a sitting position or assertion that she does not want to grow breasts or menstruate, or marked aversion towards normative feminine clothing.

In adolescents or adults, manifested by symptoms such as preoccupation with getting rid of one's primary and secondary sex characteristics (e.g., request for hormones, surgery, or other procedures to physically alter sexual characteristics to simulate the other sex) or belief that one was born the wrong sex.

C. Not concurrent with a physical intersex condition.

D. The disturbance causes clinically significant distress or impairment in social, occupational, or other important areas of functioning.

Source: American Psychiatric Association, *DSM-IV*, pp. 537–538. Reprinted with permission from the *Diagnostic and Statistical Manual of Mental Disorders*, Fourth Edition. Copyright © 1994 American Psychiatric Association.

When considering a diagnosis of Gender Identity Disorder in children, the clinician must take certain developmental factors into account. For example, there is a form of feminine dressing in boys usually limited to the wearing of undergarments or hosiery. Typically not accompanied by the cross-gender identification characteristic of Gender Identity Disorder, this behavior pattern is reported to serve a consoling, self-comforting function for the young boy. Similarly, in girls, there are cases of "tomboyism" that exhibit many of the diagnostic criteria of Gender Identity Disorder. Three criteria are purported to be of use in distinguishing between simple tomboyism and a true Gender Identity Disorder (GIDC):

> By definition, girls with GIDC display an intense unhappiness with their status as females, whereas this should not be the case for tomboys; girls with GIDC display an intense aversion to the wearing of culturally defined feminine clothing under any circumstances, whereas tomboys do not manifest this reaction, though they may prefer to wear casual clothing, such as jeans; girls with GIDC, unlike tomboys, manifest a verbalized or acted-out discomfort with sexual anatomy. (Zucker & Green, 1991a, p. 482)

Further, it is important to distinguish between developmentally appropriate gender role experimentation and true clinical cases of Gender Identity Disorder. Most children develop a sense of gender identity by age of 2½. At this point, they have a firm sense of their own gender as well as its implications. After this sense of gender identity is in place, usually during the preschool or early school years, children may incorporate gender reversal in their make-believe play. For example, a little girl may put on her father's suit jacket, pants, and tie and strut around the house saying, "I'm the daddy." A young boy may put on his mother's shoes and pretend to be "mommy going to work." The key distinction between such fantasy play and a gender identity disorder is the child's belief with respect to his or her own true gender. In the make-believe examples, the child retains a firm sense of his or her gender and never believes that he or she is truly a member of the opposite sex. In true gender identity disorders, however, the sense of gender identity is impaired, and the child believes or truly wishes that he or she were of the opposite gender.

There are several ways in which Gender Identity Disorder can present itself in adolescents. Bradley and Zucker (1990) describe four variants. In the first, the adolescent has not resolved his or her childhood gender identity issues continues to manifest gender dysphoria. For gender-disordered individuals in this classification, there is a period of at least two years during which the girl or boy is preoccupied with trying to get rid of the genitalia. In the second variant, the adolescent has a history of Gender Identity Disorder in childhood, yet has never expressed a desire for surgical or hormonal gender change. In the third, the adolescent demonstrates some form of homosexual preference. Some homosexual adolescents have a history of gender identity issues in childhood, but this is far from universal. In the fourth variant, the adolescent male obtains sexual gratification by wearing articles of women's clothing. The large majority of the time, Gender Identity Disorder of Childhood does not play a role in the clinical history of these young men.

Epidemiology

No formal studies have measured the prevalence of Gender Identity of Childhood or Adolescence in the general population, but a generally accepted estimate is 1 in 100,000 (Dulcan & Popper, 1991). Boys are referred for treatment for this disorder more often than girls, with one referral ratio being reported as 5.6 to 1 (Bradley & Zucker, 1990). It is important to note, however, that this referral discrepancy with respect to gender may represent an artifact of Western culture rather than a valid frequency differential.

Epidemiological studies focusing on transsexual or homosexual adults are of limited value in regard to Gender Identity Disorder of Childhood. The nature of any relationship among these issues is unclear.

A study based on Achenbach's Child Behavior Checklist (Pleak, Meyer-Bahlburg, & O'Brien, 1989) reports that the mother responds in the affirmative to the item "behaves like opposite sex" at rates ranging from 0.7 percent for boys ages 12 or 13 to 6.0 percent for boys ages 4 or 5. Interestingly, the rate of affirmative responses was considerably higher for girls, ranging from 9.6 percent to 12.9 percent.

Assessment

The assessment of Gender Identity Disorders in children and adolescents is characteristically multimodal in nature. In the majority of cases, the child is first brought to a clinician because of "abnormal" behavior perceived by the parents, a teacher, or some other authority figure. The clinician must evaluate the extent to which gender issues of the referring party may bias the reporting of the situation. Typically, the clinician schedules extensive clinical interviews with the parents, and with the referral source when this is someone other than the parents.

The clinical interview is the major assessment tool for gender identity disorders. The therapist discusses the perceived problematic behavior with the child or adolescent at a developmentally appropriate level. This session will yield significant data with respect to the young person's own perspective on the situation. In addition to helping with a diagnosis, this information will help the clinician design the subsequent interventions. A useful interview format adapted by K. J. Zucker was designed specifically to assess the presence of gender identity issues (see Box 8.3).

box **8.3**

Assessment of Gender Identity Disorders in Childhood

1. Are you a boy or a girl?
2. Are you a (opposite of the response to question 1)?
3. When you grow up, will you be a mommy or a daddy?
4. Could you ever grow up to be a (opposite of the response to question 3)?
5. Are there any good things about being a boy (girl)? (If yes, probe for a maximum of three responses.)
6. Are there any things you don't like about being a boy (girl)? (If yes, probe for a maximum of three responses.)
7. Do you think it is better to be a boy or a girl? Why? (Probe for a maximum of three responses.)
8. In your mind, do you ever think that you would like to be a girl (boy)? Can you tell me why? (Probe for a maximum of three responses.)
9. In your mind, do you ever get mixed up and you're not really sure if you are a boy or a girl?
10. Do you ever feel more like a girl than like a boy?
11. You know what dreams are, right? Well, when you dream at night, are you ever in the dream? (If yes, ask: In your dreams, are you a boy, a girl, or sometimes a boy and sometimes a girl?)

12. Do you ever think that you are really a girl (boy)?

13. When you were in your mom's tummy, do you think she wanted you to be a boy or a girl? What do you think about that?

14. When you were in your mom's tummy, do you think your dad wanted you to be a boy or a girl? What do you think about that?

Source: Zucker & Green, 1991a.

In spite of this emphasis on clinical interviewing, formal testing procedures have also been found useful in diagnosis and general information gathering for Gender Identity Disorders. The most useful psychological assessment instruments are of the projective type; they allow the child's gender issues to surface in a relatively unstructured setting. Several empirically based studies (e.g., Tuber & Coates, 1989; Zucker, Lozinski, Bradley, & Doering, 1992) report significant differences in the gender-related Rorschach responses of subjects with Gender Identity Disorder of Childhood. Similarly, responses on the Draw-A-Person Test, the Make-A-Picture Story Test, and other projectives have also been found to be capable of distinguishing those young people with gender identity disorders (see Rekers, Rosen, & Morey, 1990).

Etiology

It was formerly assumed that the major etiological factor in gender identity disorders was biological in nature. Working from the assumption that gender identity was genetically programmed, theorists inferred that disorders in gender identity were also biologically programmed. There is no empirically derived consensus for an exclusively biological etiology in gender identity disorders, but many biologically based theories have been proposed. One of the more popular biological theories focuses on hormonal anomalies. Some correlational studies link prenatal hormone levels and the desire for rough-and-tumble play (e.g., Coates, 1990; Eaton & Enns, 1986). Since an aversion to rough-and-tumble play is often observed in gender-identity-disordered males, these data can be interpreted as a potential hormonal link to the disorder. There are no data, however, showing a consistent hormonal variation in children diagnosed with Gender Identity Disorder.

Another set of etiological theories focuses on the interaction between the child and significant others, primarily the parents. Several empirical studies (e.g., Green, 1987) investigated the manner in which the mother conceptualized the physical attractiveness of the child. Many of these studies have shown a positive relationship between parental perception of the child in feminizing terms (e.g., pretty, beautiful) and gender identity problems in males. Closely related etiological theories attribute pathology in gender identity to selective parental reinforcement of gender-incongruent behaviors in the child.

Other theories focus on mother–son interactions. Like some theories that attempt to explain homosexuality, they propose that the son's overidentification with or closeness to the mother, as opposed to the father, plays a role in the development of gender identity disorders (e.g., Stoller, 1985). Still other theorists (e.g., Coates & Person, 1985) link the development of gender identity disorders with separation anxiety. Finally, pathology in gender identity has also been linked with other forms of psychopathology in the child and the family.

Treatment

As would be expected, the primary treatment interventions for Gender Identity Disorders of Childhood and Adolescence are psychotherapeutic in nature. Although psychoanalytic approaches have been documented, it is generally acknowledged that the most efficacious interventions employ behavioral modalities. As with the other diagnostic categories discussed in this text, however, the specific approach the clinician utilizes to treat Gender Identity Disorders depends largely on his or her theoretical orientation and concomitant conceptualization of the problem. It is important to note that although there is little empirically derived literature investigating the relative efficacy of the different treatment modalities, the majority of clinicians acknowledge that integration of some form of behavioral treatment into the therapeutic regimen is typically helpful.

The more psychodynamically oriented approaches conceptualize gender identity problems as indicative of a more serious underlying psychological disorder. Thus, foci in this type of therapy often include the relationships between mother, father, and child, as well as analysis of the child's current level of object relations. In addition to the traditional "talking cure," techniques in this therapeutic modality include play therapy, fantasy exploration, and various projective methods.

Behavioral approaches to the treatment of the gender identity disorders of childhood and adolescence usually target the cross-gender behaviors. This approach may include planned ignoring of the cross-gender behaviors, selective reinforcement for gender-appropriate behaviors, modeling, training of family members who can act as cotherapists, and training of the young person (depending, of course, on developmental level) in cognitive self-monitoring skills.

Summary

The two disorders discussed in this chapter can both be conceptualized as representing pathology with respect to the patient's sense of identity. Symptoms manifested by children or adolescents with Borderline Personality Disorder are viewed as resulting from an inadequate development of a sense of identity, which has not reached developmentally appropriate levels. Thus, the borderline child or adolescent looks to others in the environment to determine who he or she is. When the child perceives these significant others as failing to fulfill this role, borderline symptoms begin to manifest themselves. Similarly, Gender Identity Disorders reflect an impaired sense of identity, which in these cases focuses primarily on the individual's sense of gender.

The clinical manifestation, diagnosis, and even existence of Borderline Personality Disorder in children and adolescents remain controversial. The *DSM-IV* includes no specific diagnostic criteria for Borderline Disorder in children or adolescents, nor does it include any diagnostic criteria specifically relevant to children or adolescents in its description of borderline disorder in adults. Thus, assessment is based primarily on the professional's clinical judgment in terms of applying the adult diagnostic criteria to the child or adolescent. The characteristic symptoms mirror the adult symptoms, but they are modified according to the child's developmental level. Treatment for borderline disorder in children and adolescents is primarily psychotherapeutic; psychopharmacological interventions may be employed to address the more intense symptoms.

Children and adolescents with Gender Identity Disorder express a strong desire to be of the opposite sex. This desire is typically expressed in cross-gender dressing, play, and other behaviors. Some children appear to actually believe that they are of the opposite sex. When considering a diagnosis of Gender Identity Disorder, the clinician must take the patient's developmental level into account. Certain cross-gender-like behaviors may be normal at various developmental stages. Although epidemiological data report a preponderance of males with this disorder, the uneven sex ratio may reflect Western culture's greater acceptance of masculine behavior in girls as compared with feminine behavior in boys. The relationship between Gender Identity Disorder in childhood or adolescence and subsequent adult sexual adjustment has not been empirically determined. Treatment for Gender Identity Disorder can be psychodynamic or behavioral in orientation, usually including a component of familial intervention.

References

Andrulonis, P. A. (1990). Borderline personality subcategories in children. Paper presented at the annual meeting of the American Psychiatric Association in New York, May.

Bemporad, J. R., Smith, H. F., Hanson, G., & Cicchetti, D. (1982). Borderline syndromes in childhood: Criteria for diagnosis. *American Journal of Psychiatry, 139,* 596–602.

Bentivegna, S. W., Ward, L. B., & Bentivegna, N. P. (1985). Study of a diagnostic profile of the borderline syndrome in childhood and trends in treatment outcome. *Child Psychiatry and Human Development, 15,* 198–205.

Bradley, S. J., & Zucker, K. J. (1990). Gender identity disorder and psychosexual problems in children and adolescents. *Canadian Journal of Psychiatry, 35,* 477–486.

Brent, D. A., Zelenak, J. P., Bukstein, O., & Brown, R. V. (1990). Reliability and validity of the structured interview for personality disorders in adolescents. *Journal of the American Academy of Child and Adolescent Psychiatry, 29,* 349–354.

Coates, S. (1990). Ontogenesis of boyhood gender identity disorder. *Journal of the American Academy of Psychoanalysis, 18,* 414–438.

Coates, S., & Person, E. S. (1985). Extreme boyhood femininity: Isolated behavior or pervasive disorder? *Journal of the American Academy of Child Psychiatry, 24,* 702–709.

Cornell, D. G., Silk, K. R., Ludolph, P. S., & Lohr, N. E. (1983). Test-retest reliability of the diagnostic interview for borderlines. *Archives of General Psychiatry, 40,* 1307–1310.

Davenport, C. W. (1986). A follow-up study of 10 feminine boys. *Archives of Sexual Behavior, 15,* 511–517.

Dulcan, M. K., & Popper, C. W. (1991). *Concise guide to child and adolescent psychiatry.* Washington, DC: American Psychiatric Press.

Eaton, W. O., & Enns, L. R. (1986). Sex differences in human motor activity level. *Psychological Bulletin, 100,* 19–28.

Ekstein, R., & Wallerstein, J. (1954). Observations on the psychology of borderline and psychotic children. *Psychoanalytic Study of the Child, 9,* 344.

Freud, A. (1965). *Normality and pathology in childhood.* New York: International Universities Press.

Freud, S. (1916). *A general introduction to psychoanalysis.* New York: Perma Books.

Green, R. (1976). One hundred ten feminine and masculine boys: Behavioral contrasts and demographic similarities. *Archives of Sexual Behavior, 5,* 425–446.

Green, R. (1987). *The "sissy boy syndrome" and the development of homosexuality.* New Haven: Yale University Press.

Kavoussi, R. J., Coccaro, E. F., Klar, H. M., Bernstein, D., & Siever, L. J. (1990). Structured interviews for borderline personality disorder. *American Journal of Psychiatry, 147,* 1522–1525.

Lofgren, D. P., Bemporad, J., King, J. Lindem, K., & O'Driscoll, G. (1991). A prospective follow-up study of so-called borderline children. *American Journal of Psychiatry, 148,* 1541–1547.

Ludolph, P. S., Westen, D., Misle, B., Jackson, A., Wixom, J., & Wiss, C. (1990). The borderline diagnosis in adolescents: Symptoms and developmental history. *American Journal of Psychiatry, 147,* 470–476.

Pine, F. (1983). A working nosology of borderline syndromes in children. In K. S. Robson (Ed.), *The borderline child: Approaches to etiology, diagnosis and treatment* (pp. 83–100). New York: McGraw-Hill.

Pleak, R. R., Meyer-Bahlburg, H. F., & O'Brien, J. D. (1989). Cross-gender behavior and psychopathology in boy psychiatric outpatients. *Journal of the American Academy of Child and Adolescent Psychiatry, 28,* 385–393.

Reekers, G. A. (1981). Psychosexual and gender problems. In E. J. Marsh & L. G. Terdal (Eds.), *Behavioral assessment of childhood disorders.* New York: Guilford Press.

Reekers, G. A., Rosen, A. C., & Morey, A. M. (1990). Projective test findings for boys with gender disturbance: Draw-A-Person Test, IT Scale, and Make-A-Picture-Story Test. *Perceptual and Motor Skills, 71,* 771–779.

Robson, K. S. (1991). Borderline disorders. In M. Lewis (Ed.), *Child and adolescent psychiatry: A comprehensive textbook* (pp. 731–735). Baltimore: Williams & Wilkins.

Smith, H. F., Bemporad, J. R., & Hanson, G. (1982). Aspects of the treatment of borderline children. *American Journal of Psychotherapy, 36,* 181–197.

Stoller, R. J. (1988). *Presentation of gender.* New Haven: Yale University Press.

Tuber, S., & Coates, S. (1989). Indices of psychopathology in the Rorschachs of boys with severe gender identity disorder: A comparison with normal control subjects. *Journal of Personality Assessment, 53,* 100–112.

Weil, A. P. (1953). Certain severe disturbances of ego development in childhood. *Psychoanalytic Study of the Child, 9,* 344.

Zucker, K. J., Bradley, S. J., Sullivan, C. L., & Kuksis, M. (1993). A gender identity interview for children. *Journal of Personality Assessment, 61,* 443–456.

Zucker, K. J., & Green, R. (1991a). Gender identity and psychosexual disorders. In J. M. Wiener (Ed.), *Textbook of child and adolescent psychiatry.* Washington, DC: American Psychiatric Association.

Zucker, K. J., & Green, R. (1991b). Gender identity disorders. In M. Lewis (Ed.), *Child and adolescent psychiatry: A comprehensive textbook* (pp. 604–613). Baltimore: Williams & Wilkins.

Zucker, K. J., & Green, R. (1992). Psychosexual disorders in children and adolescents. *Journal of Child Psychology and Psychiatry, 33,* 107–151.

Zucker, K. J., Lozinski, J. A., Bradley, S. J., & Doering, R. W. (1992). Sex-typed responses in the Rorschach protocols of children with gender identity disorder. *Journal of Personality Assessment, 58,* 295–310.

Chapter nine
Mental Retardation and the
Pervasive Developmental Disorders

"After all," said Rabbit to himself, "Christopher Robin
depends on me. He's fond of Pooh and Piglet and Eeyore,
and so am I, but they haven't any brain. Not to notice.
And he respects Owl, because you can't help respecting
anybody who can spell Tuesday, even if he doesn't spell
it right; but spelling isn't everything. There are days
when spelling Tuesday simply doesn't count."

A. A. Milne, *The House at Pooh Corner*

Introduction

The diagnostic category of Developmental Disorders, as described by the *DSM-IV*, incorporates several different types of disorders. Mental retardation is characterized by varying degrees of impairment in intellectual functioning as well as concomitant impairment in overall adaptive functioning. The Pervasive Developmental Disorders include Autism, the most common; Rett's Disorder; Asperger's Disorder; and Childhood Disintegrative Disorder. Learning disorders or academic skills disorders are diagnosed when a child has particular difficulty with a specific skill and his or her academic progress is impeded.

This chapter will begin by presenting an overview of the concept of Developmental Disorders in general. It will then proceed with a discussion of each of the three categories of developmental disorders in terms of their clinical presentation, diagnostic issues and treatment.

Developmental Disorders as a Diagnostic Category

Developmental disorders as a diagnostic category are described in the introduction to the "Disorders of Development" section of the *Classification of Mental and Behavioural Disorders*

(World Health Organization, 1992). The *ICD-10* lists three criteria as characteristic features of all the developmental disorders (p. 233):

A.   An onset that is invariably during infancy or childhood;

B.   An impairment or delay in the development of functions that are strongly related to biological maturation of the central nervous system; and

C.   A steady course that does not involve the remissions and relapses that tend to be characteristic of many mental disorders.

Writing about the Developmental Disorders dates back to the sixteenth and seventeenth centuries, but it was not until the 1960s that the term *learning disability* was coined. During this short history of diagnostic schema, classification of the developmental disorders has been far from ideal.

With the advent of the multiaxial system employed in the revisions of the *DSM*, the Developmental Disorders were finally included in a popular diagnostic system. The *DSM-III* placed the Developmental Disorders on Axis II (the other psychiatric diagnoses are coded on Axis I), and now, using this system, the clinician had an operational means of diagnosing the Developmental Disorders with empirically and clinically derived criteria. Many practitioners still think that the Developmental Disorders are not addressed adequately in the *DSM* manuals (Cantwell, 1992). These concerns will be addressed individually in the sections of this chapter specific to each of the individual Developmental Disorders.

The etiologies of the majority of the Developmental Disorders have not been established, although heredity is thought to be the most important factor. Environmental factors are generally believed to play a lesser role in the Developmental Disorders.

Mental Retardation

Clinical Presentation

The clinical presentation of Mental Retardation is highly variable. The particular symptoms depend on the degree of Mental Retardation in the given individual. A child or adolescent with Mild Mental Retardation, with a mental age expectancy of 8 to 12 years, presents quite differently from a child or adolescent diagnosed with Moderate Mental Retardation, with a mental age expectancy of approximately 3 to 7 years; Severe Mental Retardation, with a mental age expectancy of 3 years or less; or Profound Mental Retardation.

Mental Retardation is conceptualized as a condition, not a curable or treatable disease. Patients in this diagnostic group exhibit great heterogeneity with respect to impairment, level of functioning, and overall clinical course (see Szymanski & Crocker, 1989). Several classification systems have been employed for Mental Retardation. In the early nineteenth century, Mental Retardation was already recognized as a diagnostic construct, and by the 1850s, retardation was conceptualized as a condition resulting from some type of arrest in the developmental process.

The first classification system for Mental Retardation was proposed in 1905. This four-level classification system was presented by M. W. Barr at the annual meeting of the Association of Medical Officers. The four classifications, in descending order of cognitive level, included backward/mentally feeble, moral imbecile, idio-imbecile, and idiot. The lowest-functioning category, idiot, was subdivided into profound and superficial groups. Affected children at both levels were considered to require institutional care. The first official classification system for Mental Retardation was published by the American Association on

Table 9.1 Mental Retardation Classification System

BARR (1905)	AAMR (1921)	AAMD	IQ Range
Backward	Moron	Slow	69–80
Moral Imbecile	IQ (50–75)	Mild	52–68
Idio-imbecile		Moderate	36–51
	IQ (25–50)	Severe	20–35
Idiot	Idiot IQ	Profound	Below 19

Mental Retardation (AAMR) in 1921. In this system, three classifications were offered: moron, imbecile, and idiot. These classifications were based on IQ scores, as noted in Table 9.1.

Release of the first edition of the *DSM* in 1952 brought yet another classification scheme for Mental Retardation. Under a category called *mental deficiency*, the *DSM* included three levels of severity: mild deficiency, moderate deficiency, and severe deficiency. The IQ criteria were set at higher values than those used in other classification schemes. By 1960, the AAMR and American Psychiatric Association had begun to combine their classification systems. From that time, the *DSM* system closely paralleled that of the AAMR.

In the 1960s, Mental Retardation was regarded as having a developmental basis. Classification systems incorporated functional level into their criteria as well as using standard deviations from average IQ scores for diagnosis. Five levels of Mental Retardation were defined, labeled as Borderline, Mild, Moderate, Severe, and Profound. Mental Retardation was conceptualized as a symptom rather than a disorder in and of itself.

By the 1970s, the category of Borderline Mental Retardation had been eliminated. A diagnosis of Mental Retardation required an IQ score two or more standard deviations below the mean, so the new cutoff IQ was set at 70. This change reduced the number of people diagnosed as mentally retarded by approximately 14 percent. The new criteria for diagnosis also emphasized problems with adaptive functioning as a major factor.

In a 1992 publication, the AAMR stated that Mental Retardation is not a medical or mental disorder. Instead, the key concept in defining Mental Retardation was to be the existence of cognitive limitations that compromise the individual's ability to function in everyday life: Indeed, the AAMR "requires the intellectual limitations significantly to affect functioning as a necessary criterion for diagnosis." A criterion related to adaptive functioning was first incorporated in 1959, and since then the AAMR system has been modified to assess the individual's level of adaptive functioning in relation to environmental demands. For a diagnosis of Mental Retardation, the patient must exhibit functional impairment in at least two of the following skill areas: self-care, home living, social skills, self-direction, community functioning, and health and safety. Assessment of adaptive functioning is discussed in detail in the following section of this chapter.

The AAMR and *DSM* systems in use at this time retain a four-level classification for Mental Retardation. The condition is assessed as Mild, Moderate, Profound, or Severe. In addition, an IQ of 70 remains the cutoff score for a diagnosis of Mental Retardation. Both systems, however, allow IQ scores as high as 75 if the adaptive functioning level is sufficiently impaired. Both systems regard deficits in adaptive functioning and an onset prior to age 18 as necessary inclusionary diagnostic criteria.

Another medical classification system, which takes an etiological approach, is based on a different format. This system focuses on the specific causes of Mental Retardation, dividing these etiological factors into 10 general categories and classifying the various types of Mental Retardation accordingly. Well over 200 causes of Mental Retardation have been identified. The *Manual on Terminology and Classification in Mental Retardation* (Grossman, 1977) lists the ten categories as follows:

Category 0 Mental retardation due to infections and intoxications
Category 1 Mental retardation due to trauma or some physical agent
Category 2 Mental retardation due to defects in metabolism or nutrition
Category 3 Mental retardation due to gross brain disease (postnatal)
Category 4 Mental retardation due to unknown prenatal influence
Category 5 Mental retardation due to chromosomal abnormality
Category 6 Mental retardation due to conditions originating in the perinatal period
Category 7 Mental retardation due to psychiatric disorder
Category 8 Mental retardation due to environmental influences
Category 9 Mental retardation due to other conditions

Again, individuals with Mental Retardation are not a homogeneous clinical group with a specific presentation. Further, because a diagnosis of Mental Retardation implies nothing with respect to clinical presentation aside from functional level, the psychological profile of the person with Mental Retardation ranges the entire gamut of possibilities. An individual diagnosed with Mental Retardation may also manifest virtually any of the psychopathologies discussed in this text; thus, the potential range of clinical presentations is virtually unlimited.

Thus, the only generalizations which can be offered with respect to the clinical presentation of the individual who is mentally retarded pertain to functional level and clinical course. Generally, the clinical course of Mental Retardation is strongly influenced by external (i.e., environmental) resources. The child's progression through the developmental milestones is not deviant at any level of Mental Retardation, rather it is slow. It is this slowness that characterizes Mental Retardation. Although the normal sequence of developmental stages is observed, in most cases there is a definite ceiling on achievement level. To go any further in describing the manifestations of Mental Retardation, we need to consider the degree of Mental Retardation present in particular patients.

Individuals with a diagnosis of Mild Mental Retardation typically have a rather childlike, dependent demeanor. By adulthood, most are able to achieve an academic level roughly comparable to that of a sixth-grader. With few, if any, distinguishing physical features, individuals with Mild Mental Retardation are often able to hold simple jobs, marry, and enjoy productive social lives. In terms of verbal development, speech patterns are usually unremarkable, although there is characteristically an impoverished bank of information. These individuals are able to live in the community, usually in the lower socioeconomic class, and are able to manage their own finances with minimal assistance.

Case Study 9.1

George is a 17-year-old male who was diagnosed as mildly mentally retarded at age 7, when he had difficulty with the academic demands of first grade. George is an extremely friendly person who has an active, albeit limited, social life. He is in special classes at the public high school and is doing well. After school and on weekends, he works at the local car wash, drying cars. Living at home with his parents, George takes care of his own personal hygiene and finances. When he is not working or at school, he spends time with his girlfriend, going to movies or going bowling.

The next level of severity is Moderate Mental Retardation. By adulthood, moderately mentally retarded people have attained an academic level roughly equivalent to second grade. These individuals are able to talk, but usually with impairment (e.g., lisps, poor enunciation, awkward speech patterns). The social skills of people in this group are severely limited, yet, with some training, they can become mostly independent with respect to their own personal hygiene. The typical individual with Moderate Mental Retardation is able to work in a sheltered workshop with limited task assignments. As adults most moderately mentally retarded people live in supervised settings; they are able to manage only small amounts of money ("pocket change").

Case Study 9.2

Nineteen-year-old Clara was diagnosed as moderately mentally retarded when she entered kindergarten. She is now living in a supervised setting with five other young women. Her appearance is usually unremarkable, primarily because the group home provides close supervision with personal hygiene skills every morning and at bedtime. Clara is easy to understand, but she has trouble enunciating certain words. Clara spends her daytime hours in a sheltered workshop where she stacks kitchen sponges in piles of ten. She spends evenings and weekends doing assigned domestic chores around her residence and engaging in planned recreational activities with the other residents.

Severe Mental Retardation manifests its symptoms early in the child's life. Motor development is severely impaired, as is verbal development. The child may never learn to speak. Personal hygiene tasks require supervision, and individuals with Severe Mental Retardation need to live in highly structured and supervised settings. With a maximum academic level of first grade, severely retarded adults are unable to perform any type of formal job. They are able to perform only limited tasks such as dumping trash, drying dishes, using coin machines, and bringing a shopping list to the store, and even these tasks are possible only under close supervision. Severely retarded children exhibit some of the same behaviors as autistic children, especially rocking to music.

Case Study 9.3

Twelve-year-old Nelson has been living in an inpatient facility for the developmentally disabled since he was 4. Diagnosed as having severe mental retardation, Nelson requires assistance with his personal hygiene as well as eating. His speech is severely impaired: he can say only one word, "No." When he is not occupied with some structured activity, Nelson can be found rhythmically rocking back and forth in time to the music on the radio. With close supervision, he is able to complete his daily "chore" of ensuring that all of the toilets on the living unit are flushed.

Individuals diagnosed with Profound Mental Retardation often suffer from some form of neurological deficit. They exhibit significant impairment in both cognitive and social abilities, to such an extent that they may appear to be virtually unaware of their environment and surroundings. Speech is severely limited or absent. These individuals require special care, and they may need to be restrained in chairs or beds to prevent self-injury.

Case Study 9.4

Ten-year-old Tiffany has been institutionalized in the state facility for the developmentally disabled since she was 3. Diagnosed as profoundly mentally retarded, Tiffany is not verbal. She can make her needs known only to staff members who know her well. Completely dependent on the institution staff to take care of her personal hygiene and daily maintenance needs, Tiffany spends several hours each day strapped into a wheelchair. Unless she is restrained or constantly supervised, Tiffany engages in self-abusive behavior (e.g., rectal digging, skin picking, hair pulling) that could lead to injury or infection.

Diagnosis and Assessment

The development of diagnostic criteria for Mental Retardation has traveled a rather interesting course. Until only recently, Mental Retardation was diagnosed on the basis of the clinical impression of the examining professional. Diagnosis was typically limited to only the most severe cases.

The Binet intelligence tests (Terman, 1916) introduced in the early 1900s were the first criteria for diagnosing Mental Retardation that employed any scientific standards. When these tests were administered to U.S. schoolchildren, results indicated that 3 percent of children could be diagnosed as mentally retarded, even though they might not have met the less rigorous criteria previously employed in the clinical interviews. A classification system that incorporated "mental age level" was then developed. Individuals who did not exceed a 2-year-old mental age were called *idiots;* those who reached a mental age of 4 years were *imbeciles;* and those who reached an age level of 5 years were *morons.* When this classification system was established, Terman developed his concept of IQ as being the ratio between mental age and chronological age.

By the 1960s, the AAMR proposed that IQ not be utilized as the sole diagnostic criterion for Mental Retardation. The association defined Mental Retardation as referring to "subaverage general intellectual functioning which originates during the developmental period and is associated with impairment in adaptive behavior" (Heber, 1961). Subaverage intellectual functioning was considered to be an IQ score one or more standard deviations below the mean of the intelligence test in question, raising the cutoff IQ from 70 to 85. This definition was later revised to set the cutoff score two standard deviations below the mean, so an IQ score of 70 again became the upper limit for Mental Retardation.

This cutoff score of 70 is still in use today, as is the criterion of impairment in adaptive functioning. Adaptive behavior is typically assessed via either the AAMR Adaptive Behavior Scales (Nihira, Foster, Shellhaas, & Leland, 1974) and/or the Vineland Adaptive Behavior Scales (Sparrow, Balla, & Cicchetti, 1984). These instruments request data on the individual's ability to function in day-to-day situations. Information is obtained from caretakers and/or family members. The adaptive behavior skills of infancy and early childhood involve social skills, self-help skills, sensorimotor skills, and communication skills. The adaptive functioning skills of later childhood and early adolescence include day-to-day reasoning and judgment, basic academic skills and their application, and skills involved in managing group activities and interpersonal relationships. Adaptive functioning in adolescence and early adulthood is evaluated with respect to vocational and social criteria.

In summary, then, intellectual impairment (as determined by a standardized test) and impairment in adaptive behavior (determined by a behavior assessment scale) form the basis of the diagnostic criteria for Mental Retardation. The *DSM-IV* criteria for Mental Retardation are presented in Box 9.1.

---

box **9.1**

Diagnostic Criteria for Mental Retardation

A. Significantly subaverage intellectual functioning: an IQ of approximately 70 or below on an individually administered IQ test (for infants, a clinical judgment of significantly subaverage intellectual functioning).

B. Concurrent deficits or impairments in present adaptive functioning (i.e., the person's effectiveness in meeting the standards expected for his or her age by his or her cultural group, in at least two of the following skill areas: communication, self-care, home living, social/interpersonal skills, use of community resources, self-direction, functional academic skills, work, leisure, health and safety).

C. Onset before the age of 18.

Source: American Psychiatric Association, *DSM-IV*, p. 46. Reprinted with permission from the *Diagnostic* and *Statistical Manual of Mental Disorders,* Fourth Edition. Copyright © 1994 American Psychiatric Association.

Epidemiology

Epidemiological estimates of the frequency of Mental Retardation in the general population range from 1 to 3 percent. The most commonly accepted figure is 2.3 percent. (The variation is due primarily to the definition of adaptive functioning utilized.) In the lowest socioeconomic class, the prevalence rate ranges from 10 to 30 percent. There is a predominance of males at all levels of Mental Retardation, with an overall ratio of approximately 1.5 to 1.

Think About It

Assessing Psychopathology in Mentally Retarded Children

Mentally retarded individuals may also suffer from other psychopathologies. How is the clinician to perform assessment appropriate to their developmental level? Reiss and Valenti-Hein (1994) report on the development of a psychopathology rating scale for children with Mental

Retardation. Based on the data obtained from 583 children and adolescents, the study reports that this instrument has potential in terms of screening for various psychopathologies in this population. How do you think this measure would differ from the assessment measures used to evaluate psychopathologies in nonretarded children?

Treatment

Mental Retardation is not a psychiatric or psychological disorder, so it is meaningless to discuss "treatment." Mental Retardation is not an illness that can be treated; rather, it is better conceptualized as a condition. Modifications in living situations, educational format, or vocational opportunities can accommodate the mentally retarded individual's limitations, but these approaches are not treatments; they do not alleviate any "symptoms." The condition itself is not changed.

Think About It

Effects of Residential Placement on Family Relationships of Retarded Children

Mentally retarded children and adolescents often live in institutions or group homes. Blacher and Baker 1994 investigated the effects this type of intervention has on familial involvement versus detachment. Results from interview data collected from 55 families indicated that one or two years after placement, there was no evidence of decreased involvement between the family and the child. What are some factors that might compromise the validity of these results?

Both behavior and psychopharmacological interventions are used with mentally retarded individuals. These treatments can be modified to correspond with the individual's developmental and functional levels. These interventions are employed primarily to reduce or alleviate symptom patterns characteristic of secondary psychological or psychiatric diagnoses, not to "treat" mental retardation. Again, any mentally retarded person can suffer from other psychopathologies. Appropriately modified, the same treatments used for patients in the general population can be employed for those who are diagnosed with Mental Retardation.

Szymanski and Kaplan (1991) make several excellent points in their discussion of the issues involved in the treatment of mental disorders in retarded individuals. Table 9.2 presents eight guidelines that serve as an excellent foundation for any clinical interactions with mentally retarded individuals.

Pervasive Developmental Disorders

The Pervasive Diagnostic Disorders include four named diagnoses as well as the category Pervasive Developmental Disorder Not Otherwise Specified. The *DSM-IV* lists Autistic Disorder,

Table 9.2 Guidelines for the Treatment of Mentally Retarded Persons

1. Perform a comprehensive diagnostic assessment.
2. Design a comprehensive treatment program, considering all of the patient's needs— not merely the disruptive behaviors.
3. Address causative factors.
4. Choose psychiatric treatment approaches on the basis of best benefit/risk ratio.
5. Establish target behaviors and measures to monitor them.
6. Ensure caregivers' understanding of and agreement with the treatment plan.
7. Monitor adverse effects of treatment.
8. Adhere to all ethical principles.

Source: Adapted from Szymanski and Kaplan, 1991.

Rett's Disorder, Childhood Disintegrative Disorder, and Asperger's Disorder. The current section will discuss each of these diagnostic categories individually with respect to their clinical manifestation, diagnostic criteria, epidemiology, and treatment where applicable.

Autistic Disorder

The history of Autistic Disorder as an acknowledged diagnostic entity begins with Leo Kanner's classic work, published in 1943, in which he used the term *infantile autism* for the first time. He described a group of 11 children who were thought to be suffering from early stages of Schizophrenia.

Kanner believed that the autistic syndrome occurred more frequently than it actually does. He was, however, accurate in his description of the symptomatology. Although some of Kanner's writing reflected errors because he worked with a small sample, his descriptions of autistic behavior patterns are still among the most accurate available. In his paper "Autistic Disturbances of Affective Contact," Kanner wrote that autistic children exhibited impaired spontaneity, problems in interpersonal relationships, monotonous repetition of certain noises or words, problems with language development, and an inability to tolerate change.

Later writing on Autism was mostly psychoanalytic in orientation, emphasizing the quality of parental interaction in the etiology of Autism. Parents were said to exhibit emotional alienation from their children, depression, rage, rejection of their children, and even reinforcement of the autistic symptoms, and all these were considered "causes" of autism. One psychoanalytically oriented writer seriously suggested "parentectomies" as a treatment for autistic children.

As time progressed and more data on Autistic Disorder were gathered, the psychoanalytic perspective became less accepted. It was not until the mid-1960s, however, that a book was published (Rimland, 1964) that openly asserted the cause of Autism to be organic in nature. This marked a major shift in the conceptualization of Autism, eventually weakening the theoretical connection between parental psychopathology and the development of Autistic Disorder. By the 1970s, family pathology and the development of Autistic Disorder were considered to be unrelated etiologically.

Rutter (1968) introduced the current standards for the clinical presentation of Autistic Disorder. Rutter claimed that four behavior patterns are present in all autistic children: (1) lack of social interest and unresponsiveness in social interactions; (2) impairment in language skills, with varying levels of severity; (3) bizarre motor behaviors; and (4) onset of symptoms prior to 30 months of age.

Some ten years after the publication of Rutter's work, the Professional Advisory Board of the National Society for Children and Adults with Autism offered a similar set of criteria to define the condition (Ritvo & Freeman, 1978): (1) impairment in development, both with respect to rate and sequence; (2) impairment in ability to respond to sensory stimulation; (3) problems with nonverbal communication, speech, language, and cognition; and (4) difficulties in relating interpersonally as well as in relating to events and objects. Together with Rutter's work, this 1978 revision serves as the foundation for the current conceptualization of the clinical presentation of Autistic Disorder described in the following section.

Clinical Presentation Children with Autistic Disorder manifest symptoms in different classes: social interaction, communication, bizarre behavior patterns, and cognitive behaviors. These are not the only types of symptoms presented by autistic children, but they are the most commonly observed. Autistic children are often hyperactive as well.

The autistic child's impaired ability to engage in social interaction is one of the central manifestations of Autistic Disorder. Autistic social interaction patterns are typically manifested as an overall lack of responsiveness to others in the immediate environment. These children are often perceived as extremely egocentric. Of course, developmental level will affect behavioral manifestations of impaired social skills. At any age, however, the autistic child or adolescent may appear to respond to strangers and a family members in the same way or may ignore the presence of people who are emotionally close to him or her. Autistics may appear quite content to be left alone for lengthy periods of time; they exhibit an apparent insensitivity to the feelings and/or needs of others; and they often seem to feel a greater attraction to inanimate objects than to people, including family members. They often reject physical affection.

Early descriptions of communication problems in Autistic Disorder focused on abnormal speech behaviors such as echolalia or reversal of pronouns. Subsequent work has indicated that most children and adolescents with Autistic Disorder do not speak at all. As infants, most autistics express their needs by crying and screaming. Young children communicate by pulling the adult's hand. Even in middle and late childhood, the autistic child uses gestures infrequently (although the child often understands the gestures of others relatively well). Some 50 percent of autistics remain mute for their entire lives, but some demonstrate signs of "babble" during their first year. If speech does eventually develop, it is often described as "robot-like," and it appears to be primarily self-stimulatory in function.

The manifestation of bizarre behavior patterns is one of the symptom clusters that distinguishes Autistic Disorder from the other Pervasive Developmental Disorders. The type of bizarre behavior can vary considerably. Typically, however, autistic children perform repetitive behaviors that interfere with engagement in other activities. Such behaviors include rocking, finger flicking, spinning, exaggerated reactions to trivial environmental changes, preoccupation with a particular object or a single activity, rotation of small objects, and preoccupation with certain forms of sensory experiences or certain sensory features of objects.

Seventy to 80 percent of autistic children and adolescents have an IQ below 70. The issue of cognitive impairment is significant in Autistic Disorder. Although the traditional administration and interpretation of most intelligence tests is precluded because of the verbal limitations of many autistic children, data indicate that there is a preponderance of low IQ scores among those diagnosed with this disorder. Autistic children, however, do not respond to IQ tests in the same ways as mentally retarded children. Examples of *idiot savant* behavior, as well as disproportionately high scores on visuo spatial tasks and/or short-term memory tasks, all provide supporting data for the idea that this form of cognitive impairment is qualitatively different from Mental Retardation.

Some data indicate that differences in symptomatic presentation in autistic suffers depend on IQ level (see Rutter, 1970, 1978; Bartak & Rutter, 1976). Those autistics who have IQ scores in the lower ranges tend to manifest more problems with social interaction, self-injurious behaviors, and bizarre interpersonal responses. In addition, these studies indicate that autistics with lower intelligence are more likely to exhibit seizure disorders.

Diagnosis The current diagnostic criteria for Autistic Disorder are listed in Box 9.2.

---

box**9.2**

Diagnostic Criteria for Autistic Disorder

A. A total of six (or more) items from (1), (2), and (3) with at least two from (1) and one each from (2) and (3):

1. Qualitative impairment in social interaction, as manifested by at least two of the following:

   a. Marked impairment in the use of multiple nonverbal behaviors such as eye-to-eye gaze, facial expression, body postures, and gestures to regulate social interaction

   b. Failure to develop peer relationships appropriate to developmental level

   c. Seeking to share enjoyment, a lack of spontaneous interests, or achievements with other people (e.g., by a lack of showing, bringing, or pointing out objects of interest)

   d. Lack of social or emotional reciprocity

2. Qualitative impairments in communication as manifested by at least one of the following:

   a. Delay in, or total lack of, the development of spoken language (not accompanied by an attempt to compensate through alternative models of communications such as gesture or mime)

   b. In individuals with adequate speech, marked impairment in the ability to initiate or sustain a conversation with others

   c. Stereotyped and repetitive use of language or idiosyncratic language

   d. Lack of varied spontaneous make-believe play or social initiative play appropriate to developmental level

3. Restricted repetitive and stereotyped patterns of behavior, interests, and activities as manifested by at least one of the following:

   a. Encompassing preoccupation with one or more stereotyped and restricted patterns of interest that is abnormal either in intensity or focus

b. Apparently inflexible adherence to specific nonfunctional routines or rituals

c. Stereotyped and repetitive motor mannerisms (e.g., hand or finger flapping or twisting, or complex whole body movements)

d. Persistent preoccupation with parts of objects

B. Delays or abnormal functioning in at least one of the following areas, with onset prior to age 3 years: (1) social interaction, (2) language as used in social communication, or (3) symbolic or imaginative play.

C. The disturbance is not better accounted for by Rett's Disorder or Childhood Disintegrative Disorder.

Source: American Psychiatric Association, *DSM-IV*, pp. 70–71. Reprinted with permission from the *Diagnostic and Statistical Manual of Mental Disorders*, Fourth Edition. Copyright © 1994 American Psychiatric Association.

Differential diagnostic concerns with respect to Autistic Disorder involve the following factors. Childhood Schizophrenia typically presents with thought disorders and hallucinations, which are rare in Autism. Rett's syndrome differs from Autistic Disorder in terms of clinical course, with development appearing "normal" up through 6 months of age. Asperger's Syndrome is often conceptualized as a milder form of Autistic Disorder, yet age of onset is usually later in life. Mental Retardation causes patterns of developmental impairment different from those seen in Autism, with more generalized impairment in the former. Individuals with Elective Mutism are able to speak and do speak in certain situations, whereas language impairment in Autistic Disorder is not situation-specific. Individuals with Developmental Language Disorder evidence some degree of communicative intent, unlike those with Autistic Disorder. Although symptoms of Autistic Disorder may overlap with those of other disorders, these guidelines cover the primary differential diagnostic concerns.

Assessment Three assessment instruments designed to diagnose Autistic Disorder are commonly used in clinical and research practice. The first measure attempting to provide an objective assessment of the disorder, the Diagnostic Checklist for Behavior-Disturbed Children–Form E-2, was designed in the early 1970s. It contains 80 items for parents to complete, providing information on the behaviors of their child prior to age 5. The goal of the measure is to obtain data with respect to the presence of Kanner's original symptom constellation.

Another behaviorally oriented assessment tool was published by Freeman and her colleagues. The Behavioral Observation System (BOS) was designed to assess how observable behaviors change over time. The child is rated while being videotaped in an observation room. The BOS rates the child's relations to objects, solitary behaviors, and relations to people and language. It provides ratings on 24 behaviors with respect to their occurrence in 10-second time intervals.

A similar protocol is used with the Childhood Autism Rating Scale (CARS). The child is rated while being observed in both structured and unstructured formats. Designed to be completed by clinicians, the instrument is composed of 15 scales scored along a 4-point continuum: relating to people; imitation; affective response; body use; object use; adaptation to change; visual response; listening response; taste, smell, and touch response and use; fear or nervousness; verbal, nonverbal communication; activity level; level and consistency of intellectual response; and general impression.

A Parent Interview for Autism (PIA), made up of 11 dimensions, is a structured instrument. In a study (Stone & Hogan, 1993) undertaken to examine the psychometric properties of the measure, data on 165 children under age 6 indicated that the PIA had acceptable internal consistency and test-retest reliability for 9 of its 11 measures. A revised version of the Autism Diagnostic Interview is a less structured, investigator-based interview for caregivers of children and adults suspected of suffering from Autism or Pervasive Developmental Disorders (Lord, Rutter, & LeCouteur, 1994).

Etiology Neither biological nor psychological factors have been established as having a specific etiological influence on the development of Autistic Disorders, although many etiological theories have been proposed. Early explanations of Autistic Disorder centered around pathological parent/child relationships, but subsequent studies provided no support for such an etiological relationship. Biological theories of the etiology of Autistic Disorders are currently being explored.

Biological theories of the etiology of Autism are based on correlational data from studies that determined that certain physiological anomalies are present in autistic children but are either not evident or not as pronounced in nonautistic children. Kaplan and Sadock (1991) divide these proposed biological factors into four major categories: (1) immunological factors (i.e., immunological incompatibility between the mother and fetus); (2) biochemical abnormalities (cerebrospinal fluid containing abnormal ratios of dopamine and/or serotonin metabolites); (3) organic, neurological, and biological abnormalities (perinatal complications); and (4) genetic factors.

Dawson and Castile (1992) summarize the biological factors that may contribute to the development of Autistic Disorders as follows:

Neurological findings
    Prenatal and perinatal factors
    Neurological soft signs
    Seizures
    Subcortical findings
    Cerebellar underdevelopment
    Cortical EEG findings
    Positron emission tomography (PET scan) findings
Neuropsychological hypotheses
    Frontal lobe dysfunction
    Cerebellar dysfunction
    Reciprocal subcortical and cortical influences
Genetic theories
Biochemical influences
    Serotonin
    Dopamine
    Norepinephrine
    Brain opioids

Although biological theories of the etiology of Autistic Disorder currently predominate, psychosocial theories still have their adherents. Indeed, although Kanner's early findings pointing to pathological parenting styles in parents of autistic children (e.g., obsessiveness, emotionally withdrawal and coldness) were not replicated in subsequent investigations, other of Kanner's (1954) results have been given somewhat more support by subsequent studies. For example, relatively few autistic children have parents suffering from severe (psychotic) psychopathology (see Kolvin, Ousted, Richardson, & Garside, 1971).

Another factor that supports Kanner's results is socioeconomic status. Autistic children tend to come from families of higher socioeconomic status than do children with other psychiatric diagnoses. This relationship is not found consistently, however. Hypothesizing that this trend may be an artifact of selection bias, Schopler and his colleagues (Schopler, Andrews, & Strupp, 1979) conducted a study of 264 children attending clinics for Autism and other disorders, and they found no intrinsic relationship between Autism and socioeconomic class.

Treatment Treatment for Autistic Disorder can involve both psychopharmacological and psychotherapeutic approaches. Drug interventions are not intended to "cure" the Autism or change the intensity or nature of its clinical course. Rather, psychopharmacological interventions used with autistic children are designed to control especially severe symptoms. Only a limited number of empirically sound studies have been performed, however, and their results are contradictory. No firm conclusions can be offered with respect to the efficacy of psychopharmacological interventions. Among the drugs commonly prescribed for various autistic symptoms are neuroleptics to control self-injurious behavior; vitamin B; opiate antagonists to combat withdrawal; and fenfluramine, which reduces serotonin levels. Fenfluramine was used more frequently some 15 years ago to manage several autistic symptoms.

Significantly more prevalent as a treatment modality for Autistic Disorder are the variety of treatment approaches based on behavior theory. Pioneered by Lovaas and his colleagues (Lovaas, 1977; Lovaas, 1987; Lovaas, Koesel, & Schreibman, 1979), behavior therapies have been employed with autistics to improve communication skills, to teach appropriate emotional expression, and to increase appropriate interaction with toys. Other behavioral programs for autistic children (e.g., Donnellan, Mirenda, Mesaros, & Fassbender, 1984) have focused on the reduction and/or extinction of the self-mutilating and otherwise harmful behaviors that have been observed to serve self-stimulating functions in autistics. By teaching the child to replace the negative behavior pattern with one that is less aversive, the therapist can alleviate or eliminate the more harmful symptoms of the disorder. Other behavioral methods take the form of psychoeducational modalities for family members. Special education may be provided for the autistic child, and systems-based family therapies may be employed.

Education is a major component of most treatments for Autistic Disorder, especially in inpatient settings. So-called special education can take the form of actual skills teaching for the child and/or the formation of healthy relationships with the staff. Some researchers find that a higher initial IQ has some predictive value with respect to success in the special education treatment modalities.

As the child's parents have come to be perceived less as causal factors in the development of autistic symptoms, some clinicians have developed treatment programs that involve family members. Some programs are designed to provide support and/or education for the parents, and in other programs the parents act as cotherapists. One treatment intervention that combines both of these goals is the TEACCH program devised by Marcus and Schopler (1989). Based on the principle that parents and therapists should collaborate in the child's treatment, this program involves a home teaching process as well as the providing of counseling and emotional support for the parents. The clinician avoids taking a judgmental attitude with respect to the family, focusing instead on empathic understanding of the management problems involved in dealing with an autistic child, consideration of the needs of the entire family, and a professional role as a guide rather than an expert.

Think About It

Social Services and Autism

A group of researchers (Smith, Chung, & Vostanis, 1994) evaluated the development of services and support for individuals with Autistic Disorder as well as their families over the past 20 years in England. Among the conclusions reached was that there have been some improvements with respect to younger patients (ages 1 to 9 years) but not with respect to older children (ages 10 to 20 years). How would you explain this difference?

Rett's Disorder

Not formally identified as a diagnostic entity until 1966, Rett's Disorder or Rett Syndrome is a developmental disorder with behavioral and cognitive symptoms. Since Andreas Rett's 1966 paper describing 22 girls with a characteristic neurological symptomatic presentation, hundreds of such patients have been identified.

Clinical Presentation Rett's Disorder is a neurological disorder that assumes a progressive course. Symptom presentation varies throughout the progression of Rett Syndrome. This progression, largely a function of the patient's age and the stage of the disease process, is utilized to describe the clinical presentation of the disorder. A classic paper (Hagberg, 1989) describes the four clinical stages of Rett Syndrome.

Stage I, also referred to as the *early onset stagnation period,* typically manifests itself somewhere between 6 and 18 months of age. This stage has no specific symptoms, and it is not uncommon for Rett sufferers to continue to accomplish developmental milestones during this period, though they are often delayed.

Somewhere between 1 and 4 years of age, the Rett child reaches Stage II, which is characterized by regression of abilities already acquired as well as some changes in personality. This rapid developmental regression can last from several weeks to a year. This is the stage during which mental deficiency first appears and the child loses the ability to communicate.

Stage III is referred to as the *pseudostationary period.* It can last for several years or even decades. During this stage there is some restitution of communicative skills as well as continued ambulatory ability. However, the literature reports a gradual (often inapparent) regression in neuromotor skills.

When the Rett's sufferer loses the ability to walk, Stage IV begins. In this stage of late motor deterioration, the patient becomes completely dependent upon a wheelchair. Usually first occurring during early adolescence, this stage is characterized by neuromuscular weakness and overall neurological impairment.

In addition to these progressive stages, other specific symptoms of Rett Syndrome include growth retardation (especially with respect to the feet), bruxism, epileptic symptoms, night laughing (waking up during the night laughing), changed sensitivity to pain, stereotypical hand movements (rubbing hands together and/or moving hands to mouth), bloating (assumed to be a function of air swallowing), hyperventilation, and breath holding.

Diagnosis The current *DSM* criteria for Rett's Disorder are delineated in Box 9.3

box **9.3**

Diagnostic Criteria for Rett's Disorder

A. All of the following:
   1. Apparently normal prenatal and perinatal development
   2. Apparently normal psychomotor development through the first 5 months after birth
   3. Normal head circumference at birth

B. Onset of all of the following after the period of normal development:
   1. Deceleration of head growth between ages 5 and 48 months
   2. Loss of previously acquired purposeful hand skills between ages 5 and 30 months, with the subsequent development of stereotyped hand movements (e.g., handwringing or handwashing)
   3. Loss of social engagement early in the course (although often social interaction develops later)
   4. Appearance of poorly coordinated gait or trunk movements
   5. Severely impaired expressive and receptive language development with severe psychomotor retardation

Source: American Psychiatric Association, *DSM-IV*, pp. 72–73. Reprinted with permission from the *Diagnostic and Statistical Manual of Mental Disorders*, Fourth Edition. Copyright © 1994 American Psychiatric Association.

The primary differential diagnostic issues with respect to Rett's disorder concern Autistic Disorder. A careful focus on symptomatic presentation reveals the differences between these two diagnostic categories. The Rett's-specific symptoms are seldom, if ever, observed in autistics. Further, five characteristic symptoms of Autistic Disorder—rejection of physical affection, physical hyperactivity, rotation of small objects, stereotypical play behavior, and excessive attachment to certain objects—are not seen in Rett's patients.

Epidemiology The prevalence of Rett's disorder is estimated to be 1 per 10,000 to 15,000. This diagnosis was initially considered to be limited to females, but a few male Rett's sufferers are reported in the literature. Most Rett's patients live beyond their fortieth year.

Treatment Treatment of Rett's disorder involves psychoeducational therapies as well as supportive family interventions. In addition, medical intervention is often required to attenuate the epileptic symptoms, to combat malnutrition and/or anemia, and to regulate electrolyte disturbances. Physical therapy and exercises also often play a role.

Childhood Disintegrative Disorder

Childhood Disintegrative Disorder is a new diagnostic category. Neither the *DSM-III* nor the *DSM-III-R* included it. As far back as the 1930s, however, the clinical literature reports case studies of children whose developmental process had been virtually unimpaired for at least the first three or four years of life. The terms *dementia infantilis, Heller's syndrome,* and *disintegrative psychosis of childhood* have been used. This diagnostic category is now referred to as Childhood Disintegrative Disorder in the *DSM-IV* and listed as Other Childhood Disintegrative Disorder in the *ICD-10*.

Clinical Presentation Children and adolescents with this diagnosis have an unremarkable development up to the age of 2, 3, or even 4 years. Following this apparently normal developmental process, there is an observable deterioration in skill level in the following areas: expressive and/or receptive language, play, social and interpersonal skills, bowel and/or bladder control, and overall motor skills. The *ICD-10* criteria for diagnosis require overt deterioration in at least two of these areas in addition to indications of qualitatively abnormal social functioning.

These symptoms of deterioration typically occur without any prodromal warning signs. The literature reports that these children undergo personality changes, with an increase in anxious, angry, and conduct-disordered behavior. Within a period of several months, these children lose all language and social skills. During this stage, children may manifest incontinence, and they often require assistance in feeding. In some cases, the impairment is not universal, and the child or adolescent retains "pockets" of intact functioning in certain areas. Following this phase of regression, the functional level remains relatively stable.

The period of progressive deterioration lasts from 6 to 8 months. After this phase of decompensation, the symptoms plateau. A stage of minimal improvement in symptoms may follow.

Diagnosis The *DSM-IV* diagnostic criteria for Childhood Disintegrative Disorder are presented in Box 9.4.

box**9.4**

Diagnostic Criteria for Childhood Disintegrative Disorder

A. Apparently normal development of at least the first 2 years after birth as manifested by the presence of age-appropriate verbal and nonverbal communication, social relationships, play and adaptive behavior.

B. Clinically significant loss of previously acquired skills (before age 10 years) in at least two of the following areas:

1. Expressive or receptive language
2. Social skills or adaptive behavior
3. Bowel or bladder control
4. Play
5. Motor skills

C. Abnormalities of functioning in at least two of the following areas:

1. Qualitative impairment in social interaction (e.g., impairment in nonverbal behaviors, failure to develop peer relationships, lack of social or emotional reciprocity)

2. Qualitative impairments in communication (e.g., delay or lack of spoken language, inability to sustain a conversation, stereotyped and repetitive use of language, lack of varied make-believe play)

3. Restricted, repetitive, and stereotyped patterns of behavior, interests, and activities, including motor stereotypes and mannerisms

D. The disturbance is not better accounted for by another specific Pervasive Developmental Disorder or by Schizophrenia.

Source: American Psychiatric Association, *DSM-IV*, pp. 74–75. Reprinted with permission from the *Diagnostic and Statistical Manual of Mental Disorders*, Fourth Edition. Copyright © 1994 American Psychiatric Association.

Epidemiology Because of the limited clinical and empirical data on this diagnostic category, there are no reliable epidemiological estimates of gender distribution or incidence.

Treatment The treatment of the Childhood Disintegrative Disorder is focused on managing the symptoms, usually via behavioral means; providing relevant medical care; and family intervention. For detailed descriptions of these approaches, see the subsequent section on Asperger's Disorder.

Asperger's Disorder

First formally described by a Viennese psychiatrist in the mid-1940s, Asperger's syndrome or Asperger's Disorder was first referred to as *autistic psychopathy.* There is controversy about whether Asperger's should be conceptualized as a less severe form of Autistic Disorder (as it was in *DSM-III-R*), but recent literature supports its existence as a distinct entity. Both the *ICD-10* and the *DSM-IV* acknowledge Asperger's as a diagnostic category. A recent study (Ghaziuddin, Tsai, & Ghaziuddin, 1992) based on 128 patients notes "a significant variation in terms of defining Asperger syndrome as a function of the investigation."

Clinical Presentation One feature distinguishing Asperger's Disorder from Autism is the absence of an initial delay in the development of language or cognitive skills. As noted in the next section on diagnostic issues, the Asperger's child can use individual words by age 2 and phrases by age 3. Asperger's sufferers enjoy the company of others and enjoy social interaction. The content of their verbal interactions, however, is impaired. These verbal interactions are described as stilted and awkward. A 1989 study on Asperger's syndrome reports that social interactions with these children are one-sided and that patients have, at best, a limited ability to be sensitive to the needs and feelings of others. Although they have no impairment in acquisition of verbal language, Asperger's patients often manifest delays in achieving certain developmental motor milestones. Oftentimes, these children are observed to be clumsy or awkward.

Diagnosis The diagnostic criteria in the *DSM-IV* closely resemble those in the *ICD-10*. Criteria for the diagnosis of Asperger's syndrome are presented in Box 9.5.

---

box **9.5**

Diagnostic Criteria for Asperger's Disorder

A. Qualitative impairment in social interaction, as manifested by at least two of the following:

 1. Marked impairment in the use of multiple nonverbal behaviors such as eye-to-eye gaze, facial expression, body postures, and gestures to regulate social interaction

 2. Failure to develop peer relationships appropriate to developmental level

 3. A lack of spontaneous seeking to share enjoyment, interests, or achievements with other people (e.g., by a lack of showing, bringing, or pointing out objects of interest to other people)

 4. Lack of social or emotional reciprocity

B. Restricted, repetitive and stereotyped patterns of behavior, interests, and activities as manifested by at least one of the following:

 1. Encompassing preoccupation with one or more stereotyped and restricted patterns of interest that is abnormal either in intensity or focus

 2. Apparently inflexible adherence to specific, nonfunctional routines or rituals

 3. Stereotyped and repetitive motor mannerisms (e.g., hand or finger flapping or twisting, or complex whole-body movements)

 4. Persistent preoccupation with parts of objects

C. The disturbance causes clinically significant impairment in social, occupational, or other important areas of functioning.

D. There is no clinically significant general delay in language (e.g., single words used by age 2 years, communicative phrases used by age 3 years).

E. There is no clinically significant delay in cognitive development or in the development of age-appropriate self-help skills, adaptive behavior (other than in social interaction), and curiosity about the environment in childhood.

F. Criteria are not met for another specific Pervasive Developmental Disorder or Schizophrenia.

Source: American Psychiatric Association, *DSM-IV*, pp. 76–77. Reprinted with permission from the *Diagnostic and Statistical Manual of Mental Disorders*, Fourth Edition. Copyright © 1994 American Psychiatric Association.

Differential diagnostic issues focus around confusion with Autistic Disorder and Childhood Schizophrenia. The major criterion differentiating the syndrome from Autism is the absence of delay in the development of language capacity in Asperger's sufferers. In addition, sufferers of Asperger's do not manifest the central nervous system pathologies, bizarre preoccupations, and extreme egocentrism so characteristic of Autistic Disorder. In schizophrenic disorders of childhood, the developmental history is typically rather unremarkable, quite dissimilar to the case of the developmental disorders. Similarly, psychotic symptoms such as hallucinations, pathological thought processes, and delusional ideation are not present in the Asperger's sufferer.

Epidemiology Epidemiological estimates for Asperger's range from 0.6 to 26 per 10,000 children. Despite this wide range in numerical figures, all studies support a preponderance of male Asperger's sufferers. Male-to-female ratios reported range from 3.8:1 to 10.5:1.

Think About It

Generalizing Epidemiological Data

A recent study (Ehlers & Gillberg, 1993) attempted to determine the epidemiology of Asperger's syndrome by screening all children from 7 to 16 years of age in a town in Sweden. Results supported a prevalence rate of at least 0.36 percent, with a male-to-female ratio of 4:1. What issues would need to be considered if we wanted to generalize these results to an American population?

Treatment The treatment of Asperger's sufferers requires a multifaceted approach. Psychopharmacological intervention can reduce symptoms that interfere with the child's functioning. The medications are the same ones that would be employed to treat the given symptoms if they presented themselves in other disorders. Target symptoms include anxiety, depression, attention deficit, and obsessive-compulsive presentations.

The more psychologically oriented treatment approaches for Asperger's are aimed toward the family as well as the child. Psychoeducational therapy as well as systems-oriented and behaviorally oriented approaches are employed with the goal of increasing the family's understanding of the disorder, as well as providing the family with the techniques to cope with the symptoms of the Asperger's child.

Finally, treatment approaches for Asperger's are also aimed at the social and motor skills deficits that are characteristically symptomatic of the disorder. In addition to providing therapy and training for the patient, interventions are also applied at the school level to minimize the difficulties encountered in the academic setting.

Specific Developmental Disorders

Specific Developmental Disorders, also referred to as Developmental Learning Disorders, were considered to be virtually synonymous with Mental Retardation until the 1940s. Children who had severe academic problems were classified as being emotionally disturbed, socially or culturally disadvantaged, and/or mentally retarded. However, in the mid-1940s, a new conceptualization was offered, based primarily on an etiological approach.

In consideration of the possibility that these children might suffer from academic difficulties because of neurological impairments, these disorders were conceptualized as deriving from some form of brain damage. Thus, these children came to be considered "brain-damaged," and diagnoses of *minimal brain damage* and, later, *minimal brain dysfunction* were applied to them. Subsequent classification schemes labeled these disorders in terms of the major skill deficits they presented. The most recent classifications use the term *learning disability,* focusing on the specific academic deficits.

Think About It

Learning Disabilities and Subjective Feelings in School

A recent study (McPhail, 1993) compared the subjective experiences of adolescents with Learning Disabilities with those of low-achieving and normally achieving control groups. Results indicated that the Learning Disabled adolescents reported more positive and active feelings during school hours. However, when the same dependent measures were administered after school hours, there were no differences among the three groups. How would you explain these trends?

The Developmental Learning Disorders are divided into three major categories. Language and Speech Disorders include the diagnoses of Developmental Articulation Disorder, Developmental Expressive Language Disorder, and Developmental Receptive Language Disorder. Academic Skill Disorders include Mathematics Disorder (also called Developmental Arithmetic Disorder), Developmental Expressive Writing Disorder, and Developmental Reading Disorder. A third category, Motor Skills Disorder, includes the diagnosis of Developmental Coordination Disorder. Because of the more physical nature of the symptomatology, this diagnosis will not be discussed in this chapter. Each of the other diagnostic categories is discussed in this chapter, with attention to clinical presentation and issues of diagnosis, assessment, and treatment.

Developmental Language Disorders

The clinical record of the Developmental Language Disorders goes as far back as the early nineteenth century. Clinicians then recognized that some children have difficulty understanding, using, and/or expressing speech, and, more importantly perhaps, that these children may not fit the classification of mentally retarded. Terms such as *congenital verbal auditory agnosia, acquired aphasia, language pathology, childhood aphasia,* and *congenital aphasia* have been used to refer to disorders entailing difficulties with language. As for the other Specific Developmental Disorders, conceptualizations of the Developmental Language Disorders have moved toward a greater focus on neurological influences.

Estimates of the incidence of Developmental Language Disorders in children and adolescents range from 7 to 12 percent in the general population, with estimates as high as 15 percent for Articulation Disorder. Among children and adolescents with psychiatric diagnoses, estimates reach the 15 percent figure. Gender distribution favors male predominance in the diagnoses of (Developmental) Expressive Language Disorder (4:1) and Phonological Disorder or Articulation Disorder (2:1), with the gender distribution being close to equal in Developmental Receptive Language Disorder.

Phonological Disorder

Clinical Presentation Sufferers of Phonological Disorder, previously referred to as Articulation disorder, are unable to accurately produce certain sounds of speech at a level appropriate to their expected developmental capabilities. The child will distort certain sounds, omit other sounds, and substitute one sound for another, as well as demonstrate an overall general misarticulation. Initially, the speech of children with Phonological Disorder is not substantially different from the distortions commonly heard in young children who are just learning to speak. Thus, when diagnosing this disorder, it is crucial that the clinician take the child's developmental level into account.

The clinical literature reports considerable variation in severity and general presentation of the symptoms of Phonological Disorder. Much of this variation depends on the developmental stage of the youngster as well as the intensity of the symptoms. Children who are younger or who are more severely afflicted manifest impairment in articulation of those language sounds more characteristic of early acquisition (*d, n, b, t,*). Children with a milder case have trouble only with the more complicated sounds. The severity of the disorder is positively correlated with the number of different sounds the child has trouble articulating.

Diagnosis The diagnostic criteria for Phonological Disorder are presented in Box 9.6.

---

box**9.6**

Diagnostic Criteria for Phonological Disorder

A. Failure to use developmentally expected speech sounds that are appropriate for age or dialect (e.g., errors in sound production, use, representation or organization such as, but not limited to, substitutions of one sound for another [use of /t/ for target /k/ sound] or omissions of sounds such as final consonants).

B. The difficulties in speech production interfere with academic or occupational achievement, or with social communication.

C. If Mental Retardation, a speech-motor or sensory deficit, or environmental deprivation is present, the speech difficulties are in excess of those usually associated with these problems.

Source: American Psychiatric Association, *DSM-IV,* pp. 62–63. Reprinted with permission from the *Diagnostic and Statistical Manual of Mental Disorders,* Fourth Edition. Copyright © 1994 American Psychiatric Association.

Expressive Language Disorder

Clinical Presentation Children with Expressive Language Disorder manifest difficulties in the ability to express themselves via language. Unlike the problems described in the section on Developmental Articulation Disorder, the impairments in Expressive Language Disorder do not primarily involve the actual pronunciation of words or syllables. Rather, these children manifest an impairment that appears to be more cognitive in nature, with symptoms reflecting difficulties in conceptualization and expression.

Presentation can vary considerably, both in terms of severity as well as the actual symptoms exhibited. The child may have a limited vocabulary. He or she may exhibit difficulties with word retrieval, poor word substitution, grammatical problems, strange word combinations, difficulties with changing and/or focusing on topics, and incorrect word ordering. In most cases, all forms of expressive language are affected, although to varying degrees.

Diagnosis The *DSM-IV* diagnostic criteria for (Developmental) Expressive Language Disorder are presented in Box 9.7.

---

box **9.7**

Diagnostic Criteria for Expressive Language Disorder

A. The scores obtained from standardized individually administered measures of expressive language development are substantially below those obtained from standardized measures of both nonverbal intellectual capacity and receptive language development. The disturbance may be manifest clinically by symptoms that include having a markedly limited vocabulary, making errors in tense, or having difficulty recalling words or producing sentences with developmentally appropriate length or complexity.

B. The difficulties with expressive language interfere with academic or occupational achievement, or with social communication.

C. Criteria are not met for Mixed Receptive/Expressive Language Disorder or a Pervasive Developmental Disorder.

D. If Mental Retardation, a speech-motor or sensory deficit, or environmental deprivation is present, the language difficulties are in excess of those usually associated with these problems.

Source: American Psychiatric Association, *DSM-IV*, pp. 57–58. Reprinted with permission from the *Diagnostic and Statistical Manual of Mental Disorders*, Fourth Edition. Copyright © 1994 American Psychiatric Association.

Mixed Receptive/Expressive Language Disorder (Developmental Receptive Language Disorder)

Clinical Presentation This final diagnostic category in the classification of Developmental Language Disorders is typified by problems in the actual understanding of language. As with Expressive Language Disorder, the symptomatology is quite variable. As in the two other diagnostic categories in this classification, much of this variation is a function of the degree of severity with which the specific child is afflicted. As is the case with Developmental Articulation Disorder, the more severe cases tend to be diagnosed earlier than the milder forms. Finally, it is important to note that many children with Mixed Receptive/Expressive Language Disorder meet the diagnostic criteria for Expressive Language Disorder as well.

Impairment in the ability to understand language may occur in any or all of the various aspects of comprehension. Actual language usage, grammar, vocabulary, and/or the ordering of words are all potential areas of impairment in individuals suffering from this diagnosis. Not only the specific aspects of language comprehension but also the manner in which these impairments manifest themselves will vary from patient to patient.

Diagnosis The diagnostic criteria for Mixed Receptive/Expressive Language Disorder are presented in Box 9.8.

---

box **9.8**

Diagnostic Criteria for Mixed Receptive/Expressive Language Disorder

A. The scores obtained from a battery of individually administered standardized measures of both receptive and expressive language development are substantially below those obtained from standardized measures of nonverbal intellectual capacity. Symptoms include those for Expressive Language Disorder as well as difficulty understanding words, sentences, or specific types of words, such as spatial terms.

B. The difficulties with receptive and expressive language interfere with academic or occupational achievement, or with social communication.

C. Criteria are not met a Pervasive Developmental Disorder.

D. If Mental Retardation, a speech-motor or sensory deficit, or environmental deprivation is present, the language difficulties are in excess of those usually associated with those problems.

Source: American Psychiatric Association, *DSM-IV,* pp. 60–61. Reprinted with permission from the *Diagnostic and Statistical Manual of Mental Disorders,* Fourth Edition. Copyright © 1994 American Psychiatric Association.

Academic Skill Disorders

Previously classified as learning disabilities, the Academic Skill Disorders refer to those clinical conditions in which the child or adolescent experiences difficulties in a specific academic area. This impairment cannot be considered to be a function of Mental Retardation, sensory deficits, neurological problems, or inadequate schooling. Three diagnostic categories are listed under this heading, and each refers to the skill area in which the child is impaired: (Developmental) Reading Disorder, Disorder of Written Expression (Developmental Expressive Writing Disorder), and Mathematics Disorder (Developmental Arithmetic Disorder). Assessment of these disorders involves psychological testing (e.g., the Weschler series or the Stanford-Binet series), achievement testing (e.g., the Wide-Range Achievement Test (WRAT) or the Peabody Achievement Test), and educational-diagnostic testing (e.g., the Woodcock battery or the McCarthy scales).

(Developmental) Reading Disorder

Clinical Presentation Also referred to as Dyslexia, Specific Reading Disability, and Developmental Reading Disorder, this diagnostic category of Developmental Reading Disorder is characterized by impairment in the individual's ability to read. More specifically, Developmental Reading Disorder entails problems in reading comprehension as well as the ability to recognize words. When the child with Developmental Reading Disorder reads aloud, he or she manifests unusually slow speed as well as distortions, substitutions, and omissions of words and phrases. In order for this diagnosis to be made, the impairment must interfere with day-to-day activities as well as academic achievement. This disorder is typically diagnosed by age 7, and in the more severe cases as early as age 6.

Diagnosis The diagnostic criteria for (Developmental) Reading Disorder are presented in Box 9.9.

---

box **9.9**

Diagnostic Criteria for (Developmental) Reading Disorder

A. Reading achievement, as measured by an individually administered standardized test of reading accuracy or comprehension, is substantially below that expected given the person's chronological age, measured intelligence, and age-appropriate education.

B. The disturbance in Criterion A significantly interferes with academic achievement or activities of daily living that require reading skills.

C. If a sensory deficit is present, the learning difficulties are in excess of those usually associated with it.

Source: American Psychiatric Association, *DSM-IV*, p. 50. Reprinted with permission from the *Diagnostic and Statistical Manual of Mental Disorders*, Fourth Edition. Copyright © 1994 American Psychiatric Association.

Differential diagnostic issues primarily involve Mental Retardation. In cases of Mental Retardation without a concomitant Reading Disability, however, the individual's reading ability corresponds to his or her abilities in other areas. In contrast, for those cases of "pure" Reading Disability and/or Reading Disability in conjunction with Mental Retardation, the individual's reading ability is significantly lower than his or her ability in other areas.

Assessment To make this diagnosis, the clinician evaluates the child's performance on a standardized test, analyzing whether the patient's reading skills shows significant disparity from his or her performance on tasks measuring other abilities. The child's developmental level is of course taken into account.

Epidemiology The incidence of developmental reading disorder in the general population is estimated at 2 to 8 percent.

Treatment In some ways, the term *treatment* with reference to the various developmental learning disorders is a misnomer. Indeed, none of these conditions can be "cured" in the real sense. However, it is important to note that the specific symptoms do indeed respond positively to appropriate interventions.

For (Developmental) Reading Disorder, as with the other specific developmental learning disorders, special education is the primary approach. In cases of Reading Disorder, the educational approaches are redesigned to maximize use of the child's assets with the eventual aim of teaching the child to employ associations between sounds and letters.

"I wish they made 'My First Reader' into one of those audio books."

Reprinted with special permission of King Features Syndicate.

Disorder of Written Expression (Developmental Expressive Writing Disorder)

Clinical Presentation Gregg (1992) summarized the major clinical, conceptual, and research issues pertinent to Disorder of Written Expression. (At the time Gregg wrote, the disorder was referred to as Developmental Expressive Writing Disorder.) Gregg classified the symptoms of this disorder into three major areas: grammatical disorders, phonological disorders, and visual/spatial symptoms. A list of the potential symptoms, along with the *DSM-IV* diagnostic criteria in Box 9.10, will describe this clinical disorder.

box**9.10**

Criteria for Disorder of Written Expression

A. Writing skills, as measured by an individually administered standardized test (or functional assessment of writing skills), are substantially below that expected given the person's chronological age, measured intelligence, and age-appropriate education.

B. The disturbance in Criterion A significantly interferes with academic achievement or activities of daily living that require the composition of written texts (e.g., writing grammatically correct sentences and organized paragraphs).

C. If a sensory deficit is present, the learning difficulties are in excess of those usually associated with it.

Source: American Psychiatric Association, *DSM-IV,* p. 53. Reprinted with permission from the *Diagnostic and Statistical Manual of Mental Disorders,* Fourth Edition. Copyright © 1994 American Psychiatric Association.

The first set of symptoms revolves around grammatical difficulties. In addition to distorting the order of words, the child may omit, add, or even substitute a pronoun, noun, verb, adverb, adjective, preposition, or any other grammatical entity for the correct word.

Examples
The bird flew the tree. (preposition missing)
If you must run that please be careful. (adverb missing)
Go and tell the what you did. (object noun missing)

The second set of written errors involves phonological issues (sounds). The child may substitute, omit, or transpose sounds or syllables.

Examples
What are you do? (syllable omission)
Why are you indo that? (syllable transposition)

The third set of written errors that often characterizes the writing of children and adolescents suffering from Disorder of Written Expression involves impairment of visuospatial perception. Symptomatically, this problem is manifested in the writing of these individuals by inversion, deletion, substitution, and transposition of letters as well as a delayed rate of visual perception.

Examples
Wher are you going tonit?
Whta is the prupose of this?
Why are you criyng?

Assessment   No single clinical assessment tool can diagnose the presence of this disorder. Learning disabilities involving writing must be evaluated on the basis of the child's performance on several writing tasks, including dictation, copying, and spontaneous writing exercises. Gregg (1992) recommends assessment of spelling; written syntax, including grammar ties, transitional ties, lexical ties, and coherence; and general text organization, including sense of audience, social cognitive skills, ideation/abstraction, and handwriting.

Treatment   Interventions for Expressive Writing Disorder typically take two basic forms. In the first, the clinician works with the patient in an individualized program of writing instruction and practice, focusing on the child's area of difficulty. Special provisions are usually made in the child's classroom setting to aid him or her in coping with daily academic demands. Such interventions may include help from note takers, use of laptop or notebook computers and/or typewriters, and/or altering the demands placed upon the child to minimize the amount of writing required.

Mathematics Disorder (Developmental Arithmetic Disorder)

Clinical Presentation Mathematics disorder (referred to previously as Developmental Arithmetic Disorder) is applied as a diagnosis when the child's mathematical ability is both significantly below his or her capabilities in other areas and significantly below that expected at the child's developmental level.

The degree of impairment can vary dramatically. There are four basic factors involved in the mathematical process (see Johnson, 1988): language skills; visuospatial skills, verbal ability, and ability to reason quantitatively. A vast range of symptomatic presentation is possible within this single diagnosis. The *ICD-10* lists the following symptoms as typical of children and adolescents with Mathematics Disorder:

Failure to understand the concepts underlying particular arithmetical operations

Lack of understanding of mathematical terms or signs

Failure to recognize numerical symbols

Difficulty in carrying out standard arithmetical manipulations

Difficulty in understanding which numbers are relevant to the arithmetical problem being considered

Difficulty in properly aligning numbers or in inserting decimal points or symbols during calculations

Poor spatial organization of arithmetical calculations

Inability to learn multiplication tables satisfactorily

Diagnosis Box 9.11 presents the *DSM-IV* diagnostic criteria for Mathematics Disorder.

---

box**9.11**

Diagnostic Criteria for Mathematics Disorder

A. Mathematical ability, as measured by individually administered standardized tests, is substantially below that expected given the person's chronological age, measured intelligence, and age-appropriate education.

B. The disturbance in Criterion A significantly interferes with academic achievement or activities of daily living that require mathematical ability.

C. If a sensory deficit is present, the learning difficulties are in excess of those usually associated with it.

Source: American Psychiatric Association, *DSM-IV*, p. 51. Reprinted with permission from the *Diagnostic and Statistical Manual of Mental Disorders*, Fourth Edition. Copyright © 1994 American Psychiatric Association.

Assessment The disorder is assessed through use of a standardized intelligence test such as the WISC-3 or the WRAT. Data obtained from the measure of choice are analyzed in terms of the child's absolute and relative strengths and weaknesses.

Treatment As with the other learning disabilities, treatment interventions focus on special education aimed at facilitating the development of the mathematical skills that are deficient.

Summary

The Developmental Disorders are best conceptualized as conditions rather than disease entities. Mental Retardation, the Pervasive Developmental Disorders, and the Specific Developmental Disorders have a presumed organic etiology. Clinical symptoms of these disorders reflect some type of cognitive impairment. Treatment approaches, which vary both across syndromes as well as within a single syndrome, depend on the severity of impairment as well as the manifest symptomatology.

Mental Retardation itself cannot be treated as such, although the child's environment can be modified to accommodate impairments in functioning. The most severely retarded are usually placed in group homes where their needs for constant care and supervision can be met. Moderately retarded children and adults may be able to do simple jobs, but they are not able to manage independent lives. Mildly retarded people are often able to live in the community, although they may need some assistance with finances.

The Pervasive Mental Disorders cover a wide range of diagnoses. Autism, Rett's Disorder, Asperger's Disorder, and Childhood Disintegrative Disorder all involve major disruptions in normal mental functioning. These conditions cannot be cured, although psychopharmacological and behavioral interventions may ameliorate some of the symptoms. Family involvement in therapy is often helpful as well.

Specific Developmental Disorders (learning disorders) may involve speech, writing, reading, or mathematical skills. These disorders may coexist or may appear singly; they do not indicate that the patient is mentally retarded. Special education methods have been designed to help these children overcome the difficulties they face in acquiring academic skills.

References

American Association of Mental Retardation (AAMR). (1992). *Mental retardation: Definition, classification and systems of supports* (9th ed.). Washington, DC: Author.

Barr, M. W. (1905). Classification of mental defectives. *Journal of Psycho-Asthenics, 9*(2), 35.

Bartak, L., & Rutter, M. (1976). Differences between mental retardation and normally intelligent autistic children. *Journal of Autism and Childhood Schizophrenia, 6,* 109–120.

Blacher, J., & Baker, B. L. (1994). Family involvement in residential treatment of children with retardation: Is there evidence of detachment? *Journal of Child Psychology and Psychiatry and Allied Disciplines, 35,* 505–520.

Cantwell, D. P. (1992). Foreword. In S. R. Hooper, G. W. Hynd, & R. E. Mattison (Eds.), *Developpmental disorders: Diagnostic criteria and clinical assessment* (pp. ix–xvi). Hillsdale, NJ: Erlbaum.

Dawson, G., & Castile, P. (1992). Autism. In C. E. Walker & W. C. Roberts, (Eds.), *Handbook of clinical child psychology* (2nd ed.). New York: Wiley.

Ehlers, S., & Gillberg, C. (1993). The epidemiology of Asperger syndrome: A total population study. *Journal of Child Psychology and Psychiatry and Allied Disciplines, 34*, 1327–1350.

Donnellan, A. M., Mirenda, P. L., Mesaros, R. A., & Fassbender, L. L. (1984). Analyzing the communicative functions of aberrant behavior. *Journal of the Association for Persons with Severe Handicaps, 9*, 201–212.

Ghaziuddin, M., Tsai, L. Y., & Ghaziuddin, N. (1992). Brief report: A comparison of the diagnostic criteria for Asperger syndrome. *Journal of Autism and Developmental Disorders, 22*, 643–649.

Grossman, H. J. (1977). *Manual on terminology and classification in mental retardation.* Washington, DC: AAMD.

Hagberg, B. A. (1989). Rett syndrome: Clinical peculiarities, diagnostic approach and possible cause. *Pediatric Neurology, 5*, 75–83.

Heber, R. (1961). Modification of the *Manual on terminology and classification in mental retardation. American Journal of Mental Deficiency, 65*, 499–500.

Hooper, S. R., and Willis, W. G. (1989). *Learning disabilities subtyping: Neuropsychological foundations, conceptual models, and issues in clinical differentiation.* New York: Springer-Verlag.

Johnson, C. N. Theory of mind and the structure of conscious experience. In J. W. Astington, P. L. Harris, & D. R. Olson (Eds.), *Developing theories of mind* (pp. 47–63). Cambridge: Cambridge University Press.

Kanner, L. (1943). Autistic disturbances of affective contact. *Nervous Child, 2*, 217–250.

Kanner, L. (1954). To what extent is early infantile autism determined by constitutional inadequacies? *Association for Research on Nervous and Mental Diseases, 33*, 378–385.

Kaplan, H. I., & Sadock, B. J. (1991). *Synopsis of psychiatry: Behavioral Sciences—Clinical Psychiatry* (6th ed.). Baltimore: Williams & Wilkins.

Kolvin, I., Ousted, C., Richardson, L. M., & Garsice, R. (1971). Studies in childhood psychoses. Part 2. The phenomenology of childhood psychoses. *British Journal of Psychiatry, 118*, 396–402.

Lord, C., Rutter, M., & LeCouteur, A. (1994). Autism Diagnostic Interview–Revised: A revised version of a diagnostic interview for caregivers of individuals with pervasive developmental disorders. *Journal of Autism and Developmental Disorders, 24*, 659–685.

Lovaas, O. I. (1977). *The autistic child: Language development through behavior modification.* New York: Irvington.

Lovaas, O. I. (1987). Behavioral treatment and normal educational and intellectual functioning in young autistic children. *Journal of Consulting and Clinical Psychology, 55*, 3–9.

Lovaas, O. I., Koegel, R. L., & Schreibman, L. (1979). Stimulus overselectivity in autism: A review of research. *Psychological Bulletin, 86*, 1236–1254.

Marcus, L. M., & Schopler, E. (1991). Parents as co-therapists with autistic children. In C. E. Schaefer & J. M. Briesmeister (Eds.), *Handbook of parent training.* New York: Wiley.

Nihira, K., Foster, R., Shellhaas, X., & Leland, H. (1974). *AAMD Adaptive Behavior Scale—1974 revision.* Washington, DC: American Association on Mental Deficiency.

Reiss, S., & Valenti-Hein, D. (1994). Development of a psychopathology rating scale for children with mental retardation. *Journal of Consulting and Clinical Psychology, 62,* 28–33.

Rett, A. (1966). *Ueber ein cerebral–Atrophisches syndrome bei hyper-ammonamie.* Vienna: Bruder Hollenck.

Rimland, B. (1964). *Infantile autism: The syndrome and its implication for a neural theory of behavior.* New York: Appleton-Century-Crofts.

Ritvo, E. R., & Freeman, B. J. (1978). National Society for Autistic Children definition of autism. *Journal of Autism and Developmental Disorders, 8,* 162–167.

Rutter, M. (1968). Concepts of autism: A review of research. *Journal of Child Psychology and Psychiatry, 9,* 1–25.

Rutter, M. (1970). Autistic children: Infancy to adulthood. *Seminars in Psychiatry, 2,* 435–450.

Rutter, M. (1978). Diagnoses and definition. In M. Rutter and E. Schopler (Eds.), *Autism: A reappraisal of concepts and treatment.* New York: Plenum.

Schopler, E., Andrews, C. E., & Strupp, K. (1979). Do autistic children come from upper-middle-class parents? *Journal of Autism and Developmental Disorders, 9,* 139–152.

Smith, B., Chung, M. C., & Vostanis, P. (1994). The path to care in autism: Is it better now? *Journal of Autism and Developmental Disorders, 24,* 551–563.

Sparrow, S., Balla, D. A., & Cicchetti, D. V. (1984). *Vineland Adaptive Behavior Scales.* Circle Pines, MN: American Guidance Service.

Szymanski, L. S., & Crocker, A. C. (1989). Mental retardation. In H. I. Kaplan & B. J. Sadock (Eds.), *Comprehensive textbook of psychiatry: Vol. 5.* Baltimore: Williams & Wilkins.

Szymanski, L. S., & Kaplan, L. C. (1991). Mental retardation. In J. M. Wiener (Ed.), *Textbook of child and adolescent psychiatry.* Washington, DC: American Psychiatric Press.

Terman, L. M. (1916). *The measurement of intelligence.* Boston: Houghton Mifflin.

Waterhouse, L., Wing, L., Spitzer, R., & Siegel, B. (1992). Pervasive developmental disorders: From DSM-III to DSM-III-R. *Journal of Autism and Developmental Disorders, 22,* 525–549.

Yirmiya, N., & Sigman, M. (1991). High functioning individuals with autism: Diagnosis, emipirical findings and theoretical issues. *Clinical Psychology Review, 11,* 669–683.

Young, J. G., Newcorn, J. H., & Leven, L. I. (1989). Pervasive developmental disorders. In H. I. Kaplan & B. J. Sadock (Eds.), *Comprehensive textbook of psychiatry: Vol. 5.* Baltimore: Williams & Wilkins.

Chapter ten
Disruptive and Attention Deficit Behavior Disorders

"He was the sort of tigger who was always in front when
you were showing him the way anywhere, and was generally out of sight when at last you came to the place and
said proudly 'Here we are.'"

A. A. Milne, *The House at Pooh Corner*

Introduction

Disruptive and Attention Deficit Behavior Disorders are similar in the nature of their general symptomatic presentation. For both diagnoses, some form of disruptive behavior is the primary presenting symptom. Although behavior is affected by virtually all psychopathologies of childhood and adolescence, in the case of these two diagnostic categories, behavior is the major presenting symptom.

The diagnoses of Conduct Disorder and Oppositional Defiant Disorders, frequently considered as representing an extreme of misbehavior, are applied to those children and adolescents whose behavior severely impairs the sense of well-being experienced by those around them. The diagnosis of Attention Deficit Hyperactivity Disorder (ADHD) is applied to children who are unable to focus their attention or who manifest developmentally inappropriate symptoms of impulsivity and/or activity. These symptoms affect the child's ability to function within social and/or academic realms. As with the diagnoses of Conduct Disorder and Oppositional Defiant Disorder, the overt symptoms of the ADHD child frequently affect other people in negative ways.

First we will discuss Conduct Disorder and Oppositional Defiant Disorder, considering clinical presentation, epidemiology, diagnostic issues, and treatment of each of the two diagnoses. Next we will cover Attention Deficit Hyperactivity Disorder.

Conduct Disorder

Concepts

Conduct Disorder is the most common clinical problem in both child and adolescent patients. A diagnosis of Conduct Disorder is applied when a child or adolescent chronically presents a behavior pattern that involves either violating the basic rights of other individuals or violating societal age-appropriate norms and rules. This definition, however, leaves room for subjectivity. First, the specific behaviors that are considered crucial in making this diagnosis depend on the norms established by the given culture and/or society. Second, the clinician must exercise judgment regarding the length of time required for symptoms to be considered a "persistent pattern." For these and other reasons, the classification of Conduct Disorders has long been recognized as a problematic issue.

The first edition of the *DSM*, which did not specifically address the psychopathologies of childhood and adolescence, did not contain diagnostic criteria for Conduct Disorder. The *DSM-II* included a diagnostic category called Unsocialized Aggressive Reaction of Childhood or Adolescence in the more general category of Behavior Disorders of Childhood and Adolescence. Not surprisingly, the diagnostic criteria utilized to describe Unsocialized Aggressive Reaction of Childhood or Adolescence were more pejorative than objectively scientific in character, describing these children and adolescents as manifesting "disobedient, quarrelsome, aggressive, or destructive behavior."

The *DSM-III* included two separate descriptions of the diagnostic criteria for Conduct Disorder. One was classified in "Disorders Usually First Seen in Childhood," and the other was considered a childhood version of the adult Antisocial Personality Disorder. The childhood criteria described four subtypes of Conduct Disorder: Undersocialized Aggressive, Undersocialized Nonaggressive, Socialized Aggressive, and Socialized Non-Aggressive. As criteria for the diagnosis of Childhood Antisocial Personality Disorder, the *DSM-III* included delinquency, school suspension, promiscuous sexual misconduct, and underachievement, in addition to eight of the symptoms characteristic of conduct disorder.

The *DSM-III-R* published in 1987, modified the classification of the conduct disorders into one diagnostic category with three subtypes: Group, Solitary Aggressive, and Undifferentiated. A diagnosis of Childhood Antisocial Personality remained in this classification system; however, the diagnostic criteria were modified somewhat.

The *DSM-IV* eliminates the subtypes of Conduct Disorder, with the exception of those specifying severity (i.e., mild, moderate, severe) and age of onset (i.e., childhood onset type, adolescent onset type). The specific criteria are listed in the section on diagnostic issues.

Clinical Presentation

The clinical presentation of children and adolescents with Conduct Disorder varies according to developmental level as well as gender. In fact, conduct disorder has been conceptualized as the "application of the concept of antisocial behavior to a developmental stage" (Malmquist, 1991).

Clinical symptoms of Conduct Disorder in the preschool age range consist primarily of an exaggeration of developmentally expected temper tantrum behavior. Typically, this is accompanied by general oppositional and/or negativistic behavior, poor impulse control, motor activity impairment, and inattentiveness.

Case Study 10.1

Four-year-old Johnny was brought to a psychologist by his parents because of severe behavioral difficulties. According to his parents, for the past 8 months the child has been impossible to manage. His behavior is very different from the typical "terrible two's" behavior he manifested some 18 months ago. The parents say that Johnny is "out of control." Whenever he is asked to do something he doesn't want to do, he screams "No!" and then grabs the nearest object and smashes it to the floor. When his parents attempt to restrain him, he becomes violent, hitting, punching, or flinging his arms and legs around wildly.

Elementary school Conduct Disorder patients tend to be more blatantly aggressive than preschoolers. Physical and verbal aggression, both with peers and toward parents, is the primary behavioral symptom. At this age, conduct-disordered children are likely to begin stealing, first from the home and later from others outside the home. They often begin lying and cheating, and intentional cruelty to animals is common. These children are very likely to be disruptive in school.

Case Study 10.2

Eight-year-old Lori has been referred to the school psychologist because of some intractable behavior patterns that have been worsening over the past few months. Besides attempting to disrupt class virtually every day, Lori takes personal belongings from other children's desks. When interviewed, Lori's parents report that small sums of money have been missing at home.

By the time the conduct-disordered child reaches adolescence, physical acting out decreases in frequency, but when it does occur, it is more intense. Truancy becomes more prevalent, as does acting out within a group context. Prevalent symptoms of conduct-disordered adolescents are vandalism, sexual acting out, and substance abuse. Those adolescents whose Conduct Disorder had its onset in childhood tend to manifest more serious symptomatology than those with a later onset.

Case Study 10.3

Mr. and Mrs. B. received a call from their son's guidance counselor, who told them that their son Lee, age 15, had not been in school for the past three days. The reason for the call, however, was that Lee was found spray-painting obscenities on the outside walls of a vacant building two blocks from the school. This was not the first time that Lee had been truant; however, the parents had never received any reports of vandalism previously.

Diagnosis

The *DSM-IV* diagnostic criteria for Conduct Disorder are presented in Box 10.1.

box**10.1**

Diagnostic Criteria for Conduct Disorder

A. A repetitive and persistent pattern of behavior in which the basic rights of others or major age-appropriate societal norms or rules are violated, as manifested by the presence of three (or more) of the following criteria in the past 12 months, with at least one criterion present in the past 6 months:

Aggression to People and Animals

1. Often bullies, threatens, or intimidates others
2. Often initiates physical fights
3. Has used a weapon that can cause serious physical harm to others (e.g., a bat, brick, broken bottle, knife, gun)
4. Has been physically cruel to people
5. Has been physically cruel to animals
6. Has stolen while confronting a victim (e.g., mugging, purse snatching, extortion, armed robbery)
7. Has forced someone into sexual activity

Destruction of Property

8. Has deliberately engaged in fire setting with the intention of causing serious damage
9. Has deliberately destroyed others' property (other than by fire setting)

Deceitfulness or Theft

10. Has broken into someone else's house, building, or car
11. Often lies to obtain goods or favors or to avoid obligations (i.e., "cons" others)
12. Has stolen items of nontrivial value without confronting a victim (e.g., shoplifting, but without breaking and entering; forgery)

Serious Violations of Rules

13. Often stays out at night despite parental prohibitions, beginning before age 13 years
14. Has run away from home overnight at least twice while living in parental or parental surrogate home (or once without returning for a lengthy period)
15. Is often truant from school, beginning before age 13 years

B. The disturbance in behavior causes clinically significant impairment in social, academic, or occupational functioning.

C. If the individual is age 18 years or older, criteria are not met for Antisocial Personality Disorder.

Source: American Psychiatric Association, *DSM-IV,* pp. 90–91. Reprinted with permission from the *Diagnostic and Statistical Manual of Mental Disorders,* Fourth Edition. Copyright © 1994 American Psychiatric Association.

Potential alternatives to a diagnosis of Conduct Disorder are quite numerous. Some clinicians consider the range of alternatives as encompassing the entire diagnostic spectrum of child and adolescent psychopathology (Lewis, 1991). Many of the other diagnostic categories include maladaptive behavior or conduct problems as part of their manifest symptomatology. Indeed, almost any psychopathology of childhood and adolescence can present as a behavioral and/or conduct disturbance. Some of the more commonly encountered pathologies that must be distinguished from Conduct Disorders are Mood Disorders, Substance Usage, Psychotic Disorders, Learning Disorders, Oppositional Defiant Disorder, Mild Mental Retardation, Adjustment Disorders, Seizure Disorders, and Attention Deficit Hyperactivity Disorder.

In the majority of cases, the issue of differential diagnosis for Conduct Disorder revolves around the question of the etiological nature of the symptomatology. To make decisions regarding differential diagnosis, the clinician must determine whether the conduct problems are primary in nature or secondary to another disorder. Thorough assessment of the history, frequency, intensity, and overall pattern of the symptoms is likely to answer this question.

The relationship, if any, between the occurrence of conduct disorders and psychopathy is an often investigated topic of research. This issue is well represented in the adult literature, but it is just beginning to be investigated with respect to children and adolescents. One group of researchers (Frick, O'Brien, Wootton, & McBurnett, 1994) examined the relationship between psychopathy and conduct problems in a sample of 95 children ages 6 through 13 years referred to a clinic, concluding that psychopathy and conduct problems are independent but interacting constructs.

Assessment

In a discussion of the diagnostic criteria for Conduct Disorder and its clinical assessment, Routh and Daugherty (1992) summarize the types of assessment instruments pertinent to Conduct Disorder: parent measures (e.g., Children's Assessment Schedule, Conners Parent Rating Scale, various standardized parent interviews); teacher ratings and measures of school behavior (e.g., Conners Teacher Rating Scale, Revised Problem Checklist); child interviews and questionnaires (e.g., Child Assessment Schedule, Diagnostic Interview for Children and Adolescents); and standardized behavioral observation systems (e.g., Dyadic Parent-Child Interactive Coding System). Another method entails obtaining information from the child's peer group. Clinicians and researchers agree that most individuals completing these assessment measures tend to underreport the child's symptoms, so it is generally recommended that data be obtained from more than one source (Robins, 1991). Of course, the analysis of any discrepancies in data obtained from different sources also provides valuable clinical information (see also Hinshaw, Han, Erhardt, & Huber, 1992).

Epidemiology

Epidemiological estimates put the prevalence of Conduct Disorder in the United States at around 10 percent, with a predominance of males over females for violent behaviors (8:1) and vandalism (4:1). This discrepancy in gender distribution becomes less dramatic (2:1) when the source of the epidemiological data is primarily self-report (Dulcan & Popper, 1991). Estimates of incidence in European and Canadian populations are somewhat lower, ranging from 3.2 to 6.9 percent (Robins, 1991).

Etiology

Theories about the etiology of Conduct Disorder are varied. The more biologically oriented theories rely on the fact that Attention Deficit and Conduct Disorders often coexist in the same child. These theories are discussed in the section on the etiology of Attention Deficit Hyperactivity disorder.

Other theories of the etiology of Conduct Disorder take a psychosocial approach. Sociocultural perspectives explain conduct problems as arising from the limitations placed upon the child because of his or her socioeconomic status. Because it is difficult for these children to make socially expected achievements, they attempt to reach for status through more aggressive means. A cultural issue arises because behavior conceptualized as conduct disordered by the society at large may simply represent the norms of the child's peer group.

A closely related line of reasoning looks to the familial situation as a primary factor in the etiology of Conduct Disorder. The relationship between a disruptive family situation and Conduct Disorder can be attributed to any of several factors. Whether the major problem is parental psychopathology, substance abuse by family members, physical or emotional abuse, pathological interaction patterns, or simply familial dysfunction, any combination of these factors can contribute to the development of Conduct Disorder. Both modeling theory and psychodynamic theory regard parental antisocial behavior as an etiological factor in the development of conduct disorder; for example, psychodynamic theory posits that children unconsciously act out the wishes of their parents.

Another theory that takes psychosocial factors into account focuses on risk factors. Rather than conceptualizing psychosocial factors as directly causing the development of Conduct Disorders, this theory regards certain environmental variables as making the manifestation of Conduct Disorder more likely. Many risk factor studies focus on the development of antisocial behavior, then extrapolate their findings to child and adolescent conduct disorders. Such data are far from conclusive, but therapists need to be aware of which environmental factors are most commonly considered to be risk factors. Malmquist (1991) summarizes these influences as follows: family conflict, familial psychopathology, birth position (with middle children at greater risk than firstborn, youngest, or only children), large family size, harsh or inconsistent disciplinary techniques, poor quality of schooling, and low socioeconomic class.

Think About It

Biochemical Factors Associated with Conduct Disorder

A recent publication reported the results of an investigation into the association between various biochemical factors and Conduct Disorders in boys. One reported result was that the blood level of homovanillic acid was significantly lower in conduct-disordered boys under age 12 than in normal boys in the control group. Does this study confirm that homovanillic acid is involved in the etiology of Conduct Disorder?

Treatment

Not surprisingly, the treatment approaches for children and adolescents with Conduct Disorder are predominantly behavioral in orientation. There is significant variability with respect to therapeutic technique, however; this orientation encompasses "pure" behavioral techniques as well as cognitive behavioral techniques. In addition, the format of the therapy varies, ranging from traditional individual therapy to more systems-oriented approaches involving the entire family as well as other people in the patient's academic environment. In one variation, the therapist trains the parents and/or teachers to act as cotherapists for the conduct-disordered child. Empirical studies are just beginning to investigate the dynamics underlying the relative efficacy of each of these methods (e.g., Szapocznik, Kurtines, Santisteban, & Rio, 1990).

The "pure" behavioral approaches to the treatment of Conduct Disorder are based on the principles of operant conditioning. With the primary goal being the reduction or elimination of the problematic behavior patterns, the clinician devises selective reinforcement programs. After operationally defining the target behaviors, the therapist compiles a list of reinforcing experiences for the child. Such behavioral therapies often incorporate an element of contingency management, frequently employing response cost or similar techniques that serve as punishing experiences designed to eliminate the problem behaviors. Behavioral approaches to the treatment of Conduct Disorder do not limit their focus to the child's behavior. Indeed, a major goal of such interventions is to alter the child's social environment as a means of achieving desired behavioral changes.

Cognitive-behavioral therapies utilize a wide variety of methods that attempt to modify the target behaviors by working therapeutically with the associated cognitions. Methods used in the cognitive-behavioral treatment of Conduct Disorder include video-mediated recall; thought-listing procedures (Sanders & Dadds, 1992); self-statement modification, used independently or combined with problem solving and/or relaxation training; silent reading of an instructional set (Baer & Nietzel, 1991); training in coping and problem solving; modeling; self-reinforcement for appropriate behavior; and coping self-statements (Kendall, Reber, McLeer, Epps, & Ronan, 1990). Clearly, the cognitive-behavioral strategies and the operant-based models are complimentary. Elements of the latter are found in the cognitive approaches.

The family is given a pivotal role in the operant and cognitive-behavioral approaches. Although only the more recent approaches acknowledge parents as cotherapists in the treatment of their offspring, clinicians have always recognized the necessity of familial support and direct family involvement in any behavioral therapy.

Partially because of this growing acknowledgment of the parents' therapeutic role, over the past few years several empirical studies have attempted to examine the parents' role in the treatment of Conduct Disorder from a more systematized perspective (Roberts, Joe, & Rowe-Halbert, 1992). Despite earlier findings to the contrary, formal parental involvement tends to generalize positively to the school setting; that is, the child's behavior improves in environments outside of the home (McNeil, Eyberg, Eisenstadt, Newcomb, & Funderburk, 1991).

Oppositional Defiant Disorder

Concepts

Somewhat similar to the symptoms of Conduct Disorder, the major characteristics of Oppositional Defiant Disorder center around problematic behavior patterns in the child or adolescent. Although children with Oppositional Defiant Disorder (ODD) do not exhibit the inappropriate violation of interpersonal rights (e.g., cruelty, coercion, property damage)
characteristic of Conduct Disorder, ODD individuals are typified by an overall pattern of defiant, oppositionally negativistic, and hostile behavior, most often directed toward adults in authority (usually teachers and/or parents).

Although some investigators conceptualize the history of American child psychiatry as primarily the history of the diagnosis and treatment of children with ODD (Cantwell, 1989), this
diagnosis was not listed in the first two editions of the *DSM*. The *DSM-III* first presented diagnostic criteria for Oppositional Disorder. The *DSM-III-R* renamed this entity as Oppositional Defiant Disorder, grouping it under the general heading of Disruptive Behavior Disorders. Some children with ODD, however, develop symptoms of Conduct Disorder as they
mature.

Clinical Presentation

ODD children and adolescents exhibit a chronic defiance of requests, rules, or demands is-
sued by those in authority positions. These children seem to be purposefully intent on annoying others with their noncompliance, yet their behavior seems to be more passive than the annoying behaviors in Conduct Disorder. Rather than engaging in overtly aggressive physical
acting out, the ODD child tends to express his or her pathology in a somewhat more passive
manner, predominantly by refusing to be cooperative.

Symptom presentation varies greatly among ODD individuals. Symptomatology consists of
exaggerated versions of typical problems, which depend on the child's developmental level.
When symptoms of ODD appear at an early age, parents often perceive the child to be "bad"
or "tough." This perception initiates a cycle in which the parents' demeanor toward the child
is altered, in turn affecting the child's subsequent behavior.

No single area of oppositional behavior predominates in ODD individuals. The symptomatic behavior changes with environment and developmental level. Oftentimes, the major issue of opposition is as simple as the most recent parental demand. With a pattern of "forget-
ting" and/or "not hearing" requests, the ODD child or adolescent continually provokes adults,
who respond with punitive and hostile behavior. Typically the ODD child blames other people
for the problem and then loses control.

ODD children and adolescents have considerable difficulty in interpersonal relationships.
They often feel victimized by those in authority as well as by their peers. Perceiving the world
as being unjustly critical and punitive, they feel constantly attacked and generally suffer from
low self-esteem (Egan, 1991). Another characteristic of ODD children in their interpersonal
relationships is a self-sabotaging approach to disagreements and power struggles. The issue of
"winning" an argument often takes on a life of its own, and the ODD individual will lose
something he or she wants in order to be perceived as victorious in the power struggle (Dulcan & Popper, 1991).

Case Study 10.4

**Eight-year-old Arthur was referred to a private psychologist at the recommendation of his
school guidance counselor. For the past several months he has refused to do any assign-**

ments in class, and he has repeatedly sabotaged the teacher's lessons. Arthur claims that nobody in school likes him, and he says that the teacher "picks on him" the same way his parents "mistreat" him at home. When Arthur's parents were consulted, they said that their son is no problem unless he is asked to do something he does not want to do. If a request is made of the boy, he first pretends not to hear. If the parent persists, Arthur gives several reasons why someone else should do the task instead of him. He typically escalates into a temper tantrum, prompting the parents to begin yelling at him. Once the parents demonstrate significant upset, Arthur seems to calm down almost automatically and returns to whatever he was doing prior to the request.

Diagnosis

The *DSM-IV* presents the diagnostic criteria for Oppositional Defiant Disorder listed in Box 10.2.

box **10.2**

Diagnostic Criteria for Oppositional Defiant Disorder

A. A pattern of negativistic, hostile, and defiant behavior lasting at least 6 months, during which four (or more) of the following are present:

1. Often loses temper
2. Often argues with adults
3. Often actively defies or refuses to comply with adults' requests or rules
4. Often deliberately annoys other people
5. Often blames others for his or her mistakes or misbehavior
6. Is often touchy or easily annoyed by others
7. Is often angry and resentful
8. Is often spiteful or vindictive

Note: Consider a criterion met only if the behavior occurs more frequently than is typically observed in individuals of comparable age and developmental level.

B. The disturbance in behavior causes significant impairment in social, academic or occupational functioning.

C. The behaviors do not occur exclusively during the course of a Psychotic or Mood Disorder.

D. Does not meet criteria for Conduct Disorder and, if the individual is 18 or older, criteria are not met for Antisocial Personality Disorder.

Source: American Psychiatric Association, *DSM-IV,* pp. 93–94. Reprinted with permission from the *Diagnostic and Statistical Manual of Mental Disorders,* Fourth Edition. Copyright © 1994 American Psychiatric Association.

Therapists must differentiate cases of ODD from those situations in which the child or adolescent is simply manifesting behavior difficulties characteristic of a specific developmental stage. Individuals with a valid diagnosis of ODD differ from those who exhibit the expected parenting challenges that typify the "terrible two's" or adolescence, for example. Thus, the clinician must consider both the quality and the severity of the target symptomatology within the framework of developmental stages prior to applying a diagnosis of ODD. Episodes of oppositional behavior that occur in reaction to stress and/or trauma in a child's life are often more appropriately diagnosed as an Adjustment Disorder. The 6-month criterion for duration of ODD is typically sufficient to differentiate these other disorders.

Comorbidity issues are also important for differential diagnosis. Quite commonly, symptoms of ODD are manifested in children or adolescents with Depression, Attention Deficit Hyperactivity disorder, Hypomania, Mental Retardation, some psychotic disorders, and Separation Anxiety Disorder. In such situations, it is clinically relevant to determine whether the ODD symptoms are indeed the primary issue or are secondary to some other psychopathology.

Epidemiology

Estimates of the prevalence of ODD range from 2 to 20 percent of the general population. With respect to gender distribution, there is a male predominance of between 2:1 and 3:1.

Etiology

To some degree, the etiological theories of Oppositional Defiant Disorder parallel theories of Conduct Disorder, differing only in their specificity with respect to oppositionalism. Traditional psychoanalytic theory looks to unresolved conflicts during the anal stage of development (specifically conflicts around control issues) as a contributing etiological factor. According to this perspective, if these issues remain unresolved, the child carries them throughout life, and they manifest themselves as problems with authority figures.

Behavioral theories see Oppositional Defiant Disorder as emanating from the parents' unintentional reinforcement of oppositional behavior. This reinforcement is most often in the form of attention and/or yielding to the child's wishes, out of frustration or desperation. Once this pattern is established, the child soon learns to obtain what he or she wants by acting in a certain (undesirable) manner.

Finally, the more biologically oriented approaches explain ODD as the result of heredity or biological factors that predispose the child to develop the disorder. For example, temperament theorists purport that certain children are more strong-willed than others. If such children are born to parents for whom power and authority are important issues, power struggles will develop, which can result in the development of Oppositional Defiant Disorder. In addition, children suffering from certain traumas (e.g., Mental Retardation, physical anomalies) may develop an oppositional style of interacting as a means of defending against their feelings of helplessness and/or inadequacy (Kaplan & Sciatic, 1991).

A recent study (Grizenko & Pawliuk, 1994) investigated the risk factors and protective factors for disruptive behavior disorders in children. Comparing 50 children diagnosed with Conduct Disorder (mean age 9 years) with 50 control subjects, the study reported learning difficulties, hyperactivity, school failure, perinatal complications, and maternal depression as being significant risk factors.

Treatment

Treatment approaches for ODD closely resemble those employed for the other conduct disorders. Behavioral and cognitive-behavioral approaches are utilized within an individual, family systems, or parent training format, with the goal of minimizing and eventually eliminating the undesirable behavior patterns.

Think About It

Efficacy of Parent Training Approaches

As parent training interventions have become more popular treatments for the various conduct disorders, the long-term efficacy of such treatments has come into question. Several researchers (Long, Forehand, Wierson, & Morgan, 1994) conducted a 14-year follow-up study of 26 individuals ages 17 to 22 years who participated in a parent training–based treatment intervention when they were young children (ages 2 to 7). When these subjects were compared with a matched control group on measures of delinquency, emotional adjustment, academic progress, and relationship with their parents, no difference was found between the two groups. Although these data can be interpreted as supporting the efficacy of parent training programs, what other factors need to be investigated before we can make such a conclusion?

Attention Deficit Hyperactivity Disorder

Concepts

Phil stop acting like a worm
the table is no place to squirm
Thus speaks the father to his son
severely say it, not in fun.
Mother frowns and looks around
although she doesn't make a sound.
But Phillip will not take advice
he'll have his way at any price.
He turns and churns
he wriggles and jiggles
here and there on the chair.
Phil these twists I cannot bear.

This excerpt from a nineteenth-century German poem is quoted in a chapter on Attention Deficit Hyperactivity Disorder (Weiss, 1991, p. 544) designed to describe the syndrome to psychiatry students. Few childhood psychopathologies have generated as much controversy— or as many research articles—as Attention Deficit Hyperactivity Disorder (ADHD). ADHD is the most common diagnosis in child psychiatry clinics.

The multitude of diagnostic labels that have been applied to this syndrome reflects the changes in its conceptualization over the past century. Some diagnostic labels refer to brain pathology (e.g., Minimal Brain Damage, Minimal Brain Dysfunction); other labels focus on the agitated behavior of these children (e.g., Hyperactivity Syndrome, Hyperactive Impulse Disorder, Hyperactive Child Syndrome, Hyperkinetic Syndrome); and other labels are simply pejorative (e.g., Defective Inhibition, Impulsive Insanity). In the past three decades, the conceptualization of ADHD as a brain disorder began to give way. The *ICD-9,* published in 1965, and the *DSM-II,* published in 1968, relabeled the disorder as Hyperkinetic Syndrome of Childhood, emphasizing the agitated behavior of these patients as a primary symptom.

In the *DSM-III,* the description of symptoms moved away from the emphasis on restlessness and focused more on the individual's inability to modulate his or her own attention and arousal impulses. The diagnosis was renamed Attention Deficit Disorder, modified to indicate the presence or absence of the hyperactivity component. The *DSM-III* divided symptoms into three components: inattention, impulsivity, and restlessness.

Publication of the *DSM-III-R* in 1987 reflected the return in the conceptualization of this disorder to an emphasis on exaggerated motor activity, restlessness, and impulsivity. Changing the diagnostic label to Attention Deficit Hyperactivity Disorder and eliminating the category of Attention Deficit Disorder without Hyperactivity, the *DSM-III-R* listed 14 diagnostic criteria, of which at least 8 were required to make the diagnosis.

Clinical Presentation

As is common in the psychopathologies of childhood and adolescence, the clinical presentation of ADHD varies as a function of the developmental status of the individual. In a manual designed to provide practical information to parents of ADHD children and adolescents, Liden, Zalenski, and Newman (1989) provide checklists of symptoms considered typical of ADHD children at different ages. These symptoms, presented as warning signs, so to speak, yield a thorough description of how this disorder presents itself throughout the life span.

For the toddler (age range 1 to 3 years), the following symptoms are characteristic of this disorder: excessive moving about, apparently unfocused; seeming to be "accident-prone"; ingestion of nonedible household items; failing to respond to "no;" and seeming to repeatedly "get into things."

Symptoms evidenced in the preschool child ages 3 to 6 years include failure to take turns during play activities; failure to share during play; switching from one play activity to another; inability to sit at the table until the family has finished eating at mealtime; inability to maintain concentration in academic activities; seeming not to hear; failure to remain still for a story or puzzle activity; impulsive hitting, pushing, or biting of others; and fearlessness and recklessness during play. Parents are often asked to take these disruptive children out of preschool or day care.

The 6- to 12-year-old in elementary school typically manifests the following symptoms: failure to complete started activities, interruption of conversations, inability to take turns, digression from topic of conversation, switching from one play activity to another, failure to make eye contact in conversation, inability to complete basic chores without constant supervision, poor appearance, walking into doors and furniture, being accident-prone, getting into frequent fights, having friends who are either much younger or much older, and a general failure to respond to discipline. In school, these boys and girls tend to rush through their work without checking it over; they fail to finish schoolwork, partly because they are disorganized partly they make careless errors on simple problems; they talk out of turn in class; they forget and lose things, especially assignments; and they tend to lose their place during reading.

As the ADD patient reaches adolescence, the following symptoms tend to be characteristic: substance usage, extending beyond the experimentation level characteristic of this age group; truancy; legal difficulties; impairment in comprehension of higher-level reading materials; poor organizational and planning skills; poor attention to personal hygiene; poor social skills; impulsive behavior; temper outbursts; poor responsibility skills; interruption of others in conversation; and inability to remain on a topic when conversing.

Despite the variable presentation of this disorder, which differs with developmental level as well as gender, there is a core of symptom patterns based on those generally representative of the 6- to 11-year-old age group. This age group is chosen for two reasons: (1) this is the most frequent age of referral, and (2) the majority of clinical and empirical knowledge has been obtained from work with children in this age group. The seven core symptoms are conceptualized by Weiss (1991, p. 547) as follows:

1. *Inappropriate or excessive activity, unrelated to the task at hand, which generally has an intrusive or annoying quality*
2. *Poor sustained attention*
3. *Difficulties in inhibiting impulses in social behavior and on cognitive tasks*
4. *Difficulties getting along with others*
5. *Other, coexisting externalizing behavior disorders (i.e., oppositional defiant disorder or conduct disorder) and, frequently concomitant specific learning disabilities*
6. *School underachievement*
7. *Poor self-esteem secondary to the above*

A recent study (Mantzicopoulos & Morrison, 1994) compared normal children to those with attention deficit problems. The children ranged from kindergarten age through second grade. The researchers compared performance on various academic and behavioral variables. Subjects who were labeled "at risk" for attention deficit exhibited more behavior problems, showing an increase in these problems from kindergarten to second grade. There were also statistically significant differences in reading achievement and certain processing tasks.

Think About It

Developmental Level and Diagnosis of ADD

To what degree should clinicians consider the developmental level of a child who is being assessed for an ADD diagnosis? Pearson and Aman (1994) investigated this issue in a sample of 113 children ages 5 to 16 years and found a consistently negative correlation between chronological age and severity of hyperactivity symptoms. However, no such relationship was found when investigating the relationship between symptom severity and "mental age" of the child. How would you interpret this apparent discrepancy in results?

In addition to the confirming symptoms viewed as characteristic of ADHD itself, recent research consistently finds that these children are more likely than those in the general population to suffer from other psychopathologies. Although the symptoms of ADHD can also be indicators of other diagnoses, there is a clinical and statistical propensity for ADHD patients to carry other psychological diagnoses.

Diagnosis

The *DSM-IV* diagnostic criteria for Attention Deficit Hyperactivity Disorder are presented in Box 10.3.

---

box **10.3**

Diagnostic Criteria for Attention Deficit Hyperactivity Disorder

A. Either (1) or (2):

1. Six (or more) of the following symptoms of *inattention* have persisted for at least 6 months to a degree that is maladaptive and inconsistent with developmental level:

Inattention

   a. Often fails to give close attention to details or makes careless mistakes in schoolwork, work, or other activities
   b. Often has difficulty sustaining attention in tasks or play activities
   c. Often does not seem to listen when spoken to directly
   d. Often does not follow through on instructions and fails to finish schoolwork, chores, or duties in the workplace (not due to oppositional behavior or failure to understand instructions)
   e. Often has difficulty organizing tasks and activities
   f. Often avoids, dislikes, or is reluctant to engage in tasks that require sustained mental effort (such as schoolwork or homework)
   g. Often loses things necessary for tasks or activities (e.g., toys, school assignments, pencils, books, or tools)
   h. Is often easily distracted by extraneous stimuli
   i. Is often forgetful in daily activities

2. Six (or more) of the following symptoms of *hyperactivity–impulsivity* have persisted for at least 6 months to a degree that is maladaptive and inconsistent with developmental level:

Hyperactivity

   a. Often fidgets with hands or feet or squirms in seat
   b. Often leaves seat in classroom or in other situations in which remaining seated is expected
   c. Often runs about or climbs excessively in situations in which it is inappropriate (in adolescents or adults, may be limited to subjective feelings of restlessness)
   d. Often has difficulty playing or engaging in leisure activities quietly

e. Is often "on the go" or often acts as if "driven by a motor"

f. Often talks excessively

Impulsivity

g. Often blurts out answers before questions have been completed

h. Often has difficulty awaiting turn

i. Often interrupts or intrudes on others (e.g., butts into conversations or games)

B. Some hyperactive-impulsive or inattentive symptoms that caused impairment were present before age 7 years.

C. Some impairment from the symptoms is present in two or more settings (e.g., at school [or work] and at home).

D. There must be clear evidence of clinically significant impairment in social, academic, or occupational functioning.

E. The symptoms do not occur exclusively during the course of a Pervasive Developmental Disorder, Schizophrenia, or other Psychotic Disorder and are not better accounted for by another mental disorder (e.g., Mood Disorder, Anxiety Disorder, Dissociative Disorder, or a Personality Disorder).

Source: American Psychiatric Association, *DSM-IV*, pp. 83–85. Reprinted with permission from the *Diagnostic and Statistical Manual of Mental Disorders,* Fourth Edition. Copyright © 1994 American Psychiatric Association.

Issues of differential diagnosis with respect to ADHD are especially relevant for several reasons. As mentioned earlier in this chapter, several other diagnoses have symptoms of ADHD as part of their presentation, and it is not uncommon for ADHD to exist concomitantly with other psychopathologies. Further, it is imperative that parents, school personnel, and clinicians be familiar with the developmentally appropriate behavior for children in different age group so as not to pathologize age-appropriate overactivity.

Among the major diagnostic categories that can be confused with ADHD are Adjustment Disorders, distinguishable from ADHD by the shorter duration of symptoms and later age of onset; Conduct and/or Oppositional Defiant Disorders, distinguishable by the lesser severity of the attention deficit symptomatology; and specific learning disabilities, wherein the attention deficit symptoms are a result of the child's boredom due to specific cognitive difficulties. It is also important to note that psychotic disorders, Mania, Major Depression, and various anxiety disorders can also present with symptoms of ADHD.

Think About It

The ADD Spectrum

Is ADD a single disorder, or is it more accurately conceptualized as three separate entities (i.e., inattentiveness, impulsivity, and hyperactivity)? This was the issue investigated in a re-cent study (deQuiros, Kinsbourne, Palmer, & Rufo, 1994) of 116 children ages 6 to 16 years. Analyses revealed that children who manifested these three groups of symptoms were simi-lar on several measures. The authors therefore concluded that the three symptoms are best viewed as differing clinical presentations of an ADD spectrum. From what you have read and whatever contact you have had with ADD children, what is your opinion on this matter?

Epidemiology

Estimates of the prevalence of ADHD in the general population range from 3 percent for girls to 9 or 10 percent for boys. When the sample population is restricted to child psychiatric out-patients, the overall figure increases to 40 to 70 percent (Dulcan & Popper, 1991).

Assessment

Perhaps to a greater extent than with other psychopathologies of childhood, a multidiscipli-nary assessment approach is crucial in the evaluation of the presence of ADHD. Weiss and Hechtman (1993) emphasize the necessity of formulating a treatment plan that focuses on the child's familial and/or school environment, as needed. Included among the suggested ar-eas to address in a multidisciplinary assessment battery are developmental history (including pregnancy, delivery, and developmental milestones); assessment of the child's pathological be-havior patterns; educational assessment to detect any specific learning disabilities; psycholog-ical assessment focusing on the child's cognitive processes; assessment of familial interaction patterns; assessment of the child's classroom environment; and a neurological evaluation, when indicated.

Another multidisciplinary assessment protocol was proposed by Weiss in an earlier work (1991). Consisting of six major components, this protocol includes a parent interview ad-dressing developmental history, behavioral symptoms, medical history, learning history, family stressors, disciplinary methods, possibility of child abuse, parental history of ADD or ADHD, antisocial personality and/or alcoholism, and recent changes in the family; a child interview addressing target symptoms, the child's explanation of the symptoms, the child's perception of his or her role in school and in the family, the history of the child's social interactions, the child's ability to relate to the clinician, and any concurrent psychopathologies; a family inter-view; administration of standardized rating scales (e.g., Conner's Scales, Rutter's Scales); ob-taining information from the school; and assessment of the child's cognitive functioning.

Etiology

Although psychosocial environmental factors have, in the past, been postulated as etiological factors in ADHD, the current literature focuses more on biological influences. It is important to note, however, that the controversy regarding the causes of ADHD is far from over. The eti-ological theories presented here are in development rather than empirically proved facts.

One group of theories about the etiology of ADHD dates back to the early 1900s. Viewing the disorder as a form of minimal brain dysfunction, early theorists conceptualized ADHD as stemming from some type of brain injury. When subsequent studies showed that the majority of ADHD children (with the exception of the 5 to 10 percent of ADHD patients who have damaged prefrontal limbic areas) do not have any form of brain pathology, the focus moved to other neurological factors. Thus, current explanations invoke neurological imbalances, retardation in the maturation of the central nervous system, and dysfunction in the prefrontal lobes of the brain or the limbic system.

Another group of biologically oriented theories postulate the disorder to be related to neurotransmitters. Wender (1978) hypothesized ADD to be related to the neurotransmitter dopamine. Relying on animal studies that report ADD-like symptoms in dopamine-depleted subjects, such theories regard ADD as caused by problems in dopamine metabolism. These ideas are difficult to evaluate empirically because brain dopamine levels cannot easily be obtained.

Other researchers have put forward developmentally oriented theories of the etiology of ADD. The nature of ADD symptomatology has led them to suggest that the disorder is due primarily to a developmental delay. This theory has been extensively investigated using different methodological approaches. Some researchers have compared the level of activity of control and ADD children at different ages (e.g., Achenbach & Edelbrock, 1981), and others have examined brain wave responses to various stimuli (e.g., Buchsbaum & Wender, 1973).

Other researchers have investigated the influences of toxic chemicals in the child's environment on the development of ADD. A theory proposed in the mid-1970s (Feingold, 1975) claimed that the additives and chemicals in certain food substances were sufficient to initiate attention disorder symptomatology. The Feingold diet was reported to control symptomatic behavior. Empirical data on this topic are contradictory; some studies (e.g., Swanson & Kinsbourne, 1980) find that removal of certain chemicals from the diet is helpful in symptom reduction, whereas others (e.g., Conners, 1980) show no significant effects.

Another theory regards lead as a primary cause of ADHD symptoms. Ingestion of lead can cause swelling of the brain, in turn impairing brain function. Many studies have demonstrated a correlation between ADHD and higher lead levels in children's blood (e.g., Gittelman & Eskenazi, 1983). The data, however, merely indicate that these conditions often coexist—these studies have not proved that lead causes ADHD.

Genetic theories rely on evidence that there is an increased incidence of ADHD in the parents (e.g., Morrison & Stewart, 1974) as well as the biological relatives (e.g., Frick, Lahey, Christ, Loeber, & Green, 1991) of ADHD children. Twin studies and studies of siblings show high concordance rates (e.g., McMahon, 1980); this research supports the idea that ADHD may have a hereditary component.

Other theories of the etiology of ADHD are psychologically based. Many focus on the interaction between the parents and the hyperactive child. Two recent papers (Danforth, Barkley, & Stokes, 1991; Fischer, 1990) review the current research investigating the reciprocal effects between the behavior of the child or adolescent diagnosed with ADHD and the behavior of the parents. As we intuitively expect, parents of ADHD children manifest increased stress, increased marital discord, and psychopathology that may be independent of that of the child. More research is clearly necessary, but current data may support a child-to-adult direction of cause and effect.

Think About It

Parents' Ratings of the Behavior of ADD and Non-ADD Children

A recent study investigated whether parents' concern about their children's behavior was actually related to ADD. Using a sample of 245 children ages 4 to 15 years as subjects, the authors quantified and categorized the concerns of the children's parents and then related these data to the children's clinical diagnoses. Interestingly, although parental concern about one or more symptoms of ADD identified virtually all of the children with an ADD diagnosis, such concerns were by no means limited to those children with ADD. How would you interpret these results?

Treatment

Children with ADHD are treated through psychopharmacological and/or behavioral modalities. Beginning in the 1960s and 1970s, several studies reported the efficacious use of stimulant medication for the treatment of ADHD, claiming a 70 percent success rate. Behavioral therapy was coming into its own at about the same time, and it seemed to be a "natural" treatment for this disorder. Today, some 30 years later, a review of the literature on ADD and ADHD reveals that these are still the primary modes of treatment.

Psychopharmacological Approaches ADHD is one of the few psychopathologies of childhood and adolescence for which psychopharmacological treatment is not viewed as a last resort. Indeed, approximately three-fourths of all ADHD children respond positively to a treatment regimen of either psychostimulants or antidepressants.

Perhaps the most popular of the stimulants prescribed for the treatment of ADHD is methylphenidate (Ritalin). Despite its classification as a stimulant, Ritalin induces positive behavioral changes in the ADHD individual, including improved focusing ability, increased alertness, a decrease in impulsive behavior, and an improved attention span. Some studies have also reported improvement in academic performance and peer relationships. Although the majority of ADHD sufferers respond positively to a Ritalin treatment regimen, the amount of improvement varies. A child who does not improve on Ritalin may benefit from another medication.

Beneficial effects of a dose of Ritalin can be observed within 20 minutes. Maximum drug concentration in the blood is reached some 60 to 150 minutes after administration, so Ritalin is usually administered just before the child goes to school and sometime during the lunch break. Ritalin use can result in a rebound effect. Children who take their medication early in the day may exhibit an exacerbation of their symptoms in the late afternoon or early evening. This problem arises as the serum level of Ritalin drops. It can be alleviated by altering the dosage schedule. Ritalin is now available in time-release capsules that prolong its effects for 8 to 10 hours. Although this drug is not indicated for children under age 6, it is without question the most commonly prescribed drug for the treatment of ADHD. The initial dosage is usually 5 mg once or twice daily; the drug can be increased to no more than 60 mg per day.

When stimulants result in untoward side effects (e.g., tics, seizures) or the rebound effect is intense, antidepressant medications can be prescribed. Tricyclic antidepressants, especially imipramine, are among the most commonly prescribed for ADHD. Although imipramine does not have FDA approval for the treatment of ADHD, it is generally considered the drug of first choice if stimulant treatment is not successful (Green, 1991). Other alternatives or supplements to the stimulants are beta blockers such as Inderal or Nadolol.

Despite the impressive benefits of psychopharmacological intervention in the treatment of ADHD, drug treatment has limitations. Pelham and Hinshaw (1992) list three negative effects of psychopharmacological intervention, specifically, the use of psychostimulants: (1) This type of treatment does not work for all individuals, and even in those for whom psychostimulant intervention is considered effective, there are clear limitations to the results expected in terms of interpersonal and academic functioning. (2) The beneficial effects are observed only during those times when the drug is at a certain level in the individual's system. Thus, there is a limited period during which the patient can benefit from the intervention without administration of subsequent doses. (3) The empirical studies that are currently available do not support improvement and/or efficacy on a long-term basis.

The limitations of drug treatment do not mean that behavioral interventions should be used alone. Research (e.g., Horn & Ialongo, 1988) supports the superiority of treatment protocols that combine pharmacological and behavioral approaches. Toward this end, the following section will present a brief summary of those nonpharmacological treatment methods most commonly utilized in the treatment of ADHD.

Psychological Approaches The most popular nonpharmacological treatments for ADHD include several types of behavioral therapy, cognitive-behavioral therapy, parent training, family therapy, social skills training, and dynamically oriented individual psychotherapy. The efficacy of dynamic psychotherapy in the treatment of ADHD has not been established, so this discussion will focus on the other approaches. Again, the most efficacious treatment modality for most children and adolescents with ADHD incorporates some type of psychosocial method with psychopharmacological intervention.

Traditional behavioral therapy uses contingency management involving the child's parents and teachers. The child is reinforced and/or punished for certain behaviors in accordance with a mutually agreed-upon plan. Research has yielded conflicting data on the overall efficacy of this approach, but the general consensus is that this approach leads to considerable improvement with respect to functioning (Atkins, Pelham, & White, 1989).

One criticism of the more traditional behavior therapy approaches that utilized contingency management procedures is that the responsibility for the behavioral intervention is somewhat removed from the child. In response to this criticism, cognitive-behavioral strategies, using techniques such as self-talk, self-guidance, cognitive self-monitoring, and training in problem-solving skills, have been integrated with the basic behavioral protocol. Surprisingly, despite the theoretical soundness of such an approach, the efficacy is less than optimal (see Abikoff, 1987).

Parent training programs (e.g., Anastopoulos & Barkely, 1989; Horn, Ialongo, Greenberg, Packard, & Winberry, 1990; Pisterman et al., 1992) involve instruction modules designed to train the parents as cotherapists in their children's treatment. Parents are instructed in the basic principles of behavioral therapy so that they can help in achieving the desired results with their children. Parents are taught to use strategies at both preventive and reactive levels of intervention. To use preventive strategies, the parents make modifications in the home environment as well as in their own approach to the child before any ADHD behavior manifests itself. Reactive strategies, which are used after undesirable behavior is manifested by the child, involve modifications to the environment and responses directed toward the child. Time out, overcorrection, differential attention, and ignoring are all used. Reactive strategies tend to be punitive (Goldstein 1988).

Russell Barkley (1987) published a training program designed for parents of children between 2 and 11 years of age who have problems complying with rules, regulations, and/or requests. The first part of the program teaches the parents basic skills for dealing with inappropriate behavior in the child; the second half instructs the parents in the management of a token economy milieu, in which the children are given chips or tokens to help them develop self-control and planning strategies. Barkley's program is designed to be completed with the aid of a clinician over an 8- to 10-week period. After the parents have completed their training module, the therapist spends some time working with the family as a unit, guiding the parents in utilizing their newly learned skills. Although Barkley's program is probably the best-known, others are also available (e.g., Forehand & McMahon, 1981).

Recent literature on ADHD focuses on the interpersonal difficulties encountered by these children and adolescents (e.g., Moore, Hughes, & Robinson, 1992). Social skills training is being integrated with increasing frequency into treatment plans for these individuals. A variation on the cognitive-behavioral model, this approach attempts to facilitate accurate self-perceptions in ADHD children via self-monitoring and practice (role playing, modeling) in different social situations. It is not recommended that social skills training be employed as a single modality, but preliminary data indicate that it has potential as a significant adjunct in the treatment plans of many individuals.

Over the past few years, so-called bibliotherapy modalities have become available. These materials are directed primarily toward the ADHD patient. Some of these are listed in Table 10.1.

Table 10.1 Resource Materials Designed for the ADD Patient

Survival Guide for College Students with ADD or LD by K. G. Nadeau (Magination Press, New York, 1994)

Putting On the Brakes by P. O. Quinn and J. M. Stern (Magination Press, New York, 1991)

Putting on the Brakes Activity Book by P. O. Quinn and J. M. Stern (Magination Press, New York, 1993)

Otto Learns About His Medicine by M. R. Galvin (Magination Press, New York, 1996)

Brakes: The Interactive Newsletter for Kids with ADD Magination Press (212) 924-3344

Evaluating Treatment of ADD Researchers who try to evaluate the relative efficacy of the various treatment approaches to ADHD find it difficult to arrive at any conclusive statements regarding the superiority of one approach over another. A recent article (Whalen & Henker, 1991) emphasizes that the practitioner should focus separately on each symptomatic component of ADHD, formulating treatment programs relevant to each type of symptom.

Whalen and Henker also propose several criteria the clinician might employ to evaluate the relative efficacy of a given treatment modality or treatment program for a particular child or adolescent. Their criteria could be applied to clinical interventions designed for other disorders as well (see Table 10.2).

Table 10.2 Criteria for Evaluating Psychotherapeutic Treatment

Criterion	Questions
Applicability	What types of problems can be treated? Over what developmental range is the method effective?
Adaptability	Is the method flexible? Can it be modified to fit different needs?
Communicability/teachability	Can the method be taught to nonprofessionals?
Availability	Is the method suitable for nonlaboratory conditions?

Controllability	Can the method be administered consistently?
Compatibility	Can the method be integrated with other modalities?
Durability	Are the effects of treatment stable in the long term?
Generalizability	Is the method valid in different situations?
Constrainability	Do intense or significant secondary effects limit applicability of the method?
Feasibility	Does the method impose on the patient and the family?
Visibility	Will the patient be stigmatized by treatment?
Palatability	Does the method fit with the patient's and the family's values?

Source: Adapted from C. K. Whalen & B. Henker (1991).

Summary

The disorders discussed in this chapter all involve the overt behavior of the child or adolescent, which has a negative effect on other people at home and in school. Included among these diagnoses are Conduct Disorder, Oppositional Defiant Disorder, and Attention Deficit Hyperactivity Disorder.

Conduct Disorder characterized by severe "acting out" behavior patterns, which vary as a function of the child's developmental level. Overt behaviors range from chronic negativity to vandalism. Individuals diagnosed with Oppositional Defiant Disorder are a bit more passive in their pathological behavior patterns. Problems seem to manifest most frequently around issues of compliance, with tendencies to "forget" or "not hear" requests from adults in authority. For both Conduct Disorder and Oppositional Defiant Disorder, the treatment of choice is generally behavioral. A relatively recent innovation is the use of the parents as cotherapists.

Attention Deficit Hyperactivity Disorder is commonly addressed in the clinical and empirical literature. ADHD was initially conceptualized as resulting from a form of brain pathology. Clinical knowledge about this disorder has developed considerably over the past several decades. Currently, the disorder is viewed as having three major components of manifest symptomatology: impaired ability to maintain attention, impulsivity, and hyperactivity.

Treatment of ADHD usually includes a behavioral as well as a psychopharmacological component. Either psychostimulant or antidepressant medication may be used, with psychostimulants being more commonly prescribed. Because of the inherent limitations of psychopharmacological interventions (especially stimulants) in the treatment of this disorder, various forms of psychotherapeutic interventions are often applied in conjunction with drug treatment. Symptomatic presentation varies from patient to patient, so it is necessary to formulate a treatment plan specific to the individual's needs.

References

Abikoff, H. (1987). An evaluation of cognitive-behavior therapy for hyperactive children. In B. B. Lahey & A. E. Kazdin (Eds.), *Advances in clinical child psychology.* New York: Plenum Press.

Achenbach, T. M., & Edelbrock, C. S. (1981). Behavioral problems and competencies reported by parents of normal and disturbed children aged 4 through 16. *Monographs of the Society for Research in Child Development, 46,* Serial No. 188.

Anastopoulos, A. D., & Barkley, R. A. (1989). A training program for parents of children with attention-deficit hyperactivity disorder. In C. E. Schaefer & J. M. Briesmeister (Eds.), *Handbook of parent training: Parents as cotherapists for children's behavior problems.* New York: Wiley.

Atkins, M. S., Pelham, W. E., & White, K. J. (1989). Hyperactivity and attention deficit disorders. In M. Hersen (Ed.), *Psychological aspects of developmental and physical disabilities: A casebook.* Newbury Park, CA: Sage.

Baer, R. A., & Nietzel, M. T. (1991). Cognitive and behavioral treatment of impulsivity in children: A meta-analytic review of the outcome literature. *Journal of Clinical Child Psychology, 20,* 400–412.

Barkley, R. A. (1987). *Defiant children: A clinician's manual for parent training.* New York: Guilford Press.

Buchsbaum, M. S., & Wender, P. (1973). Averaged evoked responses in normal and minimally brain dysfunctional children treated with amphetamine: A preliminary report. *Archives of General Psychiatry, 29,* 764–770.

Cantwell, D. P. (1989). Conduct disorder. In H. I. Kaplan & B. J. Sadock (Eds.), *Comprehensive textbook of psychiatry/V.* Batimore: Williams & Wilkins.

Conners, C. K. (1980). *Food additives and hyperactive children.* New York: Plenum.

Danforth, J. S., Barkley, R. A., & Stokes, T. F. (1991). Observations of parent-child interactions with hyperactive children: Research and clinical implications. *Clinical Psychology Review, 11,* 703–727.

deQuiros, G. B., Kinsbourne, M., Palmer, R. L., & Rufo, D. T. (1994). Attention deficit disorder in children: Three clinical variants. *Journal of Developmental and Behavioral Pediatrics, 15,* 311–319.

Dulcan, M. K., & Popper, C. W. (1991). *Concise guide to child and adolescent psychiatry.* Washington, DC: American Psychiatric Press.

Feingold, B. (1975). *Why your child is hyperactive.* New York: Random House.

Fischer, M. (1990). Parenting stress and the child with attention deficit hyperactivity disorder. *Journal of Clincial Child Psychology, 19,* 337–346.

Forehand, R., & McMahon, R. J. (1981). *Helping the noncompliant child: A clinician's guide to parent training.* New York: Guilford Press.

Frick, P. J., Lahey, B. B., Christ, M. A. G., Loeber, R., & Green, S. (1991). History of childhood behavior problems in biological relatives of boys with attention-deficit hyperactivity disorder and conduct disorder. *Journal of Clinical Child Psychology, 20,* 445–451.

Frick, P. J., O'Brien, B. S., Wootton, J. M., & McBurnett, K. (1994). Psychopathy and conduct problems in children. *Journal of Abnormal Psychology, 103,* 700–707.

Gittelman, R., & Eskinazi, B. (1983). Lead and hyperactivity revisited. *Archives of General Psychiatry, 40,* 827–833.

Goldstein, M. J. (1988). The family and psychopathology. *Annual Review of Psychology, 39,* 283–300.

Green, W. H. (1991). *Child and adolescent clinical psychopharmacology.* Baltimore: Williams & Wilkins.

Grizenko, N., & Pawliuk, N. (1994). Risk and protective factors for disruptive behavior disorders in children. *American Journal of Orthopsychiatry, 64,* 534–544.

Hinshaw, S. P., Han, S. S., Erhardt, D., & Huber, A. (1992). Internalizing and externalizing behavior problems in preschool children: Correspondence among parent and teacher ratings and behavior observations. *Journal of Clinical Child Psychology, 21,* 143–150.

Horn, W. F., Ialongo, N., Greenberg, G., Packard, T., & Winberry, C. S. (1990). Additive effects of behavioral parent training and self-control therapy with attention deficit hyperactivity disordered children. *Journal of Clinical Child Psychology, 19,* 98–110.

Horn, W. F., Ialongo, N., Popovich, S., & Peradotto, D. (1987). Behavioral parent training and cognitive-behavioral self-control therapy with ADD-H children. *Journal of Clinical Child Psychology, 16,* 57–68.

Kendall, P. C., Reber, M., McLeer, S., Epps, J., & Ronan, K. R. (1990). Cognitive-behavioral treatment of conduct-disordered children. *Cognitive Therapy and Research, 14,* 279–297.

Lewis, D. O. (1991). Conduct disorder. In M. Lewis (Ed.), *Child and adolescent psychiatry: A comprehensive textbook.* Baltimore: Williams & Wilkins.

Liden, C. B., Zalenski, J. R., & Newman, R. L. (1989). *Pay attention: Answers to common questions about the diagnosis and treatment of attention deficit disorder.* Monroeville, PA: Transact Health Systems.

Long, P., Forehand, R., Wierson, M., & Morgan, A. (1994). Does parent training with young noncompliant children have long-term effects? *Behaviour Research and Therapy, 32,* 101–107.

McMahon, R. C. (1980). Genetic etiology in the hyperactive child syndrome: A critical review. *American Journal of Orthopsychiatry, 50,* 145–150.

Malmquist, C. P. (1991). Conduct disorder: Conceptual and diagnostic issues. In J. M. Wiener (Ed.), *Textbook of child and adolescent psychiatry.* Washington, DC: American Psychiatric Press.

Mantzicopoulos, P., & Morrison, D. (1994). A comparison of boys and girls with attention problems: Kindergarten through second grade. *American Journal of Orthopsychiatry, 64,* 522–533.

Moore, L. A., Hughes, J. N., & Robinson, M. (1992). A comparison of the social information-processing abilities of rejected and accepted hyperactive children. *Journal of Clinical Child Psychology, 21,* 123–131.

Morrison, J. R., & Stewart, M. A. (1974). Bilateral inheritance as evidence for polygenicity in the hyperactive child syndrome. *Journal of Nervous and Mental Diseases, 158,* 226–228.

Pearson, D. A., & Aman, M. G. (1994). Ratings of hyperactivity and developmental indices: Should clinicians correct for developmental level? *Journal of Autism and Developmental Disorders, 24,* 395–411.

Pelham, W. E., & Hinshaw, S. P. (1992). Behavioral intervention for attention deficit-hyperactivity disorder. In S. M. Turner, K. S. Calhoun, & H. E. Adams (Eds.), *Handbook of clinical behavior therapy* (2nd ed.). New York: Wiley.

Pisterman, S., Firestone, P., McGrath, P., Goodman, J. T., Webster, I., Mallory, R., & Goffin, B. (1992). The role of parent training in treatment of preschoolers with ADHD. *American Journal of Orthopsychiatry, 62,* 397–408.

Roberts, M. W., Joe, V. C., & Rowe-Halbert, A. (1992). Oppositional child behavior and parental loss of control. *Journal of Clinical Child Psychology, 21,* 170–77.

Robins, L. N. (1991). Conduct disorder. *Journal of Child Psychology and Psychiatry, 32,* 193–212.

Routh, D. K., & Daugherty, T. K. (1992). Conduct disorder. In S. R. Hooper, G. W. Hynd, & R. E. Mattison (Eds.), *Child psychopathology: Diagnostic criteria and clinical assessment.* Hillsdale, NJ: Erlbaum.

Sanders, M. R., & Dadds, M. R. (1992). Children's and parents' cognitions about family interactions: An evaluation of video-mediated recall and thought listing procedures in the assessment of conduct-disordered children. *Journal of Clinical Child Psychology, 21,* 371–379.

Swanson, J. M., & Kinsbourne, M. (1980). Artificial color and hyperactive behavior. In R. M. Knights & D. Bakker (Eds.), *Rehabilitation, treatment, and management of learning disorders.* Baltimore: University Park Press.

Szapocznik, J., Kurtines, W., Santisteban, D. A., & Rio, A. T. (1990). Interplay of advances between theory, research, and application in treatment interventions aimed at behavior problem children and adolescents. *Journal of Consulting and Clinical Psychology, 58,* 696–703.

Weiss, G. (1991). Attention deficit hyperactivity disorder. In M. Lewis (Ed.), *Child and adolescent psychiatry: A comprehensive textbook.* Baltimore: Williams & Wilkins.

Weiss, G., & Hechtman, L. T. (1993). *Hyperactive children grown up* (2nd ed.). New York: Guiliford Press.

Weiss, G., Minde, K., & Werry, J. S. (1971). Studies of the hyperactive child: A five-year follow-up. *Archives of General Psychiatry, 24,* 409–414.

Wender, P. H. (1987). *The hyperactive, child, adolescent and adult.* New York: Oxford University Press.

Whalen, C. K., & Henker, B. (1991). Therapies for hyperactive children. *Journal of Consulting and Clinical Psychology, 59,* 126–137.

Chapter eleven
Disorders of Eating and Elimination in Childhood and Adolescence

Two days later, there was Pooh, sitting on his branch, dangling his legs, and there, beside him, were four pots of honey...

Three days later, there was Pooh, sitting on his branch, dangling his legs, and there, beside him, was one pot of honey.

Four days later, there was Pooh...

A. A. Milne, *Winnie-the-Pooh*

In this chapter we will explore two classifications of disorders as they manifest themselves in childhood and adolescence. The Eating Disorders include Pica, Rumination Disorder, Feeding Disorder of Early Childhood, Anorexia Nervosa, and Bulimia, and the Disorders of Elimination include Encopresis and Enuresis. Each of these will be discussed in terms of their clinical presentation, diagnosis, epidemiology, and treatment.

Eating Disorders of Childhood and Adolescence

Introduction

Before 1980, few professional publications dealt with eating disorders. After two of the eating disorders, Anorexia Nervosa and Bulimia Nervosa, attracted the attention of professionals and the lay public, the diagnostic grouping of eating disorders became a focus of clinical, empirical, and popular interest.

The eating disorders are found in two separate sections of the *DSM-IV.* Pica, Rumination Disorder, and Feeding Disorder of Infancy or Early Childhood are listed in the category of Disorders Usually First Diagnosed in Infancy, Childhood, or Adolescence. Anorexia Nervosa and Bulimia Nervosa are listed in the section on Eating Disorders, which are not conceptualized as disorders of childhood and adolescence.

Pica

Clinical Presentation Pica is described as the persistent eating or ingestion of nonnutritive substances. It may well be one of the strangest eating disorders (or even psychopathologies) of childhood and adolescence. The name *pica* is derived from the Latin word for "magpie," a bird that eats a wide variety of substances. The diagnosis needs to be distinguished from certain ingestive behavior which is characteristic of various developmental stages. Children 18 months and younger often indiscriminately ingest nonfood substances. Thus, 18 months is the critical age after which ingestion of nonfood substances is considered pathological.

CURIOUS AVENUE copyright © 1992, 1993 TOLES. Reprinted with permission of Universal Press Syndicate. All rghts reserved.

A child with Pica is likely to eat about three different nonfood items (see Singhi & Singhi, 1983). Among the most common items are leaves, grass, sticks, insects, buttons, hair, string, cloth, plants, stones, crayons, pieces of plaster or paint, clothing, sand, animal droppings, and pebbles. Surveys indicate that the majority of children diagnosed with Pica are under age 6, with a peak in incidence around age 2. The range of materials ingested decreases from age 1 to age 6.

Not all published research on this pathology limits the conceptualization of Pica to the ingestion of nonnutritive substances. Mayes (1992) found that 18 percent of the articles on Pica published between 1972 and 1978 defined the disorder as incorporating the compulsive ingestion of food items as well as repeated ingestion of nonfood substances.

Case Study 11.1

Five-year-old Yolanda was referred to the school nurse and later to the school psychologist because she has been eating pieces of crayon and chalk in her kindergarten class. Yolanda's parents have never noticed her ingesting any nonfood items, but they have found small pieces of crayon in strange places around the home—under the little girl's pillow, in her pajama pockets, and so on. When confronted by her parents and her kindergarten teacher, Yolanda admitted that she eats crayons and chalk "sometimes," but she was unable to talk about this habit in any more detail.

Diagnosis The diagnostic criteria for Pica are presented in Box 11.1.

---

box **11.1**

Diagnostic Criteria for Pica

A. Persistent eating of nonnutritive substances for a period of at least 1 month.

B. The eating of nonnutritive substances is inappropriate to the developmental level.

C. The eating behavior is not part of a culturally sanctioned practice.

D. If the eating behavior occurs exclusively during the course of another developmental disorder (e.g., Mental Retardation, Pervasive Developmental Disorder, Schizophrenia), it is sufficiently severe to warrant independent clinical attention.

Source: American Psychiatric Association, *DSM-IV,* p. 96. Reprinted with permission from the *Diagnostic and Statistical Manual of Mental Disorders,* Fourth Edition. Copyright © 1994 American Psychiatric Association.

Differential diagnosis for Pica is not complicated; no other diagnoses have similar clinical manifestations. It is important to note, however, that several associated symptoms and syndromes often occur concomitantly with Pica. Mental Retardation, organic impairment, behavioral problems, Conduct Disorder, Schizophrenia, various psychosocial stressors, and familial psychopathologies (Mayes, 1992) have all been associated with Pica.

Epidemiology Epidemiological data indicate that between 10 and 20 percent of all children will experience Pica symptoms at some point in their lives. Although there is no significant difference with respect to gender in terms of incidence, a disproportionately greater number of Pica sufferers come from families in lower socioeconomic groups.

Etiology Theories of the etiology of Pica are rather varied. Theories based on animal studies often propose dietary deficiencies as a major etiological factor, specifically, deficiencies of iron, zinc (see Woods & Weisinger, 1970), or calcium (see Jacobson & Snowdon, 1976). More psychodynamic approaches explain Pica as being the result of unresolved feelings of parental abandonment, using the ingestion of various substances as a defense against such feelings (see Millican, Layman, & Lourie, 1979). Some research (e.g., Singhi & Singhi, 1983; Singhi, Singhi, & Adwani, 1981) has provided support for this theoretical perspective in that Pica has been found to be associated with families in which there was emotional and physical neglect or abuse by the parents.

Treatment Treatment of Pica focuses initially on its accurate diagnosis. Quite frequently, children with Pica are brought for treatment of other conditions, and unfortunately, the Pica symptoms are overlooked. Systems-based treatments entail education of the parents with respect to nutrition, appropriately stimulating play opportunities for the child, and child-care techniques. Direct behavioral intervention strategies employed with the child include differential reinforcement, education or differentiation training with respect to edible versus nonedible foods, overcorrection procedures, and contingency management (see Finney, Russo, & Cataldo, 1982; Madden, Russo, & Cataldo, 1980).

Rumination Disorder

Clinical Presentation Rumination Disorder entails the intentional and pleasurable regurgitation of food. This is typically followed by reingestion and reswallowing or spitting out of the same food. There appears to be a self-stimulatory quality to the behavior; the individual manifests an obvious sense of satisfaction and psychological involvement in the activity. No visible upset is manifested on the part of the individual. To the contrary, clinical and empirical reports indicate an observable sense of pleasure and contentment during and following the behavioral sequence. This syndrome does not usually occur in infants under 3 to 12 months of age, and unless some developmental disorder is involved, Rumination Disorder tends to resolve itself by 3 or 4 years of age.

This Rumination Disorder behavior pattern is entirely self-induced. An observer may see the patient insert objects into his or her mouth to induce the regurgitating, or there may be no overt inducing activity. Should the behavioral cycle be interrupted by another individual's presence, the patient will temporarily cease the activity and will resume the rumination cycle as soon as the individual leaves.

Rumination Disorder takes two general forms. The first type of rumination disorder occurs in developmentally intact infants, the second in mentally retarded individuals of various ages. In otherwise normal infants, the disorder may be caused by pathology in the infant-caretaker relationship. The infant turns to internal sources of gratification when the environment provides insufficient psychological and physical stimulation. In mentally retarded individuals, the symptoms appear to be related to other self-stimulating behaviors so characteristic of the severely or profoundly retarded.

When Rumination Disorder occurs in adolescents, the clinician must rule out physiological causes such as esophageal motility. In such cases the behavior pattern is involuntary. In other cases of adolescent rumination, the true diagnosis is Anorexia Nervosa and/or Bulimia. These disorders are discussed later in this chapter.

Case Study 11.2

Five-month-old Shakita is causing her mother a great deal of distress. Whenever the baby is fed, she eats quite well, and she gurgles and coos appropriately in response to her mother's attentions. After her mother returns Shakita to her crib, however, the little girl regurgitates her food. Shakita then picks up the regurgitated food in her hands, smiles contentedly, and proceeds to eat it.

Diagnosis The diagnostic criteria for Rumination Disorder are presented in Box 11.2.

box **11.2**

Diagnostic Criteria for Rumination Disorder

A. Repeated regurgitation and rechewing of food for a period of at least 1 month following a period of normal functioning.

B. The behavior is not due to an associated gastrointestinal or other general medical condition (e.g., esophageal reflux).

C. The behavior does not occur exclusively during the course of Anorexia Nervosa or Bulimia Nervosa. If the symptoms occur exclusively during the course of Mental Retardation or a Pervasive Developmental Disorder, they are sufficiently severe to warrant independent clinical attention.

Source: American Psychiatric Association, *DSM-IV,* p. 98. Reprinted with permission from the *Diagnostic and Statistical Manual of Mental Disorders,* Fourth Edition. Copyright © 1994 American Psychiatric Association.

Differential diagnostic concerns primarily focus on ruling out the various medical disorders that could manifest similar symptomatology. Another differential diagnostic issue centers around observing the patient's reaction to the regurgitation behavior. In cases of true Rumination Disorder, there is no observable distress or sense of the disorder being at all ego-dystonic, unlike the reactions to regurgitation or vomiting symptoms characteristic of other disorders.

Epidemiology Although no data are available for the incidence of Rumination Disorder in infancy, estimates of prevalence among institutionalized mentally retarded individuals range from 6 to 10 percent (Rast, Johnston, Drum, & Cibrubm, 1981).

Etiology Etiological theories relevant to Rumination Disorder are rather limited. Most focus on a pathologically inadequate relationship between the child and the primary caretaker. Using a psychodynamic conceptualization, the disorder is seen as a child's attempt at self-stimulation as a result of inadequate nurturing (see Chatoor, Dickson, & Einhorn, 1984).

Treatment Treatment approaches for Rumination Disorder center around improving the relationship between the infant and the primary caretaker and/or selective reinforcing of non-rumination behavior. Instructing the caretaker in performing reinforcing behaviors (e.g., cuddling, hugging, talking, playing) around mealtime is often a primary treatment intervention. Combining such methods with some aversive conditioning (e.g., putting the child down when a rumination cycle begins), a commonly employed program of contingency management rewards the infant for nonrumination. At times, parent training is also incorporated into the treatment regimen. When parents react less dramatically to the infant's ruminating behavior, the child is less likely to perceive their reaction as reinforcing. Parents can also learn better feeding and caretaking skills.

Feeding Disorder of Infancy or Early Childhood

Clinical Presentation This new diagnostic category, first published in the recently released *DSM-IV,* encompasses older diagnoses of Reactive Attachment Disorder, Nonorganic Failure to Thrive, and Psychosocial Dwarfism. The symptomatic profile in these syndromes, all described in the early 1900s, was rather similar: retardation in physical growth, problems with interpersonal interactions, pathological child-caretaker relationship, and various associated psychological symptoms (Mayes, 1992).

However, because of the newness of the diagnostic category of Feeding Disorder of Infancy or early childhood as such, discussion in this chapter will be limited to a statement of the diagnostic criteria.

Diagnosis The diagnostic criteria for Feeding Disorder of Infancy or Early Childhood are presented in Box 11.3.

---

box **11.3**

Diagnostic Criteria for Feeding Disorder of Infancy or Early Childhood

A. Feeding disturbance as manifested by persistent failure to eat adequately with significant failure to gain weight or significant loss of weight over at least 1 month.

B. The disturbance is not due to an associated gastrointestinal or other general medical condition (e.g., esophageal reflux).

C. The disturbance is not better accounted for by another mental disorder (e.g., Rumination Disorder) or by lack of available food.

D. The onset is before age 6 years.

Source: American Psychiatric Association, *DSM-IV*, pp. 99–100. Reprinted with permission from the *Diagnostic and Statistical Manual of Mental Disorders*, Fourth Edition. Copyright © 1994 American Psychiatric Association.

Anorexia Nervosa

Clinical Presentation

A young woman thus afflicted, her clothes scarcely hanging together on her anatomy, her pulse slow and slack, her temperature two degrees below the normal mean, her bowels closed, her hair like that of a corpse—dry and lusterless, her face and limbs ashy and cold, her hollow eyes the only vivid thing about her—this wan creature whose daily food intake might lie on a crown piece, will be busy with mother's meetings, with little sister's frocks, with university extension and with what you please else of unselfish effort, yet on what funds God only knows.

Allbutt, 1910

This description written over 80 years ago was chosen to begin a recent book chapter on Anorexia Nervosa (Herzog & Beresin, 1991, p. 398). Although several decades old, this excerpt has poignant clinical relevance to any contemporary clinical or empirical description of the disorder. Similarly, Herzog and Beresin mention other historical depictions of this same syndrome: the female saints whose fasting was equated with holiness, the "miraculous maids" of the sixteenth-century Reformation who demonstrated their humility and purity by fasting, and the Victorian era's "Welsh fasting girl."

Moving beyond the historical context, the contemporary syndrome of Anorexia Nervosa is characterized by a self-imposed preoccupation (some would say obsession) with being thin. With this preoccupation as the underlying dynamic, the individual who has Anorexia stubbornly refuses to eat, resulting in weight loss of varying degrees of severity. In females, the associated endocrine changes result in amenorrhea; in males, there is an analogous impairment in erectile ability. Patients whose onset of Anorexia is prior to puberty may not actually lose weight; rather, they may fail to gain weight as expected during the period of active growth. Individuals with Anorexia are typified by a distortion in their perception of their own weight and appearance (see Cooper & Fairburn, 1992; Pumariega et al., 1993; Thompson & Heinberg, 1993).

Approximately half of patients diagnosed as having Anorexia exhibit bingeing and purging symptoms either during the course of the disorder or during treatment and recovery (Casper, Elke, & Halmi, 1980; Garfinkel & Garner, 1982).

In addition to the psychological symptoms, patients with Anorexia often exhibit an inability to tolerate cold temperatures, constipation, abdominal discomfort (including bloating), dry skin, lanugo (baby-fine body hair), sleep difficulties, diarrhea, and dizziness. A characteristic hyperactive demeanor typifies the person with Anorexia, with an almost hypomanic energy level. Palla and Litt (1988) include the following physical signs and symptoms: dehydration, anemia, abnormal glucose tolerance, hypothermia, low basal metabolic rate, cardiovascular problems, and electrolyte imbalance. The vast range of medical complications can escalate to potentially fatal levels.

Onset of Anorexia Nervosa typically follows the pubertal weight gain during adolescence. In other situations, the onset follows a successful dieting regimen in a previously slightly overweight individual. The clinical course of this disorder is rather prolonged, often lasting several years. Research indicates that approximately three-fourths of the sufferers eventually attain a normal weight yet retain pathological eating patterns throughout life.

Empirical evidence accumulating in the literature suggests that the clinical course of Anorexia may differ in male and female patients. A recent study (Romeo, 1994) compares the clinical course of the disorder in boys and girls. This report indicates that a major factor contributing to the development of Anorexia in young men is the "cultural, physical and psychological pressures on vulnerable adolescents and young adults."

Case Study 11.3

Thirteen-year-old Alyssa has been diagnosed by the school psychologist as having Anorexia Nervosa. The adolescent is furious about the diagnosis, and she says she wishes that people would "just mind their own business." Two years ago, Alyssa went on a weight reduction diet and lost 15 pounds. However, she continued to restrict her food intake, and she is now 25 pounds below her ideal weight. She has not menstruated for the past 4 months and complains of feeling cold all the time. When confronted about her Anorexia, however, Alyssa insists that she still needs to lose "only a few more pounds."

Diagnosis The diagnostic criteria for Anorexia Nervosa are presented in Box 11.4.

box **11.4**

Diagnostic Criteria for Anorexia Nervosa

A. Refusal to maintain body weight at or above a minimally normal weight for age and height (e.g., weight loss leading to maintenance of body weight less than 85 percent of that expected; or failure to make expected weight gain during period of growth, leading to body weight less than 85 percent of that expected).

B. Intense fear of gaining weight or becoming fat, even though underweight.

C. Disturbance in the way one's body weight or shape is experienced, undue influence of body weight or shape on self-evaluation, or denial of the seriousness of the current low body weight.

D. In postmenarcheal females, amenorrhea, i.e., the absence of at least three consecutive menstrual cycles. (A woman is considered to have amenorrhea if her periods occur only following hormone, e.g., estrogen administration.)

Source: American Psychiatric Association, *DSM-IV*, pp. 544–545. Reprinted with permission from the *Diagnostic and Statistical Manual of Mental Disorders*, Fourth Edition. Copyright © 1994 American Psychiatric Association.

When addressing differential diagnosis for Anorexia Nervosa, the clinician needs to consider three major issues: normal thinness, other psychiatric or psychological disorders, and physical disorders. With respect to differentiating between Anorexia Nervosa and nonpathological thinness, the clinician must take a careful history, perform a thorough interview, and possibly administer one or more of the diagnostic scales designed to assess the presence of anorexia. Data obtained are to be compared against the clinical criteria put forth in the *DSM-IV* to determine whether the individual is simply thin or whether he or she has the concomitant symptoms required for a diagnosis of Anorexia.

Included among the psychiatric and psychological disorders that can manifest symptomatology similar to that of Anorexia Nervosa are Depression, Phobic Disorders, paranoid ideation, Psychotic Depression (with delusional ideation around food), and chronic vomiting secondary to conversion disorder. The physiological diagnoses that could potentially manifest in a manner similar to Anorexia include hyperthyroidism, various endocrine disorders, chronic infections, malignancy, and certain gastrointestinal disorders (Dulcan & Popper, 1991).

Epidemiology Estimates of the lifetime prevalence of Anorexia range from 0.1 percent to 0.7 percent. Current data indicate that 90 to 95 percent of the sufferers are female, although this figure may be an artifact. Some clinicians suspect that young men are able to mask symptoms of this disorder more easily than women. Onset can be anywhere from age 8 to the mid-30s, although there are two peaks of onset at ages 13–14 and 17–18. Over 50 percent of the cases are manifest before age 20, with approximately 75 percent having their onset before age 25.

Etiology The authors of one recent study looked at risk factors associated with the development of eating disorders (Leon, Fulkerson, Jayne, Perry, & Dube, 1994). The authors interviewed the parents of 136 girls and 46 boys in grades 7 through 12. Girls in the high-risk groups rated their families on factors such as family cohesion, parent/adolescent communication, and family functioning and considered their families more dysfunctional than girls in the control groups considered theirs. The data support some gender differences—no such variation between the high-risk and control groups were found in the male subjects. Further, it is interesting to note that these trends were supported by the ratings provided by the mothers but not by the fathers.

With respect to etiology, data in the clinical literature associate sexual abuse and/or familial pathology with the subsequent development of eating disorders (see Hall, Tice, & Beresford, 1989). Oftentimes, problems in the family center on control issues. That is, the sexually abused child feels she has little control over many significant aspects of her personal life, so she attempts to assert control in terms of her food intake. Although this theory has some intuitive face validity, studies report conflicting evidence.

Minuchin and his colleagues are well known for their work exploring the nature of the family of the sufferer of Anorexia. Minuchin (1984) emphasizes the family's need to present a "healthy" and "well-adjusted" face to the world around them. This image, however, is merely a well-constructed facade designed to mask familial conflict, enmeshment, overprotection, and poor problem-solving skills. Using a systems type of orientation, Minuchin views the individual with Anorexia as serving the function of diverting attention away from the family's pathology. Further, as the patient becomes increasingly ill and requires medical care, her ability to become independent of the family structure is severely compromised, so her condition serves to maintain the enmeshed status quo.

More psychodynamically oriented theories of the etiology of Anorexia focus on the patient's pathological relationship with the mother. For example, object relations theorists view Anorexia as the patient's attempt to rebel against and express anger toward the mother in an extremely enmeshed situation. Similarly, "self-psychology" conceptualizes the anorexic condition as an attempt to delay the sexual development associated with adolescence. That is to say, a poor relationship with the mother will lead to an overly close relationship with the father. The relationship with the father could be threatened by the budding sexuality of adolescence, but the physical effects of Anorexia can guard against this (see Geist, 1984).

Treatment Cases of Anorexia Nervosa are complicated by the fact that in the vast majority of situations, the patient does not feel any need for treatment. The disorder is ego-syntonic, and most individuals with Anorexia feel that others misperceive the existence of pathology. They believe that treatment is not necessary. The patient's distortion of body image will often translate into perceiving the self as overweight. Ramifications of this perception include resentment of professionals and/or relatives who attempt to encourage weight gain. Primarily for this reason, the individual with Anorexia often does not reach a treatment facility until the medical condition is serious. Thus, the first step of treatment is usually to do everything possible to bring on weight gain, often in an inpatient facility. Generally speaking, a weight gain averaging 0.1 to 0.2 kg/day is recommended. This gradual weight gain is both medically indicated and psychologically recommended in that it assuages the individual's fear of loss of control over weight gain. Regardless of the seriousness of the current weight loss, the overall goal of all treatment approaches is to encourage eventual weight gain. All of the following treatment approaches can be utilized with minor modifications in an inpatient or outpatient setting.

Individual psychotherapeutic interventions for Anorexia Nervosa all focus on alteration of the patient's eating patterns. Because of the ego-syntonic nature of the disorder, it is crucial that the clinician operate respectfully within the patient's own value system. Although the clinician need not validate the patient's distorted body image, it is important not to automatically dismiss the patient's perceptions as pathological. Rather, the practitioner should offer therapy that respects the patient's beliefs and feelings. Therapy may involve cognitive-behavioral treatment to restructure the patient's cognitions about her body structure and the necessity of being thin; psychodynamic or supportive treatment; psychoeducational treatment to educate the patient and family about the disorder and about nutritional issues;

and behavioral treatment to promote the initial weight gain. All treatment modalities have the same long-term goal of restoring the individual to physiologically healthy weight levels and confronting the individual and familial psychological issues that form the core pathological dynamics supporting the eating disorder.

Familial interventions are usually essential, both as a means of helping the patient understand the origin of the eating disorder, and as a means of maximizing the chances of continued compliance with treatment after the patient leaves the clinician's office. Systems theory therapists work with the family to reframe the "problem" as involving pathology in the family rather than a single dysfunctional individual. This approach empowers the patient to focus on pathological interpersonal patterns within the family unit (see Minuchin, 1984).

Psychopharmacological intervention for the treatment of Anorexia Nervosa is typically limited to the treatment of other psychopathologies that accompany the illness. Thus, the patient with Anorexia may be medicated for Obsessive-Compulsive Disorder or Depression, but the medication is not aimed at the direct treatment of the Anorexia.

Bulimia Nervosa

Clinical Presentation Although case studies depicting Bulimia Nervosa go back to the early 1900s, Bulimia has been formally acknowledged as a *DSM* diagnosis only since 1980. Although the incidence of Bulimia Nervosa appears to have been increasing significantly since the 1970s, this increase may be an artifact of increased reporting rates as more people have become aware of this disorder.

The symptomatic presentation of Bulimia Nervosa includes two components: episodic uncontrolled eating referred to as bingeing, characteristically followed by self-induced vomiting, use of laxatives or diuretics, or other attempts by the bulimic individual to prevent any weight gain as a result of the binges. Foods ingested during the binges tend to be high in calories, sweet, and smooth-textured. A depressive period (referred to as postbinge anguish) will often follow this cycle.

Like individuals diagnosed with Anorexia, bulimics tend to be pathologically preoccupied with their own body weight. There is some controversy, however, as to whether this is true for all bulimics and whether individuals who otherwise fit the criteria but do not manifest this preoccupation should be diagnosed as bulimic. Bulimia and Anorexia may occur separately, concurrently, or sequentially in the same patient.

Barber (1991) describes bulimic individuals as being characterized by a preoccupation with body weight, body appearance, and food in general, spending some 85 percent of their waking time focusing on these issues. The self-esteem of bulimics is typically low. These individuals usually work below their capacity, and they are overly concerned about others' perceptions of them. The binge-purge cycle, usually engaged in privately, results in secrecy, sneakiness, and social isolation in the patient. Interpersonal relationships are further compromised because a significant portion of the bulimic's time and money is spent obtaining foods for the binges. These factors, in turn, can precipitate feelings of guilt and shame, further intensifying the patient's low self-esteem and guilt feelings.

Unlike the typical patient with Anorexia, the typical bulimic individual is not pathologically thin. Again, unlike the nonbulimic individual with Anorexia, bulimic individuals are likely to be sexually active and to acknowledge pleasure from the behavior of eating. The clinical course of Bulimia is typically a chronic one, with repeated relapses throughout the individual's life. Like Anorexia, Bulimia is associated with several medical, psychological and psychiatric complications.

Case Study 11.4

Fifteen-year-old Curlane was referred to a private psychologist because of her sporadic eating binges. During periods of stress, she might eat three to five pints of ice cream in one night, then spend 20 minutes in the bathroom vomiting. Curlane had been extremely secretive about these episodes. However, when she went for a dental check-up, the hygienist noticed some tell-tale signs of Bulimia as he examined her teeth. Her parents acknowledged that the girl seemed to eat a lot of ice cream, but they were unaware of her purging behavior. Since Curlane was diagnosed, she has isolated herself from her peers. She secludes herself in her bedroom, refusing to interact with her family.

Diagnosis The diagnostic criteria for Bulimia Nervosa are presented in Box 11.5.

box **11.5**

Diagnostic Criteria for Bulimia Nervosa

A. Recurrent episodes of binge eating. An episode of binge eating is characterized by both of the following:

1. Eating, in a discrete period of time (e.g., within a 2-hour period), an amount of food that is definitely larger than most people would eat during a similar period of time and under similar circumstances

2. A sense of lack of control over eating during the episode (e.g., a feeling that one cannot stop eating or control how much one is eating)

B. Recurrent inappropriate compensatory behavior in order to prevent weight gain, such as self-induced vomiting; misuse of laxatives, diuretics, enemas, or other medications; fasting; or excessive exercise.

C. The binge eating and inappropriate compensatory behaviors both occur, on average, at least twice a week for 3 months.

D. Self-evaluation is unduly influenced by body shape and weight.

E. The disturbance does not occur exclusively during episodes of Anorexia Nervosa.

Source: American Psychiatric Association, *DSM-IV*, pp. 549–550. Reprinted with permission from the *Diagnostic and Statistical Manual of Mental Disorders*, Fourth Edition. Copyright © 1994 American Psychiatric Association.

Differential diagnostic concerns are similar to those relevant to Anorexia Nervosa. Although not frequently encountered, the following disorders may manifest symptom presentations similar to that of Bulimia: Schizophrenia, Kleine-Levin syndrome, Parkinson's disease, and various endocrine problems.

Epidemiology Epidemiological estimates of incidence of Bulimia range from 1 to 4 percent for adolescent females in the United States, with an estimate of 1.9 percent for the general population. These estimates are probably low because of the shame and covert behavior typical of bulimics. The peak age of onset is late adolescence or even early adulthood, considerably later than the peak ages of onset of Anorexia Nervosa.

Think About It

Anorexia Versus Thinness

With the cultural emphasis on being thin and dieting, how can therapists distinguish between "healthy" eating limits and true eating disorders? Furthermore, are individuals who exhibit a preoccupation with dieting at risk for developing eating disorders? A recent study (Drewnowski, Yee, Kurth, & Krahn, 1994) used an Eating Pathology Scale to classify 557 college women in terms of their eating behavior into the following groups: nondieters, casual dieters, intensive dieters, dieters at risk, and bulimics. Over a 6-month period, 58 percent of bulimic subjects moved to the at-risk or intensive dieter categories. In addition, 4 percent of intensive dieters and 15 percent of dieters at risk became bulimic.

Etiology Childhood physical or sexual abuse is suspected of playing an etiological role in the development of Bulimia. One study (Rorty, Yager, & Rossotto, 1994) compared the history of childhood sexual, physical, and psychological abuse in women with Anorexia and those without. Those with Bulimia reported a higher level of all forms of abuse than women who did not suffer from Bulimia. However, the frequency of abuse was not correlated with eating disorders.

Treatment As in the treatment of Anorexia, the first and primary goal in the treatment of Bulimia is the restoration of physical health, to minimize the chances of subsequent or increased medical illness. Therapy usually focuses on the cessation of the binge-purge cycles, with the goal of eliminating the problems arising because of the behavior. A vast range of treatment approaches have been utilized; all have been effective to varying degrees with some patients and not others.

Most clinicians espouse a multidisciplinary approach, employing the expertise of professionals in the fields of medicine, nutrition, psychiatry, addictive disorders, and psychology. The actual techniques and modalities are similar in scope and content to those utilized with patients diagnosed with Anorexia. The one exception is the more frequent use of psychopharmacological interventions in patients with Bulimia. Although drug intervention is currently an issue of controversy, antidepressant medications, antianxiety drugs, antipsychotics, and lithium have all been used with varying degrees of success in treatment of Bulimia.

Disorders of Elimination in Childhood and Adolescence

Introduction

The elimination disorders, Encorpresis and Enuresis, refer to an inability to manage urination or defecation at an age-appropriate level. For centuries, the clinical literature has described the nature, etiology, and treatment of these disorders, but they did not achieve formal status in the *DSM* system until relatively recently. The first edition of the *DSM* made no mention of Encopresis at all, and it labeled Enuresis as a "special symptom reaction" that was classified separately from the other Axis I diagnoses. By 1968, Enuresis and Encopresis were grouped together in the category "Special Symptoms Not Otherwise Classified."

In the 1980 publication of the *DSM-III*, both Enuresis and Encopresis were classified as Mental Disorders with Physical Conditions. Perhaps more important than the actual classification, however, is the fact that this revision of the manual included the qualifier "functional" to distinguish symptoms that were not due to any recognized organic factor. The *DSM-III-R* categorized disorders as primary or secondary and subcategorized functional Enuresis into diurnal or nocturnal types.

The *DSM-IV* classifies Enuresis and Encopresis under the major category of Disorders Usually First Evident During Childhood and Adolescence, subcategorizing them as under Elimination Disorders.

Encopresis

Clinical Presentation Encopresis is the repeated, voluntary or involuntary passing of feces into places inappropriate for that purpose. The disorder is conceptualized in the *DSM-IV* as comprising two types. In those cases in which there is some evidence of constipation, either upon examination or by history, the individual is diagnosed as having Encopresis with Constipation and Overflow Incontinence. In cases without evidence of constipation, the individual is diagnosed as having Encopresis without Constipation and Overflow Incontinence. In a 1977 book chapter on fecal soiling, Hersov offered another way of conceptualizing Encopresis. The three categories he proposed include (1) individuals who have adequate bowel control and intentionally deposit feces in inappropriate places; (2) individuals who either are unaware that they are soiling or are aware but unable to control the process; and (3) cases in which the fecal soiling is due to diarrhea, anxiety, or constipation and overflow incontinence.

In contrast to episodes of Enuresis, incidents of Encopresis more frequently occur in the daytime than in the evening. Half of the cases of Encopresis are primary: the individual has never actually learned bowel control. In Secondary Encopresis, the individual has demonstrated continence for at least a 1-year period and then regressed.

The symptomatic profile of Encopresis varies somewhat. Some children who have adequate bowel control will deliberately place feces in inappropriate locations throughout the family home as a means of expressing anger, frustration, rebellion, and/or stress relevant to the family dynamics. These children present a situation clinically quite distinct from that of children who have no control over fecal excretion and, because of intense shame and embarrassment, attempt to deny these incidents. These children hide the fecal matter and/or the soiled clothing so as not to be "found out." In still other cases, the child does not seem to have any concern or anxiety about his or her symptomatic patterns of Encopresis.

Case Study 11.5

Seven-year-old Thurmond was diagnosed with secondary functional Encopresis. This behavior came to his parents' attention when the boy's underwear was not in the laundry hamper on laundry day. The Encopresis was confirmed when Thurmond's younger brother complained that the playroom closet smelled "poopy." After his fecal soiling, Thurmond hid his dirty underwear in the toy chest.

Diagnosis The diagnostic criteria for Encopresis are presented in Box 11.6.

---

box **11.6**

Diagnostic Criteria for Encopresis

A. Repeated passage of feces into inappropriate places (e.g., clothing or floor) whether involuntary or intentional.

B. At least one such event a month for at least 3 months.

C. Chronological age is at least 4 years (or equivalent developmental level).

D. The behavior is not due exclusively to the direct physiological effects of a substance (e.g., laxatives) or a general medical condition except through a mechanism involving constipation.

Source: American Psychiatric Association, *DSM-IV,* p. 107. Reprinted with permission from the *Diagnostic and Statistical Manual of Mental Disorders,* Fourth Edition. Copyright © 1994 American Psychiatric Association.

The major issue of differential diagnosis with respect to Encopresis has to do with detecting organic anomalies or physical illnesses that may manifest themselves in a similar fashion. When considering a diagnosis of Encopresis, the clinician must also consider the possibility that Encopresis is secondary to some other psychopathology. Mental Retardation, Attention Deficit Hyperactivity Disorder, Oppositional Defiant Disorder, Conduct Disorder, Phobic and other Anxiety Disorders, Mood Disorders, and psychotic disorders can all include encopretic symptoms as secondary manifestations.

Epidemiology After the age of 5 years, approximately 1.5 percent of the general population will manifest incidents of Encopresis. The rate of incidence decreases with age. The male-to-female ratio is about 4:1. Epidemiological data also reveal a higher rate among individuals with Mental Retardation and individuals in lower socioeconomic classes.

Etiology Theories on the etiology of Encopresis are relatively sparse. Oftentimes, the disorder is conceptualized as caused by a combination of maturational and psychological factors (Walsh & Menvielle, 1991). The more psychodynamic approaches look to Freudian theory and problematic relationships with parental authorities during the anal stage of development (see Bemporad, Pfeifer, & Gibbs, 1971).

Treatment The treatment of Encopresis varies according to the specific case. The ideal approach is multidisciplinary, utilizing medical, psychiatric, nutritional, and psychological treatments as clinically indicated. The relative input of the different disciplines depends on the etiological and clinical factors involved in each case.

After the appropriate medical procedures are employed to either rule out and/or treat any organic causes, psychotherapeutic interventions are typically employed, usually behavioral or cognitive-behavioral in orientation. Suggestions are offered to help the parents and the child regulate the excretory process via structured scheduling as well as contingency management techniques. In all cases, especially when symptoms obviously reflect severe familial pathology, family therapy is indicated to address issues that influence the encopresis.

Enuresis

Clinical Presentation Enuresis is the urinary analogue of Encopresis, that is, referring to the repeated involuntary or intentional discharge of urine in inappropriate places by an individual who would be expected to have urinary control. Approximately 80 percent of the cases involve primary Enuresis. These children have never had a consistent period of being asymptomatic. Secondary Enuresis refers to individuals who have been asymptomatic for over 6 months and then again show symptoms of Enuresis. With an average frequency of 5 to 7 wetting incidents per week, individuals with primary Enuresis exhibit a high spontaneous remission rate, especially when the onset is early in life (i.e., before puberty). Cases of secondary Enuresis are often caused by an increased stress level in the child's life and/or some major change in the family system.

Enuresis is subclassified according to the times at which the inappropriate urination occurs. In Nocturnal Enuresis, the most common condition, the enuresis occurs only at night. Diurnal Enuresis refers to cases of Enuresis that occur only during the daytime. Some children manifest the symptomatology during both the night and daytime hours. Nocturnal Enuresis usually occurs some 30 minutes to 3 hours after the onset of sleep. Sometimes the child wakes up, and at other times the child sleeps through the incident.

The psychological issues of embarrassment, low self-esteem, familial discord, phobic avoidance, shame, and embarrassment all affect the life of the child or adolescent with Enuresis, much as they do in cases of Encopresis. One study (Baker, 1969) concluded that Enuresis is more likely to be a cause of psychological difficulties than to be a result of them.

Reprinted with special permission of North America Syndicate.

Case Study 11.6

Six-year-old Thomas has been diagnosed with functional Nocturnal Enuresis. Although he was easily toilet trained by the age of 30 months, he resumed bed-wetting within 2 weeks after his younger sister was brought home from the hospital. Since that time (over 3 months ago), he has not had more than 3 dry evenings in a row.

Diagnosis The diagnostic criteria for Enuresis are listed in Box 11.7.

box **11.7**

Diagnostic Criteria for Enuresis

A. Repeated voiding of urine into bed or clothes (whether involuntary or intentional).

B. The behavior is clinically significant as manifested by either a frequency of twice a week for at least three consecutive months or the presence of clinically significant distress or impairment in social, academic (occupational), or other important areas of functioning.

C. Chronological age is at least 5 years (or equivalent development level).

D. The behavior is not due exclusively to the direct physiological effect of a substance (e.g., a diuretic) or a general medical condition (e.g., diabetes, spina bifida, a seizure disorder).

Source: American Psychiatric Association, *DSM-IV,* pp. 109–110. Reprinted with permission from the *Diagnostic and Statistical Manual of Mental Disorders,* Fourth Edition. Copyright © 1994 American Psychiatric Association.

As with Encopresis, the major differential diagnostic issue is that of distinguishing between the functional and organically based cases. It is essential that the child's life situation be evaluated in terms of psychosocial stressors. The clinician should determine whether the symptoms of Enuresis are secondary to some other psychopathology.

Epidemiology Sporadic Nocturnal Enuresis is estimated to occur in 25 percent of boys of all ages. When the age sample is restricted to children over age 5, the epidemiological estimate of incidence decreases to 7 percent for boys and 3 percent for girls. By age 10, both the overall incidence and the gender discrepancy decrease, with an incidence estimate of 3 percent for boys and 2 percent for girls.

Treatment The appropriate treatment modality for Enuresis depends on the cause of the disorder. Clearly, when a medical problem is present, it should be addressed first. Similarly, if the symptoms are secondary to some other psychopathology, treatment of the primary diagnosis is indicated. In other cases of functional Enuresis, psychopharmacological or behavioral therapies are employed.

Psychopharmacological interventions usually employ the tricyclic antidepressant imipramine (Tofranil). First used for the treatment of Enuresis some 30 years ago, imipramine eliminates bed-wetting in approximately 50 percent of children. However, long-term efficacy is significantly less impressive; virtually all these children regress to bed-wetting behavior within a year. This short-lived improvement, in conjunction with the potential side effects of the drug, encourages the use of psychological (usually behavioral) treatment approaches.

The earliest behavioral treatments for Enuresis were Urine Alarm Training (the bed-and-pad technique) and Retention Control Training. Houts and Mellon (1989) devised a parent-controlled program for the treatment of Enuresis (Full-Spectrum Home Training), which incorporates aspects of several behavioral methods. Table 11.1 presents a "Family Support Agreement" used in this home treatment approach.

Mowrer and Mowrer's urine alarm training technique was introduced in 1938. It continues to be utilized today as a component of various treatment regimens for Enuresis. A moisture-sensitive device sounds an alarm as soon as the child begins to wet the bed. The parents immediately take the child to the toilet when the alarm sounds. When the procedure is accurately and consistently carried out by the parents, this technique is extremely effective.

Retention Control procedures are based on the premise that individuals with Enuresis have an impaired ability to retain urine. Thus, the procedure entails daily practice in which the child (with the aid and support of the parents) ingests large amounts of fluid and practices retaining the urine for increasingly longer periods of time. Although not especially effective as a single treatment modality, Retention Control procedures are often useful adjuncts to other behavioral methods (see Shevlov, Gundy, & Weiss, 1981).

Houts, Berman, and Abramson (1994) compared the efficacy of various treatment modalities for Nocturnal Enuresis. Empirical studies that compare various treatments with each other and with no-treatment controls find that treatment in general is clinically superior to no-treatment controls. More children seem to benefit from psychological treatments than from psychopharmacological interventions. Psychological modalities that employ a urine alarm yield longer-lasting benefits.

Table 11.1 Family Support Agreement Used in Full Spectrum Home Training

1. _____ & _____ agree to carry out the training procedures exactly as described in order to accomplish the mutually desired goal of a dry bed.

2. Training will be carried out for at least 84 days (12 weeks).

3. Parents and family agree not to punish, scold, ridicule or refer to bedwetting in a negative way during the training.

4. Both parents and child understand that training is most effective when the child is not overtired or stressed.

Therefore _____ & _____ agree that _____P.M. is a reasonable bedtime, and _____ agrees to go to bed at that time every night.

5. NO RESTRICTIONS ON LIQUIDS. _____ will be allowed to drink as much liquid as desired at all times.

6. Parents and family agree to provide support, help, and understanding to_____. They will praise him/her when dry and provide encouragement that progress will be made. However, they understand that the training itself includes sufficient pressure and agree they will not urge him/her to try harder or do better.

7. Parents and family agree not to complain about the effects of the training on them or about the urine alarm, but to support and help instead. _____ also agrees not to complain about the training and to cooperate fully.

8. The family will provide a relatively stress-free environment at home during training.

9. _____ & _____ agree to participate in Self-Control Training once a day during the hours of _____ & _____ as explained in the Parent Guide.

Parents will give _____ money for each success according to the Reward Schedule for Self-Control Training.

10. _____ agrees to follow the procedure of Cleanliness Training as outlined on the wall chart and to put wet sheets and underwear in _____. Parents agree to keep clean sheets and clean underwear in the _____ in the child's room for him/her to use when remaking the bed.

11. Parents agree to wake _____ immediately if the buzzer rings and he/she does not wake up.

It is essential that the person responsible for waking the child will be able to hear and be awakened by the alarm. Nothing else should be done to wake the child during the night. The alarm must do this.

12. Parents agree to check the batteries regularly and to have replacement batteries ready when needed. Parents will also check the absorbent pockets for wear and replace these when needed.

13. _____ & _____ agree that *only* _____ will touch the alarm, except for alarm-testing as described above.

14. Parents agree to assume all responsibilities associated with training for a dry bed as spelled out in the Parent Guide.

_____ agrees to follow the Daily Steps to a Dry Bed outlined on the wall chart.

15. OVERLEARNING. When _____ has been dry for 14 consecutive nights, the Overlearning procedures will be followed until the child is dry for 14 more nights in a row. Overlearning will be explained when the child returns for the second follow-up appointment.

16. It is understood that every child has an occasional wet bed, especially when sick or under stress. Do not worry about this. Tell your child not to worry.

_____

(Child's Signature)

_____

(Parent's Signature)

_____

(Witness or Other Family Member)

Source: A. C. Houts & M. W. Mellon, (1989). In Charles E. Schaefer & James M. Breismeister (Eds.), *Handbook of Parent Training.* Copyright © 1989 by John Wiley & Sons, Inc. Reprinted by permission.

Summary

The *DSM-IV* classifies the Eating Disorders of Childhood and Adolescence into two general categories, depending on whether or not they are usually diagnosed in childhood. Those eating disorders usually first diagnosed in childhood are Pica, Rumination Disorder, and Feeding Disorder. The eating disorders included in the adult section of the *DSM-IV* are Anorexia Nervosa and Bulimia Nervosa.

Pica involves the ingestion of nonnutritive substances. Because very young children may exhibit this behavior in the absence of pathology, this disorder is typically not diagnosed prior to the age of 18 months. The range of nonnutritive substances being ingested usually decreases with increasing age. Treatment relies primarily on behavioral and psychoeducational interventions.

Rumination Disorder entails the voluntary regurgitation and reingestion of food. When this behavior does not have a physiological etiology, it may be the result of faulty parenting and, at times, neglect. In addition to selective reinforcement of nonruminating behavior, the primary treatment modalities are focused on parent training and education.

Feeding Disorder is a relatively new diagnostic category closely related to the earlier diagnosis referred to as Failure to Thrive. Children with this disorder do not eat enough to be able to develop at an appropriate, healthy rate.

Anorexia Nervosa refers to a pathological obsession with being thin. The disorder typically involves a distorted body perception as well as a tendency to diet or exercise excessively and/or starve oneself. This disorder is ego syntonic, and for that reason, it can be relatively difficult to treat. Interventions focus first on increasing the patient's body weight to a reasonable level, then on altering the individual's sense of perception and values regarding his or her own weight.

Bulimia Nervosa can occur independently or occur in conjunction with Anorexia. The central component of Bulimia is the binge-purge cycle in which the bulimic individual ingests a large amount of food and then attempts to eliminate the food from the body via forced vomiting or excretion. A sense of shame and secrecy accompanies this cycle, and the patient has low self-esteem and difficulty with interpersonal interactions. Treatment interventions for Bulimia closely parallel those for Anorexia, excepting the emphasis on weight gain.

Encopresis and Enuresis are the two disorders of elimination relevant to the psychopathology of childhood and adolescence. The former refers to inappropriate control of fecal voiding while the latter refers to inappropriate control of urination. Behavioral treatment methods are applicable to both disorders, depending on their etiological source. With respect to Enuresis, psychopharmacological interventions can also be used in conjunction with the behavioral treatments.

References

Albutt, T. C. (1910). Neuroses of the stomach and of other parts of the abdomen. In T. C. Albutt & H. D. Rolleston (Eds.), *A system of medicine* (p. 398). London: Macmillan.

Baker, B. L. (1969). Symptoms treatment and symptoms substitution in enuresis. *Journal of Abnormal Psychology, 74,* 42–49.

Barber, J. K. (1991). Bulimia nervosa. In J. M. Wiener (Ed.), *Textbook of child and adolescent psychiatry.* Washington, DC: American Psychiatric Press.

Bemporad, J. R., Pfeifer, C. M., & Gibbs, L. (1971). Characteristics of encopretic patients and their families. *Journal of the American Academy of Child Psychiatry, 10,* 272–292.

Casper, R. C., Elke, E. D., & Halmi, K. A. (1980). Bulimia: Its incidence and clinical importance in patients with anorexia nervosa. *Archives of General Psychiatry, 37,* 1030–1040.

Chatoor, I., Dickson, L., & Einhorn, A. (1984). Rumination: Etiology and treatment. *Pediatric Annals, 13,* 924–929.

Cooper, M. J., & Fairburn, C. G. (1992). Thoughts about eating, weight and shape in anorexia nervosa and bulimia nervosa. *Behavior Research and Therapy, 5,* 501–511.

Drewnowski, A., Yee, D. K., Kurth, C., & Krahn, D. D. (1994). Eating pathology and *DSM-IIIR* bulimia nervosa: A continuum of behavior. *American Journal of Psychiatry, 151,* 1217–1219.

Dulcan, M. K., & Popper, C. W. (1991). *Concise guide to child and adolescent psychiatry.* Washington, DC: American Psychiatric Press.

Finney, J. W., Russo, D. C., & Cataldo, M. F. (1982). Reduction of pica in young children with lead poisoning. *Journal of Pediatric Psychology, 7,* 197–207.

Garfinkel, P. E., & Garner, D. M. (1982). *Anorexia nervosa: A multidimensional perspective.* New York: Brunner/Mazel.

Geist, R. A. (1984). Self-psychological reflections in the treatment of anorexia nervosa: A self-psychological perspective. *Contemporary Psychotherapy Review, 2,* 268–288.

Hall, R. C., Tice, L., & Beresford, T. P. (1989). Sexual abuse in patients with anorexia nervosa and bulimia. *Psychosomatics, 79,* 73–79.

Hersov, L. (1977). Fecal soiling. In M. Rutter & L. Hersov, (Eds.), *Child psychiatry: Modern approaches.* Oxford: Blackwell.

Herzog, D. B., & Beresin, E. V. (1991). Anorexia nervosa. In J. M. Wiener (Ed.), *Textbook of child and adolescent psychiatry.* Washington, DC: American Psychiatric Press.

Houts, A. C., Berman, J. S., & Abramson, H. (1994). Effectiveness of psychological and pharmacological treatments for noctural enuresis. *Journal of Consulting and Clinical Psychology, 62,* 737–745.

Houts, A. C., & Mellon, M. W. (1989). Home-based treatment for primary enuresis. In C. E. Schaefer & J. M. Briesmeister (Eds.), *Handbook of parent training: Parents as co-therapists for children's behavior problems.* New York: Wiley.

Jacobson, J. L., & Snowdon, C. T. (1976). Increased lead ingestion in calcium deficient monkeys. *Nature, 162,* 51–52.

Leon, G. R., Fulkerson, J. A., Perry, C. L., & Dube, A. (1994). Family influences, school behaviors and risk for the later development of an eating disorder. *Journal of Youth and Adolescence, 23,* 499–515.

Madden, N. A., Russo, D. C., & Cataldo, M. F. (1980). Behavioral treatment of pica in children with lead poisoning. *Child Behavior Therapy, 2,* 67–81.

Mayes, S. D. (1992). Eating disorders of infancy and early childhood. In S. R. Hooper, G. W. Hynd, & R. E. Mattison (Eds.), *Child psychopathology: Diagnostic criteria and clinical assessment.* Hillsdale, NJ: Erlbaum.

Millican, F. K., Dublin, C. C., & Lourie, R. S. (1979). Pica. In J. D. Noshpitz (Ed.), *Basic handbook of child psychiatry: Vol. 2.* New York: Basic Books.

Minuchin, S. (1984). *Family kaleidoscope.* Cambridge: Harvard University Press.

Mowrer, O. H., & Mowrer, W. M. (1938). Enuresis—a method for its study and treatment. *American Journal of Orthopsychiatry 8,* 436–439.

Palla, B., & Litt, I. F. (1988). Medical complications of eating disorders in adolescence. *Pediatrics, 81,* 613–623.

Pumariega, A. J., Black, S. A., Gustavson, C. R., Gustavson, J. C., Gustavson, A. R., Reinarz, D., Probe, L., & Pappas, T. (1993). Clinical correlates of body-size distortion. *Perceptual and Motor Skills, 76,* 1311–1319.

Rast, J., Johnston, J. M., Drum, C., & Cibrubm, J. (1981). The relation of food quantity to rumination behavior. *Journal of Applied Behavior Analysis, 14,* 121–130.

Romeo, F. F., (1994). Adolescent boys and anorexia nervosa. *Adolescence, 29,* 643–647.

Rorty, M., Yager, J., & Rossotto, E. (1994). Childhood sexual, physical, and psychological abuse in bulimia nervosa. *American Journal of Psychiatry, 151,* 1122–1126.

Shevlov, S. P., Gundy, J., & Weiss, J. C. (1981). Enuresis: A contrast of attitudes of parents and physicians. *Pediatrics, 67,* 707.

Singhi, P., & Singhi, S. (1983). Nutritional status and psychosocial stress in children with pica. *Indian Journal of Pediatrics, 49,* 681–684.

Singhi, S., Singhi, P., & Adwani, G. B. (1981). Role of psychosocial stress in the cause of pica. *Clinical Pediatrics, 20,* 783–785.

Thompson, J. K., & Heinberg, L. J. (1993). Preliminary test of two hypotheses of body image disturbance. *International Journal of Eating Disorders, 14,* 59–63.

Walsh, T., & Menvielle, E. (1991). Disorders of elimination. In J. M. Wiener (Ed.), *Textbook of child and adolescent psychiatry.* Washington, DC: American Psychiatric Press.

Woods, S. C., & Weisinger, R. S. (1970). Pagophagia in the albino rat. *Science, 169,* 1334–1336.

Glossary

acute symptom a symptom of recent onset that will probably be of short-term duration

adiagnostic approach a perspective that minimizes the importance of diagnosis

affect external manifestation of emotional status

affective lability a condition involving the rapid and/or frequent change of an individual's emotional state in the absence of any specific environmental stimulus

akathisia motor restlessness, sometimes involving quivering

amenorrhea cessation of menstruation

American Psychological Association Ethical Principles of Psychologists a document delineating ethical principles for psychological practice

anaclitic depression severe impairment of physical and emotional development seen in infants raised in institutions

anal stage in Freudian theory, a stage in early childhood when the child's erotic focus is on excretory processes

anhedonia inability to experience pleasure

ataxia loss of muscular coordination

attachment theory a theory that regards the child's early interpersonal relationships as crucial models for later behavior

autonomic lability a condition involving a low threshold for autonomic arousal

autonomic nervous system the segment of the peripheral nervous system that controls life-maintaining, involuntary functions such as heart rate, temperature regulation, digestion, and secretion of hormones

anxiolytic drugs drugs that reduce anxiety

bell curve see *normal curve*

behavior therapy any therapeutic intervention based on the classical or operant conditioning models of behavior

beta blocker a beta-adrenergic blocking medication

bibliotherapy a treatment modality that provides the patient with educational reading materials to promote psychological health

biological theories theories that explain the development of psychopathology in terms of biological mechanisms

bipolar I disorder a diagnostic category for a mood disorder; symptoms include the presence of one or more manic or mixed episodes; a history of major depression may or may not also be present

bipolar II disorder a diagnostic category for a mood disorder; symptoms include hypomanic episodes that alternate with major depressive episodes

blunted affect manifestation of a limited range of affect; see also *constricted affect* and *flat affect*

bruxism gnashing or grinding of the teeth, most often at night

catastrophic cognitions automatic thoughts of extreme negativity, disaster, and doom; in cognitive therapy, assumed to play a strong etiological role in psychopathology

catatonia a condition in which the patient exhibits immobility, a mask-like expression, posturing, resistance to movement, and decreased spontaneity

central nervous system the brain, spinal cord, and associated neurons; contrast *peripheral nervous system*

chronic symptom a symptom or stressor that is not of recent onset and is expected to be of long-term duration; also referred to as an *enduring symptom*

classical conditioning a form of learning in which one stimulus (unconditioned) is repeatedly paired with a neutral stimulus (conditioned), resulting in the latter eventually evoking a response similar to that of the former; also referred to as *respondent conditioning*

clinical course the progression of symptoms of a disorder

cognitive behavior therapy a form of therapy that focuses on a person's belief system as it affects behavior

comorbidity coexistence of two or more disorders simultaneously

compensated a condition in which an individual's psychiatric and/or psychological symptoms are under control

concordance similarity in the frequency of occurrence of a certain disorder or cluster of symptoms between two groups

conditioned response a learned response to a particular stimulus

conduct disorder a psychopathology involving consistent, extreme misbehavior by a child or adolescent

conjoint interview an interview with the patient and the parents or other family members present

constricted affect affect with less than the normal range of expression; see also *blunted affect*

construct validity the type of validity that assesses the extent to which any given measure measures a given theoretical construct

contingency management in behavioral therapy, the regulated removal and addition of reinforcing stimuli to the environment

continuous variable a variable conceptualized in terms of degree rather than as present or not present

countertransference in psychoanalytic theory, the effects of the clinician's unresolved psychological issues on the therapeutic situation; contrast with *transference*

critical value in statistics, a probability level used as a cutoff point for making decisions

cyclothymic disorder an affective condition in which the patient alternates between depression and euphoria

delusions beliefs or belief symptoms that are not reality based

depression an affective disorder

descriptive validity the extent to which diagnostic criteria are valid in terms of differential diagnosis

developmental arrest the cessation of progress toward achievement of developmental milestones

developmental disorders a classification of disorders typically appearing during childhood or adolescence

developmental regression loss of ability to perform certain developmental tasks

developmental toxicity a negative interaction of medication with developmental processes or maturation

dichotomous variable a variable with two possible states—present or not present

differential diagnosis the process of distinguishing between two or more diagnostic categories with similar symptoms

differential reinforcement of other behavior (DRO) a technique in behavior therapy that provides reinforcement of desirable responses; that is, those responses to be engaged in rather than behaviors to be eliminated

dimensional approach a form of classifying child/adolescent psychopathology developed by Achenbach based on a multivariate statistical approach

double-blind design a research design in which neither the patient nor the researcher knows whether the patient is assigned to an experimental group or a control group

DSM-IV the *Diagnostic and Statistical Manual of Mental Disorders,* fourth edition, published by the American Psychiatric Association

dysphoria affect associated with a mildly depressed or dysphoric mood

dysthymia a mild form of depressive disorder

echolalia repetition of words spoken by other people; a symptom of schizophrenia

ego deviance a phenomenon wherein pathology intensifies when the individual is in an intimate relationship

ego-dystonic symptoms symptoms that cause the sufferer some distress; i.e., the sufferer is aware that there is "something wrong"; contrast with *ego-syntonic symptoms*

ego-syntonic symptoms symptoms that do not seem to cause the sufferer any psychological distress; contrast with *ego-dystonic symptoms*

eidetic imagery memory images that are clearer, more intense, and richer in detail than usual

Electra conflict in Freudian theory, a conflict that occurs during the phallic stage of development; the female child becomes sexually attracted to her father and jealously competitive with her mother. As the stage progresses, the child comes to identify with the mother.

emotional deprivation a lack of environmental stimulation or interpersonal interaction in early childhood; such deprivation can lead to delayed physical and mental development

enduring symptom see *chronic symptom*

environmentalist perspective an approach to the understanding of human behavior that emphasizes the influence of the environment as opposed to that of biology and genetics

erogenous zone in Freudian theory, an area of the body associated with sexual feelings

error variance that is due to technique or sampling

exclusionary criterion a symptom or other criterion whose presence excludes a particular diagnosis

etiology the cause or causes of a disorder

external validity the degree to which the results of a given measure can be generalized to other situations

extinction elimination of a conditioned response

face validity the type of validity assessing the extent to which a test "looks like" it measures what it is supposed to measure

false negative an incorrect diagnosis that no pathology is present

false positive an incorrect diagnosis of pathology

fight-or-flight reaction a physical response to danger, triggered by the sympathetic nervous system; a similar response to nonthreatening situations is maladaptive

fixation in Freudian theory, the arrest of psychosexual development at a particular stage

flat affect expression of virtually no emotion; see also *blunted affect*

free association a psychoanalytic technique designed to elicit information from the patient with little structure or direction from the therapist

functional disorder a disorder not caused by a recognizable organic factor

gender identity an individual's sense or awareness as to whether he or she is male or female

genital stage in Freudian theory, the fifth and final stage of psychosexual development, during which the individual achieves sexual maturity; achievement of this stage facilitates the eventual actualization of a mature heterosexual relationship

gender identity disorder of childhood a psychopathology in which the child or adolescent manifests behaviors inappropriate to his or her developmental stage that indicate a distorted sense of gender identity

genogram a technique used to diagram family patterns and trends

global assessment of functioning (GAF) a rating of an individual's ability to function in day-to-day situations; rated on the fifth axis of *DSM-IV*

grandiose delusions belief that one has some special powers or abilities

hallucinations imagined sensory experiences

iatrogenic illness literally, "physician-induced illness"; a condition that is caused or worsened by professional intervention or treatment

ideas of reference a patient's irrational belief that the words and actions of others are directed toward him or her

identified patient in therapy, the individual who is considered to be the one with the major symptomatology

implosive therapy a form of behavior therapy in which the patient is asked to imagine contact with a feared stimulus

inappropriate or incongruent affect manifestation of mood that is not consistent with the situation

inclusionary criteria diagnostic criteria that must be manifest in order for a certain diagnosis to be applied

individuation a process of maturation, whereby an individual becomes less psychologically dependent on his or her family and develops the resources to live as an adult

informed consent an ethics principle whereby research subjects or patients are made as aware as possible about the procedures in which they will be asked to participate

internalization integrating with and making a part of one's own personality

interpersonal theories theories that explain personality and the development of psychopathology in terms of an individual's relationships with other people

inter-rater reliability a measure of the correlation between the ratings given by two or more individuals on the same test

latency stage according to Freudian theory, the fourth of five stages of psychosexual development, in which the individual learns to direct his or her sexual energies toward socially acceptable targets

learned helplessness a phenomenon (first described by Seligman) in which individuals develop feelings of powerlessness when nothing they do seems to have any impact on the outcome of the situation

learning theories theories that explain behaviors in terms of experience and learned information

Likert scale a measure that asks for a response along a continuum, for example, on a 5-point scale

lithium toxicity a condition involving a toxic level of lithium in the patient's blood

longitudinal study a research protocol that follows the subject or subjects over time

loose associations the patient's belief in connections between topics that in reality have no relationship to each other

merged groups group therapy involving groups of patients and their parents

meta communication communicating a message on an abstract level

multigenerational model a model of therapy that focuses on the dynamics between family members, often transcending generations

neurological soft signs neurological symptoms that are not diagnostic of a particular problem but are often indicative of a deficit in sensory integration abilities

neuromotor skills skills that entail integration of neurological and motor abilities

night laughing laughing on waking from sleep; common in Rett's disorder

night terrors intense nightmares

normal curve a frequency distribution that is symmetrical and shaped like a bell

normal range of affect ability to exhibit a wide range of mood appropriate to the situation

object relations theory a theory of personality focusing on an individual's ability to form and keep mutually satisfying interpersonal relationships

observational learning a form of learning whereby organisms learn behaviors by observing one another

obsession intrusive, seemingly uncontrollable thoughts or images typically evoking a certain amount of anxiety

Oedipus conflict according to Freudian theory, a conflict during the phallic stage of development, in which the male child feels sexually attracted to his mother and jealously competitive with his father. As the stage progresses, the child moves toward identification with the father.

open-label studies a research design in which investigators know what drug a patient is taking

operant conditioning theory a theory of behavioral training that relies on rewards and reinforcement of desired behaviors; compare *classical conditioning theory*

operational definition a definition that describes a concept in objectively measurable terms

oral stage in Freudian theory, the first stage of psychosexual development, in which the young child's erotic focus centers on feeding and other activities

outcome criteria measures used to determine the efficacy or success of an intervention

overcorrection in behavior therapy, requiring the patient to perform extreme variations of corrective behaviors to "right" undesirable behavior

overproductive speech speech patterns that reflect an anxious urgency and rapid pace; a symptom of mania or hypomania

parallel-forms reliability a measure of reliability between alternative versions of the same test

parallel groups in group therapy, parents' and childrens' groups that usually meet separately

parasympathetic nervous system that portion of the autonomic nervous system that returns the body to status quo following arousal; compare *sympathetic nervous system*

pathognomic a phenomenon that is characteristic of a particular disorder

peripheral nervous system all portions of the nervous system aside from the brain, the spinal cord, and associated neurons; see also *central nervous system*

personality disorder a set of disorders diagnosed on Axis II of the *DSM-IV*, also referred to as *characterological disorders*

phallic stage in Freudian theory, the third stage of psychosexual development, in which the individual learns to obtain pleasure from his or her genitalia

pharmacokinetics the method of drug metabolism

post-traumatic stress disorder a psychopathology involving a multisymptomatic reaction to a major life stressor

poverty of content a symptom of schizophrenia involving speech that is plentiful in quantity but that says virtually nothing

predictive validity the type of validity that assesses the degree to which the results on a measure have prognostic value with respect to the results on another measure

premorbid marker a symptom or indicator occurring at a time prior to the onset of the pathology in question

prepubertal occurring prior to puberty

pressured speech see *overproductive speech*

primary symptoms symptoms that are not caused by a previously existing disorder

projective test a form of personality test that exposes the patient to purposefully ambiguous stimuli and asks him or her to "project" associations on to them

pseudohallucinations imagined sensory experiences that do not fit the criteria for true hallucinatory experiences

pseudomaturity the expression of unusual maturity in a child or adolescent; thought to mask insecurity or psychopathology rather than to indicate advanced development

psychoanalytic theories theories based on the work of Sigmund Freud and his followers

psychodynamic psychotherapy a form of dynamically oriented psychotherapy modeled on the Freudian psychoanalytic approach

psychoeducation an approach to therapy whose goal is to provide information or teach certain skills

psychogenic factor a symptom that has no demonstrable biological or physiological etiological basis

psychopharmacological approach a treatment approach involving medication that is designed to alleviate psychological or psychiatric symptomatology

psychosexual model of development in Freudian theory, the idea that personality develops by progression through stages involving erotic attachment to a specific body area

psychosocial stressors environmental factors that affect, to varying degrees, an individual's ability to function optimally

psychopharmacology see *psychopharmacological approach*

psychotherapy "talk therapy"; any form of nonpharmacological treatment that alleviates symptoms of psychopathology

rebound effect in psychopharmacology, an exacerbation of symptomatology a given period of time following administration of medication

reciprocal inhibition a behavioral technique in which anxiety associated with a given stimulus is modified by having the patient in a relaxed state

regression a process during which an individual exhibits behavioral characteristics of an earlier time of life

reinforcement any behavior whose application increases the probability of one or more target behaviors occurring

reliability the degree to which a test or assessment measure gives consistent results

response cost a behavior therapy intervention in which the patient is required to be deprived of something positive as a result of engaging in an undesirable behavior

schema a framework or outline

secondary symptoms symptoms that are caused by a previously existing condition

selection bias unrepresentative selection of subjects, leading to invalid results in research

self-fulfilling prophecy the occurrence of a certain set of behaviors that have been predicted or expected to occur

self-report an information-gathering procedure in which the individual being assessed provides the data about him- or herself

self-statements a technique used in behavior therapy and cognitive behavior therapy in which certain self-affirming statements are taught to patients so that they can repeat them to themselves at appropriate times

sensory-motor depression a condition in which a child manifests a sad, flat facial expression; delayed language development; increased sleep; lack of curiosity; an increased number of physical illnesses; and an overall delay in cognitive development

social learning theory a theory which postulates that individuals develop certain behaviors via their interactions with others, specifically focusing on identification and role modeling

somatic delusions false beliefs about one's own body

somatic nervous system the part of the peripheral nervous system that controls the voluntary activities of the body

splitting a mechanism whereby an individual attributes "good" qualities to one family member and "bad" qualities to another; often seen in dysfunctional families

stage theory a theory (usually of development) which postulates that an individual must pass through certain stages in a sequential order so that he or she can mature

strategic model of family therapy an approach that conceptualizes psychopathology as caused by maladaptive problem-solving techniques

structural approach a form of therapy that looks at the family in terms of its structural characteristics, especially as they relate to issues of authority, power, boundaries, and overall balance

sympathetic nervous system the division of the autonomic nervous system that prepares the body to react to perceived danger

systematic desensitization a behavioral treatment approach with the goal of eliminating anxiety responses by presenting the patient with anxiety-producing stimuli while the patient is in a relaxed state; the stimuli are presented in a hierarchial manner so that the least anxiety-producing stimuli are presented first

systems theory an approach to conceptualizing psychopathology that focuses on the attempt to maintain homeostasis within the subsystems in human behavior

temperament theory a biologically based theory of personality development which postulates that individuals are born with certain psychological predispositions with respect to reacting with the environment

termination phase in psychoanalytic psychotherapy, the third and final phase of therapy, marked by the accomplishment of therapeutic goals

test-retest reliability a measure of reliability that determines how reproducible scores are on successive administrations of the same test

theoretical validity the degree to which a measure or treatment intervention "fits" with a given theoretical construct

thought blocking sudden cessation of speech

thought stopping a behavior therapy technique that trains patients in techniques to eliminate the presence, or at least reduce the impact, of aversive thoughts

therapeutic alliance the therapeutic rapport between the clinician and the patient

tic disorder a psychopathology involving repetitive stereotyped behaviors

transference in psychoanalytic theory, the patient's transfer toward the therapist of feelings originally associated with significant people in the patient's life

true negative an accurate diagnosis of the absence of pathology

true positive an accurate diagnosis of pathology

true variance the proportion of variance in a test score that is not attributable to technical or sampling error

unfinished business unresolved psychological issues

validity the degree to which a test measures what it is supposed to measure; subtypes include concurrent, construct, content, convergent, discriminant, and face validity

V codes in the *DSM* diagnostic system, codes to refer to problems for which individuals seek treatment, yet are not clearly due to a mental disorder; referred to as "Other Conditions" that may be a focus of treatment

working through in psychoanalytic psychotherapy, the stage in which the therapist offers interpretations of the patient's behaviors

Credits

Chapter one

Page 5 Figure 1.2 was drawn by a 7-year-old artist Allison Nicole Marcus.

Page 9 Achenbach, T. M. (1982). *Developmental Psychopathology.* New York: Wiley. Reprinted with permission.

Chapter two

Page 28 From *Winnie-the-Pooh* by A. A. Milne, illustrated by E. H. Shepard. Copyright © 1926 by E. P. Dutton, renewed in 1954 by A. A. Milne. Used by permission of Dutton Children's Books, a division of Penguin Books USA, Inc.

Page 28 Reprinted from O. W. Goodwin and S. B. Guze, *Psychiatric Diagnosis*, Fourth Edition. Copyright © 1989 Oxford University Press. Reprinted with permission.

Pages 36–39 Reprinted with permission from the *Diagnostic and Statistical Manual of Mental Disorders,* Fourth Edition. Copyright © 1994 American Psychiatric Association.

Chapter three

Page 46 From *Winnie-the-Pooh* by A. A. Milne, illustrated by E. H. Shepard. Copyright © 1926 by E. P. Dutton, renewed in 1954 by A. A. Milne. Used by permission of Dutton Children's Books, a division of Penguin Books USA, Inc.

Chapter four

Page 64 From *The House at Pooh Corner* by A. A. Milne, illustrated by E. H. Shepard. Copyright © 1926 by E. P. Dutton. Renewed 1928 by E. P. Dutton, renewed © 1956 by A. A. Milne. Used by permission of Dutton Children's Books, a division of Penguin Books USA, Inc.

Pages 65–68 From *Ethical Principles of Psychologists and Code of Conduct.* Copyright © 1992 by the American Psychological Association. Reprinted with permission.

Chapter five

Page 92 From *Winnie-the-Pooh* by A. A. Milne, illustrated by E. H. Shepard. Copyright © 1926 by E. P. Dutton, renewed in 1954 by A. A. Milne. Used by permission of Dutton Children's Books, a division of Penguin Books USA, Inc.

Pages 94–96 Reprinted with permission from the *Diagnostic and Statistical Manual of Mental Disorders*, Fourth Edition. Copyright © 1994 American Psychiatric Association.

Page 98 PEANUTS reprinted by permission of United Feature Syndicate, Inc.

Pages 107–109 Reprinted with permission from the *Diagnostic and Statistical Manual of Mental Disorders*, Fourth Edition. Copyright © 1994 American Psychiatric Association.

Chapter six

Page 114 From *Winnie-the-Pooh* by A. A. Milne, illustrated by E. H. Shepard. Copyright © 1926 by E. P. Dutton, renewed in 1954 by A. A. Milne. Used by permission of Dutton Children's Books, a division of Penguin Books USA, Inc.

Pages 120–121, 126–127, 130–131 Reprinted with permission from the *Diagnostic and Statistical Manual of Mental Disorders*, Fourth Edition. Copyright © 1994 American Psychiatric Association.

Page 132 Adams, P. L. (1985). *American Journal of Psychotherapy, 39*. Reprinted with permission.

Pages 135–136 Reprinted with permission from the *Diagnostic and Statistical Manual of Mental Disorders*, Fourth Edition. Copyright © 1994 American Psychiatric Association.

Page 138 CURIOUS AVENUE copyright © 1992, 1993 TOLES. Reprinted with permission of Universal Press Syndicate. All rights reserved.

Page 139 CURIOUS AVENUE copyright © 1992, 1993 TOLES. Reprinted with permission of Universal Press Syndicate. All rights reserved.

Chapter seven

Page 145 "Halfway Down" by A. A. Milne, from *When We Were Very Young* by A. A. Milne, illustrated by E. H. Shepard. Copyright © 1924 by E. P. Dutton, renewed in 1952 by A. A. Milne. Used by permission of Dutton Children's Books, a division of Penguin Books USA, Inc.

Page 148 Reprinted with permission from the *Diagnostic and Statistical Manual of Mental Disorders*, Fourth Edition. Copyright © 1994 American Psychiatric Association.

Chapter eight

Page 160 From *Winnie-the-Pooh* by A. A. Milne, illustrated by E. H. Shepard. Copyright © 1926 by E. P. Dutton. Renewed in 1954 by A. A. Milne. Used by permission of Dutton Children's Books, a division of Penguin Books USA, Inc.

Pages 163–164 Reprinted with permission from the *Diagnostic and Statistical Manual of Mental Disorders*, Fourth Edition. Copyright © 1994 American Psychiatric Association.

Page 169 Reprinted with permission from the *Diagnostic and Statistical Manual of Mental Disorders*, Fourth Edition. Copyright © 1994 American Psychiatric Association.

Pages 171–172 K. J. Zucker and R. Green from "Gender Identity and Psychosocial Disorders" in J. M. Weiner (ed.), *Textbook of Child and Adolescent Psychiatry*. Copyright © 1991 American Psychiatric Association. Reprinted by permission.

Chapter nine

Page 176 From *The House at Pooh Corner* by A. A. Milne, illustrated by E. H. Shepard. Copyright © 1926 by E. P. Dutton. Renewed in 1928 by E. P. Dutton, renewed © 1956 by A. A. Milne. Used by permission of Dutton Children's Books, a division of Penguin Books USA, Inc.

Page 177 Reproduced by permission of WHO, from *ICD–10 Classification of Mental and Behavioural Disorders: Clinical Descriptions and Diagnostic Guidelines*. Geneva, World Health Organization, 1992.

Pages 182, 186–187, 191–194, 197–203 Reprinted with permission from the *Diagnostic and Statistical Manual of Mental Disorders*, Fourth Edition. Copyright © 1994 American Psychiatric Association.

Page 201 Reprinted with special permission of King Features Syndicate.

Chapter ten

Page 207 From *The House at Pooh Corner* by A. A. Milne, illustrated by E. H. Shepard. Copyright © 1926 by E. P. Dutton. Renewed in 1928 by E. P. Dutton, renewed © 1956 by A. A. Milne. Used by permission of Dutton Children's Books, a division of Penguin Books USA, Inc.

Page 215 Reprinted with permission from the *Diagnostic and Statistical Manual of Mental Disorders*, Fourth Edition. Copyright © 1994 American Psychiatric Association.

Page 217 Reprinted from *Child and Adolescent Psychiatry: A Comprehensive Textbook*, p. 544 1991:544, p. 733, by permission of Williams and Wilkins.

Pages 220–221 Reprinted with permission from the *Diagnostic and Statistical Manual of Mental Disorders*, Fourth Edition. Copyright © 1994 American Psychiatric Association.

Chapter eleven

Page 231 From *Winnie-the-Pooh* by A. A. Milne, illustrated by E. H. Shepard. Copyright © 1926 by E. P. Dutton. Renewed in 1954 by A. A. Milne. Used by permission of Dutton Children's Books, a division of Penguin Books USA, Inc.

Page 232 CURIOUS AVENUE copyright © 1992, 1993 TOLES. Reprinted with permission of Universal Press Syndicate. All rights reserved.

Pages 233–238, 241, 244 Reprinted with permission from the *Diagnostic and Statistical Manual of Mental Disorders*, Fourth Edition. Copyright © 1994 American Psychiatric Association.

Page 245 Reprinted with special permission of North America Syndicate.

Page 246 Reprinted with permission from the *Diagnostic and Statistical Manual of Mental Disorders*, Fourth Edition. Copyright © 1994 American Psychiatric Association.

Page 247 From Charles E. Schaefer and James M. Breismeister, *Handbook of Parent Training*. Copyright © 1989 by John Wiley & Sons, Inc. Reprinted by permission.

Index